D1159972

MEDIEVAL AND RENAISSANCE FLORENCE

VOLUME I

VIEW OF FLORENCE FROM THE CONVENT OF SAN FRANCESCO ABOVE FIESOLE

MEDIEVAL AND RENAISSANCE FLORENCE

VOLUME I: MEDIEVAL FLORENCE

by Ferdinand Schevill

HARPER TORCHBOOKS ▼ The Academy Library

Harper & Row, Publishers New York, Evanston, and London

To Clara

FOR WHOM THIS BOOK WAS BEGUN

AND TO WHOSE BRIGHT AND GALLANT SPIRIT

IT IS DEDICATED

First published in 1936 by Harcourt, Brace and Company under the title HISTORY OF FLORENCE *and reprinted by arrangement with the author's estate.*

Revised edition published 1961 by Frederick Ungar Publishing Co.

First HARPER TORCHBOOK *edition published 1963 by Harper & Row, Publishers, Incorporated New York and Evanston.*

LIBRARY OF CONGRESS CATALOG CARD NUMBER: *60-8571*

CONTENTS TO BOTH VOLUMES

Volume I

Volume II

LIST OF ILLUSTRATIONS TO VOLUME I

All photographs from Alinari through Art Reference Bureau, Inc.

LIST OF MAPS

Introduction: On Florentine Historiography

FIRST legend, then history—that is the inevitable succession among all groups and peoples which, by steadily advancing in the command of themselves and their environment, at last achieve a notable civilization. On reaching the stage at which history definitely rules, they usually give evidence of an increased self-esteem by somewhat contemptuously affixing to the version of the past, so long the cherished possession of their ancestors, the label "legend" and by dismissing it from consideration as the negligible offspring of ignorance and fancy. At the very least they develop a certain skepticism regarding it, simultaneously welcoming the factual and critical version of their past put forth by the representatives of the new culture. This they affirm to be history, meaning thereby a product which, in distinction from legend handed down by word of mouth and reshaped by each narrator according to his pleasure, is reliable, accurate, and certain because based on the facts as revealed by the surviving records. In short, the position of the later, more enlightened generations is that legend is fiction, history truth, and that whereas men were once content to receive the story of their past from their dreamers and poets, they now take it from their scholars and historians in command of a method of investigation calculated to yield a full and satisfying knowledge.

Although such is the view advanced societies usually entertain regarding the distinction between legend and history, it errs by drawing too absolute a line between them. This will become apparent the moment we take up an individual instance like that of Florence. In the thirteenth century when the Arno city was making rapid strides toward the conquest of that power and civilization on the strength of which it was destined in the succeeding century to become a leading world-center, the citizens were in possession of a version of their past which, to their as yet simple and untutored understanding, was a truthful record of events and therefore authentic history. It is this history which Dante Alighieri learned when he was a boy and which, never challenging, he closely reflects in his great poem. It circulated in the poet's youth in many slightly different versions, some of which have come down to us and have been made accessible in our time in printed form.

Whoever is curious about Dante's historical background cannot overlook these ancient compilations. Taking up the one which goes under the name of *Il Libro Fiesolano,*[1] we are struck at once by its palpably fabulous character. Plainly the unknown author was utterly ignorant of the Florentine past but, possessed of the literary and chivalric culture of his century, was prompted in the spirit of the contemporary romancers to entertain his audience with war and adventure on a heroic scale. So completely does the taste of readers change from age to age that it is hard for us of the twentieth century to believe that this sort of uncontrolled invention was ever considered to be entertaining. The evidence to the contrary is, however, so abundant that there is no rejecting it. With frank delight, then, the medieval reader learned from the old story-teller how Fiesole was the first town to be built after the universal flood, how the son of the first sovereign pair of Fiesole was Italo who gave his name to Italy, how a second son migrated to the east and founded Troy, how Troy was destroyed owing to the sinful love of Paris and Helen, how Aeneas made his escape from the captured city and came to Italy, how the descendants of Aeneas founded Rome, mistress of the world, and how the Romans, after taking and destroying Fiesole, laid the foundations in the plain below Fiesole of Florence, building it as the exact counterpart of their own proud capital upon the Tiber. The invention, wholly literary and fantastic, would seem to carry no single element suggestive of a genuine popular tradition.

While, owing to its total lack of verisimilitude, this version fusing universal and local history into a comprehensive unit fails to impress the living generation, we should be making a mistake to dismiss it from our attention without noting that it contains an impalpable something which should not be overlooked. Closely scanned, it communicates what to the early Florentines was without doubt the outstanding feature of their moral and political world. The young and struggling city in the valley was completely dominated by the older Fiesole on its lofty eminence, and before ambitious Florence could expand and spread its wings the dangerous rival would have to be brought low. Therefore the venerable but inconveniently close neighbor became the object of a passionate hatred; and as at the same time the memory had not died out that Fiesole was of Etruscan origin, it followed that the Florentines, so radically different in their own estimate from their despised rivals as to impose the assumption of another and a nobler race of men, were necessarily identified with the Romans,

[1] Published with two similar compilations under the comprehensive title, *Chronica de Origine Civitatis,* by O. Hartwig, *Quellen und Forschungen zur aeltesten Geschichte der Stadt Florenz.* Marburg, 1875. See also on legends and early chronicles, Santini, *Quesiti e Ricerche di Storiografia Fiorentina.* Florence, 1903.

proud conquerors in their day of Fiesole and all Etruria. In short, the Arno city was the beloved daughter and potential heir of the imperial city on the Tiber. This flattering descent the eager dreamers of the rising town pondered and poetically embroidered until it became the first and outstanding article of the civic faith with which Florence began her existence.

In the face of this patriotic kernel of the *Libro Fiesolano,* a kernel containing in terms of the imagination the most immediate and pressing reality of the youthful town, it is impossible to maintain that the past which Dante absorbed from the writings current in his day must be rated as pure romance without a shadow of historical value. On the contrary, the assertion, strengthened by picturesque particulars, of the noble Roman origin of the Florentines and of the vileness of the adder brood of the Fiesolan neighbors is without the least doubt an appreciable moral factor in that amazing energy with which medieval Florence pushed and hacked her way across every obstacle to a lofty, distant goal. Indisputably the legend carries a body of events which, historically considered, have little value or even no value at all; however, by revealing a state of mind, a psychological slant, it throws a not unimportant light on the early history of the town. We must conclude that, inasmuch as legend and history, at least in the instance under consideration, possess in certain imponderable psychological data a common denominator, they are not, as is often affirmed, two wholly diverse worlds separated by a clear-cut dividing line.

This conclusion is confirmed when we examine the Florentine work wherein for the first time and in the most decisive manner legend was replaced by history. Immediately after Dante's day, or rather while Dante was still alive, a somewhat younger contemporary, Giovanni Villani, began writing his famous chronicle.[2] We have already suggested that history as distinct from legend is at all times and everywhere recognizable by a simple criterion: it reconstructs the events with which it deals not from hearsay and dream-stuff but from the facts transmitted by the records. This test Villani successfully meets, although not consistently throughout his narrative. Leaving to one side those sections of his work which deal with the world in general and concentrating on the parts devoted to Florence—a procedure to which no one will object since it is to the Florentine material that Villani owes his fame—we are struck with the circumstance that what he has to offer of copious and well-sifted information belongs overwhelmingly to the period of his own lifetime. For this period his records or sources were his own intelligent and inquiring self, other living witnesses of the events described, and numerous official documents to which he had access. But when by way of introduction to what occurred in his day he undertook

[2] *Cronica di Giovanni Villani*. Ed. Franc. Gherardi Dragomanni. 4 vols. Florence, 1844-45.

to add the story of the birth and childhood of his beloved commonwealth, he found little else to fall back on save the legend on which he, and Dante before him, had been brought up; and having nothing better in hand, he incorporated it in his work.

In following this course Villani was troubled by no sense of incongruity. Scholars are universally agreed that his distinction as a chronicler lies in a feeling for factual reality which no medieval writer before his time possessed in the same degree. It was natural for a man so endowed to be guided by the evidence, and this was Villani's actual procedure subject to limitations beyond his control. When the records were plentiful, as in his own age, he used as many as were immediately available; and when, as for early Florence, he had access to no other records than such legendary tales as the *Libro Fiesolano,* he let himself be governed by them. In either case his method was much the same; and if he did not instinctively balk at what we recognize at once as the transparent and monstrous absurdities of the legend, we may explain this credulity in the main by his medieval simplicity. But without the least doubt it is also referable to the tone and background of the legend, which with its declaration of the Roman origin of Florence fell in exactly with his own ruling patriotic bias.

The deduction to be drawn from this kinship of Villani, first authentic historian of Florence, to the Florentine legend is so important that we must pause to elaborate it. Not only in legend but also in veritable history as well there is unmistakably something personal or subjective which is woven into the events described and is recognizable by the intelligent reader as a prejudice or a point of view or a supporting mental substructure. Even when history is composed with the most wholehearted submission to the evidence, aspiring, according to the demand of some of its most recent hierophants, to a coldly scientific attitude toward its material, the ideal is never realized. For, when the mastery of the evidence has been effected, it must, in order to be converted into a history, be shaped in the mind of the investigator; and in that process it will inevitably acquire something of the form and color of the vessel in which it was prepared. Moreover, this personal contribution is not personal in the sense of being wholly original with the chronicler or historian under consideration. As an ephemeral, and, let us add, an eminently social creature, he is the child of his environment and exhibits innumerable earmarks indicative of his particular time and place. It is for this reason we are obliged to inquire with regard to every history that comes into our hands: Who wrote it? When and where did the writer live? With what particular outlook or religion or philosophy did he face the problems of history and of life? And we shall invariably find that the answers to these questions defining the historian's individuality always enter, though not regularly in the same degree, into works passing as histories. They may have been composed with the most devoted attention to the facts, but the facts on getting themselves ordered in a logical or a chronological series have had something extraneous imposed on them, something that is not native to them as mere facts. Call this addition form, mind, interpretation—there it is! He who lacks the skill or penetration to detect this often hidden agent with his quiet manipulations and directive comment, he who reads history, any history, as if it were something impersonal communicating an absolute and final truth has never reflected on the necessary limitations of this department of literature and is likely in the end to take from it more injury than profit.

By insisting at the outset on the human equation as an ever-present element in the vast mass of Florentine historiography beginning with the earliest legend extant, we are providing ourselves with a taper calculated to shed a serviceable light throughout our journey. Although the writer of the *Libro Fiesolano* must be rated as a mere entertainer, while the first chronicler, Villani, fairly qualifies as a historian, the two have a common background of patriotic sentiment and become related to each other by this emotional tie. Nonetheless we emphatically enter with Villani into a new world which he creates by his command of the facts and his power of critically evaluating them. His immense achievement, for which we of a later period can never be too grateful, is the accurate description of the town under his eyes, his story of its trade, its industry, its social classes, its religious customs, its relation to its neighbors, its ceaseless and passionate domestic conflicts. But pulsating with life as the picture is, it is not the last word on the subject. In fact, if we have made our point, there is never any last word or final truth on any historical subject; for, even should a mistaken and self-satisfied generation think itself in possession of this truth, its successor will not fail, or at least up to the present has never yet failed, to replace it with a truth of its own.

What happened in Villani's case was that he scrutinized the Florentine scene before his eyes with a novel and amazing degree of directness and candor. While that is the first and most essential point to be noted, it is also true that his viewpoint was that of the merchant group to which he belonged and whose passionately papal or Guelph sentiments he fully shared. His whole heart goes out to the burgher republic of the merchants and artisans constituted in his impressionable youth after a long and bloody conflict with an older governing group of aristocratic and landowning families. Although his burning patriotism is rooted in class prejudice, it loses none of its sincerity on that account. This Florence, his beloved city, in becoming a merchant republic has acquired just the right constitution for its needs, although

Villani does not go the uncritical length of asserting that the individual merchants who appropriated the offices were necessarily impeccable. Living in the first half of the fourteenth century, when the new constitution was at the height of its vigor, and identifying himself with it inwardly by a solemn act of faith, he pictured it in operation with an incomparable vivacity and freshness. Because of these various circumstances weaving like a shuttle between the describer and the thing described, he created an advanced type of medieval chronicle, a chronicle which is undoubtedly on the way to becoming a coherent and critical history, although it does not quite attain its goal.

Considerable as Villani's achievement was, there is nothing mysterious or inexplicable about it. The advance signalized by him was in the air, as an examination of the work of the contemporary chroniclers throughout Italy would easily establish. In a sketch limited to Florence it will suffice to adduce the case of another Florentine, Dino Compagni. Dino wrote in Villani's day—around 1310—a chronicle[3] which represents an even more radical departure from the traditional limitations of the chronicle type than the work of his more famous fellow-citizen. In fact Dino's work, though bearing the name chronicle, is, in respect to its form, already a full-fledged history since it presents, in intention if not always in execution, a reasoned exposition of events befalling in Florence during the passionate struggle for political power between the Blacks and the Whites. Its most notable drawback is that, in contrast to the broad sweep of Villani's work, it strictly confines itself to the incidents just before and after the year 1300 in which Dino participated as a leading White. However, remarkable as the production is in itself and invaluable as throwing light on the spirit of the age, it exercised no influence on the development of Florentine historiography. For reasons of political expediency Dino's history was both during his own life and for some generations after his death kept jealously from the public eye. Even two and three hundred years after it had been penned, it circulated only privately and in manuscript form. For the world in general it cannot be said to have existed till 1726 when it was published by the great Muratori. Throughout the long period of the unfortunate suppression of Dino's amazingly original and stirring work the chronicle of Villani was in everybody's hand and was broadly utilized both for reference and imitation.

Two or three generations elapsed after Villani and Dino before the writing of history took a new turn in Florence. By that time not only had Florence reached another stage of political development but the Florentine mind, as reflected by the educated class, was dominated by very different trends.

[3] The standard edition is by I. Del Lungo, *Dino Compagni e la sua Cronica.* 3 vols. Florence, 1879-80.

Between 1400 and 1450 the movement we know as humanism had become the ruling influence among the cultivated circles on the Arno and, on the side of history, humanism in its early phase signified the conscious imitation of the classical historians, particularly those of Rome. That statement puts in a nutshell why the new or humanistic school of Florentine historiography has never been highly regarded except by its contemporaries blindly enamored of antiquity. Since it was content to imitate it took over the external characteristics of the ancients rather than their impalpable spirit and produced works which weary to exhaustion the present-day reader with their descriptions of battles, their invented rhetorical speeches, and their general failure to get below the surface of events and come to grips with reality. Two outstanding humanists tried their hands at a history of Florence. They were Leonardo Bruni and Poggio Bracciolini; and, although they deservedly hold a high place as classical scholars, by either ancient or modern standards they rate as very mediocre historians. Their accounts of Florence do not stand out by reason of new facts drawn into the light of day or of any intellectual distinction imparted to the traditionally accepted facts. As we have seen, unless the historian shines in one or the other or, better still, in both of these particulars, he will have labored in vain. Nothing illustrates more strikingly the tendency of Bruni and Poggio to succumb to false values than that, born to the racy Tuscan speech, they chose to write in the stilted Latin which the intelligentsia of their day considered a more dignified and worthy vehicle of expression. Except to pin on them their appropriate historiographical tag, there is no reason to drag them from the limbo to which they consigned themselves by their own deliberate vacuity.

The third period of Florentine historiography makes a clean break with the barren tradition of the early humanists by re-establishing an immediate contact with life. Chronologically the third period falls within the first half of the sixteenth century and is culturally identified with the later humanism of the full Renaissance. At the same time it embraces, politically, the last and dying phase of the Florentine republic. Pre-eminent among the names of the period are two that will always have a place on Clio's golden roll of honor, Niccolò Machiavelli and Francesco Guicciardini. But let us never forget that these leaders appeared among a host of hardly lesser men. Besides them, Nardi,[4] Nerli,[5] Vettori,[6] Varchi,[7] Segni,[8] and Pitti,[9] directed their considerable

[4] J. Nardi, *Istorie della Città di Firenze dall'anno 1494 fino al 1531*. 2 vols. Florence, 1858.
[5] F. Nerli, *Commentari dei Fatti Civili occorsi nella Città di Firenze*. Augsburg, 1728.
[6] F. Vettori, "Sommario della Storia d'Italia dal 1511 al 1527," *Arch. Stor. It.*, Vol. VI (1848), Appendice.
[7] B. Varchi, *Storia Fiorentina*. Per cura di L. Arbib. 3 vols. Florence, 1838-41.
[8] B. Segni, *Istorie Fiorentine dall'anno 1527 al 1555*. Florence, 1857.
[9] J. Pitti, "Istoria Fiorentina," *Arch. Stor. It.*, Vol. I (1842).

talents upon the spectacle under their eyes of the struggling but doomed commonwealth of which they were living, passionate, and suffering members. Whoever looks about to discover another city or nation which within the spread of approximately half a century harbored an equally brilliant array of historians will be put to a long and probably futile search.

Naturally this group of writers has much in common. To begin with, they all have a share, though in different degree, in the advanced thought of the Renaissance. No longer worshiping the ancients as unapproachable models, as had their predecessors of the early humanistic school, they have by reason of this very independence learned some of the finest secrets of their classical exemplars, above all, their sharp analysis of human motive. Moreover, by being confronted in their day by the extraordinary spectacle of an Italy culturally predominant but politically too feeble successfully to defend itself against the attack and invasion of the two great powers of France and Spain, they found themselves thrust, as it were, into a political laboratory in which all the doctrines of the ancients and their own as well were put to the test of practice. It was of course a terribly painful experience, this watching the slow and fateful enslavement of their country to foreigners rated by them with their greater refinement of mind and manners as rude barbarians. The spectacle wounded them profoundly and each reacted to his wound, according to his temperament and social standing, by boiling indignation, or loss of faith, or weak dejection, or frigid cynicism, or by all these moods in varying combination. But, in addition to the depressing drama of general Italian subjection, this group of Florentine historians was confronted with the no less tragic experience of Florence itself. This is particularly important, for in an Italy partitioned among a host of little states and not yet disposed seriously to entertain the thought of national unity, these men were Florentines before they were Italians. When it came to choosing a historical field on which to exercise their literary and reasoning powers, they therefore showed a preference for the theme nearest their heart and focused their attention on their narrow actual rather than on their broad ideal fatherland. In one form or another they all produced histories of Florence. This holds even of Guicciardini, although it is a notable circumstance distinguishing him that, after writing a history of Florence in his youth, he undertook in his mature years—and he was the first man who ever did so—to write a history of Italy as a political whole.[10] With the widest practical experience in political affairs of any member of the Renaissance group he came to see that, after the invasion of Italy by Charles VIII in 1494 and the consequent destruction of the old Italian balance of power, the developments in the city of Florence were unintelligible save within the frame

[10] F. Guicciardini, *La Storia d'Italia* . . . a cura di A. Gherardi. 4 vols. Florence, 1919.

of the forces operating throughout the peninsula. Machiavelli, too, rose occasionally to this larger vision as is witnessed by his famous study in contemporary government, *The Prince*. But only Guicciardini gave it expression in the novel form of a general Italian history.

Citizens of Florence and essentially contemporaries, the historians we are considering were confronted with political fluctuations in their native town involving two leading problems which never ceased to press upon and puzzle them. What were the weaknesses of the old republican constitution which had enabled the Medici gradually to replace it with their tyranny? And why, when the Medici were overthrown, for the first time in 1494 and again in 1527, had it been impossible to find a new and satisfactory constitution of a popular kind? Without an inkling of the modern view of the state as a slow and cumulative organic growth, they all regarded government as mere machinery, that is, as a product of human craftsmanship, skilled or unskilled as the case might be. It followed that they believed it could be carried to something like perfection by untiring thought and ever-renewed experimentation. They were prompted to this view, to a certain extent, by their classical exemplars, but in the main they came to it from the actual, perplexing developments of their own country. For several generations, indeed ever since the collapse of feudalism in the thirteenth century, governments devised by individuals or groups had been hopefully set up at one point or another throughout Italy only to be replaced by a fresh and more promising invention before as much as a year or even a month had gone round.

It is because of this intense preoccupation with government in general and with the Florentine government in particular that the Renaissance historians have been characterized as *statisti* (statesmen) and *politici* (politicians). Each had his own political viewpoint and in both practice and theory traveled his individual path; nonetheless they had so much in common that, by examining the procedure of one, we become measurably familiar with the leading characteristics of them all. Doubtless their most brilliant representative and certainly the one who most deeply impressed the succeeding generations down to our own time was Machiavelli. To his countrymen of the Fascist Italy of today he is more emphatically than at any earlier period *il nostro più grande politico.* While his living admirers usually base their high estimate of his talents on *The Prince,* so closely devoted to government as to be classifiable as essentially a treatise in political science, they cannot afford not to take account of his more purely narrative work, the *History of Florence.* Although indisputably a history and not a political essay, its assumptions and teachings are in no way at variance with those of *The Prince.* Having space for only a single example of Renaissance historiography, let us turn to this able, powerfully reasoned, and, in spite of innumerable errors of fact and feeble documentation, still invaluable book.[11]

Machiavelli's general attitude toward the Florentine republic during its career of several centuries is highly characteristic. He contends that the goal of every political community is unity, and that, if unity is difficult to achieve, it is because of the constant formation in the midst of every society of *sette* or parties. Parties are an affliction capable of being mastered only by good laws, from which, should they become successfully established, there results not only unity but that special reward of unity and highest goal of struggling mankind, civil liberty. To this goal the Florentines had persistently aspired, but as they had never been able to overcome the pest of parties, they had never quite achieved their aim. True, they had clung to their purpose longer than the other Italian cities, but in the end, like every community unable to cure its internal divisions, they had succumbed to the intervention of the tyrant. Between the two poles of liberty (the dream) and tyranny (the actuality) hangs suspended the world of Machiavelli's thought. Brought up in the Florentine republican tradition, he could not help putting a lingering faith in the corrective power of wise laws; but faced with the periodic and, finally, the permanent anarchy which overtook every Italian city-republic (with the exception of Venice), he was obliged by his clearness of vision and uncompromising rectitude of mind to justify the armed enforcer of laws and destroyer of parties, the prince. This meant, in the case of Florence, to declare for the Medici, certainly with no touch of enthusiasm, and just as certainly on no ground of vulgar self-interest, as has frequently been charged. The incisive but passionate thinker that Machiavelli was contented himself to present the facts as he found them and resolutely to stand by the consequences.

While Machiavelli's views on law, liberty, and parties are far from identical with those of Guicciardini, Nerli, Varchi, or any other Renaissance writer, for each of these masters reflects a very personal attitude toward the troublesome problems of Florence, nonetheless his thought and method enable us to establish the intellectual kinship existing among all the members of the group. They all saw history as limited to politics and wrote of Florence accordingly, weaving into the political narrative that particular compound of personal feeling and scientific detachment resulting from the sum of each one's qualities. Less narrators, however, than political philosophers, they accompanied the events they describe with copious reflections on governments and parties and on the actions of leaders diversely moved by jealousy, zeal, ambition, and all the other passions to which man is heir. Whoever in our day reads their books, no longer

[11] Niccolò Machiavelli, *Istorie Fiorentine*. Testo critico con Introduzione e Note per cura di Plinio Carli. 2 vols. Florence, 1927.

does so for their factual content, which is admittedly uneven and far from trustworthy, but for this savory by-product of their comment. By means of it they have thrown, as the ancients did before them, a sharp light on the personal agencies and accidents which now as then make and unmake governments and on the hidden psychological twists which have prompted and will always prompt the actions of men. And let it be once more said that although their procedure co-ordinates them historically with the ancients, they are no miserable apprentice group like the early humanists but, owing to the native vigor of their minds, a body of masters in their own right.

In the centuries that have elapsed since the Renaissance and particularly in the most recent century, the conception of history has undergone a great change. History, as the living generation understands it, embraces immense bodies of subject matter besides politics, and this enlargement of scope has brought it about that the narrowly focused Renaissance histories strike us as thin and, from the point of view of the invisible and truly determinative forces in Florentine development, as even lacking in relevance. This change in evaluation may be adduced as further proof of the theory, expounded in connection with Villani and underlying this whole historiographical survey, that each age or stage of civilization weaves a logic and mentality peculiar to itself into the texture of the facts, thus producing the history suitable to its own level of taste and experience but certain to be revised, if not rejected altogether, when another level has been reached. To the Machiavelli-Guicciardini school of thinkers the definition of history as past politics was so entirely satisfactory that they would have been unable even to conceive of a criticism inspired by another view of what it is important to know about the past. And yet another view is precisely what did come about, though only as the result of a development covering many generations. Consequently the Renaissance historians have gradually lost their vogue until at the present day they are but rarely taken from the shelves for the reason, against which there is no appeal, that they fail to supply the kind of information concerning Florence we moderns are resolved to have.

Long before rejection went this length, however, the school was subjected to adverse criticism on a ground other than that of scope. Engrossed with political reflections, deductions, and apothegms, it had only a secondary interest in the accuracy of its facts, taking them generally with the greatest unconcern and often without changing a single word from earlier authors who had gone over the same ground. Even Machiavelli and Guicciardini followed a practice which by our present standards would lay them open to a clear charge of plagiarism.[12]

[12] The habit of transcribing entire passages has been proved in the case of Guicciardini by Ranke in his *Zur Kritik neuerer Geschichtschreiber* and for Machiavelli by P. Villari in Vol. III, chaps. XII, XIII, XIV, of his *Niccolò Machiavelli e i suoi Tempi*. Florence, 1877-82.

We might not trouble ourselves about a transgression which did not rank as such in the eyes of their contemporaries were it not for important implications of the practice incapable of being overlooked. By taking much of their material bodily from selected predecessors, the Renaissance historians failed to subject their always prejudiced and often thoroughly unreliable authorities to the cleansing process of a healthy criticism; and even worse, they failed to cultivate and deepen a conviction which, astir in them, though in rudimentary form, counseled them to set the evidence of the original documents above the convenient but unsafe manuals at their elbow. We may therefore say sweepingly of them, not only that they did not go back to the primary sources, but also that they did not apply the sharp scalpel of criticism to the secondary authorities on which in the main they relied.

We must be careful to distinguish, in the case of these incisive political thinkers, between a sense of reality in which they abounded and a sense of valid historical proof in which they were conspicuously deficient. This contradiction has served to bring it about that, while their incisive intelligence has tended to secure them continued consideration, their shortcomings as investigators have raised a demand for a fuller and more reliable treatment of events. As a matter of fact it was not till the seventeenth and even the eighteenth century that such a demand made itself generally felt. Its appearance was undoubtedly owing to a novel and increasing appreciation of the value of primary sources. But so many difficulties had to be overcome before primary sources could be made broadly available that students of history only very gradually abandoned the traditional authorities and the slipshod method of getting at the facts which these authorities had hallowed. Not that there was or ever had been any lack of original documents. They were known to exist in great quantities in state, municipal, and ecclesiastical archives; but as these crowded repositories had been permitted to fall into an appalling confusion, there was required as a preliminary measure a long and costly labor of archival reorganization. Then, with the documents catalogued according to classes and periods, the difficult and interminable work of deciphering, editing, and interpreting them could at last be inaugurated. All this was something new: it was scholarship, and scholarship would have to develop its numerous special divisions and techniques before a new kind of history, consciously and solidly founded on scholarship and its inexhaustible resources, could come to birth.

It was in the seventeenth century that the vast possibilities for history of a scholarship dedicated to the recovery and interpretation of the records first dawned, not only on the Italian, but on the European mind in general. The new trend made its first appearance in the field of ecclesiastical history. This was as might be expected, since with the Reformation attacking the Catholic church on the score of its alleged perversion of the teachings of the early saints and holy doctors, the most effective defense against the charge would be an appeal to the original records. Zealous and learned Catholic champions, therefore, launched the publication of diverse bodies of ecclesiastical data such as the *Annales Ecclesiastici* undertaken by Baronius just before the close of the sixteenth century and the *Acta Sanctorum,* which began to appear in 1643. The service rendered to the Roman church by these and similar collections of source materials can hardly be exaggerated. They buttressed its weakened foundations and enabled it triumphantly to resist all later Protestant attacks. That was their immediate practical value; but, in the light of the historiographical development we are engaged in tracing, they possess the additional merit of having blazed the path for historical scholarship in general.

As soon as the value of documents for ecclesiastical history was recognized, it was inevitable that they should be demanded also for a fuller understanding of civil and secular history. Here and there throughout western Europe scattered individuals gradually caught the scent and published, at first rather as antiquarians than as scholars (for scholarship required time to develop its strict tenets), some of the secular manuscripts which they found buried in the private libraries of great lords or in neglected public archives. In Italy more than elsewhere men were carried off their feet by this novel antiquarian passion, and among its earliest evidences was a new history of Florence. Its authors were the two Ammirati, father and son, and so numerous were the new facts they succeeded in abstracting from hitherto neglected documents that their book, a recognizably novel departure, won a standing which it retained far into the nineteenth century.[13] The devotedly Christian spirit of these two sons of the Counter-Reformation is in the sharpest possible contrast to the largely pagan attitude of their Renaissance predecessors. This is worth noting as marking the effects of time; but it is more important still to take due account of their meticulous antiquarianism, which moved them to pile up their novel data in a shapeless mass instinctively repugnant to the order and clarity of the classical tradition.

Though enterprising and earnest devotees of learning, the Ammirati and the many imitative dilettanti scattered over Italy who followed in their footsteps failed to make a deep impression until that rarity, a genuinely creative scholar, came along whose genius first succeeded in giving significance to the new studies. This was the famous Muratori, who in the second quarter of the eighteenth century issued his magnificent collection of the medieval sources of

[13] S. Ammirato, *L'Istorie Fiorentine.* Con le Giunte di Scipione Ammirato il Giovane. 3 vols. (folio). Florence, 1647.

his country.[14] If his work set a scholarly mark for the other nations to aim at, that fact states its European importance; its main significance for Muratori's own people was that it made accessible for the first time and in an orderly form a sizable portion of the vast body of raw material on which a deep-delving and thoroughgoing history of medieval Italy and, above all, of that renowned medieval institution, the free commune, would have to be based. Of course even Muratori's *Scriptores* no more than blazed a trail, though a trail pointing in the right direction; and it should cause no surprise that it was only after some further generations of at first rather poorly correlated efforts that Italian and European scholarship awakened to its full responsibilities as the gateway to a new and modern type of history-writing completely liberated from the hampering conventions of the classical method and resting on its own deliberately developed preconceptions.

But this is not the place to unfold the story and analyze the stages in the development of modern historical scholarship. It is not even the intention of this Introduction to treat in exhaustive detail of Florentine historiography since from the start we have pursued no other end than the indication of the chief phases of its ebb and flow. On looking back over the road traveled thus far, we note again that a long period of flighty myth-makers was followed in the fourteenth century by a realist group of honest chroniclers, of whom the forthright, inquisitive Villani was the leading spirit. Then in the next century came the early humanists, hollow imitators of Livy and the other Roman masters, to be followed after another century by the great Renaissance writers, Machiavelli and the rest, who, while they continued to tread in the footsteps of the ancients, won a place at their side as their not unworthy compeers. But was this the end of desire? Not in a civilization which, like that of western Europe, is always pushing on to new horizons! Owing to the expansive nature of western culture and its amazing ability ever to renew itself, the seventeenth and eighteenth centuries, as we have seen, glimpsed fresh possibilities by the use of a more comprehensive and critical method than the one employed by the historians of Greece and Rome. These pioneering centuries uncovered the value of original documents and in the course of their long-continued occupation with them gradually shaped the numerous techniques which in their sum constitute our vaunted modern scholarship.

But let us make no mistake: scholarship is a portal, not a goal. It deals with the records left behind by the past, not as though they were an end in themselves, but in order that the unusual and rare scholar who combines creative gifts of mind with the stern discipline of research may set forth a more accu-

[14] *Rerum Italicarum Scriptores ab Anno Aerae Christianae 500 ad 1500.* Edited by L. A. Muratori. 25 vols. Milan, 1723-51. Completed by his *Antiquitates Italicae Medii Aevi.* 6 vols. Milan, 1738-42.

rate and authentic version of the past. Hence the modern historian, though he must be refreshed at the well of scholarship and emancipated from the narrow older methods, is still required, like the classical historians, the original inventors of this form of literature, to prove himself an artist. It is his task to take over the voluminous and sifted data of innumerable scholarly helpers and to give them an order and a meaning, rendering them intelligible and quickening to his generation. Thus both consciously and unconsciously (for much of the labor of every artist is of the unconscious kind), he impresses a particular stamp on his work which is not native to the facts. "It dates" is the current phrase by which we admit the presence in every literary production, including history, of characteristics which do not derive from the material itself but from its treatment by an individual mind. Did we not detect mind behind the legend, behind Villani's candid narrative, behind the writings of both the earlier and the later humanists? Undoubtedly we did; and when in due course modern historiography based on modern scholarship began its sway, mind or viewpoint or an underlying norm of judgment—call it what you will—continued to figure in every separate production exactly as before.

This needs expressly to be said because of the contrary claim regarding history-writing in our day which has recently been advanced by some historical practitioners and their attendant band of scholars. Conscious of the greater fullness and accuracy made possible by the vast accumulations of tested data put at their disposal through systematic research, they have set up as their ideal the history which represents the complete recovery of the past and is therefore that final and conclusive thing, the truth. They may admit that the truth has as yet in no single instance been attained; still they declare its mastery to be possible by reason of their confidence in the elaborate and impressive machinery of modern scholarship. Indeed so great is their faith in this tool that they frequently call their improved method of investigation "scientific," boldly equating it with the method of the natural sciences and claiming for it an effectiveness that is bound to find its culmination in the discovery of a body of historical laws sweepingly descriptive of the past and valid for the whole future of our human kind.

As this is not the place for a searching theoretical discussion on the nature of history, we shall content ourselves with two declaratory statements which, if they prove nothing, at least make clear the position taken by the writer with regard to the above-mentioned claim. First, we agree with the champions of the "scientific" school that modern historians enjoy an immense advantage over their predecessors through the abundant factual resources made available by the extraordinarily fruitful activities of scholarship. Secondly, we flatly reject the assertion that scholarship has put us in possession of a method capable of replacing our doubts and uncertainties about the past and our incurable igno-rance touching the future with a revelation carrying with it the implication of a final truth; and consequently we categorically refuse to assign to history which has always been and must needs remain a very personal art, the status of an abstract science. It is our opinion that these statements will be established beyond reasonable doubt by the review of the last and modern phase of Floren-tine historiography which we shall now undertake.

Modern Florentine historiography dates from the beginning of the nine-teenth century and Sismondi is its first notable representative. Although of remote Italian ancestry, J. C. L. Simonde de Sismondi was a Genevan by birth who wrote his famous *History of the Italian Republics* in his native language, that is, in French.[15] While he treated of Florence in this work, he treated of it along with all the other Italian city-republics since he was prompted to undertake his work by a very definite idea or theme. This was that the Italian communes mark the rise of human liberty out of the muck of feudal degrada-tion and tyranny. In this general story the Arno town was no more than a link in a connected chain. When Sismondi began to write, a modern tyrant, the Emperor Napoleon, dominated Europe; and since the Genevan's work with its libertarian theme had a subtle relevance to contemporary conditions, it aroused considerable interest and was widely read. But before long the critics began to busy themselves with its shortcomings and had no difficulty in demon-strating that they were neither few nor unimportant. To begin with, there was the inevitable subjective contribution. Sismondi was intellectually the child of the French Revolution and a passionate partisan of its concept of liberty. This was decidedly in his favor so far as those readers were concerned who sub-scribed to the current revolutionary doctrine; but the conservatives, who, espe-cially after 1815, were for a time in the ascendant, were repelled by an attitude which presented itself to them as a detestable mental squint. Between the two hostile camps, which respectively extolled and damned the new work, stood a small band of scholars who, dedicated to the ideal of fair play, were able with-out fear or favor to point out the extravagances and anachronisms into which Sismondi's libertarian enthusiasm had led him. In the course of time their moderate view gradually prevailed with the result that no one now disputes that Sismondi's work exhibits all the hallmarks of the political philosophy which dominated his own and the succeeding generation and which is loosely subsumed under the term liberalism. Liberalism still enjoys support in con-siderable present-day circles, but it would not occur to any living man capable

[15] J. C. L. Simonde de Sismondi, *Histoire des Républiques Italiennes du Moyen Age*. 16 vols. Paris, 1809-18.

of detached reflection to conceive of it as other than the mental product of a particular and limited phase of human experience.

Even more vigorously the critics of Sismondi's work exposed its weakness on turning to its cargo of facts. Multiplied knowledge verified by authentic documents was the shibboleth of the new school of erudition, and, although Sismondi had not failed to profit from the labors of the eighteenth-century investigators, he could not foresee the discoveries subsequent to his date of publication. But such discoveries followed without interruption, stimulated in part by his own work and the numerous historical controversies which it succeeded in stirring up. Among other questions the origin of the commune treated by him raised the issue in a nationalist-minded Europe whether the new and promising self-government of the twelfth and thirteenth centuries was the child of the free institutions carried into the Italian peninsula by the Germanic invaders or whether it was nothing other than the return to life of the Roman municipal institutions supposed long since to have perished. Scholars of great renown such as Savigny, Leo, Hegel, and Troya were drawn into this fundamental debate, and, while they were not able to bring the quarrel to a speedy settlement, they succeeded in drawing into the light of day a body of hidden material concerning the rise of the Italian communes which added invaluable details to our knowledge of the subject. The long-drawn-out battle between the champions respectively of the Roman and the German schools constitutes one of the most brilliant episodes of modern scholarship and undoubtedly carried Italian studies to a higher plane. Its leading result was that to a considerable extent the conviction gained ground that the demand of the hour was not so much a new history either of Florence or of any other medieval commune as a continued exploitation of the archives along the line of Muratori's pioneer labors. Not, however, without a different emphasis from Muratori. As the very title, *Scriptores,* of Muratori's leading work shows, the eighteenth century had given a preference to the evidence supplied by forgotten medieval chroniclers, and Sismondi had built his communal edifice largely on this class of evidence. The vigorous controversy that followed had shown the superiority of documents, which were the immediate impersonal records of political and juridical acts or of commercial transactions, over chronicles with their inevitable errors of fact and their element of personal bias. What we may call the later or nineteenth-century phase of scholarship gave precedence to documents with an official character and in the discovery, cataloguing, and interpretation of them developed an intensity and professional severity which left the scholars of Muratori's day far behind.

While no one will expect an exact date of birth to be assigned to this more intensive scholarship dedicated to sources incontestably primary, it is proper to bring out that one of its attendant features was the appearance and multiplication of professional journals. In 1842 such a journal, the *Archivio Storico Italiano,* saw the light at Florence. Planned as a co-operative enterprise for the promulgation of unpublished manuscripts and records and for minute critical monographs by and for a limited circle of experts, it scored an immediate success and has now for almost a hundred years served as a rallying-point, especially for scholars interested in Tuscan and Florentine developments. For to this field it has largely confined its attention, leaving the other provinces of Italy to other journals of a similar nature which presently sprang up. But let no one imagine that the *Archivio* sufficed as a repository for the special studies on Florence to which the confident and prolific nineteenth-century phase of scholarship gave rise. Interest in Florence became an unquenchable enthusiasm and, spreading to every country of Europe, produced a steady stream of studies, brochures, and books on every phase of the town's activities. Since, let us say, the middle of the nineteenth century these specialized contributions, which, were this Introduction a systematic historiographical survey, would have to be examined in detail, have grown to such dimensions that justice could not be done to them short of a ponderous volume. And the great flood of these publications has shown no sign of abatement to the present day.

We are but holding ourselves to our self-imposed limitations if, after indicating the nature and mass of the output of a numerous, widely scattered, and narrowly focused body of scholars, we return to our central argument and raise the question whether this devotion to the minutiae of the past has checked the production of general histories dealing with Florence. For, occupied solely with them, we have attempted to define their tendencies since the first appearance of the genre. A general history, in distinction from the highly specialized product which has without question been the most characteristic feature of history-writing in the reigning era of scholarship, represents an attempt at an intellectual synthesis of a larger or shorter period of Florentine experience, and practically all of the earlier Florentine historical literature from the birth of the legend to the rise of modern scholarship falls by our definition under this particular head. When, following the rise of a meticulous scholarship, Sismondi presented the first synthesis of the communal movement, he revealed the heavy risks to which histories of the general type would henceforth be exposed. For, owing to the rapid and ceaseless accumulation of new data, a general history was not likely to enjoy authority for any considerable length of time. But it is also true that by or shortly after Sismondi's day, Florence had taken possession of the consciousness of all educated people as a prime factor in the development of our occidental culture. This is all-important and must never be forgotten. For it was the passionate curiosity focusing on Florence that made the production of further syntheses inevitable, no matter how vigorously some perfectionists might argue that all such attempts should be abandoned until scholarship had completed its work of assembling and sifting all the available documentary material. The weakness of the perfectionist argument lies, on the one hand, in the circumstance that the labors of scholarship in their very nature can never be terminated, and, on the other hand, in the inconclusiveness of the facts, however well established, considered by themselves. Regarding this latter peculiarly important point, we must again insist that a written history is the product of an individual mind selecting and arranging the facts and that every community and generation imperatively needs such a history as an aid to its orientation in an ever-changing world. Moreover, varying and even contradictory versions arising out of varying and contradictory viewpoints are as desirable as they are unescapable. From this need and habit of a continuous working over of the past, it follows that more especially in the recent decades of accelerated change it is not uncommon for a history, which on its appearance was greeted with enthusiasm, to be regarded after the lapse of a relatively short span of years as stale, pointless, and outmoded.

We should now be prepared to understand why, even if some specialists have frankly deprecated the writing of further histories of Florence until scholarship shall have written finis under its labors, the writing of such histories has gone on in response to an ever-present demand of the human spirit. In concluding our review by considering these productions of the new age of scholarship we shall glance only at the outstanding works in order to determine their character and value. Exactly as throughout our sketch, our aim will continue to be illustrative rather than exhaustive; above all, we shall disregard every work, no matter how much esteemed in lay circles, which does not meet modern professional standards by being a significant synthesis resting solidly on the great body of minute analytical studies.

In the seventies the Frenchman Perrens began the publication of a history of Florence which was planned on a larger scale than had ever been essayed before. It appeared in two parts, the first part reaching to the Medicean domination, the second part covering the rule of the Medici to the fall of the republic in 1531.[16] At about the same time a descendant of an ancient Florentine family, Gino Capponi, put out his history representing a labor of love sustained through many decades.[17] Both of these men were able and diligent students, but diligence, however great, could not save them, as it has not saved any of their predecessors and will not save any of their successors, from being over-

[16] F. T. Perrens, *Histoire de Florence* (from the origins to 1434). 6 vols. Paris, 1877-83. F. T. Perrens, *Histoire de Florence depuis la domination des Médicis jusqu'à la chute de la République (1434-1531)*. 3 vols. Paris, 1888.

[17] Gino Capponi, *Storia della Repubblica di Firenze*. 2 vols. Florence, 1875.

taken before long by a tireless scholarship. Since the day their works first saw the light the specialists have succeeded in uncovering such a wealth of data touching every stage, and especially the earliest stages of Florentine history that the information conveyed by Perrens and Capponi has become either partially or wholly obsolete. That it took only some fifty years to bring about this result conveys a vivid impression of the tempo of modern discovery. A more melancholy implication of this accelerated motion is that all works of history produced under modern conditions are destined to have but a short life and that a literary form, which in its classical representatives still enjoys high authority, has recently taken on a tragically ephemeral aspect.

Threatened with oblivion because their scholarship is no longer abreast of the times, Perrens and Capponi have not suffered eclipse to the same extent on account of their viewpoint. True, their peculiar ideology no longer rules the day, but it is characteristic of mental formulas that they command scattered intellectual support even after they have gone, generally speaking, out of fashion. Nonetheless the outlook of each of these historians is for us of a later age very definitely the product of a "dated" mind. Perrens was close enough to Sismondi to be swayed by the same nineteenth-century philosophy of liberalism and he employed it just as confidently and jubilantly as had his predecessor for the framework of his story. As for Capponi, the born Florentine, he was the natural heir of the powerful Guelph tradition native to his city. He was the less moved to question its validity as he wrote expressly for his fellow-townsmen in their own plain speech with no other purpose than that of producing a work which they would gladly read ("una storia tutta popolana"). Capponi is throughout his narrative as consistently a Florentine Guelph as Perrens is a pugnacious, mid-century European liberal. And while each viewpoint still has followers, it no longer carries as much weight as it once did.

While these men were still engaged on their respective tasks it happened that the concept of history experienced that final expansion at which we have already glanced. In the view of the ancients history was concerned with affairs of state, and this view, taken over by the humanists, long continued to dominate the moderns. Even after the startling conquests of an enterprising scholarship and the concomitant decline of the prestige of the ancients, historians were reluctant to abandon the classical models in the matter of the definition and scope of history and continued to follow them in these particulars far into the nineteenth century. Indeed up to the very threshold of the twentieth century, Thucydides and Tacitus have in some quarters been extolled as the unrivaled and never-to-be-surpassed exponents of the literary genre called history. In the meantime, however, political economy, sociology, anthropology, and psychology had come strongly to the fore with their special discoveries regarding man and society which the historians, enamored though they might be of diplomacy and war, could not in the long run ignore. First here, then there, protests against the weight of a dead tradition made themselves heard. They swelled to an academic storm, a much more frightful phenomenon than the innocent words suggest, and, when toward the close of the nineteenth century the atmosphere began to clear, the time-honored political conception had been discarded in favor of the broader view that history should and must take account not only of government but also of commerce, industry, communications, social classes, juridical theory and procedure, the progress of the arts, and every other matter shaping the life of men. In the eyes of the reformers classical history and its more recent derivates became Old History, while the New History, offered as a substitute, proposed to regard politics as no more than the surface manifestation of much more fundamental forces stirring at the heart of the world. Interpreted in connection with the whole movement of civilization during the last half of the nineteenth century, the New History was essentially an attempt on the part of its adepts to put themselves in step with their time. Influenced though these adepts were by the important developments in both the social and the natural sciences, they were particularly impressed with the enormous and revolutionary advances made by the allied biological studies. In this connection it will serve to clarify the perspective if we remind ourselves that Darwin's epoch-making *Origin of Species* came from the press in 1859. Under the general conceptions which this book more than any other helped to popularize, government came to be viewed as a biological organism engaged in gradual evolutionary transformation; at the same time it came to be rated as a rather minor organism embraced within the much vaster social organism which gave it birth. Slowly but inevitably the attention of the historian swung from the less inclusive to the more inclusive entity, from government to society, while the purpose of the historian came with mounting insistence to define itself as the tracing of the ceaseless biological changes of the particular social organism under consideration.

The enlarged societal view of history which naturally invaded and took possession also of the Florentine field was in the nineties voiced vigorously for the first time by Pasquale Villari in the most penetrating study of the origins of the Arno town which had thus far appeared.[18] With the aid of the preparatory labors of a group of contemporary scholars he was able to go beyond any of his predecessors in reducing the struggles, triumphs, and institutions of the young commune to an intelligible unity. As is usual with fertile and original works, his book did not go unchallenged and led to an intensified exploration

[18] P. Villari, *I Primi Due Secoli della Storia di Firenze.* 2 vols. Florence, 1893-94. New edition, 1905.

of the archives and to better co-ordinated projects of publication. In fact, materials of such importance and variety were brought to light that they made possible a complete reshaping of Florentine history in accordance with the modern social and evolutionary emphasis. Prominent among this recent group of scholars working on a broader system were men such as Paoli, Gherardi, Hartwig, Santini, and Salvemini.[19] And no sooner did the older members of this group begin to pass from the scene than they were replaced by eager disciples such as Ciasca, Sapori, Ottokar, in whom the fires of politico-social research burned with undiminished ardor.

Agreeable as it would be to define the learned and often creative contribution of these contemporary or all but contemporary scholars, we shall have to content ourselves with singling out the monumental work of the greatest master of them all, Robert Davidsohn.[20] There are those who do not hesitate to hail in Davidsohn the most fruitful scholar among the many who since the revolution inaugurated by Muratori have made Florentine history their specialty. They would accord him this distinction on the strength of the vast amount of new material touching every phase of Florentine development he has uncovered not only in Florentine and Tuscan but in Italian archives in general. For within the whole peninsula there is no notable repository of materials bearing on Florentine affairs to which he has not resorted in his search for first-hand information. But if, as has happened in some cases, the critics extol his scholarship only to belittle his historical art, it is impossible to subscribe to this judgment, at least without important reservations. For Davidsohn, thoroughly imbued with the spirit of his generation, is dominated by the organic conception of society and has consistently striven to utilize the innumerable fresh data discovered by himself and others for the better understanding of the slow unfolding through the ages of the Arno commonwealth. Aiming to present an intelligible and unique whole engaged in an unbroken development under environmental stimulus as well as under its own indefinable impulsion, he has so well succeeded that, although many problems, as might be expected, have continued to baffle him, he has far surpassed in the close weave of his fabric his predecessors of every historiographical period. Indeed they make an almost painfully threadbare showing beside him enveloped in his sturdy, full-bodied garment. As the work has to date not advanced beyond the early decades of the fourteenth century, it remains to be seen if the

[19] Some of their labors may be here listed for purposes of illustration: C. Paoli, *Il Libro di Montaperti*. Florence, 1889. P. Santini, *Documenti dell'Antica Costituzione del Comune di Firenze*. Florence, 1895. A. Gherardi, *Le Consulte della Repubblica Fiorentina*. Florence, 1896. G. Salvemini, *Magnati e Popolani in Firenze dal 1280 al 1295*. Florence, 1899.

[20] R. Davidsohn, *Geschichte von Florenz*. 4 vols. Berlin, 1896-1927. Also *Forschungen zur Geschichte von Florenz*. 4 vols. Berlin, 1896-1908.

later volumes will prove equally substantial. The central organic viewpoint re-enforced by the disclosures resulting from a better co-ordinated attack on the documents was certain to prove particularly valuable for the earlier and relatively neglected stages of Florentine development. The great Renaissance writers took very slight account of these remoter phases and were content to limit their consideration of Florence to the Medicean rule. Should Davidsohn ever get to the Medici, a possibility which in view of his advanced years and the deliberate pace of publication hitherto maintained, is doubtful, he will enter more immediately into rivalry with this group of his predecessors and will find his own originality matched, on different and therefore essentially incomparable lines it is true, by theirs.

However, criticisms have been voiced against the work and may not be overlooked; for instance, against its immense, its positively astronomical scale. Although the author exercised in this respect a privilege within his choice, it committed him to a work of such spread and weight that other than specialists are not likely to read it without indulging in liberal omissions. This is regrettable, because if history is to maintain a secure position as a department of literature, it must not close the door upon the general reader. The cause of Davidsohn's imposing bulk is the absorption into his text of an immense number of details accumulated to illustrate a story of slow growth. Although from his point of view these tiny multiplied data possess each one a distinct importance, they bring it about that the large structural lines of the work at times completely disappear. While this is a drawback and a flaw, it is only intermittently disturbing, for in the long run the organic pattern, central to the whole composition, never fails to arise again from the mass, binding the profuse and usually significant matter into a finely integrated whole.

Even if Davidsohn's great work did not suffer from overspecialization and even if it went beyond the early fourteenth century to the fall of the republic, thus filling out its natural framework, it would not be the final history of Florence. For, let it be said once more, the final record of anything having, like the Arno town, a cultural significance the index of which changes with each new generation of men is an impossibility. There have therefore been histories since Davidsohn's which, though they are deeply in debt to both its facts and its viewpoint, take rank as independent works and are not just a rehash of the master-work. Perhaps the best of them is that of Romolo Caggese.[21] It exhibits a modern approach and critical spirit and, in spite of a self-satisfied and irritating dogmatism, comes off with a considerable sparkle. Moreover, it traces the story of Florence from beginning to end and even, as might

21 R. Caggese, *Firenze dalla Decadenza di Roma al Risorgimento d'Italia.* 3 vols. Florence, 1912-21.

be objected, beyond the end, since in the last volume it covers the wearisome and irrelevant stages of decay subsequent to the heroic demise of the republic in 1530. If the modern outlook requires that Florence be viewed as a social organism sustained by its native energy, there can be no valid argument for dissecting the remains after life has fled.

We have reached the end of our historiographical note, which was not intended to be and must not be confused with a bibliographical guide. Such a guide which, if ever undertaken, would win the gratitude of all serious students, will have to set itself a very broad task. Besides tracing, and far more fully than we have done, the general movement of Florentine historiography, it will have to classify, describe, and evalue all writings of every sort connected with the diverse fortunes and manifold achievements of Florence; and, because of the recent expansion of scholarly inquiry, it will have to give particular attention to the innumerable detailed studies of the last two or three generations. Our historiographical sketch was planned as an introduction to and, in a certain sense, as an explanation of, the present work. It is in no sense an apology, for an apology, if the purpose of history has been correctly set forth in the foregoing pages, is not necessary, since there is always room in a growing world for a new historical synthesis. If the synthesis is lacking in significance, the new version of an old story will quickly reveal itself as a work of supererogation. The simple criterion by which the reader of the present work may decide for himself the issue of its worth is to ask the question whether these pages revive or fail to revive the incomparable chapter of human experience that goes by the name of Florence. If the Arno city does not emerge from between the covers of this book as a living reality, if its noble civilization does not take on a fresh meaning, the author will and should be judged to have labored in vain. In that case he will have no reason to complain if his book should swiftly make its way into the capacious limbo reserved for literary efforts which have missed fire and serve no discoverable purpose.

MEDIEVAL
AND
RENAISSANCE
FLORENCE

I. Etruscan and Roman Florence

THERE is no better introduction to Florence than to mount one of the many hills by which it is surrounded and to let the quickened eye take in the noble physical setting in which the town is framed. For in the close relation of city, river, plain, and mountains lies the earliest and the most abiding clue to the history with which we are about to concern ourselves. Let us, therefore, after settling among a dozen possible lookouts on ancient Fiesole as our objective, ascend to this venerable forerunner of the more famous city lying at its foot, and having reached the wide piazza with its austere Romanesque cathedral, take the steep path that leads to the summit of the adjoining height. Here in remote Etruscan days rose Fiesole's arx or citadel. It has long since disappeared, but by a happy stroke of the magician Time its site is now occupied by the church, dormitories, and enchanted gardens of a Franciscan monastery, which, itself centuries old, goes back almost to the days of the Assisan saint.

From this incomparable outlook we command the whole dominion ruled by the Arno from the river's source in the lofty mountains of the Casentino to its junction with the Mediterranean at its journey's end. First in abrupt descents, then by more gradual inclines the crowded highlands fall away, hiding from sight the rushing river until it reaches the foothills directly under our eye and again disappears among the dense mass of roofs, domes, and towers constituting Florence. Beyond the city the valley gradually widens and the hills decline in height, though their march in ordered double file continues westward as far as the eye can reach. Between the diminishing elevations we trace the narrow ribbon of the Arno, flashing silver as it picks up the sun and sky, and visible almost to the western sea.

Turning again to the east, we note that the great chain of the Apennines, of which the Casentino range, the birthplace of the Arno, is but the central link, sweeps on proudly, not only to the south but to the north as well, curving westward around Fiesole until its columns encounter the north-south line of the marble-bearing Carrara group raising their sharp peaks along the Mediterranean shore. And suddenly we become aware that all this land of Tuscany, of which the Arno is the vivifying artery and Florence the natural focus, is a well-marked geographic unit constituting a broken plateau declining gently from the towering bastion of the Apennines to the low-lying Mediterranean Sea. While the Arno is the main stream, it has many tributaries coming from both north and south and, as the laughing landscape declares at a glance, the province is the home of a numerous and energetic farming population. An intense cultivation, conducted by means of terraces on which the vine and olive flourish, often extends to a considerable altitude before the too precipitous plunge of the upper levels with their mass of sliding rock defeats the effort of the industrious peasants to gain a living from the soil. However, only the summits of the high mountains are as a rule entirely barren, having ages ago been stripped of their waving forest crown by the improvident inhabitants. But who has time for economic regrets in the face of all this beauty? In spite of the arid mountain peaks, this Tuscany with its fertile bottom-lands, with its opulent vineyards and olive groves climbing every slope, with its industrious cities strung along the Arno from Arezzo at the source to Pisa at the mouth, with gracious Florence spread beneath our feet, with Pistoia and Lucca nestling unseen among the northern foothills, and with invisible Siena crowning the blue upland to the south over which runs the road to Rome—this seductive and infinitely various Tuscany, we are moved gladly to declare, is one of earth's garden spots in which God still walks as in the days of creation.

When in the distant ages we call prehistoric men first settled in this segment of the Italian peninsula, it was an untamed wilderness without a suggestion of its present evidences of an intense cultivation and multifold communications. Recent excavations have uncovered burial finds which make it certain that man's presence in Tuscany goes back many thousands of years. We know absolutely nothing of these first settlers of the Stone Age apart from the scant information disclosed by occasional tombs owing their discovery to the chance action of a peasant's pick or plow. The earliest inhabitants of whom we have a definite and relatively abundant knowledge are the Etruscans who have given the land and its dwellers the names whereby they have been known ever since. There is considerable likelihood that the Etruscans came to Italy by sea from Asia Minor. Supposing this migration to be a fact and to have taken place around 1000 B.C., we can without difficulty picture to ourselves the main conditions and stages under which the occupation took place. At that remote time dense forests affording excellent hunting covered all the uplands; and the many affluents of the Arno, which now are but torrents and disappear or almost disappear from view in summer, ran lustily the year round, while the Arno, itself at present no more than the ghost of a river in the torrid season, perennially rolled a broad sheet of water to the sea. There was fine fishing in these abundant streams which, in addition, served the descendants of the newcomers, as soon as they had acquired a firm footing along the bottom-lands, to float the products of the forests as well as the wheat, wine, and olive oil which they soon learned to grow to the Mediterranean Sea. Therewith the Etruscans touched a highway which they shared with many other peoples and by which they were free to exchange their native goods for the iron of Spain and the gold, silver, jewels, and pottery of those old and famous eastern centers of civilization, Egypt, Syria, and Greece.

These statements are not merely speculative; they are based on very considerable archaeological and even on some definite literary evidence. The scattered data permit us categorically to affirm not only that the ancient Etruscans were active farmers but also that they plied a busy trade with all the peoples of the Mediterranean littoral. There must too have been much warfare, for the settlers showed a decided preference for planting their towns on inaccessible hills and fortified each town with a powerful ring of masonry. At the side of this wall there regularly rose a soaring citadel. Fiesole, one of more than a score of characteristic Etruscan sites that can still be identified, bears witness in the massive remnants of its cyclopean wall to the political divisions as well as to the engineering skill and moral resolution of the Etruscan folk. A few hundred years after their arrival they had become sufficiently strong, or, to put it more correctly, a loose federation effected among some of their cities had become sufficiently strong, to assume the role of conqueror and to bring large sections of Italy, in addition to Tuscany, and more particularly Latium and Campania to the south, under their yoke. Recent investigations have established that they extended their rule over the young Latin settlement on the Tiber, called Rome, and that the kings with whom Roman history is inaugurated were probably nothing other than Etruscan tyrants who lost their throne when the Roman people rose against them and, casting them out, established a republic.

From this time on there was unceasing war between the vigorous, self-confident Roman republic and its former masters holding the hilly region to the north. For several centuries the battle swayed to and fro; but in the long run the Romans triumphed and by approximately 300 B.C. the Etruscan towns had one after the other been reduced to subjection. Thus the power of Etruria was broken and its independence came to an end. Naturally so striking a reversal may be set down as an important milestone in the resolute march of the Romans to complete domination in Italy. For us, however, who are concerned with Tuscany and not with Rome, its significance lies rather in the proof which it supplies that the old military prowess of the Etruscans had markedly declined. Their well-attested material prosperity, on the other hand, did not immediately follow the same downward curve. Indeed, owing to the greater measure of security which the firm Roman rule brought to Etruria and to the rest of the peninsula as well, production and exchange took on new life and the subjugated province became an important factor in the economic system of the expanding Roman republic.

It was under these general conditions that Florence was born. Around the year 200 B.C. the people of Fiesole, who had hitherto prudently clung to their fortified hilltop, made up their mind, since trade was now protected by a powerful central government and moved with the security provided by Roman military might along the convenient valley levels, to found a colony directly on the Arno. Somewhat to the east of the later historical Florence but within the range of its present suburban extension they built a small, strictly Etruscan settlement which prospered notably until Rome, seized with the digestive troubles growing out of its many too rapidly appropriated conquests, was convulsed with the violence of civil war. The Etruscans, among whom the memory of their former independence still lingered, sided very generally against the narrow nationalist and aristocratic faction headed by Sulla; and when Sulla was victorious they had to pay the price of defeat. For having offered a particularly stubborn resistance to the conqueror, youthful Florence, the infant of the Etruscan family of towns, was singled out as an example and in the year 82 B.C. was leveled with the ground. So complete was the destruction that it is only in recent times that the site of this first, short-lived, and Etruscan Florence has been definitely established.[1]

When after a brief interval the town arose again it was not as a colony of Etruscan Fiesole but of Latin Rome and with the conscious purpose on the part of the Latin founders of undoing the havoc caused by the recent devastating civil war. In the year 59 B.C. there was passed during the consulship and under the auspices of Julius Caesar an agrarian law which goes by his name (lex Julia) and which sketched a vigorous program of civic restoration throughout Italy. The Florentines of the poet Dante's day fondly believed that their city owed its existence to the personal intervention of the great Julius. That was a legendary exaggeration born of the desire of the medieval citizenry to be associated not only with conquering Rome but also with Rome's greatest son. However, since the founding undoubtedly took place in consequence of the reconstruction policy championed by Caesar, the medieval tradition was much less removed from the truth than most of the stories regarding the origins of the city believed in Dante's time and firmly rooted in Florentine consciousness to this very day.

The second Florence was not erected on the ruins of the first but somewhat farther downstream on the very ground which it still occupies. As no very great future was anticipated for the new venture, the ground plan, in the shape of the familiar square favored for the Roman camp, exhibits very modest proportions.[2] Its sides measured no more than five hundred meters, that is, hardly one-third of a mile. There was a wall with four main gates, one in the approximate center of each side, through which ran the north-south and east-west highways traversing the town. At their intersection and therefore in the approximate middle of the plan lay the forum or market, which for the convenience of traffic was relatively spacious. This forum corresponds to the Mercato Vecchio or Old Market of medieval times and in our day, although much enlarged by the ruthless destruction of a dark, picturesque tangle of adjoining streets, presents itself to view as the commonplace but spacious Piazza Vittorio Emanuele. The Romans erected a bridge across the Arno which, although in the course of time it had to be frequently rebuilt, is identical with the venerable, still existent Ponte Vecchio. The Ponte Vecchio served to conduct across the Arno the great northward road from Rome, the Via Cassia, which in passing through the town followed the line indicated by the

[1] The site of Etruscan Florence has been the subject of an acrimonious archaeological dispute which, in spite of the literary dust it has thrown up, is not very important. I have accepted the view of Davidsohn propounded in Vol. I, pp. 4-6, and supported by impressive evidence assembled in *Forschungen,* Vol. I, pp. 1-6. Davidsohn's opinion runs counter to the traditional view which identifies the site of Etruscan Florence with that of the later Roman Florence. Most of the local scholars such as Milani, Villari, and Santini have chosen on the basis of arguments which deserve respectful attention to adhere to the tradition. An eminently fair statement of their case is given by Villari, *I Primi Due Secoli della Storia di Firenze,* p. 61 note. New edition (1905). Santini indorses Villari in a review, *Arch. Stor. It.,* Serie 5, Vol. XXXV (1905), p. 453.

[2] A detailed plan of Roman Florence is attached to Davidsohn, Vol. I.

street now called Por Santa Maria and its prolongations. It is thus clear that Roman Florentia can still be traced in important topographical features of present-day Florence and, above all, in many of the north-south and east-west street lines.

Interesting as these identifications are, they do not permit us to deduce that the Roman town ever rose to be more than an unimportant provincial center of the greatest empire of antiquity. Like every other daughter of the great capital on the Tiber, it boasted, in imitation of the mother-city, an aqueduct, baths, a theater, and various temples to the gods. They have all completely disappeared, although their location has been determined and sections of their foundations have been uncovered by careful excavations conducted in the eighties and nineties of the nineteenth century. In the course of time and in proof of a certain modest expansion Florentia developed suburbs extending beyond each of the four main gates, and in the eastern, apparently thickly populated, suburb there was erected an amphitheater for the gladiatorial games and animal hunts which were a characteristic expression of the hard-featured warrior civilization of Rome. As the line followed by the circular outer wall of this rather ambitious monument can in part still be traced in the curve of certain house fronts in the neighborhood of the present Piazza Peruzzi, we may regard these crumbling segments of brick masonry as the most considerable single relic of the Roman city which has come down to us. In spite of the evidence that Roman Florence presented itself to view as a small-scale copy of the greatest capital of antiquity, it remains true that so long as the mother-city continued to dominate the world Florence played a humble, provincial role and fell with hardly perceptible weight into the political scales. It was rarely even as much as mentioned by the historians of the empire. Concerned with recounting the great affairs of state, they had no occasion to rescue from oblivion the happenings in the obscure and sleepy market center on the middle Arno.

On the strength of the decidedly meager body of evidence which has come down to us, we may think of Roman Florence as reaching its greatest bloom and prosperity during the early period of the empire and as then participating in the startling general decline of the Roman state and society. This was already so far advanced by the fourth century after Christ that the Romans themselves lost hope and ceased to struggle against fate. Consequently when with the fifth century there came the determined onslaught of the German tribes, the already demoralized empire went down before it like a spent fighter. It was in the year 405 A.D. that Florence experienced its first siege at the hands of an army of marauding barbarians under a Gothic leader named Radagasius. The invaders were beaten off and a great victory was won, but it is eloquent evidence of the hopeless Roman decline that the imperial armies were not led by a man of Roman birth but by Stilicho, a German tribesman in Roman employ. What is even more significant, Stilicho's victorious forces were made up entirely of hireling Goths and Huns. The battle fought on the broken terrain between Florence and Fiesole turned out to be the last crushing defeat Rome succeeded in administering to the barbarian invaders of Italy; and the only unequivocally Roman feature about the event was that of the two contending barbarian hosts the Roman state was the paymaster of the victors. Having long ago ceased to take any interest in their government, the timorous and despicable Romans had of course also broken with the custom of serving their country by enlisting in the army. This fact alone, although it appears concomitantly with a score of other evidences of moral and civic exhaustion, would serve to explain the catastrophe which overtook them and their moribund civilization. The unexampled decline constitutes an epic of disaster that concerns us only insofar as it reveals what happened in Tuscany and Florence when the last remnant of the old imperial authority broke down and successive German tribes attempted to set up their own rude barbarian government on the ruins.

But before in the following chapter we focus on these groping labors of political reconstruction under barbarian leadership, we must take account of the last great event which befell within the Roman world before its dissolution and which, because it gradually drew the conquering German tribes within its orbit, is absolutely basic to the whole subsequent development of Italy and Europe. This monumental event is the coming of Christianity. After slowly gaining a footing in the Mediterranean world, where it was obliged to meet the competition of a large number of rival oriental faiths, Christianity in the fourth century won a complete victory and swept not only its other eastern rivals but also ancient Roman paganism from the field. Three landmarks may be set down here to help us recall the almost vehemently sudden triumph. In 313 A.D. the new faith was for the first time conceded complete toleration by an imperial decree (Edict of Milan); a little more than a decade later, in the year 325, the first General Council of the Christian church met at Nicaea in Asia Minor under the presidency of Constantine the Great, the first Roman emperor to profess Christianity; and before the close of this same century the Christian victory achieved its logical conclusion in the outlawry of every other form of divine worship. While the rival faiths, and especially Roman paganism, undoubtedly continued to thrive under cover for a long time to come, Christianity had gained a legal monopoly which gave it an incontestable authority and prestige.

Contrary to the flattering legend which gained currency among the Florentines in the Middle Ages, the new faith did not establish itself solidly on the banks of the Arno till at a relatively late period and long after the days of the apostles. Moreover, the first authentic Christians who appear as residents of the provincial Roman city were not even native Florentines but itinerant traders from the eastern Mediterranean. They were either Greeks or Hellenized Asiatics from Syria and Asia Minor. This closely falls in with what we might expect when we recall that Christianity came to birth in a small Jewish community of the east and that it gained its gentile following by gradually spreading into the surrounding areas of Greek culture. It was the slow but steady expansion of the gentile element that before long made Christianity a formidable influence. Under these circumstances we need feel no surprise to learn that it was Greek, Syrian, and Jewish merchants who, having adopted the new faith, first carried it, along with their more material wares, into the Latin west. Wherever, in pursuit of profit, these easterners formed a commercial settlement, they created a Christian nucleus which acted as a more or less powerful center of attraction on the Italian, Spanish, and Gallic natives among whom they dwelt. That the probably feeble Greek colony in pagan Florence for a long time had very little success in making converts is indicated by the fact that in the persecution of the Emperor Decius in 250 A.D. the single Arno inhabitant to suffer martyrdom was Minias—a Greek. He was buried on the hill to the east of the town which afterwards received his name (San Miniato). To him and to his place of burial we shall have occasion to return in connection with the medieval awakening of the city.

It took another hundred years after the martyrdom of Minias before native Florentines were won to the novel oriental faith in large numbers; and it was not till the end of the fourth and the beginning of the fifth century that paganism was sufficiently discredited to be completely routed from the town. The leading figure in this final stage of the Christian triumph was none other than the most vigorous and shining exponent of Christianity in that period, Bishop Ambrose of Milan. In 393 A.D. this great man, distinguished among his contemporaries as both a practical statesman and a fiery Christian evangelist, fled from Milan, owing to a conflict in which he had become involved with the reigning emperor, and sought refuge in Florence until the storm had blown over. During his stay on the Arno of over a year he performed a historic act of which we have accurate knowledge: he dedicated the church of San Lorenzo, the simple forerunner of the church of that name which still stands.[3] Furthermore, he consecrated as bishop of the city a certain Zenobius, who is sometimes called the first bishop of Florence, although this honor can hardly, strictly speaking, be his, since for the year 313 there is mention of an earlier bishop by the name of Felix. If the document which mentions Felix is authentic, Florence already had a Christian bishop some eighty years before the time of Zenobius. Be that as it may, the Florentine bishopric was in all probability not solidly established until Zenobius became its incumbent and made the newly dedicated church of San Lorenzo his episcopal seat. This view is strengthened by the circumstance that his fellow-citizens so fondly cherished the memory of Zenobius that his fame survived the obliterating darkness which after his time descended on Florence and all Italy in the train of the rude Germanic invaders. The victorious persistence of the bishop's reputation can best be explained on the hypothesis of his services to the enfeebled city. More particularly it may have sprung from his having been still in office as the spiritual ruler of Florence during the terrifying first siege, in the year 405, which the hitherto safe town underwent from a mixed army of pillagers under Radagasius. The long period of Roman decline preceding the siege had been an age of waxing superstition and miraculous interventions. Consequently when, as already noted, the plunderers were disastrously beaten in battle, the good bishop, who, as the story went, had promised his people rescue through divine intervention, was, together with the God whom he worshiped, given full credit for the outcome. Although almost everything connected with Zenobius remains conjectural, it is clear that Christianity was

[3] On St. Ambrose's Florentine sojourn see Davidsohn, Vol. I, pp. 34-36.

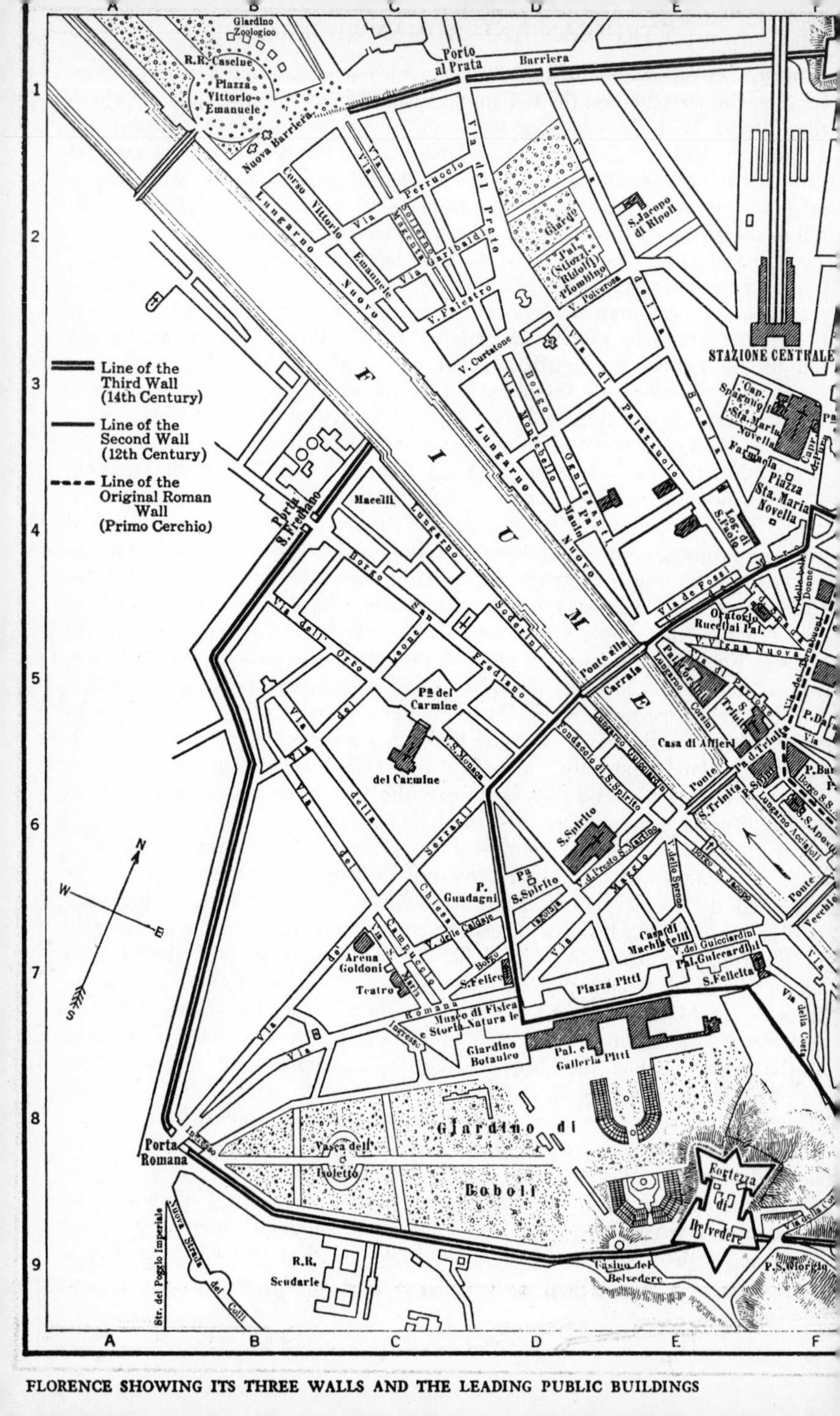

FLORENCE SHOWING ITS THREE WALLS AND THE LEADING PUBLIC BUILDINGS

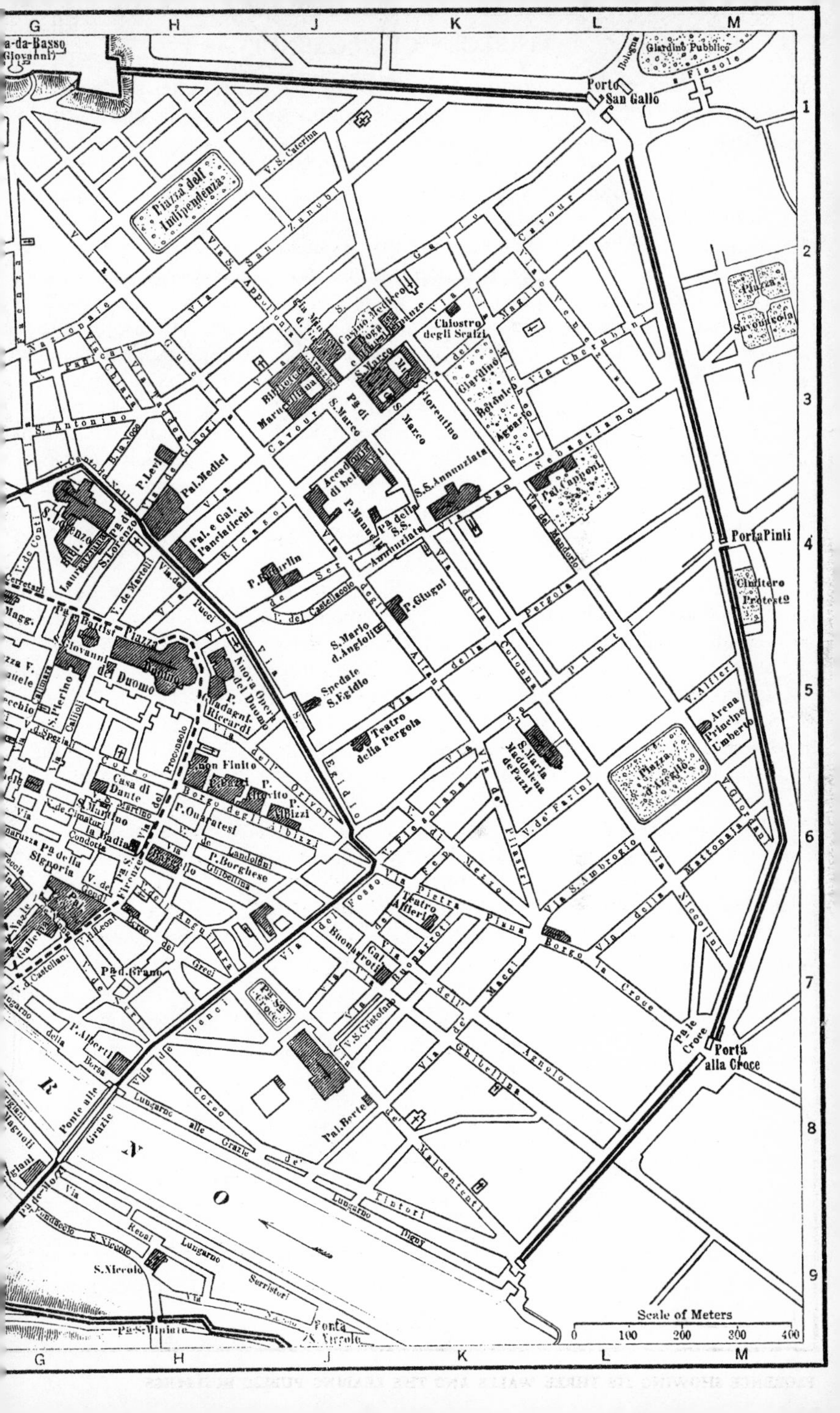

Porta San Gallo
Giardino Pubblico
Piazza dell' Indipendenza
Piazza Savonarola
Chiostro degli Scalzi
Casino Mediceo
Biblioteca Marucelliana
S. Marco
Pa di S. Marco
Giardino Botanico Agrario
Pal. Capponi
Pal. Medici
P. Levi
Pal. e Gal. Panciatichi
Accademia di belle Arti
S.S. Annunziata
Pa della S.S. Annunziata
S. Lorenzo
Bibl. Laurenziana
Pa di S. Lorenzo
P. Riccardi
P. Buturlin
Porta Pinti
Cimitero Protest.
P. Giugni
S. Maria d. Angioli
Spedale S. Egidio
Pa S. Giovanni
Battist.
Piazza del Duomo
Duomo
Nuova Opera del Duomo
P. Riccardi
Teatro della Pergola
S. Maria Maddalena de Pazzi
Arena Principe Umberto
Piazza d'Azeglio
P. non Finito
Casa di Dante
S. Martino
Badia
P. Quaratesi
P. Albizzi
P. Borghese
Pa della Signoria
Bargello
Teatro Alfieri
Gal. Buonarroti
Pa S. Croce
Pa d. Grano
P. Alberti
Pal. Berte
Porta alla Croce
Pa le Croce
Ponte alle Grazie
ARNO
S. Niccolo
Porta S. Niccolo
Pa S. Miniato
Scale of Meters
0 100 200 300 400
G H J K L M
1 2 3 4 5 6 7 8 9

so greatly strengthened during his incumbency that shortly after the beginning of the fifth century we may regard paganism as having become virtually extinct on the Arno.

Under these prospering circumstances the location of the episcopal seat outside the city, at San Lorenzo, where the great Ambrose had consecrated Bishop Zenobius, was bound to be challenged. Clearly a cathedral church ought to lie within the town serving as the capital of the diocese. Nothing was done to mend the awkward situation until the seventh century when a bishop, whose name has not come down to us, boldly transferred his seat from San Lorenzo to the newly risen church and baptistery of San Giovanni, just inside the city wall. At the same time he established his personal residence among the ruins of a Roman bath directly west of San Giovanni on what is now, owing to the leveling of the original building, an open piazza serving as approach to the present episcopal palace. When San Giovanni (which still stands) became too small for the growing town and in its turn failed to satisfy the needs of a new age, the cathedral was again moved. This time the church of Santa Reparata was selected as the central church of the Florentine diocese, and Santa Reparata, afterward rebaptized Santa Maria del Fiore, has retained its primacy to this day.

The three successive seats of the Florentine episcopal see, San Lorenzo, San Giovanni, and Santa Reparata, are enumerated at this place chiefly for the purpose of calling attention to the inconspicuous saint for whom the first small church to occupy the site of the present imposing cathedral was named. It was because the later Florentines knew nothing whatever of Santa Reparata and became secretly ashamed of having their leading house of worship named for an insignificant and unfamiliar resident of heaven that they renamed their cathedral after the most popular intercessor of the culminating Middle Ages, the Virgin Mary.[4] The interesting fact for us, who are engaged in tracing the earliest beginnings of Christianity in the Arno city, is that the historical Reparata was a lady who at a very early date suffered martyrdom in distant Caesarea in Asia Minor. If she was held in high esteem in Florence and, as can still be proved, in a large number of other trading centers of Italy and southern France, that was because the men who dedicated churches to her were visitors from the orient, fellow-countrymen of hers, who came to the Latin west to earn a living by trade but who at the same time, as sincere Christians, erected the first churches to serve the religious needs of themselves and of such native converts as they might succeed in bringing into the fold.

That Christianity was first brought to Florence by Greek, Syrian, and Jewish merchants is an interesting but relatively unimportant fact. What alone really matters is that Florence became wholeheartedly and unanimously Christian at the very time when the Roman state crashed to the ground. Rome perished, but Christianity, the youngest child of Rome, survived. The cultural catastrophe was therefore not so complete as appeared at first glance. For

[4] Villani, VIII, 9, tells us that the church of Santa Reparata received its new name of Santa Maria del Fiore in the year 1294 (actually 1296), but that the common people continued to cling to the familiar name. It took more than a hundred years for the new name to displace its homely predecessor.

Christianity, beginning, like all other mystery religions, as a faith and an aspiration, had under Roman legal influence expanded into a vast organization, a universal church, in which important elements of Mediterranean civilization were incorporated and by which they were cherished and preserved. The energetic new institution, famous as the Roman Catholic church, became the point of departure of the new or western civilization destined in the course of time to take over and develop the Mediterranean heritage. In the creation of the new culture the city of Florence, whose role in the vanished classical world had been entirely negligible, took a most active part. Indeed so significant was the Florentine contribution that to define and appraise it is the leading purpose of this book. We may therefore agree that the true starting-point of our venture is the Germanic conquest of Italy by which Roman Florence was engulfed and in the course of which it physically disappeared. But in taking leave of Roman Florence we should never forget that from the dying civilization to which it belonged was salvaged the youngest and sturdiest feature of the Roman state, the Christian faith and church. It was with this singularly fruitful endowment that Florence entered on the new or medieval phase of its existence, a phase destined to lift it to a place of unsurpassed distinction among the famous cities of the world.

II. Italy and Her Invaders

IF DURING the Etruscan and Roman periods Florence led an obscure provincial existence, the situation for a long time experienced no substantial change when the coming of the German barbarians put an end to the Roman empire in the west and inaugurated the new period of history we call the Middle Ages. This meaningless term has got itself so firmly established in the English as well as in all the other European tongues that it is futile to attempt to displace it. However, from any angle taking account of fundamental social processes it is clear that what we call the Middle Ages is nothing other than the first stage of a new civilization, which slowly got under way on the dissolution of the great classical civilization and which, by a steady unfolding of its energies through the succeeding centuries, has culminated in that occidental or western civilization which, for better or for worse, has in the course of the most recent generations spread over the whole world. Although the expression Middle Ages will have to be retained, it is important to understand that it will be used here to designate a period in which the birth and death of social forms mingled as they always do, but in which, from the viewpoint of the subsequent development of Europe, the significant and outstanding feature is the appearance of vigorous, fresh shoots destined to become a magnificent and richly individual growth on the imperishable tree of life.

In thus asserting in regard to the Middle Ages that they are the earliest phase of the new civilization which arose on the ruins of the Roman empire, we date them as beginning approximately with the fifth century and as continuing into the eleventh century, that is, we hold that they embrace the years from about 500 to 1000 A.D. These five centuries, constituting the deep Middle Ages, are followed by the later Middle Ages which extend from about 1000 to 1300. They may be considered a period of transition as they prepare the ground for what is commonly called the Renaissance. The Renaissance is, organically considered, the second main stage of western civilization and may be held to cover the period from 1300 to 1550. Because the precise division into periods here suggested is likely to give a distorted picture of the nature of social change, it should not be taken too seriously. The excuse for it is that for both historian and reader it constitutes a useful and even indispensable chronological device.

Now during the five hundred years of the deep Middle Ages our city of

Florence remains as completely hidden from view, and may therefore be presumed to have been as unimportant a human center, as during the preceding five hundred years constituting its Roman period. But in the case of this second five-hundred-year period we cannot with the same ease of conscience evade the obligation of attempting to penetrate behind the veil. For during the deep Middle Ages there took place the events and there were generated the forces which prepared the ground for the emergence of Florence not only as a powerful political entity but also as one of the leading agents of the new civilization which was slowly disengaging itself from the turmoil of the times. It is the Florence rising into view after 1000 A.D. with which this book is mainly concerned, and a close scrutiny of the slight data bearing on its dark gestation during the immediately preceding period becomes as legitimate as it is unescapable. But before we embark on this task it will be necessary to accept the obligation of presenting in swift, summary form the vicissitudes of the whole peninsula of Italy following the Germanic conquest. It is this conquest which contributed important elements to medieval society, more particularly by introducing those politico-social changes which alone made it possible for Florence to rise from impotence to power, from the darkness of obscurity into the light of fame.

The mixed army of barbarians led by the Goth, Radagasius, which in 405 A.D. was defeated outside Florence, was the forerunner of a long succession of German invaders whom the enfeebled Roman empire, never again defeating, proved itself unable to resist. Like the provinces of Gaul, Spain, and Britain and simultaneously with them, Italy fell gradually a prey to the barbarians. After seventy years, in 476, a crisis was reached in this process of barbarization which cannot be overlooked. In that year Romulus Augustulus, the last Roman emperor of the West, was forced to yield his shadowy authority into the hands of a German chief, Odoacer, and was peremptorily ordered by him to descend from the throne. True, the Roman emperor of the East, seated in his capital of Constantinople, entertained the view that the western provinces were by this usurpation only temporarily alienated and that, ideally at least, they still belonged to the one and indivisible *imperium romanum,* of which he was the lawful head. If, owing to pressing difficulties nearer home, he did not promptly defend his constitutional rights, that would not hinder a successor from defending them the moment a more favorable opportunity should arise. Under Emperor Justinian, as we shall see, that auspicious day dawned, and Italy became once again by conquest through an imperial army an immediate province of the Roman realm. Justinian's triumph turned out to be ephemeral and the barbarians speedily retrieved their fortunes. Nonetheless, it is a fact of the greatest importance for the history of medieval Italy first, that the empire of the East did not for many centuries cease to lay claim to the peninsula, and second, that for many generations after Justinian's time it retained within its grasp, even though that grasp was steadily weakening, scattered segments of the Italian coastal area. In short, in one way or another the Eastern empire continued to figure as an element in the complicated play of Italian medieval forces which must always be reckoned with.

Brushing aside the detailed comings and goings of the roving barbarian hordes who plundered Italy at will during the harassed fifth century, we shall come at once to the Ostrogoths, who in the year 489 crossed the northeastern Alps under their king, Theodoric. They are important for us because, coming less to plunder than to colonize, they set up the first Germanic state on Italian soil. They succeeded in this purpose because they had at their head a sovereign who, in addition to being the typical brave warrior of the period of the migrations, was a man of such exceptionally broad and enlightened views that he may without fear of contradiction be called a statesman. That Theodoric, the Ostrogoth, should have succeeded in mounting to a political level high above the average barbarian chieftain, he probably owed to his having been exposed by a long residence at Constantinople during his youth to the declining but still irresistible attractions of Roman civilization. In this manner, while continuing to share the contempt with which every German leader regarded the decadent Romans, he acquired a feeling almost akin to religious awe for the great organized structure of the Roman state. His highest ambition came to be to enter the service of this majestic creation and to perpetuate its power. It throws an interesting light on his attitude that he did not enter Italy with his swarming followers till he had received a formal commission to this effect from Emperor Zeno. Thus fortified, he successfully disposed of Odoacer, the German tribal chief who since the usurpation of 476 had been holding the land in subjection, and set up his own rule at Ravenna. He chose Ravenna as his seat because during the final phase of the Western empire it had served as the administrative capital of Italy and further, because by means of this residence, he could palpably present himself before the inhabitants of the peninsula as the representative of the legal sovereign. Far from irregularly robbing the natives and subjecting them to the capricious violence of his warriors, as all his German predecessors had done, he honestly and sincerely desired to bring them peace and security. In this he succeeded so well that during the thirty-odd years that his reign lasted his Roman subjects enjoyed an ordered existence such as they had not known for several generations. To effect this considerable change he was obliged, as the first item of his policy, to put an end to the long succession of raids which in recent decades had been devastating the peninsula. The only available instrument for bringing this about was his own Gothic host. According to the program which he put into effect, his stalwart people were to be the missing army of the Roman community of Italy. With protective garrisons stationed at all the strategic points the peninsula would be secured against further Teutonic invasions, thus permitting the natives to go peacefully about their various occupations much as in the great days of the empire.

It was a program devised to bring into a practical interdependence the two realities of contemporary Italy, the Roman state and society which was without military might, and German military might which, in a civilized sense, was neither a state nor a society. Theodoric was the point of junction of the two realities which otherwise had nothing in common and were by their nature mutually exclusive. As soon as the occupation was effected the king provided for his land-hungry Goths by assigning to them for their support a third of the property of the great landowners. That was an incisive but not an unreasonable measure when we consider that the Goths, though technically *hospites* (guests), were in reality conquerors, that they had to be provided for somehow, and that in return for a regulated maintenance they were required to render a primary social service. Having satisfied the demand of his warriors for an adequate means of support, Theodoric refused to entertain any further dispossession of his Roman subjects. In fact he did not scruple to use his practically unlimited power as commander-in-chief to keep his Goths strictly within their assigned bounds. They were the military arm of the state living on Roman soil by the labor of Roman hands. Their continued separateness as a people was indicated by their subjection not to Roman but to the tribal Gothic law which they had brought with them. The civilized Romans on the other hand lived under the familiar Roman law administered by Roman judges. It will be readily believed that the two juxtaposed but distinct societies regarded each other with spontaneous aversion. And it will also be conceded that they would not have remained harnessed together for a day, had it not been for the genius of their common sovereign. No sooner therefore had the great Theodoric died in 526, leaving his power to his grandson, a boy of ten years for whom his mother acted as regent, than this very personal system disastrously collapsed.

The minority of the new king and the clamorous incongruity of the Roman and Gothic societies were not the only factors in the overthrow. Although the Goths had been converted to Christianity even before they entered Italy, they were Christians of the Arian sect and, branded as heretics by the dominant Catholic church, invited the scorn and hatred of the Catholic Romans. This religious division was another and very potent influence accounting for the Gothic disaster. The final and most decisive factor in their overthrow, however, was the Emperor Justinian, a man of great energy and far-ranging views, who had mounted the throne of the Eastern empire a year after Theodoric's demise. Gazing intently westward, Justinian came to the conclusion that the moment had come for reassuming the direct rule of Africa, Italy, and, if possible, of the other alienated western provinces as well. Accordingly, he embarked on a policy of conquest which put a sudden end to such pacification as had been achieved by Theodoric's system and which transformed Italy into a bloody battlefield for the next twenty years. Successful beyond expectation in his first assault on the Goths, Justinian learned to his sorrow that his opponents were a sturdy people of undaunted courage and abundant resilience. Again and again he had to send his armies, first under the famous general, Belisarius, and then under the even more capable Narses against the dwindling but stubborn hosts of the enemy; and when finally, a little past the middle of the sixth century, the last remnant of the Goths had been annihilated, it was a ravaged, depopulated, and tragically exhausted Italy which had been brought back into the Roman fold.

Even so, not for long. From a country reduced to the utmost misery by the terrible Gothic war, Narses, the emperor's viceroy and alter ego, had to extract the taxes necessary to pay for a costly army and administration. As a devoted servant of a distant and autocratic master he wished to prove not only that conquered Italy was self-supporting, but that it could even contribute to the maintenance of the luxurious imperial court on the Bosporus. To this end he unscrupulously applied the tax-screws; and as he could not count overmuch on the fidelity of the native Italians, he employed, especially in the upper categories of his administrative service, a host of imported Greek officials. It was frankly a Greek or Byzantine, that is, a foreign government that Narses conducted at the capital city of Ravenna. Undeniably the fast-ebbing Roman civilization was benefited by the influences which radiated from the Greek officials, who still moved on a culture level high above the debased Latin west. The churches of San Vitale and San Apollinare in Classe, which still adorn the now shrunken and provincial city by the Adriatic, furnish impressive evidence of a creative vigor which continued to characterize the east at a time when the west had already definitely lost its moral, intellectual, and artistic energy. But it may be doubted that the Italians took pleasure in the cultural superiority of the new rulers. Brought forcibly back into the empire, they learned that they had merely exchanged a Byzantine for a Gothic master and that they were no better off than before.

Then with the suddenness that had marked the long series of their sufferings since the first failure of the Roman strength, a new catastrophe befell. The great statesman, Emperor Justinian, died in 565, leaving the throne to his nephew, Justin II. Almost the first act of the new sovereign was to supplant the victorious and too self-reliant Narses with a more pliant tool. Encouraged by the confusion caused by this change of governors, another mass of German barbarians gathered behind the curtain of the Alps and in 568 descended into the northeastern plain. The new invaders were the Lombards, one of the most backward, undisciplined, and brutal of the northern peoples. For some generations before their appearance in Italy they had been pushing gradually southward from their home along the shores of the North and Baltic seas in the hope of casual loot and, more important still, of fertile lands capable of furnishing them with a steady and abundant supply of food.

The story of the Lombard conquest raises many puzzling questions which can only be answered partially or not at all. Since these newest Germans were a poorly organized horde constantly threatened with falling into independent units under rebel leaders, how did they have any success at all? And having gained a foothold at one or another point of the valley of the Po, how did they with their meager administrative experience manage to keep control? Why did the Byzantine army content itself with a purely defensive policy and from first to last offer so despicable a resistance? Putting these questions to one side as incapable of better than a speculative answer, let us note that the conquest was like the inundation of a river which floods a considerable area and, after an occasional halt or even a recession, against every reasonable expectation begins to mount again. In simple truth the capricious Lombard inundation of the Italian peninsula continued for generations and at no time, not even at its height some two centuries after its beginning, did it ever completely cover the land from the passes of the Alps to the straits of Messina. The feature above all others that needs to be observed about this particular and doubtless most important of all the German invasions is its geographic limitations. Starting at the foothills of the Alps the Lombards gradually occupied the Po Valley and on reaching the Apennines pushed along their ridges far into the south. Because they constituted a primitive army ill equipped to carry on siege operations and, owing also to their lack of ships, they were unable to capture any seaport which offered resolute resistance. Unexpectedly feeble as the Byzantines proved themselves on land, they possessed the valuable asset of a fleet and were thus able to maintain themselves in the Venetian lagoons, at their capital of Ravenna, at Rome and its environs, at Naples, and around the whole bend of the southern coast. The aim of the Lombards from the first was and never ceased to be the possession of the whole peninsula; but even under their greatest king, Liutprand, who reigned from 712 to 744, they did not gain control of the coveted coastal areas. True, shortly after Liutprand's death they had the satisfaction of capturing Ravenna and its dependent district, thus bringing almost all of northern and central Italy into the kingdom. The duchy of Rome held by the pope and serving as the capital of Christendom they never brought under their yoke. And they never acquired Naples and the stretch of seacoast that outlines the foot of the long Italian boot. Because the Lombard conquest thus fell short of its object, it divided Italy—tragically as most Italian historians affirm—into three political areas which it is startling to observe remained separate and distinct throughout the medieval and modern periods down almost to our own day. There was first the Lombard kingdom comprising the bulk of the peninsula; next came the duchy of Rome, nucleus of the later State of the Church ruled by the pope; and finally there was the south, where the Greeks long continued to hold sway and where, after the dislodgment of the Greeks, a succession of other conquering powers, of which we need not take account at this point, gained control.

If the Lombard conquest was geographically less extensive than that of the Ostrogoths, even a superficial investigation will serve to show that it had social and economic consequences which were far more profound and lasting. To begin with, the Lombards did not, like the Goths, come to Italy as allies of the Roman emperor to settle and rule the peninsula with his consent. On the contrary, they came as his enemies and, being ruthless barbarians, who, unlike the Goths, had not previously experienced any of the refining (and enfeebling) influences of Mediterranean culture, they were prompted by no higher motive than the gross desire to possess themselves of the lands and chattels of their victims. To them the Roman state, more enduring than brass according to its classical encomiasts, appeared as a thing of lath and plaster, and they swept it aside more from a childlike passion for destruction than from any deep-laid political plan. In effect they wrote finis under the long and impressive history of Roman civil administration. But if this administration now disappeared from public view, that does not necessarily mean that it was utterly destroyed in all its numerous ramifications. Haphazard survival at scattered places of some of its institutions is more than probable; but in view of the mental backwardness of the Lombards and of the furious war they waged with the Roman empire represented by Byzantium, it is certain that they did not repeat the Gothic experiment of two juxtaposed societies, each supreme in its own field. Italy was their prize and by means of sword and fire they broke down every resistance to their will in order to get and retain possession.

The chief objective of the barbarians was the land, for the land would support them by the labor of the slaves and serfs (*coloni*), who, under the long imperial regime, had cultivated it for the benefit of the great landlords. We must understand that these three terms, slaves, serfs, landlords, describe the outstanding social elements of the late-Roman agrarian system. The Lombards had only to get rid of the landlord class, either by outright murder or by driving its members into exile, and success was theirs. Without further ado they would acquire title to the expropriated fields, while the slaves and serfs, left undisturbed, would work the farms exactly as before except that the surplus product of their labor would now go to another set of masters. That this social revolution was attended by horrible excesses against the Roman upper class is attested by the echo still audible in the records which have come down to us; but it is more than probable that the Lombard violence hardly touched the great mass of the agricultural population. The rude government which the barbarians set up in measure as they took over the control of the country was founded wholly on Lombard experience and Lombard tribal law. According to this law only the Lombards were free, that is, they alone enjoyed full citizen rights. The former Roman freemen, the landowners, no longer cumbered the earth, or, if they did, can only have escaped destruction by absorption into the class below them, the lowly coloni. Under the Roman system there had been of course a legal distinction between this agricultural group, which may be broadly described as serfs, and the still lower group of the slaves. While the imposed Lombard law did not fail to take account of this distinction, nonetheless both classes were bondsmen in its eyes, and the sole body in the state enjoying the rights of freemen were the victorious invaders. The quality of freedom pertained to the individual Lombard by virtue of his twofold capacity of warrior and landlord.

The Lombard state signified the forceful imposition on Italy of a harsh, cruel, and primitive politico-social system under which the peninsula made its final plunge into barbarism. The conquered Romans themselves became barbarized and the last dim tapers of classical culture guttered and went out. Then, after a hundred years of all but complete darkness, there came, hardly perceptible at first, a turning-point. When after three generations of practically continuous warfare with the invaders the Byzantine empire had failed to cast them out, the eastern government declared itself ready to make peace on the basis of each warring party keeping as its own what it happened at the time to hold. The treaty—it was signed around 677—for the first time gave the Lombard conquest an unambiguous legal standing and by encouraging personal and commercial intercourse among the hitherto hostile groups closed the first and utterly brutal period of Lombard history. Another circumstance tending to improve peninsular conditions was that after a hundred years of residence on Italian soil the Lombards themselves were no longer what they had been when they first arrived. Under the immediate pressure of geographic conditions they had at a relatively early stage accommodated their northern dress and diet, unsuited to the Italian climate, to the native standards. Soon after this change they became bilingual; and after a further lapse of time they replaced their Germanic tongue entirely with the more cultured and flexible Latin idiom of their subjects. Already very dissimilar from its classical prototype, this idiom was rapidly assuming the characteristics of that offshoot of the Latin speech which came to be known as Italian.

But the circumstance offering the most convincing indication that the Lombards were being slowly reshaped by their social environment was their gradual absorption into the fold of the Catholic church. Before coming into Italy, like many of the other wandering German tribes, they, too, had become converted to Christianity. Superficial Christians no doubt, they were—a much more serious failing according to current views—also false Christians of the same Arian type as their Germanic predecessors, the Ostrogoths. In the eyes of the Italian natives, who were Catholics, and especially and implacably in the eyes of the Catholic pope, their heterodoxy was a heinous offense. Even before the important accommodation with the emperor of 677 the Lombard royal family had become persuaded that it was the part of political wisdom to abandon a faith productive of the rancorous resentment aroused by Arianism. With the rulers making spiritual submission to the pope, their Lombard subjects speedily followed the same road. By 700 A.D. at the latest, the Lombard state had become organized ecclesiastically in dioceses under orthodox Catholic bishops who accepted the pope as their divinely appointed head.

These developments, considered in their totality, permit us to conclude that by the eighth century a fusion between conquerors and conquered was definitely under way. It took the form of the gradual absorption of the thin upper stratum of the ruling Lombards by their more numerous subjects in town and country. In short, the Lombards went through a process of Romanization or, since they in their turn helped impress a changed physical and moral character upon the natives, we may with even greater propriety speak of an amalgamation effected between the two groups. The product of the fusion was essentially a new people, the medieval Italians. It would be rash to say that by the eighth or even the ninth century this new people has stepped upon the scene invested with all the characteristics that afterwards distinguished it; but it is entirely permissible to insist that by the above-mentioned centuries all the forces were already busily at work from the interplay of which the medieval Italians arose. Undoubtedly they would owe most of their traits to the Roman side of their inheritance. Their speech and their religion and all the subconscious habit-elements that these subsume derived exclusively from that source. Moreover, under King Liutprand (of the first half of the eighth century) the submerged Roman law began to reassert its latent energy. Since it had never been relinquished as the basis of its organization by the Catholic church, it followed that when the Lombards finally adopted Catholicism they were obliged to accord the Roman law formal recognition by permitting the Catholic clergy to live under it. A close scrutiny of the juridical situation reveals that in other ways besides ecclesiastical usage the Roman law experienced a revival, for the statutes issued by King Liutprand accepted it as the personal law of occasional individuals among his subjects who were not of clerical standing. Thus by almost imperceptible stages it took its place at the side of the hitherto exclusively dominant Lombard law. While this revival of Roman legal norms indicates conclusively that by Liutprand's time the Lombard kingdom had broadened its cultural basis, it becomes clear from other evidence which has reached us that it was also becoming politically stronger and better consolidated. Under King Liutprand there functioned an improved administrative machine which gave him for the first time since the coming of his people into Italy an effective sovereignty over his state.

Without the least doubt it was precisely this auspicious development of the Lombard state which caused its overthrow. For, prompted by a sense of increased authority, King Liutprand took the natural but hazardous step of resuming the interrupted conquest of Italy. His immediate goal became the old imperial and present papal capital, the city of Rome. In spite of repeated attacks he did not succeed in capturing this august center, but he imposed his design as a primary duty to the state on all the sovereigns that came after him. Theoretically in King Liutprand's day Rome and its immediate environment constituted a duchy subject to the Eastern or Byzantine emperor; but as the enfeebled emperor was no longer able to protect his dependency, its defense against Lombard aggression fell automatically to the lot of the leading local figure, who was, of course, the pope. But the pope, too, lacked the means with his own unaided strength to resist a long-continued Lombard pressure; and when he became persuaded that the Eastern emperor either would or could not help him, he appealed for succor to the most powerful of the Germanic kingdoms founded on Roman soil, the kingdom of the Franks.

Therewith we encounter a turning-point in early medieval history, for we have reached the famous alliance between the popes and the Frankish mayors of the palace for their mutual advantage. In return for the pope's crowning the great palace official, Pippin, king of the Franks, thereby enabling him to displace the legitimate Merovingian line, the usurper twice crossed the Alps with an army and obliged King Liutprand's successor, Aistulf, to desist from his stubbornly renewed attacks on the papal capital. As an additional measure of punishment Pippin took from the defeated Aistulf the province of Ravenna and presented this territory, familiarly called the exarchate, to his papal ally (756). The famous so-called donation of Pippin has ever since been regarded as the rock on which the popes were enabled to erect their temporal power. When a new king, Desiderius by name, mounted the Lombard throne, he stubbornly resumed the now traditional anti-papal policy of his predecessors. The new attack on Rome drew Pippin's son and successor, Charles, across the Alps; and Charles, determined to have done with half-measures, continued the war against Desiderius until he had forced him to abdicate the throne. In 774 the Lombard kingdom passed into Charles's hands, and thus, after two hundred years, the Lombard chapter of the German invasions of Italy came to an end.

The victory of Charles the Great—the towering Charlemagne of medieval poetry and legend—inaugurated the Frankish phase of Italian subservience. The new sovereign saw no reason to change greatly the administration which the Lombards had gradually evolved. Originally the kingdom had been divided into provinces ruled over by local leaders called dukes or *duces*. They exercised such extensive power within their respective jurisdictions that whenever the Lombard king was lacking in initiative, they comported themselves as practically independent rulers. For this reason the later and stronger sovereigns attempted to supplant the dukes by means of officials called *gastaldi* more immediately under royal control. Dukes and gastalds remained a characteristic feature of Lombard administration till the conquest effected by the Franks. Unhurriedly and by degrees the great Charles replaced both types of officials with Frankish counts (*comites*), in whom as his personal appointees he naturally had more confidence than in Lombard agents inherited from a discredited regime. Behind the new king and his administrative representatives Frankish adventurers poured into Italy in such numbers that some historians feel justified in speaking of a new and appreciable Germanic influx. In any case, the Franks, who, like all the barbarian peoples, carried their native law with them wherever they went, brought it about that with their advent to power the Frankish law was accorded an equal standing in the kingdom with the ruling Lombard and Roman codes.

The vigorous personality and rare executive ability of the Frank conqueror brought Italy a greater measure of peace and prosperity than it had enjoyed since the days of Theodoric. Charles continued to extend his power in Europe until the new Germanic kingdoms had one after the other passed under his control. It was his unchallenged authority over most of the former Roman provinces seized by the barbarian conquerors that now precipitated an event of the greatest significance for all subsequent history. This was the coronation of the king of the Franks as Roman emperor of the West. On Christmas Day of the year 800 Pope Leo III performed at Rome in the church of St. Peter the coronation ceremony conferring this high title on the Frankish chief. In so doing, Pope Leo set a precedent from which in later centuries his successors on St. Peter's chair drew sweeping claims of supremacy over the restored empire. Although the papal assumptions were never fully accepted by the emperors and were even frequently and emphatically denied, the popes, supported by their vast spiritual prestige, succeeded in keeping them alive. The fatal result of Leo's famous act was that pope and emperor became entangled in a relationship which made them, in spite of their theoretic partnership in the rule of Christendom, bitter and, in the end, irreconcilable enemies.

In some quarters the renewal of the Roman empire brought about by the coronation of Charles the Great has been represented as a historical delusion and absurdity. While there is much to be said against any attempted revival of a dead past, it has been argued in this particular instance that, since Charles had gained actual possession of the bulk of the western lands, he might without conspicuous impropriety employ a title which had once served to express a commensurate authority. Be that as it may, it was an unfortunate circumstance that the vast political edifice of the Frank sovereign was a personal creation which, even before he died (814), exhibited unmistakable signs of a threatening dissolution. Under his son and successor, Louis the Pious (814–40), the disintegration proceeded apace and at Louis' death led to a complete and startling collapse. This emperor had three sons who, after coming to blows over the paternal inheritance, with better sense than might be expected of their very mediocre endowment agreed to partition it among them. In 843, by the treaty of Verdun, they carved the vast Frankish state into three areas, two of which approximately corresponded to the regions later identified as France and

Germany. The third area was composed of the former Lombard kingdom with the addition of a broad belt of transalpine territory (Lotharingia) lying between the two northern shares. This third share, the largest and most important of the three, was accorded to Lothar, who, as the deceased Louis' oldest son, had already been permitted to assume the imperial crown. In this manner the Carolingian house, fallen into three branches, continued to rule over western Europe. As for the imperial title, inhering as it did in Lothar's line, the view became current and gradually hardened into a tradition that its employment was dependent on the control of Italy and the consequent coronation by the pope in the historic capital of Rome.

By his general ineffectiveness Emperor Lothar I proved himself a typical Carolingian degenerate. Already during the reign of his vacillating father, Louis, the Saracens, who for some generations had been swarming over the Mediterranean Sea, had taken to harrying the Italian coasts. For their ravages, which steadily grew worse, Lothar was unable to find a cure, and under his successors an even less effective resistance was made against the enterprising pirates than by himself. Let us be just to Lothar and remember that such strength as he and his successors might unfold depended on the concurrent action of their great feudal subjects. But these proud and selfish aristocrats refused to yield obedience to their sovereign and mockingly left him in the lurch. In 875, amidst ominous signs of waxing political chaos, the line of Italian Lothar became extinct. Thereupon the two remaining Carolingian branches, the French and the German, promptly urged their claims to the Italian crown. Representatives of these lines even crossed the Alps in the hope of adding luster to their names; but when it came to the defense of Italy against the pestilential Saracens, they refused to assume this heavy responsibility and pusillanimously retired to the safer ground of their respective northern homes. We may regard the feeble gestures they made in Italy as so much shadow-boxing and agree that the Carolingian rule of Italy terminated with Lothar's line. Through good and evil fortune it had lasted almost exactly one hundred years (774–875).

There followed a period of outright anarchy which in its turn lasted for something rather less than a hundred years. It was the mark of this perturbed era that a crass feudalism gained the upper hand, prompting every ambitious duke and count to pluck at the Italian crown. In connection with this royal symbol the interesting fact calls for notice that it was at this time, that is, it was during the latter part of the ninth century that what had thus far figured as the Lombard crown came to be designated by the more inclusive name of the Italian crown. By a related change in phraseology and thought the term *regnum lombardicum* began to yield its place in official documents to the term *regnum italicum*. We have given due weight to the fusion which, already during the Lombard period, was being effected of the diverse racial elements of which the population of the peninsula was composed. Of this uninterrupted assimilation the slight but significant modification of traditional legal forms may be adduced as effective additional evidence. Recent Italian historians have gone so far as to attribute to this period of desperate social degradation the symptoms of a dawning sense of what they call *italianità*. Italianità is not quite patriotism, much less is it what we moderns signify by the term nationalism. It is admittedly a rather indefinite sentiment, which, however, by gradually gaining ground, encouraged the inhabitants of Italy, regardless of origin, to think of themselves as a single and separate European group. The assertion in however feeble a form of italianità in the anarchic interlude we are treating is a decidedly interesting phenomenon.[1]

More immediately important than this faint flicker of a unifying purpose within the legal-minded administrative class of the peninsula are the continued devastating invasions which in this period of the utmost feudal anarchy afflicted the unhappy land. To the Saracen inroads, of which we have already heard, were now added those of another people, the Magyars. If the later Carolingians, who, in spite of their decline, still possessed some authority, had proved themselves incapable of defending the coasts, what happened during the terrible post-Carolingian confusion may be left to the imagination. With no one to oppose them, the plundering corsairs came and went at will. Established along the coasts of Africa and Spain, the Saracen pirate communities were in possession of all the western areas submerged by the great flood of conquest which in the seventh century issued from Arabia, and which in the following century brought and for many generations to come kept the Mediterranean Sea under Moslem control. It was not till around the year 1000, that is, it was not till two hundred years had passed, that the Italians set about remedying the intolerable situation by the only available means, which was to provide themselves with a navy. When that time came, it was not, as we shall learn hereafter, the central government but the maritime cities, organized as self-governing republics, which put an end to Moslem encroachments and inaugurated a new era for the commerce and shipping of Christendom.

The other body of invaders, the Magyars, represent a crisis which, though fully as sharp as that associated with the Saracens, was of far shorter duration. Not till the end of the ninth century (899), in the very midst of the period of anarchy we are here considering, did they make their appearance on the Italian scene. Swift-moving horsemen, hailing originally from Asia, they had only recently pushed into Europe, where they had taken possession of the mid-Danubian plain which their descendants, commonly called Hungarians, still occupy. Using these rich grasslands as their base, they pushed their raids frequently far into Germany and also poured periodically across the Alpine passes to burn and plunder at pleasure the villages and towns of northern and north-central Italy.

For the disastrous civil strife among the great feudality, which by paralyzing the action of the central government was chiefly to blame for the Saracen and Magyar incursions, no cure was found until one of the baronial factions drew King Otto I of Germany into Italy by appealing to him for succor against a rival group. This Otto belonged to the Saxon line which had succeeded to the German crown after the dying-out, early in the tenth century, of the German branch of the Carolingians. In response to the invitation of the Italian mag-

[1] For a suggestive discussion of these matters see L. Chiappelli in *Arch. Stor. It.*, Serie 7, Vol. X ("La Formazione Storica del Comune Cittadino"), and P. S. Leicht in *Rivista di Storia del Diritto Italiano,* Vol. III (1930), pp. 5-20.

nates he came to Italy, first experimentally in 951, and with a more clearly defined program ten years later. On this second occasion he succeeded in making himself undisputed master of what since Carolingian times was called the Italian kingdom, and with complete propriety he could therefore request the pope to invest him with the imperial crown. The ceremony which duly followed has been hailed as a second restoration of the Roman empire of the West. In close imitation of the first renewal under Charlemagne the coronation of Otto was performed at Rome in the central church of Christianity, the basilica of St. Peter.

However, it was not the Roman empire, it was not even the empire of Charlemagne that was revived on that February day of the year 962 when Pope John XII anointed Otto I and proclaimed him the successor of the Caesars. Otto already bore the title German king and, ruling Germany, possessed a land which was no more than a fraction of the vast territory subject to Frankish Charles when, over a century and a half before (800), he had been invested with the same crown. In point of power, therefore, Otto was a much less imposing figure than the towering Charles. Indeed on close scrutiny and in spite of the imperial title, Otto had accomplished no more than to bring Germany and Italy under a single scepter. Consequently the leading historical result of Otto's conquest of Italy, a conquest which logically entailed the coronation ceremony at St. Peter's, was that it inaugurated still another chapter of the long subjection of Italy to her invaders. The new chapter may be called the German phase which, beginning with Saxon Otto in 962, was, if not juridically, at least effectively terminated in 1250 with the defeat and death of the greatest of all the German medieval sovereigns, the Hohenstaufen emperor, Frederick II.

The union of the crowns of Germany and Italy effected by Otto I in 962 goes commonly under the name of the Holy Roman empire. It is a peculiarly apt designation for the political creation of the great Saxon sovereign since it takes cognizance of the fact that the new polity was sufficiently different from both its immediate Carolingian and its more distant Augustan predecessor to deserve a special appellation. The tenth century successor of the Roman empire came to be so closely tied up with concepts and conditions peculiar to the Middle Ages that this revived empire was necessarily different from its earlier manifestations. Moreover, the difference resulted so largely from the close association of the resurrected empire with the church and Christianity, that to qualify it as holy was unescapable. At the time of Charles the Great the interaction of state and church, though close, had not yet assumed the later intimacy, and consequently the revival of the Roman empire connected with his name did not quite achieve the character of sacredness associated with its Ottonian offspring. Essentially, however, this talk of holy and less holy is beside the mark. The distinction between the two Roman revivals is a matter of power and reduces itself in substance to the circumstance that Charles's authority was so great that he dominated both state and church, while Otto's position was much weaker, especially in regard to the state. While he may be said to have kept the church in considerable dependence, he was obliged to share the civil power with the great feudatories; and not very long after his death the popes began to grow so strong that the unchallenged control of the church gradually passed into their hands. For all its "holiness," in fact even because of it, Otto's empire was a far less vigorous entity than that of Charles. But this admission should not blind us to the circumstance that the Holy Roman empire was a towering structure which for almost three centuries dominated the European scene.

If long before its fall the Italians began to turn against the Holy Roman empire, that was because they had been brought to see it in its true light as a foreign conquest and were determined to be free of its control. Concomitantly with its decline in Italy the empire lost its grip also in Germany; but there, owing to its being after all the national kingdom of the Germans, it managed to survive the thirteenth century and was not finally swept into the limbo of dead dreams till the vast European revolution connected with the name of Napoleon. The successive stages of its long decline interest us, for the present at least, little if at all. We are about to concern ourselves and we shall be occupied for a long time to come with the Holy Roman empire when it was the leading power of Europe and territorially embraced both Germany and Italy. But the equality between the two members implied in this statement did not conform with the facts. In reality Germany had effected the conquest of Italy, and the complicated situation which resulted for the peninsula from this enforced foreign control justifies our calling the period from 962 to 1250 the German or Holy Roman empire phase of Italian history.

The great event of the German phase dwarfing all others is the slow rise of Italian national feeling resulting at last in the overthrow of the German domination. The political instrument through which the national victory was brought about was the self-governing town, called by the Italians the commune. The multiplication of communes, the growth of their commerce and industry, the increase of their wealth and power enabling them to challenge the emperor and his feudal followers, constitute the central feature of this age. But not only does the commune signify a political and social revolution of the first order, but from it sprang also an admirable intellectual and artistic culture, the rise of which put an end to the long medieval night into which ignorance and barbarism had plunged the land. No wonder that the question as to how this dynamic institution originated became in after days an issue exciting the most passionate curiosity. From the fifteenth century, intellectually dominated by the humanists, and more decidedly from the eighteenth century, overshadowed from the point of view of historical inquiry by the great Muratori, the commune has been in the forefront of Italian medieval studies. And although only the origin of the single commune of Florence is our concern in this book, the general issue is so engrossing and at the same time so appropriate to this summarizing chapter projected as a background for the origins of Florence that a brief indication of the line which the communal inquiry has taken, especially since the rise with the labors of Muratori of modern scholarship, is indispensable.

For Muratori the question took the form of whether the Italian commune, which becomes faintly visible about the time of Otto I and multiplies rapidly after the year 1000, should be ascribed to a resurrection of the vanished Roman municipal institutions or should rather be regarded as an outgrowth of the free institutions of the Lombard and the other German invaders. Declaring in favor of a Germanic origin, Muratori took a position which was generally accepted till the beginning of the nineteenth century when it was challenged by the German historian, Savigny.[2] This scholar attempted to establish the unbroken continuity of Roman municipal institutions (and of Roman law as well). His thesis was sharply disputed by a number of German and Italian historians, among whom Troya[3] and Hegel[4] stand out most prominently. So successfully did the proponents of the Germanic origin of the free commune establish their case that their results were not called into question for several decades.

We thus come to the close of the nineteenth century when historical scholarship entered on that more intensive phase described in our introductory historiographical sketch. The new phase was made possible by the accumulation of a vast wealth of fresh documentary material and by the closer focusing by scholars on much more narrowly circumscribed bodies of fact. Under these circumstances detailed information became available that made the earlier results appear incomplete and gradually aroused the suspicion that the problem had been attacked from a wrong angle. For Muratori as well as for the investigators of the first half of the nineteenth century the question had been posed in such a way that they were bound to declare for one of two possible answers. That was the kind of simplification to which human nature is prone but which regularly fails to square with the discoveries of a more microscopic scholarship. What began to appear, first vaguely, then with more and more definiteness, was that the communes when studied individually and not in the mass failed to range themselves meekly in one or the other of two indicated categories. In point of fact it became increasingly clear that the new municipalities were not so much either Roman or German as the substantially original creations of the new era which began with Otto I and the formation of the Holy Roman empire. Since this revised position has resulted from a general movement of recent critical thought, it would be vain to attribute priority to one or another of its many representatives. But it is wholly permissible to affirm that the foremost champion of the new attitude was Robert Davidsohn. It was in 1891 that Davidsohn published his epochal article on the origin of the consulate[5] and five years later followed it up with his presentation of the origin of the Florentine commune in his *Geschichte von Florenz.*

As we shall in due time deal in some detail with Florentine origins as portrayed by Davidsohn it will suffice at this juncture if Davidsohn's contention in regard to the rise of free communal institutions in general is made clear. His starting-point is the undeniable fact that, owing to the extremely primitive conditions that prevailed in Italy during the long centuries of barbarian rule, the central government was always weak and functioned feebly or not at all in local matters. Consequently all purely local affairs, involving such indispen-

[2] F. C. von Savigny, *Geschichte des Roemischen Rechts im Mittelalter.* 7 vols. Heidelberg, 1834-51.

[3] C. Troya, *Storia d'Italia del Medio Evo.* 17 vols. Naples, 1839-59.

[4] K. Hegel, *Geschichte der Staedteverfassung von Italien.* Leipzig, 1847.

[5] R. Davidsohn, "Entstehung des Konsulats," *Zeitschrift fuer Geschichtswissenschaft,* Vol. VI (1891), pp. 22 ff.

sable immediate concerns as the upkeep of roads, bridges, and fountains, and the repair of the parish church, were left to the restricted group directly interested. This is the *vicinia* or *vicinanza,* the association of the neighbors of the countryside, which took these affairs into its own keeping and thus in an inconspicuous and almost invisible manner assumed a modest measure of self-government. In the once flourishing towns of the Roman period which had long ago dwindled to mere villages and market-places the same process is observable as in the country districts. The most familiar unit of organization within the town was the parish, and in town as well as country it was usually the parish members who made up a particular vicinia. When neighboring town parishes had common interests to debate, they would be moved to hold a general meeting, and on coming to a decision as to the action to be taken they would entrust a committee from their number with its execution. The committee members were called *boni homines* and were in effect a skeletal municipal government. With the slow but steady growth of the towns in the eleventh century the boni homines acquired a longer tenure and a greater dignity. This fresh advance was marked by the assumption on their part of the sonorous title of consuls. If we accept the advent of the consuls as a conclusive sign not only that the commune is born but that it is now a going concern, the theory of Davidsohn is that the new government springs from the earlier institution of the boni homines, who in their turn point to the neighborhood groups, the vicinie, as their vital germinal principle.

The books and monographs which during the last forty years have wrestled with Italian communal origins are literally legion. They are almost without exception well disposed to the Davidsohn theory of the commune being an original creation based on the self-help of the vicinie, but they often hesitate to accept the boni homines as the universal precursors of the consuls. And in point of fact instances have been found which do not permit the assigning to the boni homines of this decisive chrysalis role. Over and over again when the investigation focuses on a single commune some element appears which, if not entirely novel, represents a departure from the pattern characteristic of the other communes. Thus it has gradually become clear that in consequence of the barbarian invasions the conditions in Italy became so chaotic and varied so widely from point to point of even the same province that a general formula describing the evolution of communal liberty is unattainable and should be given up. The tendency prevailing at the present time is to insist on a multiple origin, that is, on the view that every commune owes its free institutions to a combination of conditions peculiar to itself. But this is not to abandon the inquiry or to leave it where it started. The gains since the famous work of Savigny have been enormous. In the first place no one any longer dreams of referring the commune flatly to either a Roman or a German origin.[6] It is admitted that Roman and German administrative institutions co-existed on Italian soil and may or rather must have entered into the new creation in a measure which it is the business of scholarship to determine in each instance.

[6] This is too absolute. Old theories die hard. Not so long ago the Roman thesis was very vigorously renewed by E. Mayer, *Italienische Verfassungsgeschichte von der Gothenzeit bis zur Zunftherrschaft.* 2 vols. Leipzig, 1909.

However, the decisive factor in the birth of the commune is a historical ***novum*** testifying to the emergence of a new vigor in Italian medieval society. It is this fresh biological energy that counts and not the occasional borrowing of Roman or Germanic forms that contended for supremacy during the dark centuries of unrelieved barbarism. And when we look for the invariable central germ of the new energy we regularly find it in the resumption of immediate self-help by small voluntary groups.[7]

This chapter has been an excursus into general Italian history planned to supply a convenient background for the unfolding of medieval Florence. Admittedly we have oversimplified, overschematized. The generous provisional acceptance by the reader of the periodization here suggested will have the advantage of enabling us to go ahead with our strictly local undertaking without too many interruptions to explain the developments within the whole peninsula.

[7] It will not be possible to do more than list a few of the works illustrative of this recent phase of the communal investigation. Davidsohn, *Geschichte von Florenz,* Vol. I, chap. 8. A. Solmi, *Le Associazioni in Italia avanti le Origini del Comune.* Modena, 1898. A. Solmi, *Il Comune nella Storia del Diritto.* Milan, 1922. L. von Heinemann, *Zur Entstehung der Staedteverfassung in Italien.* Leipzig, 1896. P. Sella, *La Vicinia come Elemento Costitutivo del Comune.* Milan, 1908. G. Volpe, *Questioni Fondamentali sull'Origine e Svolgimento dei Comuni Italiani.* Pisa, 1905. G. Volpe, *Il Medio Evo.* Florence, 1926. G. Mengozzi, *La Città Italiana nell'Alto Medio Evo.* Rome, 1914. F. Schneider, *Die Entstehung von Burg und Landgemeinde in Italien.* Berlin, 1924. L. Simeoni, *Le Origini del Comune di Verona.* Venice, 1913. L. M. Hartmann, *Geschichte Italiens im Mittelalter.* 4 vols. Leipzig, 1897-1915. L. Chiappelli, "La Formazione Storica del Comune Cittadino in Italia (Territorio Lombardo-Tosco)," *Arch. Stor. It.,* Serie 7, Vols. VI, VII, X, XIII, XIV.

III. Darkness over Florence

THE deep Middle Ages, which we have agreed cover the five centuries following on the collapse of the Roman empire of the West, constitute the long incubation period of our western civilization. During all that time Florence drowsed in the obscurity of an all but impenetrable barbarism. It was not till around the year 1000 that the darkness over the town began to lift and that the new life commenced to stir which launched Florence on its historical career. In this chapter it is proposed to treat briefly the five-hundred-year period of gloom. Fortunately it has recently been pierced by a few scattered rays from various sources enabling us to arrive at some sort of an idea of what was going on behind the veil. Outstanding among these sources is archaeology with its sheaf of very definite revelations touching the physical vicissitudes of the town. Next, there is our general knowledge of Italy and Tuscany during the Germanic invasions which permits the drawing of inferences securely applicable to our particular municipality. Finally, a few documents, chiefly of an ecclesiastical order, have been recovered yielding information of a slight but direct and indubitable nature.

Because these scattered facts have only rather recently become available, the older writers resorted to free invention to fill the gap. According to the first local chronicler of merit, Villani, Florence was, toward the middle of the sixth century, completely destroyed by Totila, one of the later kings of the Ostrogoths. As an almost incredible confusion characterizes Villani's story of the event, it is not to be wondered at that he identifies Totila, who was a man and sovereign of parts, with the much earlier Attila, king of the Huns, the terror-inspiring *flagellum dei* of his age. Following its overthrow, when "not a stone was left upon another," Florence—still according to Villani—lay in undisturbed ruin throughout the Lombard period and was not rebuilt till the time of the Franks, when none other than Charlemagne himself took the good work in hand. These statements of the chronicler are unequivocally false, for neither was Florence destroyed by a barbarous Goth nor was it rebuilt after some two hundred and fifty years of extinction by a somewhat less barbarous Frank. Villani took over the story from his immediate predecessors, the fanciful myth-makers, and they were stirred to free invention due to the circumstance that no information whatever regarding Florence during the dark period of the Germanic invasions had come down to them. Pressed to explain the puzzling silence, they postulated a dramatic Gothic cataclysm, followed, after a sleep of almost three centuries, by an equally dramatic resurrection.

What really happened at Florence during the Gothic and Lombard periods was the very opposite of striking drama, for the town obscurely vegetated in slow, uninterrupted decay. Never very important during the Roman era, it sank even lower in the social scale during the invasions, when the urban civilization of Italy, so long a-dying, went finally to pieces and the whole peninsula reverted to a rude, impoverished agrarianism. Florence repeated the experience of every town of the peninsula. The local stream of trade dried up, the population declined, the Roman public buildings, the temples, baths, and theaters were abandoned and crumbled to dust, and gardens and fields made their incongruous appearance within the narrow circuit of the walls. Too indolent and discouraged to remove the débris, the few remaining inhabitants raised such new shops and shelters as they might require on the steadily accumulating rubbish piles, until every trace of the Roman buildings had been covered up and the slowly rising medieval town was lifted to a level anywhere from four to ten feet above the level of its Roman predecessor.

All this has been fully demonstrated in recent generations by the labors of expert archaeological and historical scholars. They have established the sites of all the more important Roman buildings and have made it clear that the Roman walls, far from being leveled with the ground, as would have been the case if the reported destruction by King Totila had occurred, stood whole and unimpaired till as late as the twelfth century. Having by that time lost their usefulness, they were ordered removed because the town, now embarked on a career of rapid expansion, had burst its bounds and required for the protection of its citizens and their houses and property a second and ampler circle of walls. We may therefore fall in with Villani, after all, and agree that in the early Middle Ages Roman Florence all but completely disappeared from the face of the earth. However, instead of being destroyed by a Germanic conqueror, it perished painlessly from waxing senility, very much like the Roman civilization with which it was identified. As for the new, the medieval town, which slowly rose on the scrambled classical remains, it was for many centuries as inconspicuous and unimportant as the new European culture just beginning to rear its head.

We have already learned that it was the Lombard conquest which had more important consequences for Italy than any other German invasion. Next to the fertile valley of the Po, which from the completeness of its subjection to the newcomers came to be called Lombardy, a name it has retained to this day, it was the province of Tuscany which figured as a leading Lombard center. We have learned that these particular invaders were ferocious, plundering barbarians with no experience whatever of civilized ways, and that consequently they were slow in giving their conquest an even rudimentary organization. When something akin to order gradually emerged, we get a picture not without distinct and interesting political contours. It presents a king and court at the head of the state and residing commonly in the city of Pavia. The king was usually no more than a figurehead except in the rare instance when, endowed with great natural gifts, he was also favored by fortune. Immediately ınder him were dukes and gastalds presiding over the provinces and districts nto which the kingdom was divided. The only difference between these two ypes of high officials seems to have been that the dukes, as the older dignitaries lating from the conquest, claimed the provinces under them by hereditary ight, whereas the gastalds arose later and, serving as the personal appointees of the sovereign, were removable at his pleasure. We may fairly conclude that he gastalds indicate an attempt on the part of the later Lombard kings to cquire a more effective control of their kingdom. In Tuscany both dukes and gastalds occur and the Lombard folk took firm root in the province on the trength of a considerable influx. The invaders constituted an upper class of andholders and warriors who at the bidding of their military leaders, the king, luke, and gastald, followed them into the field.

That Florence, like every other Tuscan town, became a center of Lombard ctivity does not admit of the least doubt. Near the east wall, on land where iow stands that majestic symbol of municipal liberties, the Palazzo Vecchio, here rose the characteristic watch-tower or Gardingo of the Lombards. Its existence till a time long after the Lombard period is amply attested. Its frown-ng presence overlooking the approaches from the east proves incontestably hat Florence was one of the forts or military centers maintained by the Lom-ards to secure their rule. Other documents establish the erection under Lom-ard patronage of several churches, conspicuous among them the original Or San Michele, predecessor of the existing church of that name. If the theory warmly defended by Davidsohn is correct, no less an ecclesiastical edifice than he baptistery of St. John, one of the most famous as well as one of the most eautiful buildings still adorning the town, was erected in the Lombard era.[1] n no case is it possible to maintain that the two-hundred-year rule of the Lom-ards passed over Florence without leaving behind as much as a trace.

When in the year 774 the rule of the Franks superseded that of the Lom-ards, the administration of Tuscany underwent some changes which, at least or a time, made for a greater effectiveness. The Lombard dukes and gastalds were swept aside in favor of Frankish appointees, an official called a count eing set over each town and its dependent district. Among his other func-ions the count, who represented the sovereign, acted as judge, and in connec-ion with his judicial service we learn that, associated with him in finding the verdict, were a number of local assessors called *scabini*. The scabini were hosen from among the free residents of the town and it was by virtue of their ree status that they shared in the administration of justice. They may be ac-cepted as incontrovertible evidence of the achievement of a modest measure of nunicipal self-government as early as the Frankish period. In the age of an-rchy following the extinction of the Carolingian line the scabini are still en-countered here and there, although plainly they were no longer functioning egularly. With the advent to power (962) of Saxon Otto they vanished en-irely from the scene. We can hardly be mistaken in referring these important nunicipal officials to a movement of political self-help which manifested itself

[1] Davidsohn, Vol. I, p. 72; *Forschungen,* Vol. I, p. 24. For a detailed discussion of the origins of San Giovanni, see chap. XV.

in the Frank period. Defeated by the spread of an anarchic feudalism, the movement could be counted on to reappear with the coming of more favorable conditions, when it would dig other and more permanent channels for itself.

Another important administrative feature appearing in Tuscany during the Frank period and probably ascribable to the enfeeblement of the central power under the later Carolingians was the rise of a dignitary bearing the title of margrave. Not only did the margrave exercise rule over all Tuscany, but so powerful was he that, as had been the case in the days of the Lombard dukes, he made, or at least aspired to make, the margravial dignity hereditary in his family. For over two hundred years, till the death in 1115 of the *gran contessa,* Matilda, of whom there will be much to say hereafter, the Tuscan margraves were the most powerful feudatories of the Italian kingdom. They usually made their residence in Lucca, which by being thus distinguished became the leading town of their territory; and they preserved their margravial authority from diminution by serving as count for every town of the margraviate. However, as they could not be present in all of the Tuscan towns at the same time, they had themselves represented in the towns other than Lucca by agents who appropriately bore the designation of vice-counts.

Under the administrative system established by the Frank conquerors each town was the head of the surrounding territory, town and territory together constituting a county (*comitatus, contado*). This division of Tuscany into counties is exceedingly important for the whole later development of the province. It certainly goes back to the Frank, quite possibly it goes back to the Roman period, when an identical unit of city and outlying district was called *civitas* and constituted the basis of the old imperial administration. The cropping up after a long lapse of time of an element of the Roman system (civitas) under a name (comitatus) having reference to a Germanic administrative division may serve to remind us how Roman and Germanic elements merged in the Middle Ages, and how mistaken it is to assert categorically that the free municipal institutions which appeared later are either wholly Roman or wholly German. Much more probably, when they are not an entirely fresh growth they represent a fusion of both traditions.

In the ninth century, toward the close of the Frank period, when wildly anarchic conditions were rapidly gaining the upper hand, there took place an event which at a later time proved very advantageous for Florence. Under the Frank system Fiesole was one of the Tuscan towns which served as the administrative center of a dependent territory or county. For reasons which thus far have completely eluded the investigators, around the middle of the ninth century and certainly by the year 854 the county of the old Etruscan hill town was merged with that of Florence. Thenceforward Fiesole was a town without a county, while Florence commanded the largest contado in Tuscany.[2] The puzzling event, which apparently caused no stir, had no immediate consequences. There were as yet no municipal liberties and neighbor towns were not yet locked in mortal combat over markets and trade routes. However, when two centuries later, municipal competition had reached this stage of ferocious

[2] Davidsohn, Vol. I, p. 85; *Forschungen,* Vol. I, p. 27.

rivalry, it appeared at once that, as against not only nearby Fiesole but every other Tuscan town as well, Florence enjoyed a considerable advantage by finding itself provided with a larger dependent territory than any municipal competitor.

Admittedly the foregoing scattered data on Florence during the first five medieval centuries are too slight to give the town even the semblance of a physiognomy. Any disappointment a reader may feel will disappear when he reflects that the shrunken and barbarized Florence of that period can have had no features worth recovering. We are aiming in this book at the Florence that came to vigor after the year 1000; and the only valid reason for glancing at the stagnant period that went before is to arrive at some conception as to what the situation on the Arno may have been when the town at last awakened from its sleep and girded its loins for the race. Knowledge on this head is pertinent and even necessary; but more than from such isolated facts as those already enumerated, it will result from a general acquaintance with the conditions of the tenth century, out of which Florence, like all the other free communes, arose. To put the case as precisely as possible, we want to know the outstanding characteristics of Italian society at the time of Emperor Otto I and his immediate successors, and particularly we want to know the leading aspects of the two ruling institutions, the church and the state.

By way of introduction to such a survey we shall have to inquire how feudalism developed in Italy and what specific forms it assumed in the old core of the Latin world. Some writers are inclined to refer its origin back to the Lombards or even back of their time to the last phase of the Roman empire. In a strictly technical sense this is inadmissible, although the disorder of both the late-Roman and the Lombard period produced a condition favorable to novel and incipiently feudal practices with regard to land tenure. However, feudalism could not fully triumph until the central power had declined to the point of paralysis, and under the last Roman emperors as well as under the Lombard kings this was never quite the case. When Charles the Great took over the Lombard kingdom, the central power even experienced an increase, as appears from the merest glance at his remarkably vigorous administration. As we are already aware, his Italian kingdom was divided into counties under leading officials called counts. Not only were they appointed and removed by Charles at his pleasure, but they were also subjected to the periodic inspection of his famous traveling agents, the *missi dominici,* who were sent on their rounds for the very purpose of holding the counts in due submission to the crown.

Under the puny successors of Charles, his system of government rapidly crumbled and, before long, was succeeded by an unqualified anarchy. Then, and not till then, the last barriers of order broke down and the very complicated system of self-help we call feudalism came into being. It is not our business to describe it in this book in its innumerable ramifications. It will serve our limited purpose to call attention to some of the outstanding features of the appalling ninth- and tenth-century confusion. While there was still usually an administrative head or king, there was no king strong enough to enforce obedience. The consequence was that his local representatives, the counts, felt encouraged to make their power personal and hereditary. From having been officials subject to recall by their sovereign they aspired to become landed proprietors in their own right in enjoyment of as many farms, fields, and fortified castles as they could successfully appropriate. Voluntarily abandoning the towns or else driven out of them by the rebellious citizens, they settled in the countryside, where the estates and castles which they coveted were mainly located. Automatically by this development the church dignitaries, the bishops, became the leading personages of the towns. Without necessarily resorting to violence and often even at the pressing request of the townsmen deprived of their customary ruler, they assumed, in addition to their ecclesiastical duties, the public functions of the vanished counts. It was in the tenth century that the revolution culminated which made the spiritual lords, the bishops, also the civil rulers of the towns; and the movement, though general, was particularly characteristic of the northern, the Lombard, area of the kingdom.

In Tuscany the development took a different turn. There, as already noted, a great noble, probably himself originally a count, had succeeded during the declining years of Frank rule in bringing under his sole control the counties of Lucca, Pisa, Pistoia, Siena, and Florence. Owing to his exceptional position, he aspired to a more honorable designation than to the familiar one of count and either took, or by one of the shadowy sovereigns of the time was given, the title of margrave.[3] From the moment that he had gained a firm footing in Tuscany, the margrave exercised an authority hardly distinguishable from unqualified sovereignty. If, as happened from time to time even in the age of anarchy, an emperor-king held the throne who was strong enough to impose respect, the margrave would prudently agree to recognize him as his superior and to exercise the authority he held in the royal name. The statement holds also for the counts and bishops throughout the extent of the kingdom: they practiced independence, but if the suzerain chanced to command military resources, they did not hesitate to make a harmless profession of submission.

Now this breakdown of the central authority coupled with the rise of usurping local powers is not in itself feudalism. Feudalism is a system of order in disorder, and it arose from certain practices which the unutterably confused public situation just described brought in its wake. One of these practices is known as commendation. When the smaller landholders became aware that they were no longer protected in their rights by the king, they "commended" themselves to a more powerful neighbor, that is, in return for protection they offered the neighbor more vigorous than themselves certain specified services, above all, of a military nature. In due course the compact came to be sanctified by the ceremony and vows of homage, from which the superior emerged as "lord" and the inferior as "man" or "vassal." In measure as the great landholders, both lay and ecclesiastical, received the submission of their lesser neighbors, they acquired the character of local potentates, each potentate

[3] Not unlikely the early margraves were the counts also of the two remaining Tuscan counties of Arezzo and Volterra. That these two towns were not subjected to the rule of their bishops till around the middle of the eleventh century would appear from evidence presented by Davidsohn, Vol. I, pp. 198-99. Until subjected to their bishops, we may think of them as in all probability included in the margraviate.

commanding a company of vassals practiced in arms and prepared to follow him into the field.

The rivalry among these numerous new wielders of power was intense, the disturbances among them perennial. As is ever the case when society dissolves into its constituent atomic parts, a situation was created which cannot be better described than as a war of all against all. The conflict, turning around lands and vassals, involved the bishops no whit less than the lay lords. Possessed of vast properties, which they were obliged to defend, the bishops developed the same martial outlook as the nobles and were consequently threatened with estrangement from their original spiritual functions. And to this peril, let it be observed, the bishops of Tuscany, although they did not acquire the civil powers of the counts, were just as much exposed as the bishops of Lombardy, who in most instances did acquire them. In either case a bishop was a great landowner capable of giving protection to a smaller neighbor. That, as a great Catholic prelate, he had also a hallowed character would very probably incline the frightened possessor of a small freehold to consider that his act of submission was likely to bring him a double security.

Simultaneously with commendation feudalism took on another feature to which it chiefly owed such local vigor as it succeeded in acquiring—the feature of immunities. In measure as the central government broke down, the usurping lords took over many of its functions, especially those pertaining to war and justice. This deadly mischief the weak kings who played at royalty during the post-Carolingian anarchy were utterly unable either to hinder or undo. Indeed, in return for the small benefit of a formal recognition of their crown, they repeatedly found themselves obliged to legalize the seizure of public functions which had taken place. The usual procedure for doing this was to issue a royal charter enumerating the privileges (or immunities) of which a particular lord stood possessed. Clearly by such grants the ruler stripped himself of many essential features of sovereignty. Himself mortised henceforth into the crude system of feudalism, he exercised so strictly limited an authority that he was condemned to an all but complete impotence unless he happened to be a man of unusual ability. Ability of course performs wonders under any circumstances. In sum, power was no longer with the king but with the great landholders, lay and eccelesiastical. And because the age was characterized by religious zeal, a leading expression of which was the foundation of great monasteries, the heads of these monasteries, the staff-and-scepter-bearing abbots, also presented themselves to view as ecclesiastical landlords. Profiting by commendation and demanding and receiving immunities like the bishops, they were in every respect the peers of these older ecclesiastical dignitaries.

Such was the fluid and desperate Italian situation, when in 962 Otto I of Germany became king of Italy and Holy Roman emperor. Without any doubt he would, if he could, have re-established the vanished royal power. A real statesman, vigorous but prudent, he recognized that in the altered political circumstances such an attempt on his part would be fantastic, and that the only course open to him was to accept the accomplished feudal revolution.

Accordingly, he came to terms with the territorial magnates, the bishops, abbots, counts, and margraves, by formally enfeoffing them with their lands. In the northern or Po area he lent his support to the movement which had not yet exhausted its strength and which was pushing the bishops into civil authority in the towns. He must have reflected that with bishops who held office only for life he would not run the risk he did with lay counts of having the appointment take on a hereditary character. In consequence of Otto's policy it became the rule rather than the exception for a northern bishop to be also a civil ruler, a count. As Tuscany was under a margrave, Otto, following his policy of subscribing to the *status quo,* acknowledged the margrave, even though this nobleman, on the Saxon's descent into Italy, had sided against him. On being received back into favor, the margrave, Hubert by name, remained faithful to the new dynasty, as did his son after him. Of this son, Margrave Hugo, we shall hear later on, for it was during his reign that Florence emerged definitely into the light of history.

If it must be denied that Otto I built up in Italy an effective royal administration, he may without challenge be said to have given the troubled peninsula a greater security than it had enjoyed for over a century and a half before his advent. His most distinguished single service was to put an end to the devastating raids of the Magyars. In the year 955 he administered so capital a defeat to them on the Lechfeld in southern Germany that they lost their taste for the nomadic way of life and settled down to an agricultural existence on the Hungarian plain. Even before their incursions into Italy had ceased, we get evidence of a timid revival of trade coupled often with almost startling manifestations of fresh life in the towns. Left to themselves during the anarchy of the period preceding Otto, the towns had on several occasions given proof that they were no longer willing to play the role of mere passive victims of circumstance. After all, the ancient Roman walls, though in decay, could be restored and, in default of help from an impotent ruler, needed only to be manned by a resolute citizenry to foil the assault of the Hungarian nomads, invincible in the open country but incapable of conducting patient and extended siege operations. The habit of self-defense, once resumed, grew until it led to the creation of an organized town militia. Plainly Italian citizens who risked their lives in their own cause and who, as soon as they met encouragement from Otto's revived central government, began again to spin the threads of trade, were recovering from the cowardly dejection which had been the unbroken rule during the many centuries of the barbarian invasions. As social good and evil are in the last analysis alike referable to the quality and temper of the human spirit, we are well inspired to take account of the novel military and commercial activities manifesting themselves in the Italian towns. Without any doubt they may be signalized as marking the earliest dawn of that great communal era which was to challenge the dominant feudal order and bring it to its fall.

During Otto's reign, however, as well as during that of his successors for a long time to come, feudalism remained the characteristic institution of society and completely overshadowed the life of the peninsula in both its public and private aspects. So decisive was its dominance that it even threatened to denature and absorb the venerable and far more ancient institution of the church. For by imperceptible stages the church had become integrated with the ruling system to such an extent that bishops and abbots, and the pope as well, were no longer particularly distinguishable from the great lay nobles. By reason of their immunities they enjoyed temporal authority, and because of the conditions connected with its exercise they were involved in unceasing quarrels over lands and vassals. No wonder that, accommodating their conduct to the prevailing pattern, they assumed the brutal manners and purely military outlook of their lay rivals.

And yet the great feudalized prelates were in the first instance representatives of holy church and presumable exemplars of Christian piety and faith. True, this faith had long ceased to be the simple and naïve body of religious practices it had been in the age of the Fathers. It had become embodied in a church and, obliged to wrestle with practical necessities, it had learned that in order to carry out the vast social and religious program with which it had charged itself, it would have to have ample material resources at its disposal. This signified the possession of landed estates; and wealth in the form of land had for ages past been poured into the lap of the church as from a streaming horn of plenty. Touching these vast possessions the authoritative spokesmen of the church had never ceased to proclaim that they were under no circumstances to be understood as belonging to the clergy, the functionaries of the church, as individuals. The revenues the estates yielded were to be devoted to the maintenance of the ecclesiastical establishment, and whatever surplus there might be was supposed to be distributed among the poor. From the humblest priest to the highest prelate life was to be lived simply, even ascetically, detached from the pursuit of riches, personal ambition, and carnal delights. Such was the official doctrine, and to enforce it the popes and the councils had for centuries past enacted innumerable ordinances against every form of worldliness, and above all, against two evils to which the clergy had been found most commonly to succumb, the evils of bribery and of the flesh. Accordingly, all priests were strictly required to take the vow of celibacy and to eschew every semblance of traffic in clerical office. The latter practice was stigmatized as simony and denounced as one of the most heinous of sins.

Now it is easy to see how the clerical ideal embodied in the twofold solemn command to shun simony and fleshly concupiscence fared in the feudal age. Practically indistinguishable from their lay rivals, the great prelates tossed to the winds the obligations of their clerical status, lived in unashamed concubinage with one or more women, begot sons and daughters, for whom, as fond parents, they provided by robbing the endowments intrusted to their care, and at their death left behind a miserably depleted ecclesiastical domain. To be sure, whenever a resolute emperor assumed the scepter, and with the advent of the Saxon house there was for a time an unbroken succession of capable rulers, he would, as the official protector of the church, cancel the acts whereby an unscrupulous bishop had dispersed his possessions among relatives and favorites. Only through these repeated imperial interventions did the ecclesiastical foundations retain their character of vast landed units. That the emperor had also a personal interest in keeping them intact will be understood if we recall that they were essential elements of his power and that whenever death removed the reigning bishop or abbot, it fell to the sovereign to appoint the successor. As soon as such a demise occurred, a horde of ambitious aspirants hurried to the emperor's court and by a lavish expenditure of money and promises attempted to wring from him the coveted appointment. Not only did simony thus show its face openly, but the successful appointee would be almost sure to be a wholly worldly individual. His thought would revolve habitually around politics and war; he would make mock of his vows of celibacy; he would follow the emperor into the field clad in costly armor and attended by a clanking company of vassals; and in the occasional intervals of peace he would divert himself with the characteristic aristocratic amusement of the hunt. By the tenth century the misgoverned church had reached a degree of corruption that cried to heaven and threatened the ancient organization with an early dissolution. The very sentiment of religion, the most precious heritage of the common man and the rock on which the vast ecclesiastical superstructure ultimately rested, was threatened with complete disintegration by the spectacle of the great clerical titularies shamelessly wallowing in the black morass of a degrading materialism.

In this extremity and just in the nick of time the church was saved by one of those remarkable revivals that have been a feature of its history down to our day. That, divorced from the spirit which gave it birth, the church is no better than an empty husk will be readily admitted even by devoted churchmen; but why that spirit has repeatedly through the ages been threatened with extinction only promptly to be born again is something of a riddle. Be the cause what it may, the church has always been subject to this tidal movement. We have in this chapter dealt with a dying and dishonored church not without indicating some of the causes of its disease and shame. But around the year 1000 a revival set in which, before it had spent its force, gave Italy, and all Europe for that matter, a new religious aspect. Of particular interest to the lover of Florence is the circumstance that our town rose first and definitely into the view of history by championing the movement of ecclesiastical purification.

IV. Florence and the Religious Revival of the Eleventh Century

THE religious revival, the seeds of which were sown in the tenth and germinated in the eleventh century, was a movement as wide as the dominion of the Roman Catholic church. As this universal aspect is not our concern, as even the phenomena peculiar to Italy do not touch us except insofar as they happen to involve Tuscany, we are free to concentrate our attention on the neighborhood of Florence and to become acquainted with the character and *modus operandi* of the great revival by examining a particular instance.

Since the revival was a spontaneous movement of revulsion against the gross and palpable worldliness of the church, it was but natural that it should have had as its leaders and prophets individuals for whom the unworldly and ascetic features of Christianity constituted its vital core. Such men were likely, nay, almost certain, to be monks and hermits, that is, Christian believers who, after cutting the ties binding them to family and community, had in proof of their sincerity devoted themselves single-mindedly to the search for God. Even in the tenth century with its very general corruption men of this sort were not uncommon. To escape the temptations of the flesh they sought the solitude of mountain and forest; but often in their retreat they were visited by dreams and visions which obliged them to seek the crowded centers in order to call sinners to repentance and to proclaim the divine purpose of the Lord.

The first of these strange evangelists of whom we hear in the corrupt tenth century as carrying his message from city to city in Tuscany was a certain Romuald. Not a Tuscan by birth but a native of the Romagna, he was possessed of the fiery temper which has always distinguished the sons of this harsh Apennine soil. As is not uncommon with such enthusiasts, he had in his undisciplined youth yielded to every impulse of his passionate nature until, overwhelmed by a sense of sin, he had sought escape by prayer and flagellation. To complete his conversion from the world and the flesh he had buried himself in the savage mountains. But when, after a season devoted to his purification, he had become full to overflowing with the conviction of his mission, he was moved to seek the company of his fellows in order, like his ancient forerunners of the hills of Judaea, to discharge on his hearers the burden of God's love or, in case he found them disinclined to listen, again like his Judaean exemplars, to annihilate them with the thunders of God's wrath. It was in his own

Romagna that Romuald first testified against the terrible corruption of the clergy; but before long he crossed the mountains to carry his angry gospel along the highways of Tuscany. It is not recorded that he won any of the sin-hardened bishops to his views. But he did gradually gain a following among the common people; and surprisingly, and against all probability, he celebrated a triumph at the political and social apex of the province by bringing under his influence the margravial family.

Because of the relatively few documents which have come down to us, the line of Tuscan margraves beginning with the declining age of the Franks is imperfectly known, and those margraves whose names have been recovered pass before us like a procession of insubstantial shadows. The margrave of Romuald's day was Hugo, who held his post from about 970 to his death in the year 1001. With Hugo we come for the first time upon a margrave of whom we learn enough to arrive at some sort of opinion as to what manner of man he was.[1] His mother, Willa, on being left a widow had sought comfort in religion, and probably it was she who, first of her family, fell under the influence of the fiery hermit. A cure of the contemporary corruption much recommended by him and his like was the rearing of monasteries charged with reviving Christian zeal and serving as a retreat for holy men; and in the year 978 we hear of Willa founding at Florence, hard by the eastern wall and at the exact spot where it still stands, the famous abbey, La Badia (the abbey). It came to be called *the* abbey by the Florentines because it was for a long time the only creation of the kind within the city. Two decades after Willa's initial act Margrave Hugo in an outburst of generosity made over vast properties to his mother's foundation. As he was equally free-handed or, as we may even say, spendthrift in providing for the monastery of St. Michael at Marturi in the Elsa Valley, we may conclude that, as his life drew toward its close, he identified himself with increasing fervor with Romuald and the ascetic movement. So great was the gratitude felt for the magnanimous Hugo by the monks of the Badia that in a spirit in which we sense a somewhat too ready servility they elevated him, in the place of his mother, Willa, to the distinction of founder.

Margrave Hugo died on December 21, 1001, and was buried near the high altar of the church of the monastery which he had so richly endowed. The beautiful tomb which invites the admiration of the present-day visitor was erected almost five hundred years later. It ranks among the finest work of Mino da Fiesole. The original tomb was on a more modest but not unimpressive scale, for Hugo was laid to rest in an ancient Roman sarcophagus. The grateful brothers at once adopted the day of the margrave's death, which, the shortest of the year, was sacred to St. Thomas, for the annual memorial service of the founder. They have celebrated the event, without a single interruption, for now over nine hundred years. Dante, born within the shadow of the Badia, must have often witnessed the ceremony in his impressionable youth, for he saw fit to recall it in his immortal poem.[2]

In this same passage the poet celebrates Hugo, whom he admiringly calls *il gran barone,* as the stout trunk of the many-branched chivalry of Florence.

[1] A. Falce, *Il Marchese Ugo di Tuscia.* Florence, 1921.
[2] *Paradiso,* XVI, 128.

Doubtless the margrave, who, as his office required, was a great warrior, served in his day as the focal point of those influences from which sprang afterward the ideal of knighthood. The note of love and gratitude sounded by the verses is re-enforced from other sources. The fact is that both to Dante and to Dante's contemporaries Hugo was the earliest character of Florentine history to stand out with definite personal traits. During his long rule he had endeared himself to the citizens not only by reason of his munificence to a foundation of which they were justly proud, but also because he had given proof of a special affection for Florence by preferring it as his residence to Lucca, the traditional seat of the margraviate. Immediately after his death, stories began to circulate in his praise. In some of them he was even assigned the role, rare to the point of incredibility in a ruler of those brutal times, of champion of the humble classes against the violence of the strong. In short, since no people can flourish without heroes, as soon as the Florentines had advanced sufficiently to imagine a great future for themselves, they scanned their obscure beginnings and discovered just enough vitality in the scattered recollections of the Margrave Hugo to enable them to put his name at the head of the roster of great men required to feed their patriotic pride and spur them to great deeds.

The next name to emerge from the darkness of the age with definite individual characteristics is that of the Bishop Hildebrand. As there were excellent reasons for not hailing him as a hero, he was not, like Hugo, adopted into the official patriotic cult. Nevertheless we have such revealing information regarding him and he is so richly characteristic of his time that we cannot but profit greatly by subjecting him to a close scrutiny.

Hildebrand became bishop of Florence around the year 1008 in the manner and under the conditions inherent in the evil practice of episcopal immunities. By Bishop Hildebrand's time immunities were already of almost hoary antiquity. So far as the Florentine bishopric is concerned, we learn that as early as 874 or 875 a Bishop Andrew acquired a *privilegium* from Emperor Louis II, by which the episcopal estates were detached from the margraviate and subjected to Andrew and his successors.[3] The usual consequences put in a prompt appearance. The bishopric became the prize of ambitious, worldly men who spent their days in riotous living and squandered the possessions intrusted to their care among favorites and harlots. If the sovereign had not interfered from time to time to oblige the despoilers to return the alienated goods, the impoverished Florentine see would not have been able to fulfil its obligations to its subjects by discharging its spiritual duties. Such an imperial restorer was Otto I, who intervened vigorously against the bishop of his time, Raimbald by name, in order to force him to end his scandalous dilapidations.[4] Of course Otto was not moved by exclusively ecclesiastical considerations, for the episcopal lands constituted a fief which it was the emperor's secular interest to keep intact. In neighboring Fiesole the bishops had proved themselves even worse wolves than those of Florence, for by Otto's time the dispersion of the episcopal resources had become so complete that, in spite of his efforts and those of many of his successors, the bishopric was never restored to financial

[3] Davidsohn, *Forschungen,* Vol. I, p. 173.
[4] Davidsohn, Vol. I, p. 107.

solvency. Twenty years after Otto interfered to straighten out the tangled affairs of the Florentine church his son, Otto II, gave voice (983) to his indignation over the fresh misappropriations of Raimbald's successor, a certain Sichelmus.[5] So long as the bishops remained the frank worldings they were, it was apparently impossible to bring the episcopal finances back to health.

Steeped to their necks in feudal politics and utterly estranged from their spiritual functions, the bishops of Florence were not likely to lend an ear to the preachment of rude, skin-clad hermits who, like Romuald, descended on them from the wilderness of the Apennines. And so we come to Bishop Hildebrand, who was a most worthy successor of his immediate predecessors in that he bribed his way to office, did homage to his lord, the emperor, as though the bishopric were nothing other than an imperial fief, and played the absorbing role of feudal magnate by pursuing plans of personal grandeur and giving himself heartily to all the carnal delights forbidden to his cloth. Surviving documents inform us that whenever the emperor appeared in Italy the magnificent Hildebrand rode out to meet him at the head of his armed retainers, and that he dutifully performed all the acts required of a direct vassal of the crown. It is evident that he loved martial pomp and was insensible to the corruption with which he and his fellow-prelates were so manifestly spotted. For while he distinguished himself honorably from many of his colleagues by failing to maintain a whole harem of concubines, he did live with a woman in so frank and unconcealed a manner that he did not hesitate to sanctify his relation with her by the sacrament of marriage. The name of his wife was Alberga and she, the bishop, and their numerous sons lived together as a happy family in the *episcopium,* predecessor of the existing episcopal palace and, like it, directly west of the baptistery of St. John. Alberga must have been a woman of parts, a veritable virago. She took a passionate personal interest in all the problems of her husband's diocese. Whenever the bishop, conducting court for the purpose of giving audience to petitioners or of pronouncing judgment in quarrels brought to his attention, sat enthroned among his spiritual and temporal attendants, called in feudal language his *fideles,* Alberga brazenly took her seat at her lord and master's side. A very precious memory of such a court session has been preserved and illuminates for us as by a flash of lightning the crisis precipitated by the spreading activity of the reformers.

The scene falls approximately in the year 1020 and carries Alberga and a certain Guarinus as its leading dramatis personae. Guarinus was the abbot of a recently established monastery at Settimo, which, some five miles down the Arno, lay within the boundaries of the Florentine diocese. Bishop Hildebrand was therefore Abbot Guarinus's superior. But let the chronicler have the floor:[6]

This Guarinus made a practice of speaking openly against simoniacs and clerics living in concubinage [the regular two-point program of the reformers!]. On one occasion, having some business in hand, he sought the presence of the bishop of Florence, Hildebrand by name, and having presented his case, awaited the episcopal decision. Thereupon the wife of the bishop, Alberga, who was seated at his side,

[5] Davidsohn, Vol. I, pp. 111-12.

[6] *Vita Johannis Gualberti.* Davidsohn, *Forschungen,* Vol. I, p. 56. The *vita* is an invaluable document, owing to its preservation of the opinions current among the reformers.

Top: BAPTISTRY OF SAN GIOVANNI, EXTERIOR. *Bottom:* BAPTISTRY OF SAN GIO-VANNI, INTERIOR

Top: SAN MINIATO, FAÇADE. *Bottom:* SAN MINIATO, INTERIOR

Top: THE BARGELLO, FORMERLY PALAZZO DEL PODESTA. *Bottom:* THE BARGELLO, THE COURT

THE PONTE VECCHIO, LOOKING DOWNSTREAM. THE MODERN SUSPENSION BRIDGE IN THE DISTANCE HAS RECENTLY BEEN REPLACED BY A STONE BRIDGE

made answer: "My lord abbot, concerning this business you have brought forward, my lord the bishop has not yet been advised. He will take counsel with his *fideles* and inform you of his pleasure." At these words the abbot, fired with the zeal of God, poured out vehement maledictions on her, saying: "You accursed, sinful Jezebel, how do you dare open your mouth before this assembly of chosen representatives (*boni homines*) and priests? You ought to be burned at the stake for having presumed to asperse a creature and priest of God."

A tumult followed these wild words, but the chronicler drops the curtain and leaves us in doubt as to the issue. He does, however, vouchsafe the information that Abbot Guarinus fled to Rome and succeeded in persuading the pope to withdraw the abbey of Settimo from Florentine episcopal jurisdiction by subjecting it directly to himself. We may therefore conclude that Guarinus was not punished for his audacity; and we are justified in drawing the further deduction that reform was sweeping in like a tide and that, ominous evidence of its waxing strength, priests and leading clerics were beginning to identify themselves with the movement.

Possibly the stout old sinner on the cathedral chair began himself to be troubled, if not by mounting moral compunctions, at least by the increasing hostility of his subjects. Be that as it may, the time came when he resolved to found a monastery. It comports best with his character to refer his resolution to his active self-esteem and love of splendor, but, like other medieval men, doubtless he also hoped to have the reckoning of his sins reduced or even canceled out entirely by so signal a service to the Christian faith as the founding of a monastery was universally held to be. Although the exact moment of Bishop Hildebrand's determination to win renown as an ecclesiastical benefactor cannot be ascertained, it is certain that it antedates by some years the above-recorded outbreak against himself and his august lady. His first step was to choose as the site for his establishment the low hill overlooking Florence from across the Arno to the east and designated by tradition as the burial place of the first—and apparently only—Florentine martyr, San Miniato.

As we are aware, Minias or Miniato suffered death in 250 A.D. in the persecution of the Christians instituted by the Emperor Decius and was buried on the slope of the hill that afterward received his name. When, in the following century, Christianity was legalized, a small chapel was erected over the confessor's grave. The Minias worship, however, never became popular, for, when some five or six centuries later we get news of the chapel, we learn that it had been permitted to fall into decay and the instituted service to be neglected. Let the fact remind us that the Italians by no means uniformly cherished the memory of the early heroes of the faith. In the case of Miniato neglect and indifference went the extraordinary length of permitting, apparently without a protest, a relic-hunting German bishop of the entourage of Otto I to exhume the bones of Miniato and carry them off in triumph to distant Metz in Lotharingia.[7] In the countries north of the Alps, where martyrs were relatively few, they enjoyed an esteem in inverse ratio to their number. In consequence of this unfortunate abduction, Bishop Hildebrand faced a serious difficulty as soon as he

[7] Davidsohn, Vol. I, pp. 110-11. The removal took place about 968.

approached the execution of his grandiose design. A monastery dedicated to the Florentine saint must imperatively possess his sacred remains. For a less resourceful man than Hildebrand the problem might have proved unsolvable. He was favored by the circumstance that the saint's removal by the Lotharingian bishop half a century before had caused so little stir that either it had never become known or else it was no longer remembered. When, therefore, the cunning bishop ordered a search for Miniato's bones to be conducted over the hillside, his pick-and-shovel squad found them without any difficulty. While the initial act connected with the great project was thus a pious fraud, that did not fall heavily into the scales in an age which, gladly credulous, was not troubled by a scrupulous sense of fact.

Planning an abbey on a truly liberal scale, the powerful patron endowed it richly with possessions. The dormitory was intended to serve a goodly body of monks, and the adjoining church was to be the most imposing edifice to be found within the whole Florentine diocese. After a few years construction had gone far enough to permit the buildings to be put to use. Consequently, on April 27, 1018, the church was formally consecrated. This dates the famous structure which, still standing on its lovely hill, holds an important place in the history of medieval architecture. However, the edifice was far from finished at the time of dedication. With building operations continuing during the following decades in measure as funds became available, it was not till past the middle of the century that the church of San Miniato presented itself to view essentially as we see it today.

As Bishop Hildebrand appears in the records for the last time in 1024, in which year we may assume he died, we have the assurance that he lived long enough to see his undertaking well established. The credit for this pioneering work in medieval architecture is therefore indisputably his. His largeness of view arouses even greater respect when we recall that maritime Pisa, the most populous and opulent town of Tuscany at this time, did not feel prompted till half a hundred years later to undertake in its celebrated cathedral a comparable monument. While the cathedral of Pisa marks a striking advance in scale, daring, and beauty, to concede as much is not to deprive San Miniato either of its historic or its aesthetic distinction. Not its least merit is that it was a courageous venture undertaken at a time when Florentine society was still unbelievably poor, crude, and backward. Undoubtedly eager for the sumptuous effect produced by polished marble, the bishop to his regret found marble too expensive a material to use other than sparingly. Accordingly we find it employed in but two places, on the façade and along the inner wall of the apse, and there only as a thin covering or veneer. Conclusive evidence of the reigning poverty is furnished by the fact that the walls were erected throughout of irregularly sized blocks of stone. Even the tall columns of the nave were built up with these same small blocks, although, having at a later time been given a coat of marbled stucco, they deceive unwary present-day visitors into thinking that they are marble. Once again we may convince ourselves that the vanished Roman Florentia had been a mean city, since its ruins, which we may be sure were diligently combed for suitable remains, yielded the builders of San Miniato only the scantiest harvest in the form of a few undistinguished columns and capitals. They were incorporated in the lofty choir and in the low crypt beneath the choir, where they can still be identified.

An act of the doughty warrior-bishop, which still remains to be mentioned, was his appointing as the first abbot of his proud establishment a priest, Drogo by name, whom he instructed to prepare a life worthy of the holy proto-martyr supposedly buried under the high altar. As the only biographical material at Drogo's disposal were a few scant notices touching the saint handed down from the distant past, the task assigned to him was, historically speaking, incapable of solution. But Abbot Drogo had a mind above evidence. As he was also very proud of his Latin learning, he looked upon his commission primarily as a call to exercise his rhetorical powers. The result was a biography of San Miniato in which every son of the Arno city could take legitimate pride. To this day the popular histories of Florence, and often the so-called scientific histories as well, purvey Drogo's fables as the unvarnished truth. As might be expected, such works recount with particular unction the wonderful concluding feat of the martyr, who, when his head had been cut off outside the east gate of the town, picked it up with the greatest composure and, flying with it across the river, deposited it, together with himself, on the exact spot where he wished to be buried. The colorless original, from which Drogo was supposed to derive his facts, had the saint decapitated on the hill and prosaically buried where he fell.[8]

The biography of Abbot Drogo supports the contention put forward in the Introduction of this book that legend is the forerunner of history, and that what is properly called history is not born until society develops the habit of critical and analytic thought. Although legend and history are thus sharply distinguished, they stem from a common mental root and are both divisions of literature. For this reason Drogo's biography of San Miniato, while pretending to be history, which it is not, is, as a work of the imagination, indubitably literature. Viewed in this light, it is not without distinction. For as the first literary work accredited to a Florentine citizen, it stands at the head of a magnificent tradition culminating three centuries after Drogo in the famous trinity of Dante, Petrarch, and Boccaccio.

The events clustering around Bishop Hildebrand can leave no doubt in our minds that Florence had awakened from its long, medieval sleep, that it had in fact become a leading center of the impending spiritual conflict. In the years following the splendor-loving founder of San Miniato the conflict grew steadily more intense until it became the central concern of the citizens and drew Florence into the vortex of world-happenings. Nothing demonstrates the uninterruptedness of the movement better than the appearance, not long after the magnificent prelate had passed from the scene, of a man resolved to carry on the war against all that the bishop had stood for with as much and more of the vehemence of the Abbot Guarinus. The new head of the reform movement was Giovanni Gualberti.

Giovanni was the son of a small nobleman of the Pesa Valley and, like the ruling class throughout Europe, was brought up to the profession of arms. If

[8] Davidsohn, Vol. I, p. 135; *Forschungen,* Vol. I, p. 34. Consult also *Acta Sanctorum,* Octobris Tomus Undecimus, pp. 415-32.

we place his birth around the year 1010, we become aware that he grew up in the atmosphere dominated by the engrossing issue of ecclesiastical reform. The wind raised by the heated conflict between the saints and the sinners stirred his susceptible spirit to its depths. Therefore, no sooner had he attained manhood than he decided to abandon the military life and become a monk. As a resident of the countryside about Florence he shared with his countrymen their pride in the new foundation of San Miniato. He turned his footsteps thither and assumed the cowl.

The monk Giovanni at once gave evidence that his was the active, not the contemplative, religious temper. For, although self-condemned to a cell, he could no more avoid a life of combat than if he had never abandoned sword and buckler. At the head of San Miniato at this time was a successor of the literary Drogo, the Abbot Hubert. He owed his appointment to his patron, the bishop of Florence, to whom he had made the usual "presents" in recognition of the honor conferred on him. As soon as the militant Giovanni gained positive assurance that his spiritual chief had thus tainted himself with simony, he began to denounce him; and when the Florentine bishop, Hatto by name, himself a simoniac like the long line of his immediate predecessors, sided with the abbot as he was in duty bound, Giovanni without hesitation attacked Hatto also. It took a courageous fanatic to challenge these two dignitaries, mighty men in the first place and, in addition, the young monk's ecclesiastical superiors. Grimly resolved to see the struggle through to whatever issue it might bring, he determined to draw the people into the controversy by haranguing them at street-corners about the sins of their spiritual leaders. In an uprising produced by him in the heart of Florence, in the Mercato Vecchio, he received a severe beating at the hands of the partisans of the bishop and betook himself in search of convalescence to the solitudes of Vallombrosa (1035?). This was, and in part still is, a densely wooded mountain district of the Arno Valley to the east of Florence. Joined before long by numerous youthful enthusiasts, he collected them into a monastic foundation of his own. It grew rapidly in the following years until, under the name of the Vallombrosan Order, it had spread in numerous dependencies throughout Tuscany and central Italy. Thus was the rebel of a corrupt monastery visibly rewarded from on high by becoming the father of a whole congregation of monasteries dedicated to purity and incorruption.[9]

As head of a powerful order called into being by his religious ardor, the Abbot Giovanni was able to carry the campaign against simony and clerical concubinage far and wide in Tuscany and, like many another hard, uncompromising fighter, lived to see the triumph of his cause. Long before his death

[9] My account has omitted the celebrated story of Giovanni Gualberti's conversion, according to which he spared an enemy delivered into his hands by an accidental encounter, when the frightened victim threw himself on the ground and with extended arms presented the figure of a cross. On going, deeply stirred, into a nearby church to pray, the crucifix over the altar solemnly inclined its head in sign of approval of his generous act. The upshot was that he renounced the world and became a monk. This impressive story was cut out of whole cloth by Giovanni's first hagiographer. Taken in connection with Drogo's free inventions in behalf of Miniato, it drives home the point that we are dealing with a credulous age endowed with the will to believe and as yet undisturbed by intellectual doubt. On the several "Lives" of Giovanni Gualberti see Davidsohn, *Forschungen,* Vol. I, pp. 50 ff.

the movement had spread into every corner of Italy, arousing repercussions that made themselves felt through the length and breadth of Christendom. However, to achieve this universal character it had to be taken up by a man of greater reach and stature than distinguished an, after all, purely provincial personage like Gualberti. This champion was none other than that fearless and towering pontiff, the famous Gregory VII. In the next chapter we shall hear how the reform movement came to a head under him, challenged the current ecclesiastical abuses in the person of their main supporter, the emperor, and filled the church in every country of Europe with new life. To our Giovanni may be conceded the by no means inconsiderable honor of being a forerunner, who with other forerunners in other parts of the world prepared the way for the triumphant Gregory. That he died in the very year of Gregory's elevation to the chair of St. Peter (1073) may be taken as the conclusive confirmation of his pioneership. Shortly before he died he enjoyed a success that must have given him immense satisfaction, for he won it in the strenuous local war, with the declaration of which he had inaugurated his religious career. The story sheds so much light on the religious situation in Florence that it cannot be passed over.

In spite of the agitation for reform, the bishopric of Florence long remained entangled in the corrupt practices which had become traditional. However, by the middle of the century the monkish party had acquired a considerable following among both laity and clergy. It had gained a foothold even in the capital of Christendom and, with occasional support from Rome itself, the agitators were able to make the situation of a proved simoniac in possession of the Florentine see highly uncomfortable. It was around the year 1061 that a certain Peter Mezzabarba became bishop of Florence through appointment by the imperial court. Unfortunately for him the usual "presents" by which he paved his way became a matter of public knowledge. The incident constituted so flagrant a case of the forbidden sin that it lashed the reformers to an unexampled outburst of fury. Immediately the alert Gualberti, now the powerful head of the Vallombrosan Order and a lifelong fighter for ecclesiastical purity, took command of the opposition. The new battle developed into the severest conflict of his career, for the erring bishop was not without numerous supporters among his fellow-bishops (like himself simoniacs almost to a man), besides having many lay noblemen and particularly the powerful Margrave Godfrey of Tuscany on his side. But Gualberti was equal to the occasion. He mobilized his ecclesiastical troops, the devoted Vallombrosan monks, and had them carry on such a frenzied campaign in Florence and throughout the diocese that the population was fanned into a white heat of religious zeal.

Thereupon the agitators played their trump card in the form of the demand that Bishop Peter submit himself to the judgment of God. That meant, according to the juridical ideas of the day, a trial by fire. When the indignant bishop refused the test, his persecutors went the length of ordering a boycott of the churches served by priests of his appointment who refused to repudiate their sinful chief. So terrible was the pressure exercised under the generalship of the fanatical Vallombrosan chief that parish after parish fell away from Peter until he stood on his episcopal eminence a man marked with a public stigma and—

alone. To clinch the now certain victory the Abbot Giovanni resolved to conduct the fire test, even though the accused party refused to participate. The excited people imperatively demanded a spectacle and, talented impresario that Gualberti was, he was more than willing to serve them.

The fighting abbot had conducted his campaign from the monastery at Settimo as his base, and it was Settimo he chose as the scene of the trial. When we remember that Settimo had been the home of that Abbot Guarinus who had begun the war against simony by attacking Bishop Hildebrand, we must concede that there was an eminent fitness in its selection, for now, after half a century of conflict, Guarinus was to receive his reward. The ordeal took place on February 13, 1068, and an incident more dramatic and at the same time more illuminative of certain dark areas of the medieval mind cannot be imagined. As soon as day dawned long lines of people from Florence and the countryside began to pour over all the roads that led to Settimo. They gathered in a dense, expectant mass around two piles of wood somewhat less than man-high with a narrow path left open between them. To represent the prosecution and bear the burden of the trial the Abbot Giovanni had chosen one of his Vallombrosan monks, Peter by name, who, as might be expected, was the most simple, guileless, and devoted member of the band. Then, after the brothers had chanted their litanies, the two piles of wood were set aflame and the great moment of Peter's life had come. He took the path indicated, was swallowed from view among the enveloping smoke and flames, and a few seconds later reappeared safe and sound. The enthusiasm of the spectators was indescribable. Their cries of thanksgiving rose to heaven and in their rush to kiss the hem of the poor monk's garment they almost trampled him to death. From that moment Peter became Fiery Peter (Petrus Igneus) for his admiring contemporaries. Before many years had passed, he was made a cardinal, and when he died he was widely adored as a saint. As for the controversy between Abbot Gualberti and Bishop Peter, which had for years turned the Florentine diocese topsyturvy, it was over, for further resistance was impossible after God himself had pronounced in favor of the abbot and against the wicked prelate. Driven from the city by a popular uprising, Peter was deposed by a papal synod and a successor ordered to be elected in strict accordance with the canons of the church.

If success ever brings happiness to men, Giovanni Gualberti must have felt richly blessed during the five years of life still vouchsafed him. Then, at the close of his days he experienced a final triumph, for he lived just long enough to see that man elevated to the chair of St. Peter who had become the champion of reform at Rome itself and who was destined to make Gualberti's Tuscan struggle as universal as the church.

V. The Countess Matilda and the Emergence of Communal Autonomy in Tuscany and Florence

THE movement of ecclesiastical reform, spontaneously inaugurated at many centers of Italy and Europe though it was, would never have acquired a unified and irresistible character if it had not been taken up by the central institution of the church, the papacy. But that the papacy of that period would ever champion the cause of reform must have seemed utterly improbable even to its most sanguine supporters, for, during the first half of the eleventh century, it was passing through one of the blackest phases of its history. True, almost from its foundation it had experienced these sudden and overwhelming calamities. They issued in the main from the circumstance that the papacy had its seat in feudalized medieval Rome, in whose passionate local issues it became inextricably entangled. Repeatedly in the past it had succumbed so completely to its environment that, in spite of its universal claim and mission, it sank lower and lower in the scale until it was, in effect, no more than a Roman municipal office, over the possession of which rival feudal families fought and intrigued without respite and without shame.

Precisely this was the situation in the days of Giovanni Gualberti's youth. Never had the chief office of Christendom reached a lower moral depth; and Gualberti and all the other leaders of the ascetic movement, anxiously noting every ailment of the church, did not fail to give moving expression to their sorrow and indignation over the disgraceful spectacle presented by the capital of Christianity. However, the spirit of reform was abroad and was spreading, and presently the reformers had the satisfaction of winning to their side a discontented element of the Roman clergy. This was an indispensable preliminary to a revolution at the corrupt heart of the Christian system. But before a moral movement of irresistible momentum could get under way, the Augean stable that Rome and the papacy had become would have to be swept clean with an iron besom. And as matters stood in the world in the first half of the eleventh century, the only possible wielder of that besom was the emperor.

The Saxon line of emperors inaugurated by Otto I came to an end in the person of Henry II in the year 1024 and was followed by the Franconian line, of which the second and greatest representative was Henry III. Raised to the throne in 1039, he did not make his first descent into Italy till seven years later. Like all the finer-fibered individuals of his age, he too had been deeply troubled by the corruption of the church, and under the influence of the reformers who, for Europe north of the Alps, had their vital center in the great monastery of Cluny, he was resolved to do everything in his power to bring the ailing institution back to health. That meant specifically that he would lend his aid in imposing celibacy on the clergy and in eliminating the worst abuses connected with nomination to clerical office. However, he would not surrender blindly to the movement of reform. While honestly resolved to serve religion and the church, he would refuse to impair his royal prerogative by giving up his customary right to appoint the great prelates. For, under the system of immunities, bishops and abbots were his immediate political subordinates, the nomination of whom he could not surrender without giving up the very substance of his power. His reform activity would therefore be strictly accommodated to his conception of his imperial authority. He would forbid "gifts" and other corrupt practices; he would have only tried and worthy men intrusted with the great ecclesiastical dignities; but he would hold fast to the view that it was his right and privilege to appoint these fit candidates and to invest them with office. Immediately on mounting the German throne he had elaborated these principles for Germany and now, on crossing the Alps, he resolved to apply them also in Italy.

On arriving in Italy Henry made his way to Rome to be crowned emperor by the pope, as custom demanded. It was the very moment the papacy had reached its most scandalous decline, for as many as three rival popes were attempting to drape themselves in the seamless mantle of Christ. The indignant and energetic Henry made short shrift of their conflicting claims. Although not clothed with such supervising powers by any ordinance of the church, he deposed all three contestants tainted alike with simony, and seated on the papal throne a German bishop, whom he could trust to live up to the obligations of his new office. It was from this personal appointee, Clement II, that he received the imperial crown. When Clement II died after a few weeks, the all-powerful emperor raised his successor to office; and he continued to exercise this unwarranted authority till a total of four popes owed their elevation to his intervention. The issue of simony was not raised nor can it be said to have been involved, for he exacted no money from his appointee. Nonetheless there was a new abuse of the greatest gravity in that the church had at its very crown and apex been brought under the control of a temporal lord. If this usurpation aroused at first only secret clerical opposition, the adversaries were the more dangerous as they were the very reformers whom the honest intentions of the sovereign had for the first time put in the saddle at the capital of Christendom.

As long as the formidable Henry dominated the scene, his opponents hesitated to show themselves in the open. Hardly had he died (1056), however, at the early age of thirty-nine, when the reformers were encouraged to repudiate the imperial hegemony and to carry through the reorganization of the church according to their own views and under their own authority. The bold resolution was greatly favored by the troubles which impaired the royal power in Germany immediately on Henry's death. As his son and heir, Henry IV, was only six years old, his mother exercised the rule in the capacity of regent. Not only was she too feeble to keep the reins firmly in her hands but, like all the German sovereigns before and after her, she suffered from the geographical handicap of being too far removed from Italy to bring such power as she had to bear upon the situation. When, before long, Germany was convulsed with a succession of revolts that paralyzed the central authority, the Roman reform party recognized that its hour had come and set about the execution of its plans without concerning itself further with the shaky pretentions to ecclesiastical supremacy of the distant German court.

The head of the Roman clerical party and formulator of its independent policy was a man who by all but universal consent is the greatest figure of his century. Hildebrand, born of an obscure family of southern Tuscany, had as a youth gone to Rome and become a monk in response to an urge of purification shared by so many of his best contemporaries. Joining at once the as yet insignificant party of the reformers, he succeeded in acquiring a much wider survey of the human scene than was common among his Roman friends by visiting the monastery of Cluny beyond the Alps and making his home for a while in that most dynamic of all the centers of the religious revolution. While the heart of Hildebrand glowed with religious zeal, he also felt strongly the need to busy his mind with practical affairs. This preoccupation with both heaven and earth is his outstanding characteristic and supplies us with the key to his historic eminence. Pushed by his rare executive ability into the fields of diplomacy and administration, he gradually gained such considerable influence over the far-flung business of the papacy that, long before the world in general had heard his name, he was recognized at Rome as the most important member of the papal court, the invisible director concealed under the mantle of the successive popes who sat upon St. Peter's chair following the death of Henry III. It was Hildebrand who, during the eclipse of the imperial power, took the reform movement in hand and gave it its final expression. It had started with a passionate outcry against simony and concubinage, and from these demands, received from his predecessors, Hildebrand never departed. But because of his long and agitated personal experience at the capital of Christendom he now added a specifically papal feature to the program which pushed the reform into the arena of European politics and ended by making the pope the arbiter of the western world.

While living in Rome as a young monk, Hildebrand had been outraged by the spectacle of the papacy perpetually fought over by rival feudal factions immediately on the ground. This condition was made possible by the traditional manner of election, according to which each new incumbent of St. Peter's chair owed his elevation to the action of the clergy and people of Rome. So loose an arrangement was bound to produce disturbances, and in point of fact a papal election regularly gave rise to political machinations, armed intervention, and bloody riots. To a man of Hildebrand's temper a system provocative of such ever-recurrent evils was monstrous and unbearable. Therefore, when Henry III put an end to it, the reformers applauded him to the echo; but on the emperor's then arrogating to himself the right to appoint the pope, he aroused an opposition which was no less vigorous for being kept discreetly under cover so long as his power lasted. He had hardly departed this life, leaving, as we have seen, the imperial power in a paralyzed condition, when Hildebrand came forward with an electoral plan of his own. By it each new pope was to be chosen by a small number of the higher clergy of Rome distinguished by the title of cardinals. Intrusted to a limited body of churchmen of high station, the election was to be taken entirely out of lay hands, whether those hands belonged to a base Roman mob, to a junta of feudal conspirators, or to a single grasping potentate.

It was in 1059, during the reign of Pope Nicholas II, that Hildebrand promulgated the decree establishing the new electoral system. Its striking success is witnessed by its having lasted in its essential features through all the succeeding centuries down to our day. But to admire the new electoral machinery is far from doing justice to the scope and logic of Hildebrand's papal program. While he desired passionately to free the papacy from the non-clerical influences which had brought confusion on its head, his leading purpose was to make it more supreme over the Christian church than it had yet been and, with the vast ecclesiastical power concentrated in its hands, to bring all temporal potentates, great and small alike including the emperor, under the control of the pope. The universal monarchy of Rome was to be revived, but not in the manner of Charlemagne or Otto. Recalled to life in a world that had become passionately Christian, it was to be identified with the church, the venerable and authoritative association of true believers. It followed unescapably that the head of the new universal state must be the pope, vicegerent of Christ and successor of the apostle Peter. But not for his personal satisfaction and aggrandizement was the Holy Father to be raised to his unrivaled eminence. He was to exercise his vast authority in order to bring God's great purpose to fulfilment by leading mankind to salvation.

Although Hildebrand did not at once publish his revolutionary program to the world, the mere fact that he nursed it, shaping every measure of the Roman court in accordance with its terms, signified that a life-and-death struggle with the emperor could not be avoided. It did not actually break out till Hildebrand himself mounted the papal throne as Gregory VII. In the year 1073 the man who for several decades had been serving as the masterful counselor of popes stepped at last into the open by himself assuming the highest Christian office. He promptly brought to a head the conflict with the temporal power for which he had been so long preparing by having a Roman synod sweepingly enact the whole reform program into law. Accordingly, the papal anathema, which already on previous occasions had been fulminated against simony and concubinage, was renewed in the most vigorous terms, while bishops and abbots who should receive their offices from lay hands, and every emperor, king, and temporal ruler who should presume to invest bishops and abbots with office were threatened with excommunication. From the Pandora's box of the papal synod of 1075 there issued for the first time in definite form the fateful issue which goes under the name of "lay investiture." Although we may agree that it was implied in the problem of ecclesiastical reform from the start, we must insist that it did not actually leap to the front till Hildebrand, become pope, made it the pivotal item in his program.

Since the time of the great Otto the emperors, practically without exception, had been extremely well disposed to the church. They had been particularly interested in providing the great body of the laity with a purer Christian minstry. But when, as now appeared, the purer ministry, to which they had given heir support, was to be achieved by the abolition of lay investiture, that is to ay, by the annihilation of their power, the reigning emperor, Henry IV, registered an immediate and violent protest. For throughout alike his German nd Italian lands bishops and abbots ruled over vast territories, and if they vere no longer to be invested with their domains by their sovereign, they vould be released from his control and he, for his part, would no longer in ny effective sense be a sovereign. When Pope Gregory VII promulgated the udacious decree of 1075 Henry IV was ruling Germany in his own name with ll the arrogance and caprice of an undisciplined young man. Without hesitaion he tossed his gauntlet to Gregory by declaring him deposed from office. The pope's answer was as prompt as it was uncompromising. He in his turn leposed Henry and, in addition, laid him under the curse of excommunication. The war for supremacy between the two claimants to the power of ancient Rome had begun. Never again would there be a durable peace between empire nd papacy until one had defeated and humbled the other.

In this fateful conflict our concern is limited to the part played in the drama by Florence and Tuscany. It happens to be important largely for the reason hat the ruler of Tuscany, who was the most powerful vassal of the emperor n all Italy, sided unreservedly with the opponent of the emperor, the pope. n order to appreciate the full significance of this action we must briefly bring he story of the Tuscan margraviate down to Gregory's time.

The Margrave Hugo, who looms so large in Florentine myth and story, died vithout offspring in 1001 and was succeeded by a number of imperial appointees with whom we need not concern ourselves till we reach Boniface II. This Boniface was invested with office by Emperor Conrad II in 1027. The new provincial chief was head of the Canossa family, already abundantly endowed with lands extending from the northern slopes of the Apennines all he way across Lombardy to the foothills of the Alps. The family took its name rom the castle of Canossa, which from its bold Apennine rock looked threateningly across the smiling plain of the Po stretching northward as far as the eye could reach. With Tuscany added to his strength by Conrad's munificence he Margrave Boniface completely dominated central and northern Italy; and ince he clung to his superior, the emperor, with more consistency than was usual among feudal magnates, he served as the main pivot of the imperial power in Italy in his day.

However, while giving the emperor his support, Margrave Boniface was not minded to let any opportunity slip by calculated to promote his personal interests. He was a grasping, iron-fisted lord who oppressed his subjects and steadily increased his possessions at the expense of both clergy and laity.[1] One gets the impression that he was an admirable embodiment of the feudal spirit n its crudest form. Before his death a little past the middle of the century (1052), he had raised his house to a position which caused it to be regarded on ll hands with mixed awe and dread. His widow Beatrice undertook to carry

[1] Falce, *Bonifazio di Canossa.* 2 vols. Reggio Emilia, 1926. The first volume is a biography of he dubious, "reconstructed" sort. The second volume, entitled *Regesto,* is a valuable digest of elevant documents.

on the government in behalf of her infant son and, when her son died pr
maturely, in behalf of the sole surviving heir, a daughter, Matilda. From fe
that she, an unarmed woman in a turbulent, arms-bearing world, would n
be able to cling to the precarious summit to which Boniface had climbed, sl
contracted a second marriage, choosing as her husband Godfrey, duke of Upp
Lotharingia. This Godfrey, every whit as lordly a man as Boniface, cham
pioned her cause so effectively that, on his death in 1069, she felt sufficient
strong to try the experiment of ruling without masculine support, in associatio
with her vigorous and rarely capable daughter. Until Beatrice herself died i
1076 mother and daughter shared the reins in unbroken harmony. These ba
facts needed to be enumerated because they explain how it happened that
woman came into possession of the margraviate of Tuscany and the va
Canossa heritage in Lombardy as well. The Countess Matilda was still youn
in office when by his bold prohibition of lay investiture Pope Gregory V
precipitated the epic struggle with the emperor.

Counting Matilda's accession to the margraviate from the death of her ste
father (1069), we note that she dominated Tuscany and central Italy for almo
half a century. To voice their feeling of respect, her contemporaries called h
the great countess (*la gran contessa*). What particularly impressed them, as
continues to impress us, was her clear-cut character, which, having prompte
her to side with Gregory the moment war was declared between him and th
emperor, kept her unalterably faithful to the papal cause. And let it not be fo
gotten that her decision imperiled both her life and her possessions, since th
emperor commanded great resources and was, in addition, her lawful overlor
The danger left her unperturbed. By taking her stand at the side of Gregor
she became the strong shield without which he might easily have gone dow
to defeat; and as if to make it clear that she was fighting, less for a perso
than for a cause, when Gregory died she made an equally uncompromisin
fight in behalf of his three immediate successors on St. Peter's throne. By thu
bracketing her name with that of the church without regard to personal co
sequences, she appeared to the party of reform as a heaven-sent champio
fighting in shining armor on the side of Christ and righteousness against th
forces of the world and Satan. Beginning even before her death, these pa
tisans made a myth of the great countess until they had transformed her int
a holy virgin in complete accord with the colorless feminine ideal cherishe
by all preachers of a perverse asceticism. This legendary portrait still looks o
at us from most of even the recent histories. It is, if not false, at least so on
sided that it invites correction by the rehearsal of some of the actual circum
stances of Matilda's life, in the light of which she again becomes an actu
woman in a living world.

Although we may assume that Matilda was born with a tender religious co
science, we have no evidence to indicate that the reformers enjoyed her suppo
in the days of her youth. In the rude society in which she lived young wome
accepted in public and private matters alike the guidance of their male relative
and Matilda was no exception to the rule. Almost the first fact we know of he
is the marriage to which she was obliged to submit to her stepfather's son an
heir, the younger Godfrey. She dutifully followed her husband to his hom

beyond the Alps, to the duchy of Upper Lotharingia, and there an emotional crisis occurred which the few shadowy details that have come down to us suffice to make reasonably clear. She was not fond of her husband who, though a famous fighter, was a hunchback and hideous to look upon. When the child born to them died almost at birth, she could not bear to continue life at his side and returned to her native land. Thenceforth husband and wife lived apart, and when in 1076 the hunchback perished at an assassin's hand, Matilda must have felt that she had been liberated from an odious yoke.

We can hardly doubt that her unhappy marriage dropped a blight into the young countess's soul, which drove her to seek refuge in religion and which, at least in part, explains how she became the devoted and ever-obedient daughter of the church. But stalwart as that devotion was, she never permitted it to interfere with the secular duties imposed upon her as the heir of a great house. She was a powerful feudal sovereign, the chief Italian vassal of her liege, the emperor, and in her public and private character she consistently maintained the style appropriate to her station. Contemporaries tell us that, clad in helmet and coat of mail, she led her forces in person into the field and that, when she required relaxation, she would eagerly indulge herself, like all the members of the ruling class, in the pleasures of the hunt. It accords well with this picture of her in her worldly aspect that in her court, famous throughout Europe for its feudal magnificence, her vassals were wont to address her on their knees. In short, to think of her, as the hagiographers would have us do, as a closeted nun exclusively occupied with thoughts of salvation, does her a wrong by blotting out her role as a great secular power.[2]

The struggle between Gregory VII and Henry IV, inaugurated by their furious declarations of war in 1075, came to a swift climax in the scene of Canossa which held and still holds captive the imagination of the world. By the universal defection of his own countrymen the conceited young sovereign of Germany was apprized that he had challenged a power before whose moral authority the sword broke in his hand. When presently he stood alone, ejected from Christian society and facing deposition, he hazarded as a last resource the journey that brought him as a humble seeker for forgiveness to the feet of his papal adversary. In the bitter month of January of the year 1077 he waited for three days in the cold and snow to be admitted to Gregory's presence. The memorable scene was laid at Canossa, the Apennine stronghold of Matilda and the home from which her race drew its name. Canossa testified to the world that the gran contessa, the most powerful sovereign of Italy, stood behind, not the emperor, but the emperor's adversary, the pope, and that she stood behind him with all her castles and all her armed men. If we agree, as agree we must, that Henry, the barefoot petitioner at the barred gate of Canossa, was not dragged from his pedestal by a manifestation of material power, we should nonetheless be blind not to perceive that Matilda's presence at her ancestral castle with Gregory was at least a not insubstantial factor in his terrible humiliation.

[2] The literature on Matilda is very considerable. A good recent work is by L. Tondelli, *Matilda a Canossa*. Reggio Emilia, 1926. The best biography in English is by Nora Duff, *Matilda of Tuscany*. London, 1909. The earliest monkish biography, an invaluable source, is by a younger contemporary of Matilda, Donizone by name. It will be found in Muratori, *Scriptores,* Vol. V.

Instead of the end, Canossa turned out to be no more than the prologue t
the great struggle over lay investiture. Henry and Gregory conducted the cor
flict so long as they lived; and when they had departed this life, it was cor
tinued by their respective successors. When both sides at last resolved to neg
tiate and effected an accommodation of their claims in the Concordat of Worm
(1122), the movement of reform had passed its apex and the world, as has bee
its capricious way from the beginning, had turned to other interests. The docu
ment signed at Worms accorded the victory to neither combatant. To the pop
it conceded the right to invest the bishops and abbots with spiritual authority
to the emperor, the right to invest them with their lands. So lame a compro
mise was possible only because, after fifty years of warfare, the reform move
ment had exhausted its energy. Before its ardor was extinguished, howeve
it had expressed itself in a movement of such importance for the civilizatio
of Europe that it cannot be overlooked. In the year 1095, at a General Counci
of the church held at Clermont in France, the reigning pope, Urban II, ha
the happy inspiration of reviving the religious fervor, which by its nature re
quires constant feeding with fresh fuel, by directing it upon a new enterpris
He proposed a war of the united Christian west against the Moslems to wres
from them the Holy Places of Palestine. His project was wildly acclaimed b
a vast multitude and led to the launching of the First Crusade. Without an
doubt the stirring war between Cross and Crescent must be accepted as th
astonishing final fruitage of the religious reform inaugurated over a hundre
years before by puritanical monks and hermits roused to indignation by th
scandalous degradation of the church.

We have lingered over the world-issues of the last quarter of the elevent
century largely for the purpose of supplying something of the background o
Matilda's personal thought and feeling. This greatest personality that had thu
far sprung from Tuscan soil will remain a stranger to us unless we grasp tha
the two materially distinct but spiritually related movements of the investitur
struggle and the crusades utterly filled her being. Just as certainly as the in
terminable war between pope and emperor wrung her soul with agony, th
war between Christian and Moslem released a holy joy, even though, as
woman, she was hindered from joining the crusading host. And yet, over
shadowing as the religious movement in its several aspects seemed to her, i
was not and could not be more than a segment of the age in which she lived
Numerous other interests were arising, which even in her day were slowl
pushing the religious issue into the background, and which in the centur
after her reign succeeded in greatly altering the face of Europe. While Matild
did not comprehend these novel agencies, they already so fully dominated th
new generation which confronted her in her old age that often she must hav
seemed to herself to be living among strangers. In sober fact in her last phas
the aging countess was as much of an anachronism as her tough, simonia
father, the Margrave Boniface, had been an anachronism in the atmospher
of religious purification steadily gaining ground during the last years of hi
reign.

The new forces announcing a new age were secular in their nature and ma
all, in last analysis, be referred to the revival of commerce. In now turning t

this engrossing movement we are obliged to make those enemies of Christendom, the Moslems, our starting-point and to recall how, after converting the Mediterrean Sea into a Moslem lake, they had filled the measure of their iniquity to overflowing by periodically harrying the coasts of Italy with fire and sword. Not till the time of Otto I and his successors did the situation register a gradual improvement. Even so, it was noticeable rather within the peninsula than upon the sea, owing to the fact that the emperors, commanding an army but not a navy, could not make their power felt beyond the shore. Indeed under an agrarian system, like feudalism, it was unlikely that the rulers would ever come into possession of a navy; and consequently, if the Moslem pirates were ever to be tamed, it would devolve upon the maritime towns to take the business in hand by means of a navy built and manned by themselves.

The Mediterranean shore of Tuscany is lacking in good natural harbors. The only seaport of any consequence it boasted at that time was Pisa, which, at the mouth of the greatest Tuscan river, the Arno, enjoyed a dominant position. With no aid to be had from the land-minded emperor, it behooved the Pisans themselves to terminate the calamities from which they suffered along with all the other dwellers on the coast. In their feebleness they made but slow headway for a long time. Both before and after the year 1000 the occasional chroniclers continue to report destructive raids on the part of the pirates against the Tuscan littoral. Conscious, however, that resistence to their encroachments was gradually becoming more resolute, the Saracens determined to nip the recovery movement in the bud by seizing the island of Sardinia, from which rising Pisa and all western Italy for that matter could be kept under convenient control. Its successful capture by the Moslems spurred the Pisans to the greatest effort they had made so far and they drove the enemy from the neighboring island. The startling victory, won in 1016, marks the turning of the tide. Encouraged by success, the Pisans now began to extend their cruises. They traded boldly along the whole Italian coast and, before many decades had passed, demonstrated their growing confidence by assuming the offensive. They leaped upon the Moslem corsairs wherever they found them, in the waters of Spain and Sicily and along the coast of northern Africa. After some generations, by the time, let us say, of the reign of the Countess Matilda, Pisa had become a thriving community steadily extending its range at sea at the expense of the Moslems and sharing with Genoa on the adjoining Ligurian shore an already all but assured primacy over the western Mediterranean.

The remarkable initiative manifested by the Pisans was no isolated phenomenon. All the other Tuscan towns, beginning with Pisa's nearest neighbor, Lucca, before long exhibited similar signs of vitality attended by an enlarged exchange of goods. But no sooner was the commercial movement well under way than the towns became aware of a monster in their path in the form of the feudal system. This so-called system was, as we are aware, a makeshift born of anarchy and never free from manifestations of war and violence. Incapable of giving security, it was bound to disintegrate the moment that the groups it oppressed acquired the courage and developed the resources successfully to organize themselves against it. Throughout Italy the most characteristic single feature of the established social order were the great lordships made up of a widely scattered aggregation of estates and castles. Under the novel conditions brought to birth by the eleventh century these vast properties were exposed to the attack, first, of the rising townsmen and, second, of the lower nobility, the *milites,* as impatient in their way as the townsmen of their dependence on the caprice and wilfulness of their hard masters. The century was not far advanced when townsmen and lesser nobility occasionally joined forces against the common enemy; and although they by no means uniformly scored a victory, they remained in touch with each other, prepared to renew the struggle the moment the occasion seemed auspicious. The best evidence of this trend is seen in the growing habit of the lesser gentry to take up their residence in the towns, where they became an upper layer of privileged, fighting citizens. Starting with the immediate practical demand of open communications for their goods and the cessation of capricious taxes levied along the highways, the townsmen before long moved on from this modest program to fairly ambitious projects of self-government. In point of fact, they began on their own authority to organize such simple municipal services as their most pressing needs required; and almost before they were themselves aware of it, they were practicing a limited municipal autonomy, for which there was as yet no basis in either law or custom.

Need we go farther to indicate the main aspects of the complex social upheaval which went on under the eyes of the Countess Matilda not only in Tuscany but at an even accelerated rate among her northern, her Lombard dependencies? And need we marvel that she, who took so clear and confident a stand in the great religious issue of the day, looked in a kind of daze on economic phenomena wholly beyond her narrow, aristocratic comprehension? Jealously bent on preserving her inherited rights, she was instinctively hostile to political change of every kind and particularly critical of what to her mind were the insolent demands and actions of the upstart townsmen. She would have preferred—this meek virgin of the legend—to lay her powerful sword to their backs, but the delicate situation stayed her hand; she had cast her fortunes with the pope and, except for some truce-like intervals devoted to negotiations, she was permanently at war with her powerful suzerain, the emperor. The merchants in control of the towns would have been obliged to deny their sharp, bargaining natures if they had not taken advantage of this conflict between their two feudal superiors. The opportunity was theirs to side with either Matilda or the emperor, depending on which was willing to pay the price. And the price, in view of the usurpation of municipal authority of which in varying measure they were all guilty, could not be other than the legalization by description in a formal charter of as much of the usurped authority as countess or emperor could be induced to concede.

The struggle between the two overlords, between emperor and countess, explains the famous charters which Henry, he of the memorable Canossa incident, issued in 1081 to Lucca and Pisa respectively.[3] Being at war with the pope and the countess, Henry badly needed the help which two such prosperous towns as Lucca and Pisa could bring to his cause. Therefore, with many com-

[3] For the charter to Lucca see Ficker, *Forschungen zur Reichs und Rechtsgeschichte Italiens,* Vol. IV, p. 124. For the Pisan charter see Muratori, *Antiquitates,* Vol. IV, p. 19.

punctions, as we may be sure, he agreed to put the seal of his approval on the municipal activities by which the two towns had partially lifted themselves out of the frame of feudalism and taken their first uncertain steps toward self-government. What Henry had thus granted, his vassal, the countess, did not have the power to revoke. To be sure, Pisa and Lucca might not, under all circumstances, be able to enforce their proud new status, but since it had been confirmed by the fountainhead of feudal law, it was difficult to see how it could ever again be successfully nullified.

In the light of these general Tuscan developments we are now prepared to narrow our inquiry to Florence and to take note of its fortunes during the long reign of the great countess. The first circumstance to leap to view is that throughout the life of Matilda the cordiality existing between her and her town on the middle Arno was never broken. Florence approved of the Matildan policy of supporting the pope and, alone of Tuscan cities, refused to listen to the overtures repeatedly made by Henry IV with a view to drawing it to his side. We shall not be making a mistake if we ascribe this fidelity to the countess as owing, in the first instance, to the devotion to the papal cause that the townsmen shared with their valiant ruler. They had become identified with religious reform in the pre-Gregorian days of Giovanni Gualberti's missionary labors, and their fervor had given their city a moral energy permitting it to radiate an influence which made itself felt far and wide over Italy. To compare it with the influence exercised by Cluny over the lands beyond the Alps is by no means an exaggeration. Then, too, there was a strong personal attachment to Matilda and her house. A little past the middle of the century, in 1057, Florence had been made the center of the margravial administration, thereby replacing Lucca as the capital of the province.[4] This was a great material advantage, and the honor that went with it was underscored by the open preference repeatedly exhibited by Matilda for the City of the Baptist. Although, like all feudal sovereigns of wide sway, she engaged in constant travel and lived in many castles, she resided for sufficiently long periods in her palace at Florence to be regarded affectionately by the inhabitants as their fellow-citizen. On the strength of this emotional bond there was gradually happening to her what had already happened to the Margrave Hugo and Giovanni Gualberti. Even before her end she was being incorporated in the steadily expanding patriotic legend of the town.

Cordial as were the relations between ruler and ruled, they did not hinder Florence from experiencing the commercial impact of the age. Somewhat more tardily than Pisa and Lucca, it is true, but no less surely, the town was going through all the changes making for burgher self-esteem and calling for the creation of new commercial, juridical, and political institutions. It is not to be supposed for a moment that the Florentine merchants nursed a greater indulgence toward the oppressive feudal system than the merchants of the other Tuscan towns or that they were less eager to promote their selfish interests. Inevitably therefore they began to perform individual acts of autonomy, with no

[4] Chiapelli, "La Formazione Storica del Comune Cittadino." *Arch. Stor. It.*, Serie 7, Vol. XIII (1930), p. 7 (footnote). My date (1057) is supplied from Davidsohn, Vol. I, pp. 203-5.

idea in their heads at first beyond the limited one of solving the problem lying immediately across their path. The haphazard procedure is illustrated by a few isolated facts of which we have certain knowledge. Thus by the year 1079 the Florentines already had their own system of weights and measures.[5] Perhaps they had acquired this privilege through a diploma issued by their friend, the countess. No document to that effect has come down to us; indeed the extraordinary dearth of documents for this period makes it impossible to come to other than very tentative conclusions regarding the advance of the movement of self-government. However, the above-mentioned proved use of municipal weights and measures signifies the exercise of a sovereign act, which, if not ascribable to a margravial concession, must be regarded as an out-and-out usurpation. A little later (1090), we hear of the city collecting a feudal due throughout its county (*comitatus*), which again signifies the assumption of a right ordinarily reserved to the margravial power. Since only a few years before this event Henry IV had so conspicuously honored Pisa and Lucca with the ample privileges of 1081, Matilda may have felt obliged to make some equivalent concession to her subjects of Florence in order to command their continued loyalty. And whether she made the concession or not, the Florentines, whose faithfulness to the countess was entirely compatible with a strong sense of their own rights, would not in the least be minded to let their political development lag behind that of the other Tuscan towns.

That, in point of fact, it did not so lag was conclusively proved not long after by the exercise of an authority entirely impossible in the old days of feudal submissiveness. Of all the symbols of sovereignty, the most imposing from the beginning of history has been the right to make war and peace. Should we therefore learn that Florence undertook to levy war without the consent of its overlord and in its own exclusive interest, we would be justified in declaring that a very respectable measure of practical independence has been won. And an unequivocal declaration to this effect is made possible by an event recorded by the earliest Florentine chronicler whose meager assortment of happenings in the life of the young commune has come down to us. In the year 1107, according to this unknown annalist, "the Florentines destroyed the castle of Monte Gualandi." [6] This castle lay some eight miles down the Arno on a hill above the existing village of Lastra and belonged to a branch of the Conti Alberti. The Alberti (or Counts Alberti) were one of the great feudal families of the Florentine county; and when we are told that a citizen army destroyed one of their castles lying along the road to Pisa, we are obliged to deduce that Florence had been annoyed by a barrier to its commerce and had leveled it with the ground. Like all the rising communes of Italy, the Florentines recognized that the prime obstacles to their development were the great feudal families and that they and their castles would have to be cleared from the path if the city was to enjoy the unhampered growth to which it aspired. The destruction of Monte Gualandi was the first step in a policy which di-

[5] Davidsohn, Vol. I, p. 270. The author's interesting discussion concerning the coming of autonomy is supported by evidence in *Forschungen*, Vol. I, pp. 62-3.

[6] Annales Florentini, II. Hartwig, *Quellen und Forschungen*, Vol. II, p. 140.

not rest until, though only after several centuries, there was not an independent feudal stronghold left in Tuscany.[7]

Some years later (1114) the same nameless annalist reports the destruction by the Florentines of another castle, Monte Cascioli. It lay on the left bank of the Arno only a short distance from the recently destroyed Monte Gualandi. The complicated provincial situation which led to this new aggression has been reconstructed by the historians of the period, such as Santini and Davidsohn. It will satisfy our limited purpose if we content ourselves with two remarks. The first is that by the early twelfth century Florence had manifestly become an aggressive community regarding war in its own interest as its legitimate province; the second makes the point that the first wars of Florence had as their objective the numerous nearby castles from which the feudal lords threatened the rising commerce of the town. It is quite improbable that the Countess Matilda was consulted in connection with these actions, which were a concern not of hers but of the trading burghers. Clearly in Florence, as everywhere else, the floodlike movement of events was pushing her aside. She may not even have been fully conscious that her power was on the wane; but such facts as these here recorded permit us to affirm that, with or without her consent, Florence, like every other city of her realm, was exercising rights which in their sum signify the assumption of a liberal measure of administrative and political autonomy.

Should anyone require additional proof regarding the decline of Matilda's authority during the latter half of her reign, let him consider an outstanding event of her very last years. In the year 1113 Pisa, risen a hundred years after its capture of the island of Sardinia to the status of a bustling and irrepressible commonwealth, organized a crusade against a band of Saracen corsairs who, from the Balearic Islands as a base, ventured to reassert an ascendancy which they had never entirely surrendered. Since the crusade, if successful, would destroy a vicious nest of pirates, all the neighboring ports and the inland Tuscan towns as well were invited by Pisa to join in the enterprise. Many towns, including Florence, responded to the call, with the result that a magnificent armada sailed westward over the sea and, after a campaign which cost three years of strenuous endeavor, captured Majorca, the main Moslem fortress.[8] True, when, with their object gained, the crusaders returned home, fresh Moslem bands from Spain resettled the islands. We hear of them as an unabated nuisance for a long time to come. Nonetheless a glorious victory had been won, bringing honor to the Tuscan towns but chiefly to sea-faring Pisa, which had captained the enterprise. A notable feature that will not escape the student attentive to political change was that the ruler of Tuscany, whose participation in such an enterprise might well be taken for granted, shone by her absence. In an expedition affecting the welfare of the whole province, the famous and authoritative Matilda had no share. Apparently no one consulted her about the venture nor did she feel a pressing desire to take charge. Perhaps her ad-

[7] The attack on Monte Gualandi was part of a complicated series of actions arising from a new phase in the war between emperor and pope. Whoever is interested in these larger implications may consult Santini, "Studi sull'Antica Costituzione del Comune di Firenze," *Arch. Stor. It.*, Serie 5, Vol. XXV.

[8] For the Balearic crusade see Heywood, *A History of Pisa,* chap. V. Cambridge, 1921.

vanced years—she was nearing seventy—caused her to be less eager than had once been the case to assert her power. In any event she does not figure in the greatest armed feat in which her Tuscan subjects had thus far engaged. On July 24, 1115, only a few months after the capture of Majorca and before the Tuscan rejoicings over the great triumph had subsided, she died at Bondeno, one of her many castles in Lombardy. Who can doubt that the church bells rung at her funeral sounded also the knell of an epoch?

We cannot close this chapter without referring to a memorial of the Balearic crusade which to this day intrigues the visitor of the Arno city. On either side of the main door of the baptistery of St. John he sees a much damaged porphyry column securely fastened to the wall by iron hoops. These two not unimpressive shafts were among the booty brought from Majorca by the Florentine contingent in that expedition and were triumphantly set up in the as yet mean and undistinguished town to commemorate the victory. After some generations had passed the ever-exuberant fancy of the burghers busied itself to twine a vine of legend around the damaged trophies. According to this invention, which has enjoyed an unchallenged currency down to our own day, the columns represented a fraud practiced by the treacherous Pisans on their unsuspecting Florentine friends and allies. Perhaps the battered appearance of the shafts suggested to a later generation that there must have been some deception, and the theory the more readily gained ground as there had meanwhile sprung up a passionate ill-will between the two towns. The fact to which to hold fast, however, is that the ill-will and hatred did not develop till a hundred years after the Balearic expedition and that they were completely nonexistent when the blackened relics first made their appearance in Florence. Instead of commemorating Pisan bad faith, they undoubtedly celebrate a mutually advantageous friendship. However, that there could ever have been a time when trust and friendship ruled between them and the Pisans, the Florentines of the subsequent centuries absolutely refused to credit; and to justify their invincible aversion of their neighbors they spun a malicious tale illustrative of the well-known and ingrained Pisan treachery.

VI. The Twelfth Century: The Consular Phase of Communal Autonomy

IN TRACING the history of Florence during the investiture struggle we learned that the town, still in shadow, though the shadow was lifting, had assumed either with or, as is far more likely, without margravial authority certain self-governing functions, and had thereby constituted itself as a commune. As at the same time many other towns in Tuscany and many scores of towns throughout Italy had done the same thing, we are confronted with the famous communal period of Italian history and, by way of overture, with the much agitated issue of communal origins. While there is no need to repeat what has already been said on the score of origins,[1] it is permissible once more to point out that the nineteenth-century conflict between the followers of the German and the Roman schools was based on what to us of a later day is a historical misconception. Inspired by a simple faith in the effectiveness of institutions in themselves, the scholars took them as their point of departure. Institutions were regarded as the deliberate invention of men, subject to modification by other men as intelligence and self-interest directed. With the adoption of the genetic approach to history characteristic of the present time the older view gradually lost favor, since the contemporary historian inclines to look behind institutions to the general social conditions producing them. He tends to regard society as an organism which periodically runs with fresh sap obliging the organism to express itself in novel forms. The sap which in the eleventh century began to fill the Italian towns was the revival of commerce; and it no sooner ran, magically multiplying both private and public activities, than it was sluiced into numerous appropriate channels. In other words, as has been the case from the beginning of time, the quickening social energies called into being the new economic, juridical, and political forms they needed in order to function. They may in some instances have utilized either a Roman or a German form, which happened to have survived and lay conveniently at hand. In that case they made institutional borrowings, but the borrowings, however definite and provable, are relatively unimportant. What alone greatly matters is the coming of new life, which, like the season of spring in the world of nature, is far more a mysterious and unfathomable process than it is a rational and analyzable one. Working with unabated but capricious energy, the commercial revival brought into being such institutions of law and government as were capable of serving its ends. This is an organic view of social

[1] Chap. II.

processes, and in its light the commune, the sum of the institutions slowly rising to view in the eleventh century, is not the revival of a dead past, Roman or German, but essentially an original creation.

However, just as spring comes slowly and hesitantly, the communal institutions had a very gradual unfolding and their hidden beginnings go far back of the eleventh century, when the commune first made its appearance as a going concern. For our town of Florence the increasing activities of the eleventh century and the barely perceptible movements of a still earlier time have been so thoroughly investigated by Davidsohn that every subsequent student must needs follow the trail he has blazed.[2] Davidsohn, with his eye directed on Florence, and the numerous scholars who, taking their cue from him, have undertaken similar investigations covering the length and breadth of the peninsula, have shown beyond challenge that in the anarchic period following the Carolingian dissolution the central government practically ceased to function and that men were obliged to shift for themselves or perish. As a result neighbors banded together to perform the absolutely indispensable services pertaining to the business of living on its simplest conceivable level. Such voluntary groups, called *vicinie* or *vicinanze,* arose spontaneously here, there, and everywhere, indicating that, just as social dissolution had reached its lowest point, a fresh and narrowly local start toward organization was made in response to such pressing necessities as could not be evaded if life was to go on. In lieu of the vainly implored help from above, the neighbors, abandoned by the government, undertook to help themselves.

If we try to picture the combined county of Florence-Fiesole during the anarchic ninth and tenth centuries, we must begin by conceiving of Florence itself as still inclosed within its Roman walls but in other respects hardly more than a village, whose usually deserted streets were brought to a certain moderate animation on the customary market days. The hilly country round about was still heavily wooded, with its extensive clearings worked by peasants who were held in the many degrees of dependence characteristic of serfdom by a thin upper layer of feudal lords. The status of these latter as a ruling class of warriors is indicated by the fact that they bore arms and were housed for safety in rude castles of stone. It is still possible to prove from documentary references that even after the communal age had got well under way, in the twelfth century, there existed in the single contado of Florence as many as one hundred and thirty castles. The actual number at that time and during the immediately preceding centuries, which we are here considering, must have been far greater. In fact, there is every reason to believe that our rolling comitatus and, for that matter, the whole variously contoured province of Tuscany carried a castle on every hill offering a fair prospect of safety from marauders. But these rude defensive structures were not for the lords alone. A castle consisted of a tower with barns and stables inclosing one or more open courts and with a sturdy wall, unscalable except with ladders, enveloping the whole compound. To this fortress-like residence, as soon as an enemy appeared, the cultivators of the surrounding fields flocked for safety, bringing with them all they held dear, their families, their animals, and their chattels. In the frequent, sudden emer-

[2] Davidsohn, Vol. I, chap. VIII.

gencies of that lawless epoch the peasants of whatever degree served as the garrison of the castle, performing the military duties required by the occasion; and in return for this service they were endowed with a number of rights, among them the very important right to appoint a gateman or *portinarius* to act as caretaker of their goods. Here, then, in connection with the castle of the countryside we encounter one of the earliest forms of the vicinia: agricultural neighbors resorting to military self-help in times of unusual stress.

Another form of the vicinia may be noted in connection with the *populus* or parish. The well-knit ecclesiastical organization of Italy did not break down when the civil administration failed. Indeed, with other institutional props disastrously giving way, men looked with increased affection to the parish church, which with its solemn ceremonies of baptism, marriage, and burial gave spiritual strength and moral sanction to the primal social unit, the family. After celebration of the mass on Sunday or on holidays, the neighbors of the parish would meet in the open space in front of the church and take council together concerning the repair of God's house, or the maintenance of paths and roads, or the upkeep and increase of the water supply.

In Florence too, ecclesiastically divided from the early days of Christianity into parishes, the parish neighbors on coming together after mass would deliberate concerning their common interests. However, when it came to defense against a sudden assault upon the town, the parish meeting was not the proper court of appeal. To meet a situation of equal importance to all the parishes there had sprung into being an organization expressive of the circumstance that Florence was a walled town entered by four dangerously exposed gates. In case of attack every male inhabitant was required to report with such arms as he possessed at the gate to which he belonged in order to render military service as the member of a gate company. Like the meeting of the parish neighbors, who would name a committee to carry out the measures they had adopted, the four gate companies would intrust the conduct of their business to leaders or captains elected by the group. Such agents were commonly called *boni homines* and, after performing the service for which they were appointed, these true and honorable men would report to their respective assemblies and, if their service was approved, would be discharged with thanks.

When this extremely primitive social situation experienced the economic recovery setting in with the eleventh century, the first effect was a rapid increase in the neighborhood activities attended by the need of their better coordination from the point of view of the town as a commercial and political unit. Neighboring parishes or neighboring gate companies would find themselves obliged to act together in a matter of common concern. To this end they would consult regarding the appointment of boni homines of broader scope than had hitherto been usual until this development would inescapably terminate in boni homines representative of the whole town. We should not think of these representatives of wider scope as acquiring at once a permanent character. They long continued to function as a purely provisional executive and, their task completed, they would vanish from the scene. Let us never forget that everything was fluid, experimental, and haphazard in this inchoate and still profoundly disturbed society. On this very account, however, the advantages of a firmer organization would not fail to impress themselves, and uncertain steps aiming at a continuous and improved control would be gradually taken, although it is no longer possible to trace them in detail. With commerce steadily expanding and bringing up new problems we cannot doubt that officials uninterruptedly engaged upon their growing tasks became an urgent necessity. There would have to be—to mention only the most indispensable requirements—a secretary to keep the communal records, a treasurer to assemble and disburse the communal funds; and there would also have to be a town hall to house these earliest officials of the emerging commonwealth, even though at the beginning it might be represented by nothing more than a single rented room in a private house.

Municipal rudiments of the haphazard and experimental order indicated were probably in existence in Florence by the middle of Matilda's reign. They can be proved for other Tuscan towns, such as Pisa and Lucca, where organization had already by that time gone so far as to give the central executive committee of boni homines something more than a purely temporary, *ad hoc* character. As soon as this particular advance had been made, whether in Tuscany, Lombardy, or elsewhere, it became customary to call the boni homines by a more dignified name, by the name of consuls. The title, harking back to the republican days of Rome, stirred a proud, never wholly forgotten memory in Italian bosoms and gained an immediate popularity throughout the communal area. Without hesitation the rising towns fastened on the Roman term; and its adoption appeared so significant to later generations that it became usual to date the achievement of full self-government on the part of any town from the first accredited use of the consular title. This was anything but a sound procedure, for while, on the one hand, self-government of a loose provisional sort antedated by a good deal the appearance of consuls, on the other hand, the presence of these officials is no assurance of autonomy, much less of sovereignty, fully achieved, since for a long time after consuls can be proved for a given commune, the commune was still, both theoretically and practically, dependent on the emperor and, on the rare occasions when the emperor was strong, might actually find itself thrust back into full feudal subjection.

Provided we make due allowance for the constant fluctuations and incurable uncertainties inherent in the communal situation, there is no reason why we should not join in celebrating the institution of the consuls as a considerable political advance indicative of a new and higher stage of municipal organization. But at this point we are met by a fresh difficulty springing from our inability to date exactly the arrival of consuls in even a single instance. The best we can do is to fall back on their earliest mention in a document. Thus in the case of our town of Florence the first authoritative reference to consuls belongs to the year 1138.[3] For Siena we have documentary proof of their existence by 1125;[4] and for Pisa and Lucca the evidence reaches well back into the previous century. As there was, in spite of the admittedly

[3] Hartwig, *Quellen und Forschungen*, Vol. II, p. 185. Santini, *Documenti dell'Antica Costituzione*, etc., Introduzione (p. XXVI).

[4] Pasqui, *Documenti per la Storia della Città di Arezzo*, p. 573.

earlier self-governing activity of Pisa and Lucca, an essentially parallel political development of all the Tuscan towns, we may safely affirm that Florence had consuls for some time before 1138, probably from the death of Matilda in 1115, and not improbably even before that.

Once established, the consular executive, generally speaking, lasted well through the twelfth century. While many details regarding the consular system as operated in Florence and Tuscany remain a complete puzzle, we know enough confidently to essay a general description. The consulate is always a multiple executive, twelve being the more usual number of consular associates. They served commonly for one year and were invested with the power to negotiate treaties, to lead the urban host in war, and to preside at the highest municipal court. The method of election is wholly conjectural. The consular system recognized a general meeting of the citizens called *parlamentum* or *contio* or *arringhum* and presided over by the consuls. This was its democratic feature, of which a great deal has always been made by passionate proponents of the democratic principle. But although the parlamentum was commonly asked to approve treaties and to acclaim the new consuls on their assumption of authority, it is not at all likely that it had a hand in electing these officials. Consuls issued so regularly from the highest stratum of the citizens that we are obliged to define the consulate as an essentially aristocratic institution carefully manipulated in the interest of the leading families. In the unwieldiness of the parlamentum lies the probable explanation of its largely ornamental character. No orderly election of executive officials is possible in a mass meeting nor can a mob function as a satisfactory legislature. Therefore, if the Florentine or any other Tuscan parliament ever had any legislative authority, it yielded it at an early date to a council (*concilium, consiglio*) of approximately one hundred and fifty members. As the council, too, was drawn regularly from the same well-to-do element as manned the consulate, we can hardly escape the conclusion that, contrary to a still prevalent fiction, the consular constitution of the young communes did not have its root in the people but functioned as an oligarchy coated with a thin democratic veneer. Owing to the fact that many generations passed before the town equipped itself with adequate public buildings, the early parlamentum of the Arno town met either in the cathedral or on a public square under the open sky, while the early council assembled in one of the lesser churches such as San Piero Scheraggio. At an early date it became customary to define the authority committed to the consular officials in a *breve consulum*. On this document the incoming consuls took the oath of office for their term. Periodically revised and enlarged, the breve grew until it became, but not till the following century, a fully elaborated constitution.[5]

An examination of the social structure of Florence in the twelfth century makes it absolutely clear why the political government could not be other than aristocratic. The most conspicuous social group were the lesser nobles, the knights or *milites*. Endowed with lands in the immediate vicinity of the town, they had probably always lived within the walls. However, during the con-

[5] A breve consulum for Florence cannot be proved before 1159. As to the certainty of earlier brevi and the manner of their expansion into a constitution see Davidsohn, Vol. I, p. 665.

sular regime their number steadily increased by the policy of the victorious commune to oblige the conquered possessors of more distant castles to become Florentine citizens and to manifest their acceptance of the new situation by residing for at least a part of each year in the town. Immediately after this dominant group came the prosperous merchants. Their wealth enabled them to intermarry with the knights so that they became imperceptibly merged with them in a single class of the rich. The knights for their part made fusion easy since, having breathed town air from their birth, they were far from exhibiting any insuperable aversion for trade. In possession of all the wealth there was, in possession of both fixed and fluid capital, this upper crust enjoyed a prestige which made it possible for them to monopolize the communal offices without any difficulty. There would have to be a large and active population of shopkeepers and artisans before the political control of the oligarchs could be challenged with any chance of success. And as yet these two classes were extremely feeble. Indubitably they had begun to increase in the century under discussion, but their number did not reach a sufficient figure to unsettle the social balance. The remaining elements composing the population were the clergy, the physicians, the men of law, and the common laborers. The clergy were a numerous and highly respected class made up of the bishop and the cathedral canons, the parish priests, and a great variety of monks and nuns. As members of the Roman Catholic church, an institution which had achieved a status on a par with and outside of civil society, they were indeed sheltered and protected by the commune, but they were not a political part of it. Physicians were as yet few in number; men of law, made up of notaries and judges, were far more plentiful. Rapidly gaining in authority, they will by the following century have become an indispensable adjunct of a society given to an ever-increasingly eager pursuit of wealth. As to the laborers, dependent for a living on daily wages, while their number was undoubtedly expanding through immigration from the farms, neither now nor as long as Florence continued to figure as an independent commonwealth did they exercise an influence remotely commensurate with their numbers.

The associative impulse, which had given birth to the commune in the first place, long continued to manifest itself as the fundamental energy of society. Until a strong government had arisen, prepared to guarantee life and property, individuals would be prompted to make agreements with other individuals to gain security for their persons and to promote their material interests. Hence the extraordinarily complicated network of social, economic, and religious bonds which underlies medieval society everywhere. Throughout the twelfth century Florence gave birth to new and ever newer associative phenomena. Very early in that century, perhaps even in the previous century, the resident knights constituted themselves as a *societas militum,* to which members of well-established merchant families were after a delay admitted on a basis of equality. Although the miles or knight was originally a lesser nobleman, a sub-vassal who rode to war in the service of a greater lord, by the consular age any citizen rich enough to own a helmet, spear, sword, coat of mail, and of course a horse, might aspire to qualify as a miles. While the Florentine knights, accoutered in the manner indicated, have the look of a military aristocracy and were pleased to display the martial manners of such a class, let us never forget that from a purely economic angle they were simply the men of means, the rich.

The remaining citizens, naturally the vast majority of the population, made up the foot-soldiers, the *pedites*. They were originally assembled in companies according to the parish in which they resided. In the course of time, but not till the next, the thirteenth, century, they were amalgamated into a *societas peditum*, which, under the more expressive term of a *societas populi*, was destined to challenge and, in the end, to overthrow the military aristocracy. Cavalry and infantry together made up the communal army which, when an expedition was ordered, took the field under the command of the consuls. Of course the cavalry, composed of men dedicated to arms as a profession, were a far more effective force than the infantry, who, called from their shops and benches by the ringing of a bell, fought without armor and with such improvised, casual weapons as their slender means permitted them to provide. The greater value on campaign of the well-born and wealthy horsemen must be set down as a weighty factor in their long-continued political ascendancy. It is highly characteristic of the still purely private nature of the public activities of the citizens in the consular age that, while the obligation to serve in the army was general, and while the army was the most perfect expression of the unitary will of the new political entity, the commune, each inhabitant provided his own military equipment and was a horseman or a foot-soldier according to his private resources.

When the communal army was mobilized for war it took with it into the field as a symbol of the new and precious union of the citizens the car of state, the *caroccio*. This consisted of a platform on four wheels carrying suspended from a mast the banner of the commune, not yet the famous Red Lily on a white field but a simple cloth of two stripes, one red, the other white.[6] The car was drawn by one or more pairs of white oxen which, like the vehicle itself and its troop of attendant grooms, were swathed in rich crimson stuffs. Since the caroccio, far from being a destructive engine of war, was a cumbersome contraption which seriously interfered with the mobility of the citizen army, we can account for its existence only by referring it to the zest and swagger which were the pardonable accompaniment of the commune's adolescence. Around the caroccio, far visible with its waving communal banner, the youth of Florence gathered, when the battle raged, prepared to defend this ark of the covenant with the last drop of their blood.

The massing of the milites, the men on horseback, in a single society conveys the impression of a unity among them which was clamorously denied by the facts. Nothing was more characteristic of the upper class than their implacable feuds. On account of the strong call of the blood among medieval men they accepted the family bond as something irrevocable and hallowed. Long after the commune with its public responsibilities had raised its head the family with its ancient obligations of a private nature exercised an undiminished sway. Therefore whenever a quarrel occurred between two young swordsmen and braggarts, it automatically involved their respective families; and if it chanced that blood had been spilt in the course of the argument, blood was

[6] Villani, IV, 7; also VI, 43.

called for in return. Love of fighting for its own sake, fortified by the solemn family obligation of vendetta, explains a type of association interesting in itself and doubly interesting because it provided twelfth-century Florence with its most characteristic physical feature. Still an almost unbelievably primitive community, the town boasted, with the exception of the handsome baptistry of St. John, not a single church conspicuous for either size or beauty; it had not a single civic building, for civic organization had not yet advanced to the point of requiring a special structure; and it housed its poor, which means the overwhelming majority of the population, in wretched wooden hovels among conditions of indescribable squalor. But if from a neighboring hill, like San Miniato, we could have looked down on this Florence contained as yet within the narrow circuit of its Roman walls and presenting to view a huddle of mean structures, largely of wood and dangerously inflammable, we would have broken into a spontaneous cry of surprise over the sight of scores of towers of brick and stone soaring high above the surrounding roofs.[7]

These towers were the property of related groups of noble families or, in a few instances, of a single particularly powerful family. Without any doubt whatever they originally served as residences, although in the course of time the families that owned them commonly provided themselves with more habitable quarters erected at the side of the towers. In that case the tower became the fortress whither the family retreated the moment that a vendetta developing with a rival family precipitated private war. Families sharing the possession of a tower formed a tower association (*consorteria*), and the towers, constituting a series of town castles, served as military supports in the battles that periodically raged up and down the narrow streets. Throughout the twelfth century, and for most of the following century as well, the municipal government was far too feeble to suppress the savage extravagances perpetrated by the upper class in pursuit of mere private hate and vengeance. For many generations it did not even try to do so, for the communal government itself at first had the character of a private association exercising strictly limited local powers, among which the dissolution of the consorterie did not figure. Besides, the government was in the hands of the very people who gloried in the towers as an expression of class and family pride. Under these circumstances the towers may be thought of as symbols of a lawless upper caste ruling the town in its own interest and indulging itself in practices which were a constant menace to the safety of the common people. We may conclude without fear of contradiction that if Florence was ever to be established as an orderly burgher community, the towers, the tower associations, and the nobles themselves would have to disappear. A clean sweep would have to be made and indeed was made, as we shall learn; but happily, we are moved to declare, it was not so clean a sweep that numerous towers, prudently deprived of their threatening upper stories, have not survived. In the consular age the towers rose thick as a canebrake, especially in the Mercato Vecchio and along the street leading to the Old Bridge, called Por (for porta) Santa Maria. Along this street and its lateral feeders, streets which in our day better than any other

[7] Davidsohn is of the opinion that around 1180 the towers of Florence numbered over one hundred. Davidsohn, Vol. I, p. 554.

surviving Florentine district preserve the peculiar aspect of the medieval town, many of these towers may still be identified by the attentive visitor. They will appeal to his awed imagination as the impressive remains of an age when the recently formed commune was governed by a feudal caste and was exposed daily and even hourly to the shock of arms.[8]

If the tower associations enshrined an important aspect of the feudal governing class, the newly risen classes, falling in with the active spirit of the age, formed equally characteristic associations of their own. Since the main transforming influence of society was commerce, the merchants were the outstanding *novi homines* and to protect their interest formed a *societas mercatorum,* in sum, a merchant gild. While the records are too defective to permit any positive assertions, it is not open to dispute that from an early time there existed a powerful gild of merchants, on whose shoulders rested the rising prosperity of the town.[9] Its members, either as individuals or through partnerships, dealt indiscriminately in all the goods which were in demand, particularly in cloth, dyes, hides, and spices. With money coming more and more into use as the medium of exchange, they concerned themselves also with the current coins, the silver *denarii* (pennies), put out by the various governments of Europe, as well as with the practice of borrowing and lending. Thus almost unconsciously they launched into the business of banking. Since these rising merchant-bankers, when they were rich enough, intermarried with the knights, and since, owing to this relationship, the knights established a direct contact with trade, it commonly happened that the merchant gild bore on its roster the names of numerous members of the tower families. Let the fact confirm the fusion, already noted in the case of the societas militum, of the two urban groups possessed of wealth; and let it at the same time serve to refute the hoary fiction, imbedded in all the older histories of Florence, that the citizens who comported themselves as feudal lords proudly spurned the vulgar allurements of commerce. True, this stubborn aloofness does seem to have characterized the leading noble family, the rather grandiose Uberti; certainly the rest of the local gentry showed no aversion whatever to participating in merchant enterprises in the hope of sharing the consequent profits. In the consular age and for the following ages as well it is quite impossible to draw a sharp dividing line between a nobility concerned alone with fighting and a bourgeoisie devoted exclusively to trade.

With trade breathing life into the activities of the town, the crafts came into being; and no sooner were there crafts than there were also craft gilds or, to use the Italian term for gilds, there were *arti* (arts). In attributing craft gilds to the Florence of the twelfth century we are obliged to resort to conjecture or else to argue from analogous data supplied by other towns. However, just before the close of the century, in 1193, we get an unmistakable notice proving

[8] The many interesting aspects of the tower societies and, above all, their legal aspect, are treated by Santini, "Società delle Torri in Firenze," in *Arch. Stor. It.,* Serie 4, Vol. XX, pp. 25-58, 178-204.

[9] Davidsohn, Vol. I, p. 667. The earliest surviving reference to a merchant gild belongs to the year 1182. It occurs in the submission to Florence of Empoli. Santini, *Documenti dell'Antica Costituzione,* etc., No. XII.

the existence of an undetermined number of craft gilds.[10] It has been assumed that their number in the above-mentioned year was seven, but the probability is great that they ran to a much higher figure. Be that as it may, the total importance of these minor gilds, compared with that of the single powerful merchant gild, remained small for long years to come.

The summary information supplied in this chapter on the political, social, and economic developments in Florence during the twelfth century is intended to serve a double purpose. While the reader has been made acquainted with the main domestic concerns of the still embryonic commonwealth, a picture worth getting for its own sake, he has also been provided by means of a body of social-economic data with the leading clue to Florentine foreign policy. To this policy we shall now turn and begin with the assertion that, from the moment the Arno city became autonomous, it aimed at something better than autonomy: it aimed at complete independence. It did not take this stand from any abstract love of freedom, but because in its immediate practical affairs it found itself obstructed at every point by the feudal system in which it was imbedded. Feudalism was an agrarian development with no comprehension for, nor sympathy with, trade; and when Florence, the very life of which was commerce, discovered that feudalism regarded commerce as an upstart to be kept down and exploited without mercy, the resolution gradually took shape that feudalism would have to go. Under these circumstances the main feature of Florentine foreign policy became a relentless combat with this proved and self-confessed enemy.

Now the visible representatives of the feudal system were the emperor, the margave of Tuscany, and the nobles, great and small alike, but more particularly the great nobles since the sub-vassals were often so hostile to their superiors that they did not hesitate to seek the protection of the towns in the vicinity of which their possessions lay. We have seen that Florence had an upper layer of nobiliary citizens and we have not failed to note that most of these had made submission to the commonwealth of their own volition in the hope of escaping the exactions of their immediate overlord. It need hardly be expressly said that the conflict between vassals and sub-vassals was of decisive advantage to the towns. Even more advantageous was the falling out, already mentioned, between the emperor and the margrave over the investiture issue. However, the death of Countess Matilda in 1115 created a new situation. With it as our starting-point, we shall resume our interrupted political narrative and carry it through the century under consideration.

Emperor Henry V, son of the man who had stood as a humble penitent at the gate of Canossa castle, was not minded to let the new margrave, whom the death of Matilda gave him the right to appoint, play the same hostile role as the great countess. To this end he adopted a new policy. He was the more inclined to consider a change as Matilda, being the last of her race, had made a testament, transferring all her allodial property to the chair of St. Peter, that is, to the pope.[11] In this she was acting entirely within her rights, although we

[10] A. Doren, *Entwickelung und Organisation der Florentiner Zünfte in 13. und 14. Jahrhundert* (Schmoller's *Forschungen*, Vol. XV), pp. 8-11.

[11] Matilda made two testaments to the above effect dated respectively 1077 and 1102. Davidsohn, Vol. I, pp. 259, 290.

must understand that she could not—and did not—assign to the pope the estates with which she had been enfeoffed by the emperor and which were attached to the margravial office. True, there might be a difficulty in distinguishing in every case between what was feudal and what was allodial property, but the difficulty did not at once put in an appearance. It failed to do so because Emperor Henry V completely ignored the testament and appropriated the whole inheritance for himself. The papacy, temporarily enfeebled, did not even register a protest. But when its fortunes rose again in the eternal ebb and tide of Italian politics, it presented its claim, and the later emperors, enfeebled in their turn, were obliged to reopen the question. There can be no doubt that the Matildan inheritance added fuel to the always either smoldering or blazing fire lit by the irreconcilable ambitions of the two heads of Christendom, but that it was to any considerable degree a determining factor in the conflict which, off and on, raged between them for another two hundred years must be denied. The vicissitudes of the inheritance have been carefully traced by Overmann.[12] Whoever is interested may follow them in minute detail under his guidance. For the general reader it will suffice to learn that, while the quarrel between the two contestants of the will dragged on interminably, a third party—the usual mischievous *tertium gaudens*—with no claim at all except his strong right arm, possessed himself of the lion's share of the prize. That third party was, for the Lombard properties, the various Lombard communes; for the Tuscan properties, the various Tuscan communes. In the course of the many years during which the quarrel continued the masterful young republics quietly appropriated by far the greater portion of the margravial estates, whether feudal or allodial, thus clearly revealing not only the strength of the communal movement but the relative political weakness compared with it of both pope and emperor.

No less than in the absorption of Matilda's inheritance Emperor Henry V was interested in a successor to the margraviate who would prove steadily subservient to his authority. With this object in mind he resolved to replace the hereditary margraves of Italian nationality with German appointees removable at his pleasure. The very first German, a certain Rabodo, transferred the margravial administration from Florence, where it had rested since 1057, to San Miniato situated on a hill high over the junction of the Elsa with the Arno, in the very center of Tuscany. Owing to its association in the mind of the natives with a foreign domination the new capital acquired the designation of San Miniato del Tedesco, under which name it still lifts a tall, dark tower, like a warning finger, over the smiling valley at its foot. Rabodo had no luck in enforcing his authority, for when, in the name of the empire, he occupied Monte Cascioli, recently taken by the Florentines, their citizen army descended on him, retook the castle by assault, and buried Rabodo among the ruins (1119).

Thereupon another margrave was sent from Germany, indeed a long succession of them, of all of whom it may be reported that they had as little success as the unfortunate Rabodo in maintaining the imperial authority

[12] Overmann, *Gräfin Matilde von Tuscien: Geschichte ihres Gutes von 1115-1230*. Innsbruck, 1895.

against the rising communes. Whenever the emperor himself appeared at the head of an army, as he did from time to time, it was, to be sure, a different story. Before this exhibition of irresistible force the young republics drew in their horns. But no sooner had he vanished behind the snows of the Alps than they showed renewed disrespect for his representative by refusing to pay him the monies which were his due or to make war at his bidding. Under the circumstances the margrave dwindled to a pallid and harmless official without a following in the province; and although it is a fact that he figures in Tuscan history to the end of the century and that a succession of German margraves has been recovered from the documents as long and shadowy as the line of kings following in the wake of Banquo's ghost, we are justified in thinking of the margravial office as having the great countess as its last effective occupant.

The practical disappearance of the margrave left the emperor and the great nobles as the sole defenders of the feudal system and opponents of the revolutionary communes. And again these latter greatly profited from the fact that, owing to the only occasional presence of the emperor in Italy, the feudal defenders did not steadily and solidly stand together. Except under the emperor's immediate command the self-willed feudatories could not be persuaded to present an undivided front to the enemy. In spite of poor team play, however, they continued to wield a considerable power which, whenever it was co-ordinated by the emperor's personal intervention, swelled to formidable proportions. It is therefore proper that we look somewhat more closely at the great feudality; but as we wish to view them from the angle of our city of Florence, we shall take as our point of departure the doctrine firmly held at Florence in the communal age regarding the normal relationship between town and countryside.

Every Tuscan town of the eleventh century thought of itself as identified with its county, in spite of the fact that actually the county was and had been for some time past in the hands of the great feudality. Perhaps a memory persisted of the comitatus of the Franks, perhaps even an older memory of the civitas of the Romans had again come to life in the hearts of the townsmen. It was the special feature of both of these former administrative units that they emphasized the identity of the town and its immediate countryside. However, should the memory of the Frank and Roman divisions have dropped from the mind, there, in effective visible operation, were the dioceses of the church, which in the main still followed the boundaries of the old Roman civitates. Since the town, in the person of the bishop, ruled the contado ecclesiastically, it seemed logical that, as soon as the town became a responsible governing entity, it should rule the contado also politically. On this consummation the townsmen of the twelfth century had so set their hearts that war between them and the feudal powers in actual possession of the contado was unavoidable.

The outstanding feature which met the eye, scanning not only the Florentine diocese but also that larger unit born of an obscure event of the ninth century, the united county of Florence-Fiesole,[13] was that diocese and county

[13] See chap. III, p. 32.

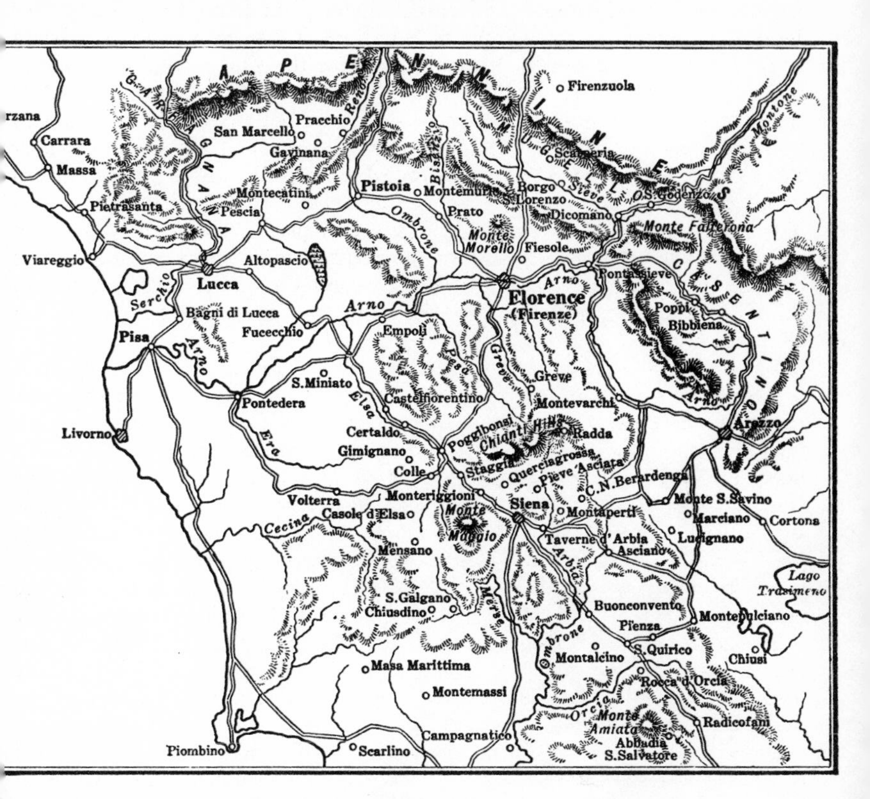

CANY SHOWING THE CHIEF TOWNS, RIVERS, ROADS, AND MOUNTAINS

were dominated by three great feudal magnates. One of these was the bishop himself; the other two were the respective heads of the great Guidi and Alberti families.[14] If not the immediate, the ultimate aim of the townsmen was to destroy the long string of castles by which the lords maintained their power and to draw their innumerable estates within the jurisdiction of the commune. But from the first a distinction was made between the bishop and the two lay rulers. We are aware that the bishop, owing to the system of immunities, was also a lay ruler; but not for a moment are we permitted to doubt that his newer, political power was less essential to him than his older, spiritual power, sole source of his vast moral authority. In his spiritual capacity the Florentines sincerely venerated their bishop and had no desire to deprive him of the revenues which he drew from his estates. He was the most distinguished resident of the town and was expected to maintain a dignified court in his spacious palace lying just west of the baptistery. But the Florentines also contended, and with the greatest vigor, that civil rule over his estates was not inherent in his episcopal office and that it rightfully belonged to them. With astonishingly little conflict, at least of an open nature, their viewpoint gradually prevailed. In the course of the twelfth century the bishop let himself be divested of the civil jurisdiction over his lands for reasons which are not difficult to recover. For one thing, he lacked the military strength necessary to meet the communal challenge; and for another, as long as the townsmen guaranteed him his undiminished revenues, he may even have welcomed a development that enabled him to devote himself exclusively to his strictly clerical duties.

Not content with dealing with their bishop in the cavalier manner indicated, the Florentines resolved to use him as a cloak to hide their policy of expansion. A difficulty in which this policy entangled them from the start was that they obliged such lords as they conquered to become their subjects, although these lords were legally the subjects of the margrave and the emperor. The subjection was therefore an offense to the constituted powers, whose wrath it was to the advantage of the burghers to avert until the time when they had become strong enough no longer to fear it. To this end they bethought themselves of a fiction by which they might give a certain air of respectability to their bold usurpations. In the charter of surrender they would require the conquered nobleman to certify his submission, not to themselves, but to the cathedral church and to its patron saint, St. John the Baptist; and further, in visible sign of his submission, they would require him to make an offering of wax candles on the Baptist's annual festival. As this fell on the twenty-fourth of June it came about that once every year Florence witnessed a spectacle that swelled the bosom of the citizens with barely controllable pride. For, forming a line which grew longer with every decade, on each St. John's day the conquered noblemen of the contado, in gala raiment and bearing lighted candles in their hands, presented themselves in solemn procession at the portal of San Giovanni to signify their subjection to the victorious commune.

[14] Santini, "Studi sull'Antica Costituzione del Comune di Firenze," *Arch. Stor. It.*, Serie 5, Vol. XXV (1900). An accompanying map shows the location of the many fiefs of the three lords in question.

It cannot be said that the emperor or anyone else was deceived by the subterfuge. However, as it was employed not only by Florence but by all the other Tuscan communes as well, it must have had some value as a legal device to bridge over the gap between a society that was slowly dying and its successor that was just as slowly coming to birth.

The bishop, then, in spite of his numerous well-distributed estates, was no obstacle to the plan of the citizens to govern their county. The opposition came, in the main, from the two ancient and powerful families, the Guidi and Alberti, with their literally scores of castles scattered chiefly over the county of Florence but to be found also, especially in the case of the Guidi, the more formidable of the two clans, in many adjoining counties. In sign of their ancient blood and long exercise of authority the members of both families bore the title of count. As the Alberti owned many castles almost within sight of Florence, the earliest clashes of the ambitious commune befell with them. When in the year 1107 the Florentines inaugurated, so far as we can now see, their expansion policy, they captured Monte Gualandi, a castle of the Alberti; and when, six years later, they celebrated a second triumph of this sort at Monte Cascioli, they moved against a family with which the Alberti were closely leagued. Thus reluctantly were these counts moved to acquire respect for the upstart commune, an attitude greatly furthered by the circumstance that the new German margraves sent to Tuscany as successors to the Countess Matilda were without adequate resources and the emperor too far away to give effective aid. Consequently the Alberti were often in a mood to seek an accommodation with the Florentines; and as the Florentines, for their part, were frequently in serious straits because of having too many irons in the fire, they welcomed intervals of peace in their relations with the counts. This must be grasped if we are to understand the bewildering surface changes in the attitude of Florence toward the Alberti. Without ever losing sight of its fixed purpose, the prudent commune was prepared to reckon with the shifting currents of practical politics and to reach the goal of its ambition slowly and by devious paths. To follow the perpetual alternations of good and bad neighborhood relations between the commune and the Alberti would lead us into a maze as confusing as it is unprofitable. Suffice it that the Alberti, although often defeated by the commune and manifestly on the wane, continued to cut an important figure in Florentine and Tuscan politics throughout the consular age.

The same is true of the Guidi, a family credited at the meridian of its power with the possession of three hundred castles distributed, we should never forget, almost as widely over the Romagna as over Tuscany. The Guidi were perhaps the greatest feudal family of all central Italy. Hostilities with them did not become chronic until the Alberti were already hard pressed; but, the battle once joined, it never again rested, although it was not continuously waged and was even punctuated with intermittent periods of amity. On purely rational and material grounds the two great clans should always have stood shoulder to shoulder, but there was too much jealousy between them for this to be effected. Of this extremely fortunate division Florence took full advantage by frequently using one group against the other. However, as often as the emperor arrived in Tuscany, Alberti and Guidi alike crowded to his service, whereupon the stock of the feudality would suddenly rise, while that of the communes would score a corresponding decline.

The emperors who immediately followed Henry V were Lothar III (1125-37) and Conrad III (1138-52). They showed less interest in their Italian kingdom than their immediate predecessors had done; and although they visited it, largely to effect the coveted imperial coronation at Rome, they did not linger long and, giving only half-hearted attention to the problem created by the rising communes, avoided precipitating the conflict between the old and new order which, in the long run, was inevitable. Not till the reign of Frederick I was the rising new order effectively challenged. Elevated to the German throne in 1152, Frederick came to Italy two years later. Before considering the activist policy which he at once adopted and which precipitated a tremendous convulsion, we shall have to give attention to a factor in the program of Florence which was coming more and more to the front, and which loomed as large as and, finally, even larger than its animosity against the two great feudal families.

In the very year (1107) in which Florence embarked on the conquest of the feudal castles lying athwart its road, she also made a descent on the inconspicuous, close by town of Prato and destroyed it.[15] Although Prato, a very recent creation, bore witness to the commercial spirit abroad in the world, it came into existence under the fostering care of the Alberti, who owned a castle at that point. While hostility to the Alberti doubtless figured in the Florentine attack, the destruction of the little market town was induced, at least preponderantly, by the unwillingness of the Arno city to have a possible trade rival grow up at its doorstep. That Prato lay just outside the county of Florence, in the county and diocese of Pistoia, made no difference to the merchants in control of Florentine policy. When, owing to one of the sudden, kaleidoscopic changes usual in Tuscan politics, the attention of the Florentines was drawn elsewhither, Prato was rebuilt and Florence did not again interpose its veto. For one thing, the governing class may have convinced itself that tiny Prato was not a real commercial menace; and for another, the rulers had made the agreeable discovery that Prato was a still greater annoyance to Pistoia than to themselves. Lying at the foot of the Apeninnes, Pistoia commanded the immensely important road that led to Bologna; and Florence, obliged to use that road for her steadily broadening enterprises, instinctively sensed in Pistoia a dangerous future rival. For its part, Pistoia, following the same policy regarding its county as did Florence and every other town, wanted to keep Prato in close subjection. Consequently, as soon as the Florentines discovered that the Pratesi were a major thorn in the side of Pistoia, they completely changed their attitude by lending support to their little neighbor. In their eyes the real opponent in this quarter was not Prato but Pistoia. Besides illustrating the passionate flare-up of jealousy among communal neighbors, which at an early date started dangerous fires all over Tuscany, the episode shows how the general Tuscan situation tended to become complicated by the con-

[15] Annales Florentini, II. Hartwig, *Quellen und Forschungen,* Vol. II, p. 40.

flict of every town with its town neighbors, great and small, and by the rapidly shifting alignments among the towns, which made and unmade treaties with an entire lack of scruple and with an eye directed solely to the main chance.

That the animosities among neighboring towns, largely over trade advantages, date from the very beginning of the communal movement, and that they at once assumed perfectly fantastic proportions could not be better proved than by a glance at the case of Pisa and Lucca. These two towns were the first in Tuscany to respond to the commercial stimulus, and they no sooner aimed at a greater volume of trade than they engaged in ferocious warfare with each other. Their wars ended only to begin again, and so passionate and spontaneous did the hatred between Pisans and Lucchese become that we are prepared to believe, as contemporary writers solemnly report, that they imbibed it as babes with their mother's milk. Before the twelfth century, covering the first phase of the communal revolution, was over, the Pisan-Lucchese feud had been duplicated by literally scores of similar feuds, usually between large-town neighbors, but not infrequently also between small-town neighbors and even between neighboring villages. Wherever the tide of trade flowed, there envy and jealousy raised their ugly heads. While we are concerned only with Tuscany, the statement applies with equal force to Lombardy, Venetia, Emilia, Umbria—in short, to all northern and north-central Italy. To all this area the communal spirit came with a rush indistinguishable from frenzy. Unless we steadily keep both the extent and the vehemence of the movement in mind, we shall be tempted to make the mistake of regarding Florence as a unique and monstrous instance.

We are now prepared to understand the next peculiarly ferocious act of the youthful republic. On a hill to the north and in full sight of the town on the bank of the Arno stood ancient Fiesole. There is no evidence of any rivalry between the two neighbors before the communal era; but no sooner had commerce begun to bring its benefits, and to scatter its terrible dragons' teeth as well, than Florence visited Fiesole with an inextinguishable hatred. Its echoes can still be heard in the legend which Florentine mothers of later generations recounted to the children at their knees. According to this hate-inspired invention the Fiesolans were a vile Etruscan breed, which could not possibly be permitted to exist on the same earth with Florentines, who, as authentic descendants of the conquering Romans, were manifestly a chosen people. While the legend has been completely discredited by modern scholarship, it is not wholly without significance, since it tells us of an unreasoning aversion which, itself a historical fact of no mean order, we are free to explain in our own way. For us, familiar with the behavior pattern of the rising communes, it is clear that Florence resolved to bring Fiesole under its control. Indeed, owing to the physical closeness of Fiesole, the Florentine determination would be among the earliest manifestations of its budding sovereign will.

After much precedent petty bickering, in the year 1123 the Florentines, mobilizing their citizen army of cavalry and infantry, climbed up the hill to Fiesole and laid siege to it. The first campaign was a failure, owing to an inherent weakness of the communal forces. Composed largely of shopkeepers and artisans, they could not be kept long in the field. When Fiesole did not promptly surrender, the Florentines went home. The war was renewed in the following year and in the year after that; and it was not till this third campaign that Fiesole was taken (1125). The vengeance of the victors was terrible. Not only were the Fiesolans slaughtered almost to a man, but the little town was utterly destroyed. Especial animosity was directed to the protective girdle of its walls. These went back to Etruscan days, as every visitor can still convince himself by inspecting the small section to the north which was happily spared and has survived to this day. These immense, these cyclopean blocks of stone, here as wherever we encounter them in central Italy, betray Etruscan origin and workmanship. In order not to offend the pope unnecessarily the fine Romanesque cathedral, a creation of the previous century, was also spared. All around the cathedral the ruthless victors spread a desert; and if, some years afterward, they permitted the few Fiesolan survivors to crawl back and to provide a miserable shelter for themselves among the ruins, they did so on the condition that the walls and the citadel above the town should never under any circumstances be rebuilt. Fiesole never again raised its head and to this day conveys to every sensitive visitor the impression of a community stricken with a mysterious blight.

The next stage of the Florentine advance brought the commune face to face with Siena. This town owed its commercial importance to its location on one of the main roads leading to the capital of Christendom, to Rome. At the very first appearance of communal self-consciousness it resolved, like all its neighbors, to gain the control of its county; and presently, on this very score, it came into conflict with Florence. While county boundaries coincided in the main with diocesan boundaries, this was not always the case, and in these exceptional instances the county boundary was certain to be a matter of dispute. When Florence pressed the claim that its county line toward the south reached within a few miles of Siena's northern gate, the Sienese protested, partly because the issue was in doubt, and partly because they did not feel safe with a neighbor of the mettle of Florence camped almost under the shadow of their wall.[16] The resulting animosity was stimulated by commercial rivalry until it led unescapably to war. The first certain armed conflict between the two communes occurred in 1129, four years after the destruction of Fiesole; and the fire lighted on that occasion was not effectively extinguished for many hundred years. The famous Florence-Siena feud will force itself on our attention again and again in the course of this history. It reached a degree of ferocity that obliges us to list it among the most embittered communal feuds of the period, with neither the monstrous Pisa-Lucca nor the equally terrible Pisa-Genoa feud surpassing it in implacability.

In the early twelfth century the struggle between the two towns was as yet in its infancy. Much remains dark about this phase, but it is certain that the initial conflict of 1129 was followed at irregular intervals by many others. While the issues involved have been touched upon and require no further

[16] A map throwing light on the boundary dispute will be found in Schevill, *Siena: The Story of a Medieval Commune,* p. 178. New York, 1909. The wars of the two communes are related with some detail in chap. VI.

clarification, we must understand that Siena and Florence were not concerned to bring them to a decision in single combat like a pair of duelists. As soon as a fresh conflict threatened, each contestant searched the horizon feverishly for allies and indicated a willingness to accept support from every available quarter. The two towns therefore turned for help not only to other towns within the orbit of their trade and politics but also to the surrounding feudal lords. Naturally Siena, threatened by Florence, turned to the clans of the Guidi and Alberti, who might be expected to hail with delight this opportunity to lower the pride of their communal enemy, while Florence responded in kind and sought the alliance of the great feudal clans of the Sienese contado, such as the Cacciaconti and the Aldobrandeschi. It may be left to the imagination to what an extent this situation pumped fresh blood into the veins of the declining feudatories. Just as they seemed to be doomed by the communal movement, the movement dissolved itself into a number of separate units, and against the threat of the enemy commune the magnates found unexpected protection in that commune's political rival.

If we now remind ourselves that the policy adopted by Florence and Siena closely resembled that of every other commune in Tuscany, we are prepared for a wild confusion of wars and alliances. Luckily there is no need whatever to plunge into the maze and to disengage its intolerably tangled threads. It will suffice if we master the leading forces and motives, which, operative in the case of Florence and Siena, repeated themselves at a score of other points over the face of Tuscany. The commune, every commune, had as its enemy the feudal lords and desired to destroy them; the commune, every commune, came to grips with as many of its neighbor communes as seemed to obstruct its commercial and political development. Communes and feudal lords alike invariably followed the line of immediate advantage, changing partners with the greatest ease and with an entire lack of scruple. But—and herewith we broach a matter of the greatest consequence—while fighting and intriguing among themselves without interruption, they did not fail to turn an uneasy eye in the direction of their distant common master, the emperor. For during the first half of the twelfth century the emperor was still strong enough to inspire his subjects with respect and fear. However, as we have seen, the emperors of the period, Lothar and Conrad, did not happen to spend much time in Italy; and when they came, they were too much perplexed by the situation and its infinite ramifications to attack it with vigor. As a result the local forces fought it out among themselves as best they could under the anarchic slogan of everyone-for-himself. No one won a decisive victory, but the trend of events imposed the certain conclusion that the feudal clans were a declining, the communes, in spite of their paralyzing differences, an advancing power. At this point the situation took on a new aspect by the appearance on the scene of an emperor who was resolved to break with the do-nothing policy of his immediate predecessors and to make the empire again an active force in Italian affairs.

The new emperor was Frederick I of the house of Hohenstaufen. Intelligent, vigorous, and authoritative, he had complete faith in the feudal system in which he had been brought up in Germany, where it had not yet been lisrupted by the rising power of the towns. On crossing the Alps in 1154, he et foot first in Lombardy, from the point of view of urban development the nost advanced section of his Italian kingdom. To his surprise and indignation ie noted that the many prosperous towns sown along the valley of the Po ad all become self-governing under a regime of elected consuls. This to his imple, feudal mind was rank rebellion, which he was resolved to crush without delay. He would bring the towns back to their old dependence and rest he imperial administration, in the future as in the past, on the great body f his vassals, the lords, lay and spiritual. How this reactionary policy, backed y an apparently irresistible army, at first overawed the Lombard towns; how Milan, the leading commune, on trying to resist, was obliged to surrender; iow, here and there, the resistance continued to push spasmodically to the urface; how Milan, on venturing to revolt a second time, was punished by eing leveled with the ground (1162)—all this is a passionately interesting tory which we cannot follow in detail, but which concerns us deeply because, vithout it, the Tuscan developments must remain entirely unintelligible.

Triumphant in Lombardy in his early years by a policy of war and terror, Frederick I, whom, because of his luxuriant, flame-colored beard the Italians alled Barbarossa (Redbeard), discovered even in this period of comparative elicity that he had to reckon with the ancient rival and enemy of the empire, he papacy. The emperor was engaged in making himself the unchallenged naster of the peninsula, and no incumbent of St. Peter's chair could accept hat prospect unless he was prepared to surrender all the ecclesiastical and olitical advantages gained since the great Hildebrand. As no true pope would nake that sacrifice, Frederick encountered papal opposition from the first, which with the elevation to the pontifical office of Alexander III (1159–81) ecame open and unflinching. Aware of Alexander's enmity, Frederick met it y inducing a minority group in the college of cardinals to set up a rival pope, hereby precipitating a religious schism. The device proved unavailing. The world in general paid homage to Alexander III, who both by his character as a man and by his gifts as a diplomat proved himself worthy of his most capable predecessors. His keen penetration enabled him to see that the Lombard cities needed only to stand firmly together under the patronage of an unyielding pope, and the battle would be won, though it might be hard fought and long drawn out. He advocated this associative policy year in, year out, until he overcame all effective opposition to his plan. Under papal inspiration the Lombard towns at last agreed to form a single overwhelming league; and in 1176, a date so important for Italian communal history that it deserves to be inscribed in brass, they won a crushing victory over Frederick at Legnano.

Unable after Legnano to offer further resistance, the red-bearded emperor was obliged to come to terms with both his adversaries, the pope and the Lombard communes. The negotiations which he spun with Alexander III led in 1177 to a peace congress at Venice. It was opened by an act of formal reconciliation between emperor and pope in the atrium of the great church of St. Mark. Prostrating himself before his adversary to kiss his foot, the humbled Barbarossa presented a picture to the world which in the long gallery of medieval spectacles takes its place beside the memorable scene enacted at

Canossa exactly one hundred years before. In distinction from the earlier, stil exclusively feudal scene, there were present at Venice representatives of th Lombard communes, to whom on this occasion the papacy in large part owe its victory. To these spokesmen of a new social and political order the defeate sovereign was not obliged to prostrate himself as a measure preliminary to settlement; but he had to accept a truce with them on terms which, six year later, were converted into the Peace of Constance (1183). As this treaty con firmed to the Lombard towns all the essential rights of self-government, i may, though it did not quite ring the death knell of feudalism, be hailed as fundamental charter legalizing the new urban civilization.

In the epochal Lombard struggle covering over a quarter of a centur (1154–83) the Tuscan communes took no part. Neither now nor afterwar did there ever develop a sense of solidarity among the Italian towns; and national sentiment, as we understand the term, was not born till the nineteent century. As for the emperor, engaged during this period with all his resource in the struggle with the pope and the Lombard communes, he was oblige to maintain an attitude of conciliation toward Tuscany by leaving it largel to itself. Thus to be left alone was all that the Tuscan communes desired. The had their mind set on continuing the struggle among themselves and with th great barons in their midst without interference from above; and out of neces sity, certainly not from choice, Frederick I gratified their wish.

An exception to this imperial aloofness cannot, however, be passed over i silence. When in the year 1162 the emperor had destroyed Milan, he entere on an interval of comparative peace and authority in the north, which at las enabled him to take a more lively interest in Tuscany. Under the inspiratio of his chancellor, Rainald, who was also archbishop of Cologne, he worke out a plan of imperial control in this province which Rainald in person under took to carry out. While attempting to establish a kind of balance between th warring communes and the feudality, it presented as its major feature th creation of an imperial administration composed of a network of agent (*potestates*) of the sovereign spread over the whole province. The potestate were intrusted with the collection of monies owing to the sovereign and wit the maintenance of peace and were responsible to an imperial governor resid ing at San Miniato del Tedesco. Ever since the death of Matilda this little hil town over the Arno had been the capital designate of Tuscany, but not til Frederick I called into being a German bureaucracy to rule the land did i figure as the capital in a real and practical sense. The distinction thus wor it retained as long as any trace of imperial authority survived in Tuscany.

Since for the brief number of years it lasted the reorganization effected b Chancellor Rainald reduced, if it did not terminate, the anarchic confusion o Tuscany, we may fairly affirm that it sprang from a sound idea. That idea ma be defined as provincial pacification brought about by means of an authorita tive central administration; and no student of history will fail to note that thi was the road afterward traveled by every state of Europe which found a effective cure for feudalism. Rainald was therefore on the right track so far a his leading principle was concerned. But he loaded it with too many liabilities In the first place, his plan was not radical enough, since he joined it with a nachronistic attempt to preserve the feudality in all its ancient rights; in the econd place, its execution was put into the hands of a body of foreigners without any support in the country. While pointing to a possible solution, his cheme was imperfectly conceived and executed and began to go to pieces as oon as the Lombard provinces braced themselves to resume the intermitted truggle with the emperor. The new conflict, dating from 1167, was not closed ll the victory of Legnano (1176) had been crowned by the Peace of Conance. As soon as, beginning in 1167, the emperor was once more obliged to oncentrate his strength on Lombardy, he had no way of hindering the breakown of his Tuscan experiment. His potestates, no longer obeyed, ceased to unction and gradually withdrew from the province. Thereupon the various ocal powers eagerly resumed an independence which the irrepressible mutual nimosities promptly turned into the previous mad-house war of all against all.

The story of Florence may and should be seen as an illuminating instance of ne general Tuscan turmoil. The moment that Barbarossa's bureaucratic program collapsed, the liberated town returned to its previous policy of selfggrandizement, snarling and snapping at every foe whom the current atomizaon of society planted across its path. Successes, often astonishing in their romptness and magnitude, were scored in every direction. As the conquest of iesole had clearly shown, Florence was grimly resolved not to permit any of s small neighbors to develop into possible future rivals. Consequently such nconspicuous urban nuclei as Figline and Empoli, lying somewhat farther field than Fiesole, were now brought into a desired subjection.[17] In its set urpose to control its county the town was not minded to let even the smallest sh slip through the meshes of its net.

And naturally the close watch kept since the very beginning of the consular eriod on the great feudal families, the Guidi and Alberti, suffered no relaxaon. After the collapse of their suzerain's authority at Legnano, both families ere drawn into the Florentine system, though with a difference, owing to the reater subtlety of the reigning head of the Guidi clan. This was Count Guido uerra, who had been a most active partisan of the emperor during the recent ttempt to impose an imperial administration on the province. Sensing his daner under the altered circumstances, he entered into relations of amity with ne burghers which, while leaving him ostensibly free, reduced him to someing suspiciously close to subjection. In his attempt to achieve a cessaon of the warfare so destructive of his rights he even condescended (1180) ask for the hand of Gualdrada,[18] daughter of a leading citizen, Bellincione erti. The marriage succeeded in creating a kindlier atmosphere between count nd commune, and as long as the husband of Gualdrada lived, the ancient eud with the Guidi seems actually to have rested. As the more rancorous and, herefore, more foolish head of the Alberti tribe refused to abate his hostility n any way, the citizen army in 1184 stormed his great castle of Mangona in ne Apennines and took the count himself prisoner. He was not released till

[17] The subjection of Figline on the Arno above Florence occurred in 1168; Empoli on the Arno elow Florence was subjected in 1182.

[18] Gualdrada was admired for her beauty and delicate Tuscan speech. Elevated to the highest udal rank by her marriage, the *buon Gualdrada* was promptly absorbed into the Florentine patriic legend and, generations later, was respectfully saluted by Dante and Villani.

he had signed a sweeping submission acknowledging the jurisdiction over h estates of the victorious republic. With the fall of the Alberti the last imped ment had broken down, and Florence had achieved the ambition with whic she had embarked on her consular career: she was the unchallenged mistre of her county, with noblemen and small towns alike acknowledging he supremacy.

A characteristic act of this period of swelling confidence must not be ove looked. It consisted in Florence providing itself with a second and ampl circle of walls. As originally laid out by the Romans, Florentia took the shap as we know, of a small, irregular square penetrated by four gates. In spite the shrinkage of the population during the early Middle Ages, the Roman wa did not disappear. Not till the consular age did the revival of commerce brin about a noticeable increase of population, from which fact it followed th suburbs, called *borghi* in Italian, began to extend along all the roads issuin from the gates. By the reign of Emperor Frederick I the borghi had become s considerable that an enemy by attacking and setting fire to them might infli a very serious loss on the community. In 1172 the citizens set about correctin this alarming situation by undertaking a new girdle of walls planned to em brace the exposed suburbs. They took four years to complete the very consi erable enterprise. As eloquent evidence of the commune's physical growth l us note that the new wall inclosed three times the area of the first circuit an what is particularly deserving of remark, by taking in a segment of the le bank it established Florence on both banks of the river. The increased traff of the communal age is indicated by the circumstance that, whereas four gat had originally met existing needs, three times that number of gates were r quired to serve the enlarged town.[19]

At this point all the success and glory harvested by a policy of stealth sleepless encroachment upon its neighbors and competitors were imperiled b one of those sudden turns of the wheel of fortune so characteristic of the flu Italian situation. In the year 1184 the Emperor Frederick, now an old ma whose famous golden beard had long since turned silver, came again Italy; and this time he came on a mission which, at least on the surface, w eminently peaceful. He crossed the Alps in order to marry his son and su cessor, Henry, to Constance, heiress of the kingdom of Sicily. There was to b no war, if possible not even any friction, between him and his Italian subjec until the union had been effected which would establish the Hohenstaufe family in southern Italy, thus enabling its chief effectively to straddle the pe insula and keep it in secure subjection. On passing through Lombardy th emperor was received with rejoicing by the communes, which since the Pea of Constance were in legal possession of full, self-governing rights. From Lon bardy Frederick pressed southward into Tuscany, where, to his chagrin an indignation, he found the communes practicing the same freedom as the sisters in the plain of the Po. To his conservative, legalistic mind the distin tion between the two cases was that between law and rebellion; for, what th Lombard towns were doing, had been conceded to them by charter, where

[19] See map on p. 10. Attached to Davidsohn, Vol. I, is a map which traces in detail the first a the second circle of walls.

ie Tuscan towns, with the exception of Pisa,[20] could point to no document
om him to justify their usurpation. In his view the only valid system for
'uscany was the one set up by his chancellor, Rainald of Cologne, some twenty
ears before, and he proceeded straightway to put it again in operation. The
irprising thing is that the cities, of whose pride and daring we can have no
oubt, yielded without a struggle. But the surprise evaporates when we con-
der the situation. Owing to their implacable divisions, the communes were
tterly incapable of forming a union against their suzerain on the model of
ie successful Lombard league. Consequently, each town was obliged to deal
ith Frederick separately and, as he was now at peace with the Lombard
ommunes, he was for the time being irresistible.

In the course of the two years following the royal visit to Tuscany of 1185
'rederick and, after him, his son Henry, reordered the government of the
rovince along the lines with which we are familiar. A body of imperial offi-
ials, called *potestates* or *teutonici,* radiating from San Miniato del Tedesco as
ieir capital, took over the collection of taxes and the administration of justice;
ie nobles, great and small alike, were reinstated in their undiminished rights
nd possessions; and the communes, while confirmed in their local self-govern-
ient, were limited in its exercise to the actual town area or, as a special act
f imperial grace, they were permitted to include within their subject territory
ie immediate countryside to an average depth of five or six miles.[21] In 1189,
n the death of the childless King William of Sicily, Henry and his queen,
'onstance, succeeded to William's throne. Then in the following year Henry
lso succeeded his father as Holy Roman emperor. Never before had an em-
eror possessed Sicily and Naples, and therefore never before had an emperor
ominated Italy so completely as did Henry VI. The ancient rival of the em-
eror, the pope, found himself tragically eclipsed in his capital at Rome and,
t least for the time being, did not venture to offer resistance. If we remember
he conjunction of compelling circumstances which raised Henry to such
ieights, we cannot fail to understand how it came about that an administra-
ion of authoritative imperial agents could be reimposed on Tuscany to remain
ntact as long as the towering Henry lived.

A factor which came to the aid of Frederick, and to Henry after him, in
acifying Tuscany according to their conservative prescription remains to be
nentioned. At precisely this time a new wave of crusading fervor poured over
vestern Christendom, owing to the arrival of gravely disturbing information
rom the east. It was in the autumn of 1187 that the news of the capture by
he Saracens of Jerusalem the Holy spread like wild fire through the countries
of the occident. Won a hundred years before by the knighthood of the First
Crusade, Jerusalem had come to be regarded as the supreme shrine of the faith

[20] Pisa is a special case among the Tuscan communes for the simple reason that Pisa possessed
navy. From an early time the emperors were prepared to make considerable concessions to Pisa
n return for support at sea. We have seen (p. 58) that Pisa got a charter of liberties from
Henry IV as early as 1081. In 1162 it got a still ampler privilege from Frederick I conferring the
ullest self-government as well as complete jurisdiction over its county. *Mon. Ger. Hist. Legum,*
Sectio IV, Tomus I, p. 282. For significant comment see Davidsohn, Vol. I, p. 478.

[21] The charter which Henry, in the name of Frederick, conceded to Florence may be found in
Ficker, *Forschungen,* Vol. IV, p. 213. It is dated June 24, 1187, and is notable as the first imperial
privilege ever issued to Florence conferring a limited self-government.

which the infidels must under no circumstances be permitted again to ravisl
At the report of its fall such a sea of warrior enthusiasm washed over th
European peoples that their sovereigns, bowled over by its impetuous onse
were obliged to head the movement of retaliation and assume the cross. Tc
gether with the kings of France and England the now venerable Empero
Frederick was sucked into the maelstrom. In 1189, attended by a great army
he set out for the east from Regensburg in Germany. Following the lan
route, he got as far as Asia Minor, where his fate overtook him, for he wa
drowned while crossing a small stream. Although the German host melte
away at this misfortune, the kings of France and England persisted in th
enterprise. However, beyond capturing (1191) the port of Acre after a lon
siege, nothing of note was accomplished. Jerusalem was not even threatene
and continued to rest securely in the hands of the Saracens.

In the emotional crisis represented by these events our Florentines were a
deeply entangled as the rest of the western world. The crusade turned thei
eyes to a considerable degree away from the distressing domestic situation
Seizing upon this outlet for their suppressed emotions, they threw themselve
with passionate fervor into the war for the delivery of Jerusalem. In sucl
numbers did they volunteer for the crusade that, when they arrived by sea i
Syria, they were permitted to constitute a separate division of the Christia
army drawn in a besieging ring around Acre. Without any doubt they had a
honorable part in the capture of this seaport, thereby spreading the fame o
their growing city over Europe. But that their share was as decisive as thei
chroniclers were afterward so unanimous in telling the world may be doubte
without the least injury to the reputation of a brave and devoted band.

Henry, who had stayed behind as regent when his father went on crusade
ruled the empire as Emperor Henry VI for the brief period of seven year
(1190–97). Energetic, unscrupulous, and vastly ambitious, he overawed hi
enemies both in Germany and Italy and did not meet with any serious opposi
tion from his obedient province of Tuscany. Florence in particular seems t
have made up its mind that it was useless to kick against the pricks, althougl
there is evidence of occasional local disturbances indicating that the citizen
did not bear the imperial yoke without a protest. In the main, very much lik
the rest of Tuscany and Italy, the commune adopted a waiting attitude. Sud
denly, in the autumn of the year 1197, the whisper went from mouth to moutl
that the all-powerful emperor, the ferocious tyrant, had died of a fever at Mes
sina. It was true: Henry VI had expired, hardly thirty years of age, leavin
behind as his heir a boy, Frederick by name, aged three years. Henry's powe
had manifestly been a personal power and was laid with him into the grave
Nobody knew this better than the oppressed communes of Tuscany and with
out delay they determined to act.

VII. The Tuscan League of 1197; Replacement of the Consuls by the Podestà; The Religious Revival of the Begging Friars

THAT the Tuscan communes lost no time to act on hearing of the death of Henry VI is indicated by their sending delegates to San Genesio to take counsel together within a few weeks after the event. San Genesio was a small open town in the plain below San Miniato del Tedesco, and because of its central location had already on earlier occasions served as meeting-place for the Tuscan republics. And now it was seen that Henry's iron yoke had caused the bitter local feuds to be at least momentarily forgotten, for a Tuscan league, which it had never been possible to realize in the past, came into spontaneous existence. It was born too, exactly like its Lombard predecessor, under the auspices of the papacy. Two cardinals attended the sessions of the congress and committed the church to loyal support of the liberation movement. The sessions were still proceeding when in January, 1198, a new pope mounted the throne, who, under the name of Innocent III (1198–1216), revived the most exaggerated claims of his predecessors to universal empire. His accession guaranteed an alliance as firm as that famous older union between the Lombard league and Alexander III which had brought about the triumphant settlement of Constance. An immense advantage enjoyed by the latest alliance between pope and towns was that the war with the empire, which seemed to be a certain consequence of its action, did not materialize. A disputed election in Germany had carried two candidates, Otto of the house of Guelph and Philip, brother of the late emperor, into the lists against each other, and until they had settled their differences the empire was paralyzed. As this condition lasted for ten years, the Tuscan league was never subjected to the supreme test, the test of war against its feudal chief.

Even though the expected war with the empire did not take place, there was abundant work for the league of another kind. Each commune wished to get back its freedom of action and, above all, to recover the lost control of its county. Though in guarded language, this purpose was written into the agreement of November 11, 1197, which every town, nobleman, and castle was invited to sign. Even Pisa was summoned to subscribe, although it already enjoyed by imperial charter all the advantages the other Tuscan communes were combining in order to achieve. But except Pisa, which felt it had nothing to gain, the others did, either at once or in the course of the winter, attach their signatures till the document bore the names of Florence, Siena, Lucca, Arezzo, and the bishop of Volterra (signing for the town of which he was the lord).[1] What is more surprising at first blush, it bore the names also of the heads of the two great feudal families, the Guidi and Alberti. Only with the greatest reluctance could these counts have presented themselves at San Genesio to make their submission to the communes under a deceptive formula of amity. It proves that they themselves no longer entertained any doubt that the emperor was their sole support and that, on his failing them, their best course was to adjust themselves to the altered circumstances and to save what they could from the wreck. Exactly as under the similar situation of twenty years before, the Guidi fared better than the Alberti. Without a struggle they yielded the civil jurisdiction over their castles in the Florentine contado to the triumphant commune. Apparently they solaced themselves with the thought that owing to their large holdings beyond the reach of Florence on either side of the Apennines, they could still comport themselves as imperial magnates and unfold a baronial grandeur. The Alberti, more narrowly a family of the Florentine contado and more hateful to the citizens because of their long and unconcealed hostility, were subjected to a grinding humiliation. By a series of acts of the year 1200 they surrendered to Florence all the castles and way-tolls the commune demanded of them and, in substance, submitted to be rated as Florentine citizens.[2]

In the years immediately following the formation of the Tuscan league each commune tried to realize its fixed and burning ambition to conquer and rule its contado. While the feudal nobility, as the case of the Guidi and Alberti shows, was obliged at least to pretend to accept this program, this was not yet the case with the many small urban settlements scattered over the countryside. The free winds blowing vigorously over Italy had created a passion for liberty in which every hamlet, regardless of its size, had a share. It often required more than threats on the part of Florence before towns like Figline and Certaldo, of small circumference but swelling with a fresh, communal pride of their own, agreed to curb their necks under the yoke of their larger neighbor. And one of these small towns had the effrontery to put up such an audacious resistance that it obliged Florence to conduct a war requiring five campaigns before it was crowned with success. This town was Semifonte. As it presents an instance strikingly illustrative of the selfish and headstrong resolution of our pushing community of traders, the story of Semifonte is worth recounting.

The venomous character of Florentine hostility to Semifonte is not a political enigma. Semifonte was an artificial creation of those dangerous and persistent enemies of the Arno commonwealth, the Counts Alberti. Engaged in a bitter contest with a commercial community that was notably adding to its strength with every passing decade, the Alberti bethought themselves of erecting a town on land of their own which should develop into a rival of Florence and draw off some of the Florentine profits into their pockets. They selected for this purpose a high hill near Certaldo; and in the decade of imperial control coincident with the rule of Henry VI they built a town on that summit with a strong wall around it and called it Semifonte. It bloomed astonishingly to the immense disgust of its Florentine neighbors, who would

[1] Santini, *Documenti dell'Antica Costituzione*, etc., No. XXI.
[2] *Ibid.*, Nos. XXVII, XXVIII, XXIX.

ıave gone into action against it at once with sword and fire, had it not been 'or Henry's imperial officials, effective guardians of the peace of Tuscany. Then with dramatic suddenness came Henry's death, the collapse of his administration, and the Tuscan league. Therewith Semifonte, as lying in the contado of Florence, was delivered into that commune's hands as completely ıs the Alberti magnates themselves. It is interesting to note that many of the mall neighbors of Semifonte in the Elsa Valley, such as Colle and San Gimignano, either secretly or openly encouraged it to offer resistance to the town hat claimed the undisputed headship of the county. Instinctively these little ommunities sensed that their own independence was tied up with that of emifonte. However, such slight help as they managed to provide was unvailing; and although the Semifontians proved themselves a race of heroes nd held the Florentines at bay for five campaigning seasons, at last, in the ear 1202, they were obliged to surrender. While the inhabitants saved their ives in return for a promise to disperse, the town itself, delivered over to the nercy of the conquerors, was destroyed even more completely than that earlier horn in the Florentine flesh, Fiesole. So thoroughly was the work of demoliion carried out that before many generations had passed there was no longer ny memory in the neighborhood that such a town as Semifonte had ever xisted. In an effort to locate the vanished community modern antiquarians ave diligently searched the reputed site without recovering as much as a ingle stone that might with certainty be ascribed to the short-lived, upstart ival of Florence.

The immediate effect of the league of San Genesio was a general civil war ı Tuscany, or rather, in view of the permission granted each leading comıune to possess itself of its county, a series of separate and distinct civil wars etween each county capital and its dependent countryside. In spite of the aliant resistance of obstinate little centers like Semifonte, the work of subection was completed after a few seasons, with the result that the great comıunes achieved a domination which was nonetheless real for its manifest ıck of a legal basis. Then with the end gained, for the sake of which the eague in the first instance had been formed, the federation flew violently part. All the terrible interurban feuds that had come to birth in the consular ge flamed up anew exactly as if there had not been a sworn alliance and a uinquennium of ostensible brotherhood. What else was to be expected? As oon as Florence or Siena or any other town had mastered its particular condo, it faced its neighbor across a boundary which was sometimes in dispute— ıe Siena-Florence boundary was such a case—and which, whether in dispute r not, was regularly without any geographical significance. From an economic r a political point of view it was difficult, if not impossible, to call a halt at purely artificial a line; and young exultant organisms, like the Tuscan comıunes, could not be expected to do so. As a result Florence clashed with Siena ıd Pistoia, Siena with Florence and Arezzo, Lucca with Pisa and Pistoia; in ıort, all the wars broke loose again which we have already noted in our record f the previous century and which were bound to continue until one commune ould prove itself stronger than the others and by conquering them in turn 'ould at last impose an enforced peace upon the province. That one and only

solution was not even remotely in sight at the beginning of the thirteenth cen
tury. The Tuscan towns were approximately as yet of the same size an
strength and the prospect immediately ahead was a planless, internecine strug
gle conducted with blind impulsiveness and without so much as a trace o
either faith or scruple.

As long as Florence had not set its heel on Semifonte, it was at some pain
to keep on speaking terms with Siena. However, hardly had Semifonte bee
converted into a dust heap when the old bickerings were renewed over th
disputed boundary. In the hope of having the ancient quarrel adjudicated with
out war, Siena in 1203 agreed to submit the case to an arbiter and to accep
the podestà of Poggibonsi in that capacity. The result was a judgment or *lod*
which drew the boundary in every respect in accordance with the pretension
of Florence.[3] More exacerbated than ever the Sienese nursed a rage in thei
hearts which led shortly to a new war, in fact to a long succession of wars
with the details of which we shall not concern ourselves. Such significance a
they have lie in the fact that the expanding Arno city proved itself to be n
longer interested in merely its own county; it desired to extend its control int
the neighboring Sienese county by lending aid to small towns in this area lik
Montepulciano and Montalcino in their efforts to preserve their liberties agains
the encroachments of Siena. Plainly the ambition of Florence was bursting it
early, self-imposed bounds and taking a broader survey of the Tuscan scene

The deliberate selection by Florence of centers of political support in Sienes
territory was duplicated by similar action in the counties of Pistoia and Arezzo
and inescapably this reaching out farther and farther over Tuscany would be
fore long carry the Florentines to the sea. Begun modestly as purely overlan
trade, their commerce had hardly got under way when the crusades opene
up golden opportunities in the east. In view of their amazing energy, th
Florentine merchants would not be inclined for long to leave the immens
profits of this oversea traffic in the hands exclusively of the towns planted o
the coast. During the twelfth century, when Florence, not yet having acquire
much momentum, was necessarily humble in manner and restricted in out
look, it had maintained the most friendly relations with Pisa, at the mouth c
its river, content to accept such commercial favors as the much more powerfu
maritime community might concede. Pisa, in its turn, did not fail to see th
advantage of having a friend and ally in inner Tuscany. This sense of mutua
dependence led to the treaty of 1171, as important politically as it was com
mercially, for, after establishing an offensive and defensive alliance betwee
Pisa and Florence to run for forty years, it laid down a series of trade pro
visions of inestimable advantage to the inland town. The most important o
these was the obligation assumed by Pisa that Florentine merchants and thei
goods should enjoy the same rates in Pisan vessels as native goods and mer
chants.[4] There can be no doubt whatever that Florence benefited immensel
from this concession, on the strength of which it was enabled to extend it
commercial operations over the whole Mediterranean Sea. The unchecke
arrogance noticeable in the conduct of the government in the early thirteent

[3] Date of lodo, June 3, 1203. Davidsohn, Vol. I, pp. 640-1.
[4] Santini, *Documenti,* No. IV; Davidsohn, Vol. I, p. 518.

century is referable to a large extent to the ever-widening range of Florentine enterprise. Slowly but decisively the earlier attitude of deference to the great seaport began to disappear; and so slight an incident as the clash in 1220 between the Florentine and the Pisan delegations attending the coronation festival of Frederick II at Rome sufficed to release an animosity which was never again composed. The war born of this Roman episode is a milestone in Tuscan history, for with it the Florentines turned their attention to the control of the coast of their province in their own interest. With this enlargement of their already ambitious program they produced a political alignment among the Tuscan communes which remained characteristic for a long time to come. Inevitably on the transformation of Florence from a friend to an enemy, Pisa sought the company and support of Siena, while Florence, in its turn, edged close to Lucca, the ancient and uncompromising foe of Pisa. It followed from other circumstances to be recounted hereafter that Pisa and Siena with their following came to be bracketed as the imperial (later to be called Ghibelline) powers of Tuscany, while Lucca and Florence with such adherents as they commanded served as the pillars of the ecclesiastical (later to be called Guelph) cause. We shall pass over the dark intrigues and incessant, petty wars among the Tuscan towns till toward the middle of the century when they became tied up with a world-situation which has a genuine claim on our attention.

In the period of the Tuscan league and the renewed conquest by the towns of their contado, there occurred a change in their constitutional structure which has been given different and even radically opposed interpretations. The multiple executive of the consuls was replaced by a single executive called *podestà*. The word is derived from the Latin *potestas,* and potestas owed its contemporary currency to the circumstance that it was the name given by the Emperor Barbarossa to the imperial agents he established in Tuscany and elsewhere. The change from consuls to podestà was not effected at once but carried out over a period of years and had at the beginning plainly an experimental character. In Florence, for example, as early as 1193 a single Florentine citizen served as head of the government in place of the consuls.[5] After thus giving the podestàship a trial, the citizens reverted to the familiar multiple consulate. Then, as a further experiment, they summoned a foreigner to serve as podestà; and before the first decade of the new century had elapsed, the foreign podestà had won such general approval that he became a fixture. At the same time the conditions under which he served took definite shape. On assuming office for his term, which usually ran for a year, he took a solemn oath to fulfil the duties specified in the constitution and to execute that document in every particular. When his year was over, he agreed to submit, before leaving for home, to an audit (*sindicato*) and to have deducted from his salary any fines for which he may have made himself liable by transgressing his authority.[6]

Simultaneously with the change in the chief executive the whole constitution suffered certain rather minor modifications. They deserve, however, to be recorded since they mark a departure from the established consular usage. As the fruitful source of political disturbances the public assembly or parlamentum,

[5] Santini, *Documenti*. Catalogo degli Ufficiali del Comune di Firenze, p. XLI.
[6] Full details of the close supervision exercised over the podestà in Davidsohn, Vol. I, p. 697.

in which we detected the democratic base of the consular government, had already during the consulate been permitted to fall more and more into disuse. This tendency continued under the podestà. In measure as the parlamentum declined the council rose in authority, not only because it lent itself better to orderly debate, but pre-eminently because it rested securely in the hands of the leading citizen groups exercising control of the town. However, with the coming of the podestà the council experienced a bifurcation into a general and a special council. This involved no change in the ruling system since both councils continued to be recruited from the same upper strata of society. The creation of a smaller special council strengthened, if anything, the control of the government by the well-to-do, as the foreign podestà could undertake nothing without the preliminary consent of this more intimate body.

It has been hotly debated whether or not these changes may be interpreted as a democratic advance. Any question posed in this way permits the adducing of arguments favorable to either side. If, on the other hand, we drop the dogmatic point of view and agree to study the communal constitution genetically, we shall be content to see what actually happened without feeling obliged to evaluate the happening in terms of a particular theory. Proceeding in this manner and directing our attention to the special instance of Florence, we observe that the consular executive, composed usually of twelve men, had by the second half of the twelfth century developed serious imperfections. In the first place, government by a large board has always and everywhere proved unwieldy, and Florence was no exception to the rule. Next, the consular posts having become from the outset the prerogative of the leading families, two opposed high-born cliques developed, each of which tried to monopolize the consulship and to exclude from power the members of the rival clique. On the occasion of the annual elections there was in consequence a tension in the city which threatened civil war. In the year 1177, for instance, the group of consular families which cohered around the Uberti rose in rebellion against the group of which the Giandonati were the head and which had managed in the immediately preceding years to attribute the consular offices exclusively to its members. The resulting civil war lasted three years.[7] The inflamed local passions could be most satisfactorily appeased by a single executive, who, drawn from another town and province, might be expected to hold the balance between the warring groups. The single head, charged, among other duties, with the task of maintaining peace among the noble factions, would have the further advantage of appealing to the trading elements who were gaining in numbers every year and who were instinctively averse to the nobiliary excesses. Finally, since the podestà was a paid official, called by the council and responsible to it by his obligation to submit to an audit, he was under much more effective control than had ever been the case with the consuls. Whether in view of these circumstances, all of which may be thought of as having conduced to the replacing of the consuls with the podestà, the new official is to be rated as a democratic felicity or as an aristocratic menace is essentially unimportant. It is enough that the consuls had proved themselves an unsatisfactory executive and that their successor, the podestà, offered the possibility of termi-

[7] Davidsohn, Vol. I, pp. 553-59.

nating the civil war to which the local consular elections periodically gave rise. Finally, the foreign podestà was summoned as a specialist in administration and justice and filled the chief magistracy much more effectively than the consuls had done.[8]

While these developments were taking place in Tuscany, the empire was in one of its periodic swoons, owing to the disputed election following the death of Henry VI. The crisis was not terminated till 1208, when the murder of Philip of Suabia, brother of the late emperor, left his rival, Otto of Saxony, in unchallenged control. The two men represented respectively the great German houses of Hohenstaufen and Guelph (Welf), the irrepressible conflict between which was now in the third generation. For the moment at least success smiled on Guelph Otto and, securely in possession of the German throne, he set out for Italy, where, in 1209, he was crowned emperor by Pope Innocent III. This pontiff needed all his ability to steer his course safely amid the rocks that threatened him and his office. Like all his immediate predecessors he was averse to the Hohenstaufens because of the unyielding obstinacy with which since the advent to the throne of Frederick I in 1152 they had upheld the authority of the civil power against the claims of the church. The bitterness had reached its highest stage when the family, through the marriage of Henry VI with the heiress of Sicily, had gained possession of this flourishing southern kingdom. During his short reign Henry, with one foot planted in northern, another in southern, Italy, straddled Rome like a colossus and held the pope at his mercy. Without any doubt the emperor's premature death was a lucky stroke for the papacy. In fact it gave back to the head of Christendom his full freedom of action, for not only was Frederick, the three-year-old heir of Henry, eliminated, on account of his immaturity, from among the candidates for the German throne, but, on the death of his mother, which followed quickly on that of his father, he fell into unqualified dependence on the pope by becoming his ward. At this point we must recall that when the Normans conquered the Italian south back in the eleventh century, they agreed to rule it as a papal fief. Among the rights of the pope as acknowledged suzerain of the kingdom of Sicily was the exercise of wardship over a king who was an orphan and a minor. A thoroughly honorable man, the reigning pope, Innocent III, was at pains to give young Frederick a careful bringing-up; but he was equally determined that the dangerous situation in which the papacy had found itself in Henry's time should under no circumstances be permitted to return. For this reason, while prepared to let Frederick, on coming of age, mount the Sicilian throne, he was pleased to have the implacable enemy of the Hohenstaufens, Guelph Otto, wear the German and imperial crowns. Moreover, being a clever and far-seeing statesman, Innocent was resolved to make himself as sure as possible of the perpetual separation of the Sicilian and imperial scepters. Therefore, before placing the crown on Otto's head, he made him take a solemn oath that he would respect all the traditional rights of the church and particularly that he would never attempt to add Sicily to the empire.

[8] Since the towns wanted the podestàs whom they called as executives to be as expert as possible, young men began to prepare themselves for the office as for a profession. On the professional aspect, see Davidsohn, Vol. I, p. 695. It is not an exaggeration to think of some of the podestàs, the best of them, in terms of a present-day city-manager.

Following his coronation, the new emperor, Otto IV, retired to Tuscany and immediately again set up in that province the imperial administration which had collapsed so promptly and ignominiously at the death of Henry VI. If in this respect he scored an ephemeral success, he owed it, as his predecessors had done, to his military power. The communes had just finished repossessing themselves of their counties and regarded their acquisition as the apple of their eye. But there was no legal basis for the seizures they had effected; they failed to stand shoulder to shoulder, owing to their fatal disagreements; and on sober second thoughts they chose not to measure their strength at this time against that of their imperial master. It is these considerations that explain how it happened that Otto was able to call back to life a system which only ten years before, in the first flush of the triumphant Tuscan league, had seemed to have been swept away forever. From the battlements of the great tower at San Miniato del Tedesco the imperial banner with its heraldic eagle again fluttered in the wind, and from and to this tower imperial agents (*potestates, teutonici*) were in constant movement on errands of their once more triumphant lord, the emperor.

It was a triumph brief as summer lightning, owing in large measure to Otto's unfathomable falsity and folly. No sooner was he safely possessed of Tuscany than he undertook to do the very thing he had renounced under the most solemn vows. He resolved to conquer Sicily on the certainly very debatable ground that it was a subject-land of the empire. We can imagine Innocent's indignation at this base betrayal. Not only did he promptly excommunicate the perjurer, but he prepared to punish him in a more effective manner still by starting a backfire in Germany. He summoned his Suabian charge, now a youth of eighteen, to Rome and, forgetting in his wrath at Otto his fear of the Hohenstaufens, he dispatched young Frederick across the Alps to win the German throne from the Guelph incumbent (1212). At the mere prospect of this move Otto hurriedly withdrew from Italy; and hardly had his army left the Tuscan soil when the imperial administration in Tuscany once more broke down and the towns again resumed the interrupted rule of their counties. Italy was left to itself, while the Guelphs and the Hohenstaufens renewed their ancient and disastrous feud for the possession of the German crown. On this occasion it was the Hohenstaufen champion who gained the victory and in 1215 young Frederick was crowned German king at Aachen. It was only now that Pope Innocent's normal caution reasserted itself; and during the negotiations with the young sovereign in regard to his future coronation as emperor he insisted that, as an indispensable preliminary to that ceremony, Frederick would have to renounce the earlier, the Sicilian crown. The negotiations on this head were still proceeding when the masterful pope died (1216). As Germany continued to seethe with disorder, Frederick was obliged to linger in the north. Not till 1220 did he reappear in Italy, when he immediately betook himself to Rome to be formally invested with the empire. The new pope, Honorius III, a gentle soul, the exact opposite in temper to his lordly predecessor, was content to leave Frederick's renunciation of the kingdom of Sicily involved in verbal ambiguities. All his thoughts and hopes were set upon a new crusade to liberate Jerusalem; and when he had exacted a promise from Frederick to lead a Christian host against the infidel, he placed the crown upon the Hohenstaufen's head.

With the accession to the empire of Frederick II there began a new chapter in the long struggle of the Italian communes for self-determination, for Frederick did not scruple to renew the attempts of his father and grandfather to subject them to imperial control. The fresh effort to turn back the wheel of time ended in failure like all its forerunners, but it was made forever memorable by the extraordinary character and talents of the imperial incumbent. It has, besides, a special claim on our attention because of the prominent part taken in the struggle by our town of Florence. Reserving this climax of the long conflict between the two opposed systems of agrarian feudalism and urban self-government to the following chapter, we shall take up a change in the religious temper of Christianity befalling at this time which greatly contributed to the failure of Frederick II by once more endowing the church with irresistible energy. As it is the unfolding civilization and not merely the political evolution of the Arno town which is our goal, we are certainly on the right track when we propose to keep in touch with the ever-changing phases of Christian thought and feeling. For religion provided the climate in which the society of the Middle Ages had its being to a degree which the present generation can only realize by a lively effort of the imagination.

The religious movement inaugurated with the beginning thirteenth century flows from many sources and gathers around many champions; but with all due respect to its complicated character we commit no violence if we refer its decisive manifestations to the pontificate of Innocent III (1198–1216). Innocent was a sanguine, intelligent, and irrepressibly energetic man, who subordinated his ambition to his office, but whose ambition *for* his office absolutely knew no bounds. Like all the great medieval popes, practically without exception, far from falling under the type of mystic and dreamer, he was primarily an administrator, a jurist, and a statesman. He had studied canon law at the University of Bologna and his training, added to the hard, metallic quality native to his mind, inspired him with the desire to have the still frequently fluctuating practices and doctrines of the church cast into rigorous, legal form. There, for instance, was the unsettled and ever cantankerous question of the church and the state. The theory commonly held in the early Middle Ages was that church and state were independent of each other, that each was supreme in its own field, and that both derived directly from God. However impressive on paper, this equalitarian, this dualist theory had worked out very badly in practice; and church and state, instead of living peacefully side by side as partners in a common enterprise, had been perpetually at each other's throat. Under these distressing circumstances an ecclesiastical school of thought came to the front, beginning with the famous Gregory VII, which contended that the church was superior to the state and that, whenever a conflict threatened, the state must yield to the institution which possessed the greater authority because it boasted Christ himself as its founder. While this conception may be said to have been in the air since Hildebrand's time, it had never been pressed, never even been more than tentatively formulated. To Innocent's juristic temper this wavering condition was unendurable, and he resolved to put an end to it by making the church unquestionably supreme both in fact and in theory. In numerous letters and addresses he insisted that the pope was the vicar of God on earth and that, as such, he towered over all civil rulers, who henceforth would be considered to be exercising their authority subject to good behavior and at the pope's pleasure. The goal of his policy was the control by his office of all the sovereigns of Europe, and it is amazing to what an extent he realized his purpose. He made and unmade emperors, as the cases of Otto IV and Frederick II show; he obliged the king of France meekly to take back the wife whom he had repudiated; and he brought the kings of Portugal, Aragon, and England so completely to heel that they made a gift to him of their respective kingdoms and received them back at his hands as papal fiefs.

Never since its origin had the church with the tiara-crowned pope at its head been more unquestionably the ruling institution of the west than under Innocent III. But if one looked behind the brilliant façade at the Christian congregation which it hid from view, he became aware of conditions calculated to startle and alarm him. Ever since the eleventh century, which had inaugurated the revival of commerce, this congregation had been involved in a vast social and economic upheaval. The statement applies to the whole west without exception, but it is particularly true of Italy and southern France, which undoubtedly marched in the European van in respect to urban development. When the religious reform of the eleventh century declared war upon the gross worldliness which was undermining the church, it drew its main support from the new and restless elements gathered in the towns. But such success as the reform achieved rapidly evaporated in the following century. The church of the twelfth century pursued wealth, power, and display more openly and eagerly than ever, and a striking feature of the revived worldliness was that the papacy itself took the lead in the movement. The immediate successors of the ascetic Gregory VII found their main satisfaction in increasing the revenues of the Roman see and in tightening their hold on the universal church of which they were the visible head. More and more definitely they assumed the character of absolute monarchs. When at the close of the century Innocent III in characteristically arrogant terms proclaimed this achieved absolutism to the world, far from proving himself an innovator, he did no more than bring a movement of long and slow gestation to its inevitable issue.

The splendid edifice of papal power did not, however, overawe the enemies of ecclesiastical worldliness. On the contrary, more fervidly than before they uttered their protest against a development which, according to them, offended both the original spirit of Christianity and the multitude of God's poor, for whom, according to the declaration of the Fathers, the church had in the first place been established. The masses of the needy were by the twelfth century congregated in the rising towns and, frequently unemployed and always miserable, they were only too ready to listen to a preachment which fell with a peculiar flattery on their ears. When the bolder critics of the prelatical magnificence at last very positively demanded that the church divest itself of its wealth in favor of the poor and return to the simplicity and poverty of apostolic times, the great dignitaries became alarmed and promptly communicated their alarm to the pope. In the hope of silencing the opponents of the ruling trend, not one but several popes of the twelfth century publicly and unambiguously condemned as false the teaching that it was sinful for the church to be endowed with worldly goods. And when Innocent III in his day renewed the anathema in a particularly rigorous form, he was again doing no more than following in the footsteps of his predecessors. By the repeated papal declarations every preacher of, and believer in, apostolic poverty for the church automatically became a heretic.

From its earliest days Christianity had been obliged to wrestle with opinions which, failing to square with the orthodox viewpoint, were condemned as heretical and called for extirpation, at need with fire and sword. Nonetheless the sects charged at one time or another with nursing false doctrines had by no means all disappeared. Some of the more vigorous heretical groups, such as the Cathari, the Manichaeans, the Paulicians, maintained a secret, underground existence throughout the Middle Ages. When the popes of the twelfth century, culminating in the mighty Innocent III, made advocacy of ecclesiastical poverty a heresy, they rendered the older heresies, which though invisible were still alive, an unexpected service. For immediately the indignant new heretics allied themselves with the more ancient outlaws, and a fusion of forces of such dimensions took place that it became a serious threat to the church. More particularly in the flourishing town area of southern France did the movement assume alarming proportions. So numerous and confident did its followers become that they dared go so far as openly to profess their divergent faith. Called Albigenses from the town of Albi, one of the centers of their worship, the rebel believers seemed to be on the point of superseding orthodox Christianity throughout a wide section.

When Pope Innocent III became aware of the crisis which had arisen in southern France, he met it in a manner befitting the unflinching devotee of the law. Heresy had become rampant because the church had been too lenient; the quickest, the only, cure was to pluck it up root and branch. Scorning negotiations, he proclaimed a crusade against the Albigenses under the leadership of the orthodox princes of northern France; and hounded to the attack by the vicar of Christ, these warriors of the Cross turned the blooming cities of Languedoc into a shambles. However, believing also in persuasion, Innocent at the same time under the name of inquisitors dispatched missionaries into the infected area to attempt to win the heretics back to the fold by argument; and this missionary work continued long after the crusade had scored its bloody triumph. When the satisfied pope reviewed his victory, he could persuade himself that in the crusade and inquisition he commanded two tools admirably suited for dealing with religious perversity. He resolved to make the inquisition permanent and to extend its operations to the whole dominion of the church. In 1215 at a General Council held at Rome this body obediently and enthusiastically indorsed the project.

In connection with the traveling missionaries who labored in behalf of orthodoxy in southern France, a Spaniard by the name of Dominic had greatly distinguished himself. He shared the pope's horror of heresy and, like him, was not averse to employing the sword against it; but he also held that force was not enough for the work in hand and that it should not be employed at all until persuasion had been tried and had failed. Since the heretics had been manifestly led astray by evil counselors, Dominic thought it reasonable to suppose that they could be won back to the fold by the sounder arguments of the true believers. What the errant sectaries therefore supremely needed was divinely inspired teaching and preaching. To this end the eager and indefatigable Spaniard gradually gathered a company of like-minded men about him. They became the nucleus of his famous Order of the Preaching Friars. The new society won the approval of the pope, who welcomed it as a valuable ally in his declared war on heresy. As enthusiasm begets enthusiasm, recruits flowed in on Dominic from all sides. In a surprisingly short time his order had spread to every country of the west. Than these blindly devoted brothers no fitter body could be found to give effect to Innocent's expertly devised institution of the inquisition. Accordingly, it was intrusted to their care, and in every country of Europe and particularly in every commune of Italy troubled by the presence of heretics the local Dominican group was charged with a supervision of speech and conscience planned to hold the inhabitants to an unvarying orthodox course. The inquisition long retained something of the idealism associated with a missionary enterprise. More and more, however, it resorted to torture and the faggot and became a ferocious and purely repressive agency. Let no one say that force wins no victories, for after the systematic application through several generations of the inquisitorial horrors heresy lost its hold on the Italian urban elements. While uprooted in Italy, it did, to be sure, persist in other countries assuming ever novel forms determined by the place and hour. Centuries passed before it gained an irresistible momentum and scored a supreme triumph in the movement called the Protestant Reformation. All these subsequent manifestations are a separate story and do not concern us here.

While the sweeping thirteenth-century victory of orthodoxy may be attributed to the inquisition and its watchful special police, the Dominican friars, there remain other factors to be considered. They come into play because medieval Christianity was a highly complex phenomenon. Insofar as it was a church based on law and organization, the inquisition and the Dominican order, which emphasized the ecclesiastical aspect, were notable additions to its strength. But Christianity was also a sum of sentiments and aspirations turning about the love of God; in fact these sentiments constituted the original Christian core, to which the organized church had been afterward added as a convenient practical means of perpetuating the Christian community. It follows therefore that an attack on heresy to be completely successful would have to be conducted with due regard for both the church and the faith. The inquisition and the Dominicans represent the ecclesiastical attack; they signify an action by organization in behalf of organization and their achievement on the strength of the evidence must be admitted to have been remarkable. But had this been all, had the inquisition not been supplemented by a campaign of an emotional and religious character, it is highly doubtful that its success would have been other than temporary and that heresy would have been driven from the field.

And so we come to St. Francis of Assisi, the man who completed the work of St. Dominic by remembering that Christianity was not only an institution but also an unceasing personal search for God. The sole inspiration of St. Francis was the gospels. From beginning to end they spoke to him of divine love, spoke to him indeed so intimately and persuasively that he completely identified himself with their message. When followers gathered about him, they pressed him for a *regula* or rule by which to guide their footsteps. Hesitantly consenting to their request, he drew up a document to which the successor of Innocent, Pope Honorius III, gave his blessing. Thus was founded the Order of the Brothers Minor, commonly called the Order of St. Francis. Taking, like the Dominicans, the three vows of obedience, chastity, and poverty, the Franciscans indicated by the assumption of these pledges their effective derivation from the monastic movement reaching back to the distant days of St. Benedict. But, in spite of this descent, they blazed an entirely fresh trail by aiming at a very different objective from their monastic predecessors. Far from fleeing the haunts of men to seek God in the solitude of forest or desert, the brothers who wore the rough brown garb of St. Francis sought the crowded towns in order to tend the sick, to distribute alms, and to perform the many other services of Christian charity. Since the Dominicans in their earliest phase directed their efforts to preaching and instruction, there was thus a distinct dividing line between the original purposes of the two orders. In point of fact the dividing line soon disappeared, because a rivalry sprang up between them which, on the one hand, pushed the Dominicans into the service of the poor and, on the other hand, induced the Franciscans, but not till after their noble founder's death, to concern themselves with instruction and to seek the honors of scholarship. Already by the second half of the thirteenth century the rivalry was at white heat, and, although each continued to exhibit the characteristic stamp of the genius who had called it into being, both orders were by that time moving along substantially parallel lines of endeavor.

In spite of this close duplication of effort every penetrating consideration of the two orders confirms the opinion that it was not Dominic but Francis who with his message of love made religion again a living force in a doubt-troubled world. If ever teaching was evangelical, it was his, for he tried to live his life from day to day in literal imitation of the Lord Jesus. He was particularly enamored of poverty and never spoke more movingly than when engaged in its praise. But preaching poverty for his friars, he did not preach the poverty of the church, and thus avoided falling under its anathema. He had nothing but reverence for the ecclesiastical order with the pope at its head and unquestioningly held to the belief that there was ample room for his great missionary work within the church as it existed. Therefore without arousing hostility in high places he brought evangelicalism, a strictly limited evangelicalism, it is true, back into favor. In this way he did the church an inestimable service, for the masses who had become estranged from a ceremonial church ruled by great dignitaries separated from themselves by an unbridgable chasm, welcomed in St. Francis and his followers a body of lesser clerical servants, who descended to their own level and preached and practiced love of God and neighbor as the core of Christianity. It was only because the church had become empty of comfort that the people had ever turned against it; but now that comfort was again dispensed, a comfort exactly adjusted to the needs of the lowly and the overburdened, they again made their peace with the church, accepting it as the sure gate to salvation.

As the spirit of Francis shines in all he said and did, it shines also in an act by which he attached great bodies of the laity to his ideals. Not all men, even if they heard the inner call, could abandon shop and family and join the Order of St. Francis; nor could all women join the Order of St. Clare, founded by Clara, the friend and Assisan neighbor of Francis, as the female counterpart of the male order. To meet the case of innumerable devotees who could not leave the world, Francis had the happy inspiration to create a lay adjunct of the two regular Franciscan orders. It is popularly called the Third Order and its members, Tertiaries. It was open to both men and women. Tertiaries did not take the vows prescribed for the regular brothers and sisters, nor did they leave their work or surrender their place in society. They pledged themselves simply to be guided by the spirit of the founder, to live frugally, distribute alms, and love their fellow-men. Large numbers of the laity were in this manner again brought into touch with the original spirit of Christianity as unfolded in the gospels. There is no telling how much the Tertiaries added to the religious fervor of the thirteenth century, although we may guess that the contribution was large. Since the rivalry between Franciscans and Dominicans moved them to copy each other in every possible respect, it followed that the Dominicans were not slow to create a Third Order of their own. Doubtless it did its share to popularize religion and to bring it about that the Christian church of the thirteenth century was probably closer to the hearts of the people of all classes, high and low, than ever before or since.

For us engaged in tracing the many lines of Florentine development, it is a matter of no slight interest to learn how the Florentines were affected by the religious revival connected with the two great orders of begging friars. Over a hundred years earlier they had shown their susceptibility to religious emotions when, carried away by the ascetic preaching of Giovanni Gualberti, they had become the most important Italian center of the reform movement headed in its final phase by Pope Gregory VII. Since all emotions exhibit a tidal action, alternately rising and receding, we are prepared to hear that the ecclesiastical enthusiasm fanned by Gualberti gradually subsided. In the century following the struggle over lay investiture, the church came in for much criticism in the Arno city and many different kinds of heresy won a foothold within the circle of its walls. It was this ecclesiastical rebelliousness, become common throughout Italy, that both Dominic and Francis were prompted to seek out; and as their active missionary spirit kept them in almost uninterrupted movement through the cities of the peninsula, it happened that they brought their message also to Florence. Dominic entered the city apparently only once; of Francis we know with certainty that he was a frequent visitor of the City of the Baptist. It was in the year 1219 that the famous Spanish preacher entered the gates and immediately his magnetic personality caused a Dominican community to spring to life. Two years later it was put in possession of a little insignificant church, Santa Maria Novella, located in the western section of the town just outside the recently completed second circle of walls. The settlement grew rapidly in numbers, riches, and influence so that dormitories and cloisters had to be added and repeatedly enlarged. From practically the day of its founding its friars were intrusted by the pope with the work of the inquisition for the Florentine area, and by their persistent fanatic zeal they gradually overcame the early reluctance of the commune and people to approve of the eradication of dissident opinion by violent means. Before the end of the thirteenth century the Florentine Dominicans had waxed so great that they undertook to replace the inconspicuous original Santa Maria Novella with the magnificent church of that name which still stands. Its scale and grandeur may be accepted as a just index of the importance within the Florentine world which the Dominicans had by that time acquired and which they retained unimpaired for several centuries. From the great Dominican compound there radiated influences which profoundly affected the Florentine religious, moral, intellectual, and artistic development, as we shall have frequent occasion to see. Florentine politics, too, did not escape the Dominican impact. For, as devoted sons of the papacy, the brothers of Santa Maria Novella were the willing channel by which the popes brought a powerful influence to bear in their own behalf on the Arno government.

Although Francis visited Florence many times to bring to it his message of divine love; there is no record of the creation of a Franciscan community in the Arno city till two years after his death. It was in 1228 that a band of Franciscan brothers took over the church of Santa Croce for the preaching of a simple, popular character which was one of their most cherished purposes. Santa Croce was a small, undistinguished building in the eastern part of town just beyond the new or second wall. The local branches of the two great begging orders were thus as far removed from each other physically as possible. But as both equally enjoyed the favor of the citizens, the Franciscan nucleus expanded no less rapidly than the rival organization. Cloisters and dormitories were presently constructed, and just before the end of the thirteenth century the friars were able to replace their first extremely modest house of worship with the famous Gothic structure which is still one of the landmarks of the city. The significance for Florentine civilization of the great Franciscan settlement yields in no respect to that of its Dominican counterpart. Florentine manners and morals and, above all, the Fine Arts were affected at every turn by the congregation of brothers who made their home at Santa Croce. For the pope it became a second center of political support within the town. For, rivals in everything, the Franciscans did not let themselves be outdone by the sons of Dominic in unhesitating devotion to the chair of St. Peter.

From the second quarter of the thirteenth century onward we must think of Florence as provided with two new dynamic centers of religion, the one in the eastern, the other in the western, section of the town. An electric current passed from each of them to the citizen body and from the citizen body flowed back to the two centers. It was a religious and a cultural exchange of great energy which continued unabated for many generations. While both groups of friars put themselves, each in its own way, at the service of the people of Florence, they did not put themselves, at least with anything like the same devotion, at the service of the Florentine government. For, as members of the church, they enjoyed ecclesiastical immunity and dwelt outside the civil order. From the point of view of organization they looked upon themselves, and indeed were, each one a papal citadel within the rising commonwealth. From this Romeward orientation there arose no difficulty so long as the papal and the Florentine governments lived in peace and harmony; but when they disagreed, as they very often did, a grave local tension could not be avoided.

VIII. The Buondelmonte Murder; Guelphs and Ghibellines; Triumph and Failure of Frederick II

THE coming of the podestà at the beginning of the thirteenth century signified a revolution within the consular system. While its meaning has been disputed, it is reasonably clear that it represented an attempt to put an end to the ferocious factional warfare for consular honors among the upper order of the citizens, the milites. We have seen that the great body of the Florentines made up the foot-soldiers or pedites, and that through the public assembly, or parlamentum, the pedites brought a faint flavor of democracy into the consular system. Throughout the consular period, however, the political power was virtually monopolized by the wealthy burghers who rode to war on horseback and were carried on the urban muster rolls as milites. It was human, intensely human, that factions should develop among this ruling class; and in view of the vendetta obligation, which no miles could escape, and of the numerous tower associations admirably suited to give vendetta a prompt effect, it was inevitable that upper-class rivalry in connection with the annual consular elections should lead to ever-recurring civil disturbances. They became more and more numerous toward the turn of the century until a solution had somehow to be found. As other towns in the same case tried the arbiter from without, the foreign podestà, Florence tried him too. By 1207 the new era, the era of the podestà, was well under way.

We may agree that the new chief executive was in more than one respect an improvement on the consuls. That he would suddenly patch up the ancient quarrels among the magnates was not to be expected and did not follow. The quarrels, as part of the long established habits of a group feudally oriented, obstinately continued; in fact, through various circumstances to be presently related, they grew steadily more embittered until, toward the middle of the thirteenth century, a factional conflict had developed of so passionate a nature that it defied every attempt at compromise. Over this inner division the societas militum, representing the unity of the old ruling class, went to pieces; and although one of the nobiliary factions was in the end victorious over the other and the nobles as a class were not immediately wiped out, the ruin of their society must, from their class point of view, be accounted a loss which it was impossible ever again to make good.

For the common people, on the other hand, the disappearance of the society that gave the milites the character of a unified order was bound to prove an immeasurable gain. Unfortunately in the case of our city of Florence we have no evidence covering the early decades of the thirteenth century which tells us just how the pedites reacted in the face of the irritating arrogance and the civic misbehavior of their social superiors. To supply the missing information recourse may fairly be had to neighboring towns, such as Lucca and Siena, where essentially identical social conditions obtained; and in these nearby communes we learn from authentic records that the pedites developed the necessary spirit to take the protection of their interests into their hands. They did so by forming a political society of their own, a *societas populi.* Therewith they declared in substance that their numbers and importance justified their claiming a larger share in the government than had thus far been accorded them. Even though the Florentine popular movement cannot be proved to have reached this fighting stage till some decades later, we know beyond a doubt that Florence experienced a social and economic development identical with that of its Tuscan neighbors. Exactly like them, it boasted throughout the twelfth century a waxing trade, an uninterrupted increase of occupational activities, and an expanding population. Consequently there took place a steady strengthening of the common people throughout the consular age. With the advent of the podestà the Florentine popular elements may quite possibly have tried the experiment of a society of their own, which, quickly quashed by the governing group, has happened to leave no record behind. Be that as it may, at the exact middle of the century (1250) the foot-soldiers of the Arno city did at last form a societas populi of which we have definite news and which developed such amazing power that it ventured to set up a revolutionary government on the basis of its exclusive rule. True, under the stress of unexpected and incalculable forces which, after 1250, overwhelmed Florence and all Tuscany, the first Florentine democracy, celebrated in Florentine annals as *Il Primo Popolo,* lasted only a decade. How it arose and how it fell will be told in the following chapter. At this juncture we are interested in establishing nothing more than this: that the first half of the thirteenth century witnessed a significant social revolution exhibiting two distinct but subtly interrelated phenomena. The first of these was the intensification of faction among the well-to-do, the horsemen (milites), to a point which destroyed their class coherence and brought them to the verge of ruin; the second was the slow rise and gradual emancipation of the common people till with a sudden rush they were able to take over the government. It is this exciting social-political upheaval among the milites and pedites during the first half of the thirteenth century on which our interest will be centered in this chapter.

It lay in the nature of the case that the blood-feuds among the upper class were constantly nursed by fresh episodes, sometimes of a political, sometimes of a personal, character. The podestà had not long replaced the consuls when such an episode befell. Beginning as a purely personal quarrel, it took on a political color, as personal quarrels among a governing group have the habit of doing, and blazed up so prodigiously that the early chroniclers—and the poet Dante as well, who received his local history from these chroniclers—represented it as the prime cause, the veritable *fons et origo* of all the unhappy civil broils in which the town became subsequently engulfed. This is of course an exaggeration, since, conflicts among the nobility being no novelty in Florence, the new outburst was no more than a fresh link in a long chain of incidents reaching back far into the past. Nonetheless the Buondelmonte murder of the year 1216 took hold of the imagination of the citizens to such an extent that, on this ground alone, it is impossible to pass it by. We shall present it in the version of a chronicler who wrote about one hundred years after the event. His story has so authentic a ring that it has been suggested that he must have drawn upon the family records, the *ricordanze,* as they are locally called, of some memoirists close to the main participants. A notable quality of the account that no one will overlook derives from the vivid glimpses it affords of contemporary feudal manners.

A few explanatory words may bring the feudal manners revealed by our selection somewhat more into the open. The story begins with a feast offered by a new-made knight at his country seat some six miles to the west of the city. In this connection we should remind ourselves that knights were a product of the movement of chivalry which originated in northern France about the time of the First Crusade and promptly imposed itself as its most handsome decoration on the rough feudal society characteristic of the whole European west. While every Florentine who was rich enough to own a horse from the angle of civic organization ranked as a miles, not every miles by any means was a knight, that is, an accredited member of the high, informal order of European chivalry. Eligible to knighthood, like the miles of every other country the Florentine miles had to satisfy certain indispensable tests before he could be promoted to the honor to which he aspired. He might then be struck knight after appropriate games and ceremonies of which he and his family were obliged to bear the costs. As not many could afford the heavy expense of these formalities, comparatively few Florentine milites ever gained the knightly dignity; but having gained it, we may be sure that they bore themselves with an added touch of arrogance toward their humbler fellow-citizens. Since a knight continued to be carried on the Florentine official register as a miles, a certain confusion has arisen in regard to the term, as it designates both a horseman and a horseman become a knight. We need not let that particularly disturb us. For us the milites are a social order which includes the knights, the knights being just the more eminent milites who have achieved the honors of chivalry.

At the feast described by our chronicler the food was doubtless plentiful, though by our contemporary standards greatly lacking in variety; and a poverty and simplicity characteristic of the age were indicated by the circumstance that the knights at table were grouped in pairs so that a single plate might do service for two guests. This must be kept in mind if we are to understand why it was that two knights were insulted when a plate was suddenly snatched from under the nose of one of them. It was seized by a clown, one of a large company of mimes, acrobats, and minstrels who in that roving age were wont to make an appearance wherever and whenever invitations to a wedding or a knighting or any gathering whatever of notables had gone forth. If much of the fun of these wandering entertainers was extremely unrefined, its broad note harmonized admirably with the rude tone of the feudal rulers, whose chief idea of amusement was a rough horseplay calculated to evoke a side-splitting laughter. And finally we come face to face with an instance of the terrible vendetta custom. We are aware that spilt blood called for blood and that the obligation rested less on the injured individual than on the individual's family or on the group of associated families to which he belonged. By the time of the murder about to be related, an accommodation of a feud had become permissible. The compounding often took the form of a marriage arranged between members of the aggrieved families. To exorcise hatred and enmity by the merry peal of wedding bells looks like a wildly romantic undertaking. Over and over again it ended dismally in failure, but in the instance under consideration the failure assumed nothing less than tragic proportions bringing death to many and widespread ruin to the town. And now let the unknown chronicler have the floor:[1]

In the year 1216, when Messer Currado Orlandi was podestà, Messer Mazzingo Tegrimi of the family of the Mazzinghi had himself struck knight at a place called Campi, some six miles from Florence, and invited thither all the best people (*tutta la buona gente*) of the town. And when all the knights had sat down to meat, a buffoon snatched away the full plate set before Messer Uberto dell' Infangati, who was paired at table with Messer Buondelmonte de' Buondelmonti. That angered Messer Uberto greatly, and Messer Oddo Arrighi de' Fifanti, a man of valor, roughly reproved him on this account. In reply Messer Uberto told him he lied in his throat, at which Messer Oddo Arrighi tossed a plate full into his face. And the whole assembly was in an uproar. When the tables had been removed, Messer Buondelmonte struck at Messer Oddo Arrighi with a knife and wounded him severely.

As soon as all the company had returned to their homes Messer Oddo Arrighi took counsel with his friends and relatives, among whom were the counts of Gangalandi, the Uberti, the Lamberti, and the Amidei; and their advice was that peace should be concluded over the issue and that Messer Buondelmonte should take for wife the daughter of Messer Lambertuccio de' Amidei, who lived at the head of the bridge. The bride-to-be was the niece of Messer Oddo Arrighi. Accordingly, the marriage contract was drawn up and the peace arranged and on the following day the wedding was to be celebrated. Thereupon Madonna Gualdrada, the wife of Messer Forese Donati, sent secretly for Messer Buondelmonte and when he came spoke to him as follows: knight, you are forever disgraced by taking a wife out of fear of the Uberti and the Fifanti; leave her you have taken and take this other [i.e., her own daughter whom we must imagine her bringing forward at that moment] and your honor as knight will be restored. As soon as he had heard, he resolved to do as he was told without taking counsel with any of his kin. And when on the following day, the morning of Thursday, February 11, the guests of both parties had assembled, Messer Buondelmonte passed through the gate of Santa Maria and went to pledge troth with the girl of the Donati family; and her of the Amidei he left waiting at the church door.

This insult enraged Messer Oddo Arrighi greatly and he held a meeting with all his friends and relatives in the church of Santa Maria sopra Porta. When all were assembled he complained in strong terms of the disgrace put upon him by Messer Buondelmonte. Some counseled that Buondelmonte be given a cudgeling, others that he be wounded in the face. At this spoke up Messer Mosca de' Lamberti: whoever

[1] His chronicle goes under the name of *Pseudo-Brunetto Latini* and has been published by Hartwig, *Quellen und Forschungen,* Vol. II, pp. 221 ff. The translated passage begins on p. 223. The dates, given in the document in accordance with the Florentine calendar, have been accommodated in the translation to the current Christian calendar. The Florentine year began not on January 1 but on the twenty-fifth of March, the reputed day of the Annunciation.

beats or wounds him let him first see to it that his own grave has been dug; what this case requires is not half measures but clean work [*cosa fatta capo ha,* the famous phrase quoted by Dante and destined to become proverbial in the language. An equally terse translation is impossible]. Thereupon they decided that the vendetta was to be carried out at the very place where the injury had been done, when the parties had gathered for the exchange of the marriage vows. And thus it came about that when on Easter morning [with his bride at his side] Messer Buondelmonte in doublet of silk and mantle and with a wreath about his brow came riding over the bridge, no sooner had he arrived at the statue of Mars than Messer Schiatta degli Uberti rushed upon him and, striking him on the crown with his mace, brought him to earth. At once Messer Oddo Arrighi was on top of him and opened his veins with a knife. And having killed him, they fled. The ambush had been in the houses of the Amidei [who, as we have learned, lived at the head of the bridge].

Immediately there was a tremendous tumult. The body of the murdered man was placed on a bier and the bride took her seat on the bier, holding the head in her lap and weeping aloud. And in this manner the procession moved through all Florence.

Before night fell on that bloody Easter day the hostile families had taken up arms and war raged as so often before from tower to tower and street to street till the podestà interfered and imposed a truce. There was nothing particularly novel in the situation, unless it be that the incidents leading to this latest nobiliary brawl presented so many picturesque and romantic features that they became indelibly impressed on the minds of the citizens. The peace patched up by the podestà would last till a fresh event caused the slumbering passions again to flare up. Thereupon local fighting would be renewed, sometimes with the same, sometimes with a different, cast of characters. The podestà proved to be a restraining and moderating influence, and the nobles themselves, especially the older and more judicious elements among them, were loath to let the divisions in their class become irreconcilable. For, should that come about, the societas militum, the organization through which they exercised a dominant political influence, would necessarily suffer shipwreck. However, they were swept along by a current difficult, if not impossible, to control. We get a hint of the danger lying ahead from the chronicler on whom we have just drawn. He concludes his account of the Buondelmonte murder with the following startling words: "On this day . . . for the first time new names were heard, to wit, Guelph party and Ghibelline party." In sum, he lets us know that the traditional upper-class altercations were threatening to take on the character of a permanent schism; and without his expressly telling us, we are instinctively aware that, should distinct parties replace the haphazard divisions which had thus far been the rule among the magnates, their common politico-military society would have to go by the boards.

The names Guelph and Ghibelline loom so large in Italian history for more than two hundred years after this event that we must imperatively look into their origin and significance. We shall assume the obligation the more readily, as the story has its start at Florence where, exactly as the chronicler indicates, the names were first employed. This has been established in so indisputable a fashion by recent investigation that the tale can now be presented without any apologies for regrettable lacunae.[2] Let us imagine ourselves at Florence in the year 1212, some four years before the above-related murder, when Pope Innocent III, having excommunicated Otto IV, dispatched the young king of Sicily, Frederick of Hohenstaufen, to Germany to claim the crown. As to all the other Italian principalities and cities, so also to Florence Innocent issued the strict command to repudiate Otto and acknowledge Frederick. However, the Florentines were slow to obey the papal order, owing to the lively recollection among them of how shabbily they had been treated by the father and grandfather of Frederick. They felt themselves much less threatened in their self-governing aspirations by Otto, at whose hands they had recently enjoyed some not inconsiderable favors. Quite naturally therefore there formed itself in Florence a party of Otto which, since Otto was of the Welf or Guelph family, took the name of the party of the Guelph (*parte del Guelfo*). Contrariwise, those who bowed to the pope's orders and accepted Frederick as sovereign called themselves party of the Ghibelline (*parte del Ghibellino*). The Hohenstaufen family had been long associated with the castle of Waiblingen in Suabia so that "Waiblingen, Waiblingen," was one of the battle-cries with which their followers were wont to charge the enemy. Transformed by the Italian tongue into Ghibellino, this name made an appearance in Florence contemporaneously with Guelfo. Before a generation had passed both names had spread like a ripe contagion into every town and hamlet of Italy. And when the dissemination was complete the Guelphs had become aligned with the church and the Ghibellines with the empire. This is of course the familiar identification of the two terms; but in view of this very familiarity, it is rather startling to observe that on their first raising their heads at Florence the Guelphs were in opposition to the pope, while the Ghibellines, as supporters of the pope's candidate for the empire, enjoyed his hearty indorsement. We may regard this as an accidental quirk or twist resulting from Innocent's momentary support of a young and unknown Hohenstaufen against an unmasked and treacherous Guelph. On the very day on which Frederick, after winning the German crown, made it clear that he would continue the policy of his ancestors, the papal quirk disappeared. No other than the ancestral policy was open to the young Hohenstaufen, who, unless he were prepared to betray his office, would imperatively have to maintain the independence of the state against the church. However, from the moment Frederick showed his true colors, he and his supporters, the Ghibellines, were promptly denounced by the successors of Pope Innocent as persecutors of the church. At this turn of affairs the Guelphs, as opponents of Frederick, gathered under the banner of the papacy. The grouping thus achieved remained characteristic of Italian political life for all the years to come.

But this is only one aspect of the story of the Guelph and Ghibelline partisanship. It would be a grave mistake to think of the Guelphs, whom already by the middle of the thirteenth century we encounter in practically every Italian town, as organized primarily to support the church; and it would be just as erroneous to think of the equally universal party of the Ghibellines as

[2] Davidsohn, *Forschungen,* Vol. IV, pp. 29 ff. "Die Entstehung der Guelfen und der Ghibellinen Partei."

created for the single purpose of serving the empire. Deeply considered, the two parties owed their existence to the communal revolution, the problems of which were much closer to the inhabitants of the towns, and much more real to them, than the relatively remote issue of supremacy so ferociously argued and fought over by empire and church. The point we are trying to make is strikingly illustrated by the case of our very city of Florence. For a hundred years before the conflict between Otto and Frederick, and for over a hundred years after that conflict, the leading issue in Florence was without any question the purely communal problem of political independence. Throughout the consular period there had already been a citizen group which cherished independence as its dearest goal and which, recognizing the empire as the main obstacle to its ambition, opposed the emperor openly when he was feeble and secretly whenever he visited Tuscany with an irresistible army. As at the time of the conflict between Otto IV and Frederick II the imperial authority was negligible, its Florentine enemies did not hesitate to assume a bold front. By supporting Frederick's opponent and calling themselves Guelphs after him, they could even give their boldness an appearance of legality. Their intimate thoughts, we may be sure, turned, not about Otto and Frederick, but about Florence and the increase of their local authority likely to result from the success of their imperial candidate. In the same way their political opponents, the Ghibellines, were concerned, first and foremost, with the enlargement of their power at home. In Ghibelline eyes the empire was still a power to be reckoned with and in the hope of obtaining Frederick's aid for their plan of controlling the city, they ostentatiously tendered him their allegiance.

At the head of the local group of nobles which already during the consular period had built its plans of domination on Hohenstaufen support was the oldest and haughtiest family of the town, the Uberti. Never did a quarrel break out in Florence in the ranks of the governing class without their taking a hand, partly because of their violent feudal manners, partly because of their many ramifications with other leading families either through marriage or by reason of partnership in one of the soaring towers. We have just learned how the head of the house, Schiatta degli Uberti, participated in the Buondelmonte murder, although he was not immediately involved in the offense which had led to the vendetta. His action injected a non-personal, a distinctly political element into the assassination. Moreover, following the murder, the Uberti, we learn, at once took up arms; and with civil war on their hands, they would not fail to see the advantage of adding to their strength by identifying themselves with the cause of Frederick. This decision by the Uberti would of itself suffice to persuade the Buondelmonti and the Buondelmonti adherents to seek the advantage certain to accrue from adopting the opposite or Guelph cause. It will not do to press these tentative political alignments too closely. The situation was as fluid as water and long continued to remain so. But it is fairly clear that it was over nothing other than the issue of local control that the two factions of the nobility, which had so dramatically collided in 1216, tended to consolidate into parties, although the final step, from which there was no retreat, was not taken till several decades later. Only when the division had at length reached that decisive point do we find the Uberti faction definitely organized as the Ghibelline party and the Buondelmonte faction just as uncompromisingly identified with the Guelphs. Each party, though essentially local, was ready at any time to accept help from without the town, the Uberti from the emperor and his allies, the Buondelmonti from the pope and such friends as the papacy commanded; and in return for help received from outside partisans each party was of course prepared to come to the aid of these outsiders. Undoubtedly therefore both the Guelphs and Ghibellines of Florence had a foreign policy and made their influence felt beyond the limits of their city. Just the same the most ardent concern of both parties was always the domestic situation, for each aimed at the exclusive rule of the passionately loved town.

The rapid radiation of the Guelph-Ghibelline animosity from Florence over Tuscany and thence over Italy, though puzzling at first sight, is easily explained on the ground of the essentially identical conditions among all the young city-republics. In every Italian commune the governing group around the year 1200 had fallen into two rival factions; and in their struggle for supremacy each local faction eagerly sought the support of some power stronger and more permanent than itself. Within the whole peninsula there were just two powers of this kind available, the empire and the papacy. It is the tie-up effected between an infinity of circumscribed local interests and the issue of church and state, general to the whole peninsula, that gave the two parties their broadly national character. Far more surprising, on the whole, than the ubiquity of Guelphs and Ghibellines is the extraordinary rancor that marked their rivalry. Partisanship is so unfailing a feature of every great historical development that, within limits, we are prepared to accept it as a positive sign of health. But partisanship in the Italian city-republics reached such a height and frenzy of virulence that life must have been conducted perpetually at wasteful fever heat. Not content with civil warfare with its but too familiar accompaniment of riot, arson, and murder, Guelphs and Ghibellines carried their differences into every conceivable field of human expression. You knew a Guelph from a Ghibelline by the cut of his doublet, by the angle at which he wore the feather in his cap, by the shape of the battlements that crowned the family tower. Luckily these extravagances, like the parties themselves, were largely limited to the upper order; also they did not reach their climax till the passage of one or more generations had permitted the movement to gather momentum. We are here dealing with its infancy and have still to show how in this phase it was deeply affected by a great, a masterful individual. This was the Emperor Frederick II, to whom an all but universal opinion points as the outstanding personality of his age.

When, after an absence of eight years in Germany, Frederick II returned to Italy and in 1220 was crowned emperor at Rome by Pope Honorius III, he was a vigorous, self-assured young man of twenty-six. He had just assumed toward the pope, and in the most solemn manner, the obligation of leading a crusade to the Holy Land; but before setting out for the east, he obtained permission to visit his kingdom of Sicily, where his presence was required in order to revive the royal authority seriously impaired through his long absence in the north. Once in his native kingdom, he resolved to engage on a far-reaching reorganization. This domestic program of his revealed his vigorous political initiative, for it signified nothing less than the replacement of the anarchic self-government of the feudal barons with a centralized bureaucracy under royal control. So radical an undertaking could not be carried through under many years. On being reminded by the pope from time to time of his crusading vow, he excused himself by the pressure of work in his Sicilian home as well as throughout his kingdom of Italy. However, to placate Honorius he met the wishes of the Holy Father in other respects, less immediately important to himself. He agreed, for instance, to satisfy a papal demand of long standing by bringing the civil authorities into line with the ecclesiastical rulers in the uprooting of heresy. Thus it came about that Frederick became the sponsor of the most rigorous criminal code *contra hereticos* that was ever devised; and repeatedly during his reign he issued peremptory orders to the governments of all the Italian communes to incorporate this ferocious legislation in their local constitutions. It is impossible to explain this hearty seconding of the papal inquisition by a man of Frederick's skeptical and secular outlook except on the ground of political opportunism.

In the year 1227 the mild and conciliatory Honorius died and was succeeded by Gregory IX, a man no whit less imperious than the fiery Innocent III. In the new pope's view his predecessor had been trifled with by the slippery young man on the imperial throne; and when Frederick seemed to be at his old tricks with him too, Gregory promptly banned him from the Christian fold. Without waiting to have the ban removed, Frederick in June, 1228, set sail for the east, thereby affording the world the curious spectacle of an excommunicated Christian prince faring on crusade to wrest the Holy Land from an infidel foe. Europe was even more dumbfounded when, without fighting a single battle, this strange crusader, whom all the faithful were ordered to avoid like the plague, gained what thousands of earlier crusaders under the special blessing of the church had died in a vain effort to achieve. In simple fact, and in spite of his expedition in behalf of the Cross, Frederick did not at any time have his heart in the enterprise. He was just a calculating diplomat governed by common-sense considerations and, on finding the Moslem ruler over Syria disposed to come to terms, he promptly signed a treaty with that sovereign by which Jerusalem and a few adjoining districts were delivered into his hands. Thereupon he crowned himself king of Jerusalem and, with fame sounding its trumpets before him, returned to Italy. Many were rejoiced by his success but the head of Christendom was not among them. As there was no denying, however, that Frederick had brought the Holy Places of Palestine back into Christian possession, Gregory let himself be gradually drawn into negotiations. They ended in his cancelling his curse and signing a general treaty of reconciliation (1230).

The new peace between pope and emperor soon proved a sham, as had the long roster of its predecessors. So long as the empire made claims that the church would not recognize and vice versa, every treaty signed between the two adversaries could be nothing better than a truce. The new peace would last, exactly like the many that had gone before, until some fresh event deeply affected the relationship of the two parties and made them disposed to have recourse to war in the hope of improving their position. The rupture of the treaty of 1230 did not occur till almost a decade later in consequence of the open and avowed renewal, on the part of Frederick, of his grandfather's attempt to bring the Lombard cities under the imperial yoke. Without any question he had been pondering the reopening of this crucial issue ever since his coronation in 1220; but the complicated business of reorganizing Sicily and, afterward, the innumerable troubles released by the crusade absorbed his energy and he had been obliged to curb his impatience.

Frederick II was a man so responsive to the new modes of thought and feeling beginning to stir in Europe in his day that in many respects he would seem to have stepped across the threshold of the Middle Ages into the modern world. Child of a Sicilian mother and brought up in southern Italy, where Christian and Moslem influences met and mixed, he had developed an intellectual skepticism which rendered him completely immune to the religious fervor characteristic of an age of faith. Far from being a help to him as a ruler, his critical attitude of mind proved to be a heavy liability in a society which, still medieval, was just then passing through a vast religious revival championed by the two begging orders. Both Dominicans and Franciscans instinctively sensed the emperor's intellectual emancipation and worked against him secretly and openly by every means at their disposal. From pulpit and street-corner they denounced him—and in so doing they were probably not far from the truth—as a secret follower of the Arab philosopher, Averroes, and consequently as an infidel and a rationalist. Again, on grounds no less valid, they poured the vials of their wrath over him as an Epicurean and a sensualist. For, endowed with delicate senses as well as with an alert mind, Frederick delighted in all the refinements and luxuries with which the west had become acquainted since it had re-established contact with the east through the crusades. He made his court the most elaborate and exquisite of his age. In his palaces and gardens knights and ladies joined in pleasant intercourse and listened to those alluring entertainers out of the Provence, the troubadours, who sang the love of woman and gloried in the beauty of the earth. Frederick himself wrote verses in the Provençal manner and is deservedly celebrated as one of the earliest adepts of Italian lyric poetry. It was in the realm of sex that the oriental influences which he had assimilated manifested themselves in the most conspicuous manner. For by openly maintaining a harem he revealed that he had succumbed to the sensuous languors of another and a softer civilization.

This fluid individual, who succeeded in bursting through so many of the current medieval limitations, is immediately important to us only on the side of his political activity. That Frederick was capable of thinking just as fresh thoughts in the political field as in philosophy and poetry was proved by the reform he carried through in Sicily. It amounted to nothing less than replacing the loose and wasteful feudal system with an efficient monarchical absolutism. When, many generations later, absolutism revealed itself throughout the extent of Europe as the common remedy for feudal anarchy, Frederick had been long forgotten; but that cannot deprive him of the honor of having been perhaps the first European, certainly the first Italian, ruler, not merely to project, but actually to create a modern state. We hail him therefore as a political innovator but—and here we encounter one of those contradictions which no complex character seems to be able to escape—when he faced the issue raised by the prosperous north Italian towns, he was incapable of seeing it in any other than in the conservative light in which it had presented itself to his father and grandfather before him. To him, as to them, the communes were exercising or attempting to exercise self-governing rights which were an infringement on the sacred imperial authority. To be sure, the Lombard group of towns had secured an acknowledgment of their freedom in the victorious treaty of Constance (1183) and were therefore fairly within their rights; but the indisputable legality of their very substantial independence did not make it any more agreeable to contemplate. Frederick pondered the situation in the spirit of an obstinate aristocrat, whose heart stirred with contempt for upstart traders and craftsmen daring to challenge the long-established authority of their betters; and following his reconciliation with Pope Gregory IX in 1230, he made up his mind that the time had come to take the matter actively in hand. As the Lombard cities commanded great resources and were well armed, he was obliged to proceed with a considerable measure of caution. And when he was at last ready and about to strike, he was checked by a revolt which broke out in 1235 in Germany. Hurrying thither to suppress it, he did not return to Italy till two years later. Then at last the storm broke with extraordinary fury. As it broke in Lombardy, its details do not concern us. It will suffice if we trace the general course of Lombard events in order to understand the important repercussions they produced in Tuscany.

On November 27, 1237, Frederick unexpectedly fell upon the army of the Lombard league at Cortenuova and defeated it utterly. In his exultation he imagined he had reversed the decision of Legnano and had made himself master of northern Italy. He soon learned he was mistaken, for, in spite of defeat, first one town and then another defied him, obliging him continuously to hold the field and spend his energy on a succession of tedious and wasteful sieges. In this manner years passed during which the terror spread by the Cortenuova triumph gradually evaporated. Besides, in 1239 Pope Gregory terminated his neutrality and actively entered the game. We cannot but agree that it was normal for the papacy to join whatever agency was resisting its ancient enemy, the empire; and Gregory, secretly rejoicing over Frederick's waxing difficulties in Lombardy, stepped out into the open against him just as soon as the moment seemed auspicious. Less than two years after Cortenuova the pope stiffened the ranks of the Lombard opposition by once more excommunicating the emperor. At the same time those formidable cohorts of the papacy, the Dominicans and Franciscans, went up and down the land inflaming the common people against the Hohenstaufen sovereign, whom they denounced in unbridled language. They called him a heretic and limb of Satan and in their frenzy even spread the ominous whisper that he was that most fearful of all visitations, the anti-Christ, forerunner of the Last Judgment.

The considerable military power commanded by Frederick was bound in the long run to exhaust itself against the combination of Lombard resolution, papal authority, and religious fanaticism. Slowly but inexorably his cause turned to its setting. When Gregory died in 1241, he was succeeded by Innocent IV, and the new pontiff, even more grimly hostile than his predecessor, resolved to make the chasm between himself and his opponent absolutely unbridgeable. At a General Council of the church, which he summoned to meet him at Lyons in France, not only did he excommunicate the emperor anew but, as earlier popes had done with earlier emperors, he went further and declared him deposed from office (July 17, 1245). Misfortunes now crowded on the unhappy man in a bewildering succession. The pope succeeded in setting up a rival king in Germany; Frederick's army suffered a crushing defeat at Parma at the hands of the Lombards; the Bolognese captured his favorite son, Enzio, and clapped him in prison. He bore the multiplied blows of fate with unshaken fortitude and till death visited his tent kept his banners waving in the wind.

Before coming to this closing scene we must catch up with the very important developments in Tuscany and Florence. From the day of his accession to the empire, Frederick had been in the habit of sending representatives to Tuscany to exercise the rights which were his traditional due in that province. Conspicuously ignored by the expanding towns and, more particularly, by Florence, these agents led an obscure existence, far from calculated to enhance their master's credit. The terror produced by Cortenuova, however, changed this ignominious situation almost over night. A new emissary, a certain Gebhard of Arnstein, issued the command to the Tuscan towns to acknowledge the imperial authority without more ado; and the bitterly divided communes, unable to agree on united action, were obliged to obey. Proud Florence was no exception to the rule. Gebhard wisely made its submission easy by refraining from excessive demands. The Arno city was permitted to retain its constitution with the provision that the podestà, before entering on office should receive the indorsement of the emperor (1238). Presently Gebhard was replaced as legate in Tuscany, and with each new year his successors clipped from the Florentines one or another of their cherished liberties. The insidious process continued till all the boasted gains since the Tuscan league of 1197 had been cancelled and the town had been unequivocally subjected to the emperor. Florence had become a humbled Ghibelline community.

The acceptance by Florence as podestà of Frederick's illegitimate son, Frederick of Antioch, marks the culmination of the disastrous development. It was in 1246 that the younger Frederick became ruler of the city. Since his father appointed him at the same time as vicar-general in Tuscany, his rule extended over the whole province. By taking up his residence in Florence he automatically made this city, in place of the historic San Miniato del Tedesco, the focus of the imperial administration. In the name of the emperor the son, whose talents and gallantry made him a representative worthy of his famous father, appointed the podestàs, the judges, and the notaries throughout his territory. So far as it is possible to penetrate into the secret places of the emperor's mind, he seems to have planned to provide Tuscany with a bureaucratic government fashioned after the regime he had introduced into his kingdom of Sicily. If that is true, he failed to take account of the fact

hat Tuscany and Sicily were two entirely distinct societies. While the south-
rn kingdom was still overwhelmingly agrarian and feudal, Tuscany had
ecome revolutionized by commerce and took its political tone from a flourish-
ng body of irrepressible towns. From the day of his assumption of the im-
erial scepter in 1220 the weakness of Frederick's statesmanship was and
emained that he failed to appreciate the vigor, the valor, and the ultimate
ecessity of the new burgher society volcanically pushing upward through the
eudal crust. Indeed his blindness to this complex of irresistible energies gives
im, who was in so many respects aware of psychological realities hidden from
is contemporaries, something of the air of a misguided Don Quixote. It is
ertainly necessary to search far and wide in history before finding anything
nore fantastically quixotic than Frederick's lifelong labor to build a dam
gainst the vast new forces that were in his day engaged in reshaping the
vorld. They might delay their action in the deceptive manner of such forces;
ut in their own good time they would with an explosive energy that could
ot be checked sweep the emperor's puny obstructions, together with his per-
on, out of their path.

When Frederick of Antioch became the all-powerful vicar-general of Tus-
any, he found that he faced a Florentine opposition which was no less alive
or having gone temporarily into hiding. We have learned that the local
Guelphs were a group of the nobility who favored the independence of their
ity from the empire, and who in pursuit of this bold policy sought the sup-
ort of the papacy. The Ghibellines, on the other hand, leaned toward the
mpire in the hope of being rewarded for their fidelity with the rule of the
ity. We have seen that the two distinct trends went back at least to the latter
alf of the consular era, and that since the Buondelmonte murder of 1216 the
nimosities that gave them birth had steadily increased. Notwithstanding, up
o the appearance in Florence of Frederick of Antioch in 1246, the Guelph-
Ghibelline quarrel had not yet been carried to a final and irrevocable schism.
That schism was now to take place; and at the same time the common people,
ong disaffected toward the lawless and high-handed nobles in their midst,
vere to be prompted to rise in an attempt of their own to free the city from
oreign control and by that act to secure its government for themselves. As
o the common people or *popolani,* they were not, at least not yet at this time,
ither Guelph or Ghibelline. This distinction had arisen in the upper order
nd long remained peculiar to it. However, as the Florentine commoners also
avored the liberation of their city from the imperial yoke, they clearly nursed
entiments of a general Guelph nature. Consequently, in the struggle between
he two groups of nobles for control they leaned, though somewhat hesitantly
t first, toward the Guelph side. In the course of time and in measure as the
Ghibellines more and more flagrantly offended the burgher passion for inde-
endence, the merchants and craftsmen turned their backs on them, until the
our came when *guelfismo,* that is, a settled Guelph disposition of mind,
ecame characteristic of the whole population. Therefore in the days ahead,
vhen Florence, having disfranchised the nobles, became a democratically
riented society, it consistently comported itself as a Guelph commonwealth.
But this historical Guelphism must not be thought of as going back to the

first half of the thirteenth century nor should it be regarded as a blind sub
mission to the papacy. Essentially it was a passionate patriotism expressin
itself in frenzied hatred of every individual or party threatening the city
independence.

On the emperor's young son taking over the reins in Florence, he foun
himself enthusiastically but interestedly supported by the Ghibelline factio
headed by the great family of the Uberti. To put their services in the bes
light they lost no opportunity to denounce their Guelph enemies as secretl
nursing treasonable projects. And while these Guelphs may have been quie
for the moment, it was certain, even though the charge might not be possibl
to prove, that they were in touch with the papal court and its army of be
ligerent friars spread over Italy and sleeplessly busy at stirring up the excitabl
masses against the excommunicated emperor. In so nervous an atmospher
clashes between the two magnate groups within the city walls were inevitabl
Whenever they occurred, young Frederick regularly sided with the Ghibe
lines. After a particularly severe brawl at the beginning of 1248 the Guelph
in a state of panic, on Candlemas Day (February 2), abandoned the city. The
retired to the hills, where they had castles and retainers, and where they wer
better prepared to offer resistance than in their crowded city quarters. When
ever the Ghibellines organized an expedition to pursue their foes to one o
another of their many retreats, a combat flared up which threw the whol
countryside into confusion. In connection with these violent new disorder
we have mention for the first time of *capitani dei Guelfi*. The title admits c
no other interpretation than that the exiles had given themselves a party or
ganization under elected officials. And if the Guelphs now went this length
the Ghibellines must be supposed to have done the same. The division in th
magnate group, which had repeatedly threatened during recent decades bu
which had always been patched up again, thus became final, and the ol
societas militum, sign and guaranty of magnate solidarity, came to an enc
When we reflect that the nobles had been able to exercise their political pre
ponderance in the past through this class organization, we realize what a fata
blow they struck their own ascendancy by their incurable partisan hatrec
And since it is pertinent to our understanding of the situation, let us not fai
to note that even though the societas militum now vanished from the scene
the obligation of the individual miles to serve in the citizen army remaine
unimpaired. Henceforth the nobles still rode to war, the Guelphs unde
Guelph captains, the Ghibellines under Ghibelline captains, but, thus dividec
they weighed considerably less both in war and in politics.

In connection with the Candlemas Day exodus of their enemies, the Ghibel
lines were guilty of an act of vengeance which constituted an innovation i
the practices of local warfare, and which was destined in the end to be visite
on their own heads with compound interest. Unable to lay their hands on th
persons of the Guelphs, the victors vented their spite on their foes' inanimat
possessions. Some thirty-six structures, most of them towers, belonging to th
exiles were in blind fury leveled with the ground. Among them was a towe
of the Adimari over two hundred feet high. As it stood near the graveyar
adjoining the baptistry of St. John, it was called *Il Guardamorto* (Guardia

›f the Dead); and when it was brought down without damage to the town's nost beloved ecclesiastical monument, excited citizens with Guelph sympathies vho witnessed the destruction declared that they saw the falling tower de- lected in mid-course by the miraculous intervention of the Baptist himself.[3]

Owing to the manifest decline of the emperor's fortunes in the late forties, pasmodic revolts multiplied all over Tuscany and obliged the vicar-general, 'rederick of Antioch, to spend much of his time in the field away from 'lorence. One of these absences in the autumn of 1250 led to momentous onsequences. By suddenly attacking the Ghibelline host encamped at Figline bove Florence, the exiled Guelphs won a notable victory. No sooner had the iews of this rout reached the city than it encouraged the people to attempt o regain their freedom. In the course of the last decade not only had they een saddled with every form of vexatious taxation, but they had also been bliged to surrender their hard-won independence and humbly bend their iecks under an imperial governor. To the cry *Viva il Popolo* they gathered n the streets and churches, resolved to recover their liberty. Before the absent 'icar-general could assemble the necessary forces to crush the revolt he was eached by information which struck the sword from his hand. On December ;, 1250, the Emperor Frederick had died in southern Italy. Like the rest of the vorld, the son saw at once that with the death of his father the whole artificial 'rederician system was doomed and, bowing to the will of the gods, he put he spurs to his horse and rode away. Florence was therefore left in the hands f its rebellious inhabitants, and without risk of interference from on high hey set about giving themselves the kind of government they desired. As the evolution was the work exclusively of the people, and as neither the Guelph ıor the Ghibelline faction of the nobles had had a hand in it, the triumphant ommoners provided themselves with a constitution in which for the first time ince the rise of the commune the decisive influence was attributed to them- elves. The period thus inaugurated goes by the name of the First Democracy *Il Primo Popolo*).

The new government was characterized by two outstanding features. Since he people had made the revolution, and since they were aware that they could ıot retain their power except by military means, they formed themselves into wenty companies under a single leader. This was the *capitano del popolo,* vho could mobilize his companies instantly at the ringing of a bell. The capi- ano was by no means to replace the traditional ruler, the podestà, but was to unction at his side as the special protector of the people. Indeed the tradi- ional government of the podestà was left substantially intact on the under- tanding that it should henceforth be more responsive to the people, who, rganized into a military society under an elected head, had risen to a novel osition of authority. It was wholly in the spirit of this experimental age not o evolve an entirely new government from preliminary theoretical considera- ions, but, taking over the old core, to add to it the features expressive of the ıewest energies of the commonwealth. This viewpoint accounts for the second mportant element of the new constitution. Since the civil powers inherent in he office of the podestà were hardly, if at all, diminished by the rise of a popu-

[3] Villani, VI, 33.

lar official like the capitano, the sponsors of the revolution, convinced that they needed an office capable of acting as a check on the podestà, created the *anziani* (ancients). This was a body of twelve good and true men of the people, two for each of the *sesti* (sixths) into which the city was divided. They were charged with the general supervision of the state and its finances. Above all, they were expected to breathe a vivifying democratic spirit into the revolutionary system. And that they actually did so is proved by the fact that ever afterward the twelve anziani signified to the Florentines the very substance of their first democratic venture.[4]

Before taking up the exciting and colorful career of the new government we may pause to consider the death of the sovereign, on whom rumor fed so busily in his day that he threatened to become a legend while still in the flesh. Extraordinary and amazing rather than great, Frederick puzzled his contemporaries with his many unresolved contradictions, as he has continued to puzzle all the later generations. Even with his death he added to the mixture of terror, awe, and bewilderment with which he was generally regarded. He died at Fiorentino in Apulia; and fifty years later, when Villani wrote his chronicle, there still circulated a tale regarding his demise which is so revealing in respect both to Frederick's unfathomed character and to the murky atmosphere of an age whose religion was shot through with the weirdest superstitions that we must imperatively give it our attention. In spite of Frederick's rationalism, which liberated him from many of the prejudices of his time, he continued to hold firmly that the stars controlled the lives of men and, consequently, he governed himself as far as possible in accordance with the prognostications of his court astrologers. Now these magi of his had frequently warned him against Florence (Fiorenza), because in Florence he would meet his death. He scrupulously obeyed the admonition; and although he moved tirelessly up and down Italy throughout his life and was repeatedly in Tuscany, it is an established fact that he never set foot within the Arno town. But no one can escape his destiny. Consequently when the emperor died, it was indeed not in the Tuscan commune but in a small Apulian town with an all but identical name (Fiorentino). Good old Guelph Villani fully believed the current tale, especially as he too had complete faith in the astrological mysteries. He took exception, however, to one point. Instead of the emperor's receiving the warning from honorable astrologers, he had received it from one of the demons with whom he, as an indubitable son of Satan, habitually consorted. And the chronicler closes his account with this gloating comment: "Ill did he understand the lying word of the demon, which bade him beware of dying in Fiorenza but not of dying in Fiorentino."[5]

[4] The constitution of 1250 has not survived. It has been carefully reconstructed from other documents by Davidsohn, Vol. II[1], pp. 367-73.

[5] Villani, VI, 41.

IX. Il Primo Popolo or The First Democracy (1250–60)

EMPEROR FREDERICK II had filled so large a place during his life that his death created an immense vacuum. It was as if he had taken the empire with him into his tomb; and although he was survived by one legitimate and several illegitimate sons, so complete was the collapse of his power that few contemporaries believed it could ever, even in part, be revived. His legitimate son and acknowledged heir was a young man, who, having been crowned king of Germany in Frederick's lifetime, was known as Conrad IV. During his father's last phase he had represented the emperor in the northern kingdom. But the excommunication and deposition of Frederick decreed by the council of Lyons had broken Germany into factions and rocked it to its foundations. Conrad might conceivably have triumphed over his many difficulties, had he not preferred to rush to Italy on his father's death in order to assume the Sicilian inheritance. Sicily, too, was in turmoil, owing to a baronial uprising provoked by the pope. Conrad had a difficult fight on his hands; and hardly had he mastered the situation when he died (May 21, 1254), a victim, like his grandfather, the mighty Henry VI, of the fever which has frequently been the best ally of this southern people against an intruder from the north. While Conrad's son and heir, Conradin, a mere babe in arms, was growing up in Germany, the maintenance of the Hohenstaufen cause in Sicily devolved on Manfred, the emperor's illegitimate son and uncle of the distant Conradin. Manfred's position, however, was highly precarious, for, more firmly than ever, the pope was resolved to transfer the crown of Sicily to some other house than that of Suabia. Therefore, under the most favorable circumstances, a struggle awaited the Hohenstaufen champion which would engage his attention for years to come. The bare facts here recited should make it clear that for some years following the demise of Frederick II the imperial cause was prostrate throughout Italy, and that Florence, the great rebel community of mid-Italy, was free to realize its ambitions without interference from above.

Although the new Florentine government was a democratic innovation and represented a revolt against the traditional ascendancy of the nobles, it took over the foreign policy of its predecessor without changing it by a hair's breadth. That policy went back in a straight line to the earliest days of the commune. In the initial stage its aim had been the mastery of the Florentine county by clearing it of the oppressive feudal lords. But no sooner had this purpose been achieved than, the appetite growing with what it fed on, the neighboring counties began to look desirable; and by the time the podestà replaced the consuls Florentine ambition ventured to lift its eyes to Tuscany itself as the goal of its endeavor. Toward the middle of Frederick II's reign and just before that emperor, following the battle of Cortenuova, turned his attention to the control of Tuscany, Florence had already won a dominant position in the Arno Valley. When this not only had to be given up but was replaced by an abject subservience to the emperor's agents, a despair settled on the city which at last found vent in the explosion of 1250. Taking over at once and without opposition the rule of its county, the new government, which from the first day exhibited an amazing daring and vitality, returned to the program of the pre-Frederician period and resumed the struggle, to which Frederick had put a stop and which aimed to bring all Tuscany under Florentine control.

In our own time we call such a policy imperialism and recognize that it is primarily prompted by the energy of an expanding commercial community. It is therefore highly probable that what we may call the Florentine imperialism of this and the subsequent centuries was a response primarily to the demands of an enterprising merchant class. However, as the imperialist trend goes back to the consular age, although in those early days it was but a feeble plant, we are driven to the conclusion that the nobles whose names were prevalent at the head of the government were *themselves* the great merchants who were already at that time the hidden directive force of the state. When after the revolution of 1250 the victorious democracy without delay struck out on the same path, we must again conclude that, the new popular apparatus notwithstanding, it was still the bankers and foreign traders who imposed their policy on the government. If this is true, the continuity of Florentine foreign policy, just noted, loses its quality of mystery. Regardless of the forms successively assumed by the government, the merchants would seem to have been and, as we shall have occasion to see hereafter, would seem to have remained, the controlling factor. In the case of the Primo Popolo, with which we are dealing in this chapter, the artisans and shopkeepers undoubtedly shared in the government and thereby gave it a popular character; but there was nothing in the system to keep the great bankers and merchants from exercising hidden, essential control and, in the sacred name of home and country, persuading the whole citizen body to make the merchant policy its own.

By its very first act in the foreign field the new government committed itself to a policy of bold aggression. It persuaded a count of the great Aldobrandesca family, which held a position in the Sienese region analogous to that of the Guidi clan around Florence, to lease the port of Talamone to the Arno city. True, Talamone was a miserable little village with a silted harbor which has defied the many efforts made in the course of the ages to render it practicable; but its obstinate resistance to improvement had not yet been established, when in the spring of 1251 a sudden diplomatic stroke established Florence on the coast of the Maremma. While the action was particularly resented by Siena, which on geographic grounds regarded the Maremma coast as lying within its sphere of influence, it also alarmed Pisa with the prospect of the creation of a rival port to its immediate south. The prompt result was a defensive league of the two towns, to which Pistoia, perpetually threatened by nearby Florence, joined itself as a third member. Inasmuch as these three towns had usually in the past sided with the empire, theirs was naturally a Ghibelline league, to which Florence, the confirmed enemy of the empire, opposed just as naturally the Guelph league of itself and Lucca. Since Ligurian Genoa was always ready to unite in any action aimed at its maritime rival, Pisa, no difficulty was encountered in adding Genoa to the Guelph combination. Tuscany, thus divided, was threatened with a struggle which would not leave the remotest village undisturbed.

The war broke out at once and lasted for four years. Its most outstanding feature was the unbounded energy displayed by democratic Florence. Although neither Lucca nor Genoa withheld their aid, Florence engaged in the conflict with such sustained fervor that the victories won over each of the Ghibelline foes in turn or over all of them in combination were primarily the work of the Arno city. From the start it aimed its attack at the weakest link in the Ghibelline chain, at Pistoia. Blockading the town and cruelly harrying the countryside, the Florentines usually waited till the Sienese and Pisans brought up a relieving army, when they would throw themselves on the advancing forces with ferocious impetuosity. It was the tactics of an unwavering offensive admirably expressive of the indomitable mood of the people. Under these circumstances little Pistoia was after a few campaigns reduced to the last extremity and obliged to sue for peace. Signed on February 1, 1254, the treaty spelled, in substance, submission to Florentine control.

It was now Siena's turn. The Florentines invaded the Sienese contado and systematically laid waste its fields and olive orchards. After appealing in vain to Pisa which, caught in a vise between Lucca and Genoa, was unable to render help, the exhausted Sienese offered to come to terms some five months after the surrender of Pistoia. The main demand of the Florentines was that the small hill towns of Montalcino and Montepulciano, lying in the southern part of Siena's county, should be given their independence. The stipulation admits of no other interpretation than that the victors planned to use the two liberated communities as points of support for their own ultimate expansion into southern Tuscany. Thus only Pisa remained to be dealt with. Cruelly pressed by her three enemies without and paralyzed by an outbreak of factions within, Pisa broke down in its turn, hardly more than a month after Siena had yielded to Florentine might. The leading article of the treaty signed with Pisa was a plain indication that Florence had already convinced itself of the vanity of its Talamone plans; for, by this article Florence fastened on Pisa as its best possible outlet to the Mediterranean markets by acquiring the privilege of importing and exporting its goods *via* Pisa free from all customs dues. For the elated Florentines the year 1254 became and remained ever afterward "the year of victory." It did not detract from the glory won in that *annus mirabilis* that the Pisans, consumed by chagrin, delayed the execution of the peace for a number of years. In the end they had to swallow their pride and acknowledge that the hegemony in Tuscany, so long enjoyed by them, had passed to the upstart inland rival.

On the inauguration of the war in 1251 Florence had attempted to win the support of the common people throughout the Tuscan world by proclaiming that she was fighting the battle of democracy. By coming to the aid of Montalcino and Montepulciano in their struggle against Siena she could with a certain plausibility establish the added claim that she was the champion of the small Tuscan towns against the greed of their larger neighbors. In a struggle for power an alert and unscrupulous opponent will not neglect to avail himself of the imponderable moral values. When, however, with the victory won Florence surveyed a submissive Tuscany, she cast the mask aside and frankly revealed her plan of complete Tuscan control. With the large towns prostrate the small towns, at least all those within convenient reach, were absolutely at her mercy. At a nod from the imperious democracy they came to terms; and when a nod did not suffice, they yielded precipitately before the threat of military action. The most important single area of small towns was the hill region of the Elsa Valley, where the spheres of influence of Pisa, Florence, and Siena met and overlapped. Here three towns, Poggibonsi, San Gimignano, and Volterra had taken advantage of the balance hitherto maintained among their three large neighbors to set up independent governments, behind which they put all the unreasoning fervor characteristic of the communal age. In the eyes of their citizens life without independence or, as they preferred to call it liberty, lost half its value. However, when victorious Florence had become queen of Tuscany, the independence could not be sustained, and the three towns were obliged, with what deep heart-burnings the future would reveal again and again, to accept their fate.

For the Arno city, still young in conquest, it now became imperative to work out a method of control for its dependencies. It is interesting to observe how the early measures dealing with this problem had a purely empirical character and differed considerably in detail. A usual requirement was that the subject town should accommodate itself to the Florentine political system, preferably by taking over bodily the constitution of 1250. It was an ingenious procedure calculated to make Tuscany, along with Florence, safe for democracy. Another demand commonly imposed was that the chief local official, the podestà, should be selected from among the citizens of Florence. Finally, as a safeguard against rebellion, which had always to be reckoned with, the dependent community was required either to demolish its walls or to suffer a fortress, a so-called *cassero,* to be built at a strategic point within the walls and to be garrisoned by Florentine troops. The latter measure was imposed on Volterra, the former on Poggibonsi and San Gimignano.[1] One procedure was probably as successful as the other so long as the hegemony of Florence remained unchallenged; but let her rule appear to be shaken and straightway hope would visit the unreconciled spirits of her subjects and move them, regardless of the risk they ran, to attempt to strike off their chains.

The triumphs of 1254 were still on every tongue when Florence supplemented the peace treaty with Siena by a treaty of alliance (1255). By its terms the City of the Virgin, as the Sienese delighted to call their town, accepted

[1] Davidsohn, *Forschungen,* Vol. IV, p. 115. "Die erste Unterwerfung von Pistoia, Poggibonsi Volterra und San Gimignano (1253-57)."

: SANTA MARIA NOVELLA, LOOKING TOWARD THE HIGH ALTAR. *Bottom:* CATHEDRAL OF SANTA MARIA DEL FIORE, LOOKING TOWARD THE HIGH ALTAR

Top: SANTA CROCE, LOOKING FROM THE HIGH ALTAR. *Bottom:* THE PA
VECCHIO, FORMERLY THE PALACE OF THE PRIORS

OR SAN MICHELE. *Bottom:* OR SAN MICHELE. INTERIOR, SHOWING THE
RNACLE BY ORCAGNA

Top: THE CAMPANILE OF GIOTTO. *Bottom:* THE LOGGIA DEI LANZI, FORMER[LY]
THE LOGGIA DEI SIGNORI

very detail of the Tuscan reorganization which Florence had recently effected. urthermore, the two towns agreed to come to each other's help in time of var and in time of peace to live on such good terms that neither would re- eive the political exiles (*fuorusciti*) of the other. In short, the upland town ound itself to undertake nothing calculated to disturb the achieved ascendancy f its lowland rival. Immense must have been the prestige of the City of the aptist and great the terror that went before its name for Siena ever to have een induced to sign a paper testifying to the abdication of its ancient claims o political equality.

To its achievements in politics and war the Florentine democracy added in his triumphant period a no less notable body of achievements in the broad ivil field. Our concern being with the total cultural activity of Florence, hey may by no means be overlooked. Up to this point the emergence of the olitical sovereign unit has chiefly engaged our attention. With the advent f the democratic regime, however, a change may be noted, and so many vidences of an uncommon mental and spiritual vigor began to accumulate hat we must needs take account of them, partly for their own sake and, even nore, as an earnest of the far greater developments to follow. Agreeing that hey are of varying importance, we shall set them down in the haphazard way n which they thrust themselves into the situation.

One of the first acts of the proud and self-conscious democracy was to give o Florence the famous coat-of-arms which is its emblem to this day: the red ily on a white field. The adoption was occasioned by an incident which arries to a striking degree the peculiar flavor of the age. We have heard that vhen the caroccio was decked out for war, it bore suspended from a tall mast wo long, narrow stripes of silk, one red, the other white. This simple device vas the earliest banner of the young commonwealth and remained in use as ong as the caroccio itself was mobilized for war. But in an age given to olorful self-expression in heraldic language, this single banner was not enough, nd the rising commune had adopted, as a second emblem, a white lily on a ed field. This, as abundantly picturesque, had swiftly gained the general avor. Now in the year 1251, when the war for the control of Tuscany began, he Florentine Ghibellines committed an open act of treason by joining the nemies of their native city. The motive for their act was not Ghibelline in the enerally accepted sense of the word, for the empire had vanished from the cene at the death of Frederick. What irked these noble gentlemen was the riumph of democracy in their home town; and they calculated that if Florence vere defeated in the field, they might come back into power on the wave of an motional reaction. Accordingly, they rode forth from the city, and on the arro- ant assumption that they were the legitimate commune, they took along with hem the municipal banner, displaying it vaingloriously at the head of their avalcade. The undismayed democracy met the challenge with inventive romptness. Abandoning the white lily on a red field to the noble traitors, it eversed the color scheme and declared that henceforth the red lily on a white ield should be the emblem of the commune. At the same time the common eople, who, as we are aware, had organized themselves as a militia under the apitano del popolo, adopted the lion (*marzocco*) as their particular group device; and lion and red lily from this time on served as the beloved symbols by which the Florentine commoners demonstrated to themselves and to the world their devotion to their city.

To complete the tale of the Ghibelline exodus with its attendant theft of the town banner we must not omit to note the complete failure of the action. Unable to stay the Florentine tide of victory, which set in with the very first year of the war, the Ghibellines, prompted by discretion, offered to come to terms, and a year after their treason to their home town committed a second treason by deserting the Pistoia-Siena-Pisa alliance, to which they were under solemn engagement. It obliges us to hold the shrewdness of the commoners in high regard that they were willing to let by-gones be by-gones in the hope—vain as it turned out to be—of welding the citizen body into a solid unit. Re-admitted to favor (1252), the Ghibellines returned to Florence, although it was perfectly clear that, unless they should cease thinking of themselves as a caste born to rule, they would repeat their felony at the earliest opportunity.

One of the signs in every river town of a growing animation is the multiplication of bridges. The oldest bridge across the Arno, the famous Ponte Vecchio went back to Roman times. On its solid Roman foundations it rested immutable till 1178; at least there is no record of a collapse until that year when as an annalist informs us, it was washed away in a frightful inundation. On being rebuilt it lasted for one hundred and fifty years, when it again collapsed (1333), owing to torrential rains, which almost drowned the whole population and of which we shall hear later on. Not till the first half of the thirteenth century did the need of crossings over the Arno supplementary to the Ponte Vecchio make itself felt. In 1218 a second bridge, afterward known as Ponte alla Carraia, was undertaken; it was followed in 1237 by a third bridge, originally called Rubaconte, in honor of the podestà under whose rule it was begun, but familiar to later generations as Ponte alle Grazie. To these three bridges, already in existence at the time of the revolution, the new democratic government added, in 1252, a fourth bridge, which from its vicinity to the church of that name was called Ponte Santa Trinità. It gives a measure of the rapid advance made by Florence in the first half of the thirteenth century to be reminded that by 1252 the City, once of the White but now of the Red, Lily, was already provided with all the bridges it ever boasted during the period of its greatness. Of the four the Ponte Vecchio still is nearest the heart of the Florentines because, as the oldest bridge, it is enveloped with a particularly luminous mist of memories. Strangers, too, are greatly drawn to it, more especially by reason of the quaint shops with which it is lined. In medieval times this was not the unusual feature it has become in our day, since shops were often installed on Italian bridges and, for that matter, on bridges throughout Europe. The Florentine commune, eager for revenue, did not feel it could forgo the rentals accruing to it from the wooden *botteghe* which, if picturesque, were far from safe and not infrequently were swept by a devastating fire.

Of all the domestic measures of the Primo Popolo none added so much to the reputation of the city as the issuance of a new and famous coin, the gold florin. The history of Tuscan money is a story which this is not the place to unfold in detail.[2] Suffice it for the present to relate that the current coin of medieval Tuscany was the silver penny (*denarius*). It was minted first at Lucca, the margravial capital, and later at Pisa and other places on the strength of an imperial privilege. In view of the fact that coinage was a prerogative of the crown, a town could not issue its own money without a document affirming the consent of the sovereign. Although Florence, so generally in opposition to the emperor, never gained the concession, nonetheless a little before or after 1235, having for the time being nothing to fear from Frederick II, it boldly usurped this right and issued as its first coin not a silver penny but a silver florin. This, let it be observed, was an innovation, for the silver florin was worth twelve silver pennies. Commerce which had by this time far outstripped the penny stage, so heartily welcomed the newer and more convenient unit that the silver pennies of Lucca, Pisa, and Siena, hitherto dominating the Tuscan markets, lost much of their prestige. Not only did the minting of the new coin, in view of its illegality, reveal the daring of the Florentines, but it also disclosed the commercial sagacity of a people who, when the traditional monetary unit proved inadequate in the face of the increasing magnitude of commercial transactions, invented a more suitable coin twelve times the value of its Tuscan predecessors.

Continuing on the bold path blazed by the government of the podestà, the new democratic government resolved to carry Florentine initiative to a still higher level and in 1252 began the issue of the gold florin. It bore the image of the lily on one side and, on the other, that of John the Baptist, patron saint of the city. Before this time only the Emperor Frederick II among occidental sovereigns had issued a gold coin, and with his death his mint had completely shut down. With merchants confronted with the difficulties caused by innumerable pennies of varying silver content, we need not wonder that the appearance of the gold florin, a beautiful shapely coin, studiously kept by an enlightened government at its full value, was hailed as a light shining in darkness. Here was the stable standard which commerce imperatively required for the handling of the steadily increasing volume of international trade. The new gold florin was worth twenty silver florins, and since a silver florin (or *solidus*) was the equivalent of twelve silver pennies, the gold florin had a value of two hundred and forty pennies. In a surprisingly short span of time the gold florin was adopted as the coin in which prices were quoted and transactions consummated throughout the western world. For several centuries its authority was much like that of the English pound in the period before the World War. As indicative of how fame in a world dedicated to and living by trade grows out of economic prestige, we note, not without a measure of dismay, that neither Dante nor Giotto nor the whole succession of quattrocento painters did so much to carry the name of the City of the Red Lily to the ends of the earth as the little, convenient invention, the *fiorino d'oro,* which commerce hailed as a compass incomparably useful in helping it to steer its difficult, international course.[3]

[2] For a fuller account see chap. XVII.
[3] Davidsohn, Vol. II[1], p. 411.

As our last evidence of the vitality of this government we point to the new official home it erected for itself and which, begun in 1255, was brought to completion in the course of the next few years. Up to this time the podestà had been quartered in a private dwelling rented for the purpose, while the councils had utilized the various churches as their meeting-places. The proud democracy in control of the town felt that this haphazard method of housing its representatives no longer satisfied the dignity of the commonwealth and erected the impressive Palazzo del Popolo which still stands. For Florentines of a later period it became the Bargello; and Bargello it is still called in spite of its conversion in the second half of the nineteenth century, into a National Museum of Sculpture. Ecclesiastical construction had begun long before in Florence, as such buildings already in existence as San Giovanni and San Miniato al Monte sufficiently disclose. Private building was as yet represented by nothing better than the rude palaces and soaring towers of the military families. With the new communal residence, the Palazzo del Popolo, civic architecture came to life, producing as its first handiwork an impressive, fortress-like structure crowned with battlements and tower. The Italian towns had arisen as a protest against the feudal system, but in Florence as everywhere else, the earliest expression of their spirit in stone and mortar took rather incongruously the form of a feudal castle.

Florence had for some years ruled a largely dependent Tuscany, when what had been long a faint vapor to the south began to darken and fill the sky with warnings of a storm. We left Manfred, Frederick's illegitimate son, charged with defending the claims of the Suabian house to the kingdom of Sicily. Difficult as his situation was in the face of the always recalcitrant barons, it was rendered almost untenable by the resolution of the papacy at all costs to dispossess the family from which it had suffered so many indignities. In pursuit of this aim, in the year 1255, the pope offered the Sicilian crown to the king of England. This was Henry III, who not only promptly accepted it for his second son, Prince Edmund, but agreed besides to aid the pope in squeezing vast sums out of the English church with which to fit out a papal army of conquest. Manfred had a hard stand, but was so consistently successful against the invaders that by the summer of the year 1258 he felt strong enough to crown himself king at Palermo. In doing so, he ignored the rights of his nephew, the boy Conradin, possibly, as his enemies declared, owing to his vaulting ambition, but possibly too because he believed he had won the realm for himself by force of arms. In any case it was far more likely that the barons would be faithful to him than to a distant boy relative, whose German bringing-up made him a complete stranger to the south.

The effect on Tuscany of Manfred's coronation was electric. The animosities secretly nursed against the hegemony won by the Florentine democracy ventured into the open and one of the earliest evidences of the hopes awakened by the *biondo e bello* son of the unforgotten Frederick was furnished by the ever-restive Ghibellines of Florence. Although they had been forgiven their treason of 1251, they had not renounced any of their aristocratic pretensions. They were Ghibellines, not, or at least not primarily, because they were attached to the empire but because they regarded the empire as the most likely means to win back their privileged position in their native town. We shall see later on that the Florentine Guelphs dwelt on no higher moral plane, since they were Guelphs mainly by reason of their expectation of realizing their dream of Florentine ascendancy through the backing of the pope. In the summer of 1258 the Florentine Ghibellines, wildly elated by the rise of Manfred, made an attempt to overthrow the hated democratic government and, on failing to realize their aim, promptly withdrew from the town. This time the aroused citizens, egged on by the Guelph faction, knew no mercy. Throwing moderation to the winds, they decreed the destruction of the houses and towers of the Uberti, Lamberti, and the other fuorusciti, thereby dotting the town with unsightly rubbish heaps that long remained untouched in order to serve as a warning to traitors. For the Guelph nobles it was the revenge long overdue for the destruction wrought on their houses by the Ghibellines some ten years before. The largest single area of destruction was the site once covered by the houses of the proudest of the magnate families, the Uberti. When after more than a generation it was at length cleared of its ruins, it was converted into a magnificent central square, the present Piazza della Signoria.

Exiled a second time the Florentine fuorusciti withdrew as before to Siena; and, in spite of the fact that since 1255 Siena and Florence had been allies and that one article of the treaty expressly forbade either town to give shelter to the rebels of the other, when the fugitives, headed by the bold Farinata degli Uberti, knocked at the Sienese gate, they were promptly admitted. Here was a most acceptable *casus belli,* in case the Florentines were looking for one. On second thoughts they preferred to ignore the incident, possibly on the calculation that Manfred's swollen power would collapse as rapidly as it had gathered. The Sienese, on the other hand, reckoned with the opposite probability and looked upon the Sicilian sovereign's south Italian dominance as the certain herald of an early Tuscan intervention. More hotly than ever they avowed their Ghibellinism for the reason, the sole reason, that the representative of the Hohenstaufen cause was the only means at hand for overthrowing the hated primacy of Florence. It is as foolish to predicate of the Sienese a love of the empire for its own sake as it is absurd to credit the Florentines with a blind devotion to the church. We are dealing with two young sovereignties, each of which was supremely concerned with its own selfish ends and each of which hated the other with elemental fury because it lay across the path of its ambition.

Impatient to inaugurate its war of liberation against Florence, Siena sent an embassy to Manfred's court which engaged to swear fealty to him in return for the promise of military aid. Manfred accepted the offer and in May, 1259, dispatched a first small troop of horsemen, Germans and South Italians, to Siena as an earnest of his good will. When these were followed in December by an impressive force of German mercenaries under Manfred's relative, Count Giordano, the cup of the Sienese overflowed and they gave the stalwart band a delirious welcome. Giordano displayed a patent from his master naming him vicar-general of all Tuscany. With Siena as his rallying-point he was empowered to assemble the scattered supporters of the empire throughout the province in the hope of putting an end to Florentine control.

Even now, when it was plain that war was no longer avoidable, the Florentines, instead of striking at once, displayed an unusual hesitation. They permitted the Sienese, aided by Giordano's cavalry, to assume the offensive by attacking the small towns and castles in their neighborhood devoted to the Florentine interest. Several of these, including the important Grosseto in the Maremma littoral, had fallen before the Florentine host, in April, 1260, was at last mobilized to check the Sienese action. At that moment the main body of the auxiliaries under Count Giordano, supported by a section of the Sienese militia, was laying siege to the strong fortress of Montemassi, not far to the north of vanquished Grosseto. Entering the Elsa Valley, the Florentines pushed on as if bent on the relief of the beleaguered Montemassi. Suddenly they swerved from their track and struck straight at Siena in the hope of taking the city by surprise. On May 17 they made their appearance on the heights to the west of the town; but when on the next day they pushed forward against the Porta Camollia, they were thrown into great confusion and all but routed through a sudden furious sortie conducted by a small band of German troopers who had been left behind to guard the town when Count Giordano departed on the Montemassi expedition. The failure of their ruse discouraged the Florentine leaders, and in an access of caution they led the army home. It had been a typical democratic campaign in that, begun with enthusiasm, its energy rapidly evaporated on meeting with unexpected difficulties. No matter how loudly the good burghers crowed victory on their return to their wives and children, the spring offensive had been an expensive failure.

The first effect of the Florentine retreat was that the defenders of Montemassi surrendered. This gave Siena unchallenged control of the Maremma. Her next step was to bear down on the small towns of Montalcino and Montepulciano, particularly hateful because, although lying in the Sienese contado, they were always treacherously leagued with Florence. In July Montepulciano yielded, making the best terms it could; but Montalcino, sending up sharp cries to heaven and to Florence for aid, stubbornly continued to resist the Sienese assault. In order to provision the beleaguered town and balk the Sienese of their prey the Florentines during the summer prepared a new campaign, and toward the end of August started from their city. No pains were spared to provide the most elaborate equipment with which a Florentine army had ever yet set forth. The details are preserved for us in the famous official record, the *Libro di Montaperti*.[4] Its abundant documents afford a degree of illumination touching the art of war as practiced by communal Florence which leaves little to be desired. The whole male population between the ages of fifteen and seventy, with the exception of the sick, the disabled, and certain exempt groups required for necessary work at home, was liable to service in the field; and on a typically hot, late summer day the burgher host, fully mobilized, marched out of the southern gate. At places appointed beforehand the Florentine forces were swelled by the contingents of the allied and subjected towns, Lucca, Pistoia, Prato, Arezzo, Volterra, San Miniato, and San Gimignano. We get a vivid impression of the authority enjoyed by Florence when we hear that

[4] *Il Libro di Montaperti*. Per cura di Cesare Paoli. *Documenti di Storia Italiana,* Vol. IX.

Bologna and Orvieto, lying well beyond the confines of Tuscany, were prompt, at the bidding of the Red Lily, to come to her assistance and make a stipulated contribution to her masterful host. An army of probably seventy thousand fighting men moved on Siena, without comparison the largest force medieval Tuscany had yet seen in action. Indeed this army *was* Tuscany, which under the guidance of its foremost town marched forth resolved to coerce its one erring member into joining the provincial fold. For, excepting the eight hundred horsemen under Count Giordano, the handful of Florentine Ghibellines under Farinata degli Uberti, and the contingents of a few small dependent neighbors, Siena stood absolutely alone. Even Pisa, as consistently Ghibelline as Siena and ever ready in the past to side with the City of the Virgin, on this occasion either refused or was unable to render aid.

On the closest possible calculation the Sienese must have been outnumbered some two or three to one. Owing probably to this circumstance the Florentines considered that they ran no risk of being attacked if they passed under the very nose of Siena on their way to Montalcino. For the reprovisioning of that hill town and for the support of the great army on its march the fighting forces were attended by an immense train of twenty thousand pack animals. With all this unexampled magnificence—the numerous allied contingents under their waving banners, the rich equipment of arquebuses and other war machines, the countless beasts of burden laden with supplies—the Florentines hoped to overwhelm the imagination of the Sienese when they mounted their walls and other vantage points to watch the enemy file by. Some of the more sanguine leaders of the Arno town seem even to have entertained the delusion that their discouraged antagonists would in the face of all this *pompa e grandigia* surrender without more ado. May the purpose of the march past Siena have been what it will, on the afternoon of September 3, 1260, the allied Tuscan army pitched camp among the bare, chalk hills of the Arbia Valley, only a few miles distant from the eastern gate of Siena. It was a dangerously exposed position, only slightly improved by the seizure and occupation of Montaperti, the only fortified castle of the immediate neighborhood. As the sun went down the Florentines could see the towers of lofty Siena silhouetted like serried spears against the sky and its formidable, rose-tinted walls of brick rising and dipping with the undulations of the ground.

If anything was needed to convert the normal courage of the Sienese into frenzy, it was this mocking bravado. In the dusk they marched forth from their city to camp in the fields, and when the next day's sun arose, the clear, hot sun of Saturday, September 4, they streamed in a solid mass of cavalry and infantry across the Arbia, shallow with the summer's drouth, and rushed with maddened shouts upon the enemy. Of what followed the Sienese and Florentine chroniclers have left us widely different accounts.[5] Under the delirious excitement of a hand-to-hand combat the fancy of men is wont to blossom so exotically that it is doubtful if the true picture of any battle that was ever fought can be recovered twenty-four hours after it is over. Nor does it much matter except perhaps to men who follow war as a profession. In the case of

[5] For the Sienese version with its inflamed patriotism and manifestly legendary touches see Schevill, *Siena,* pp. 175 ff.

Montaperti an examination will show that, while the Florentine and Sienese versions emphasize each a particular set of determining circumstances, these are not necessarily contradictory. Granted that the victory won was not wholly, as the Sienese asserted, a matter of the impetuous charge by Count Giordano's German horse supported by the crushing momentum of the patriotically inflamed infantry; and granted that the contention of the Florentines that they lost solely through treason in their own ranks is equally one-sided, there is nothing to hinder us from holding that these factors operated together to produce the result. Let us frankly concede the possibility of treason in view of its extraordinary persistence in the political framework of the age; and since we are following the history, not of Siena but of Florence, let us see what the prudent but certainly not unprejudiced Villani has to say of an episode which the Sienese for their part consistently bury under silence.[6]

Before giving in his famous chronicle his version of Montaperti, Villani offers copious details touching the political maneuvers and military ruses during the campaign of 1260 of the Sienese and their Ghibelline guests from Florence. Much of this is doubtless mere gossip; on the other hand, we must never forget that the Florentine exiles were unscrupulous adventurers who plucked at every means calculated to put them back in power and who certainly maintained unbroken secret communications with their partisans at home. In this connection it must further be kept in mind that, while some Ghibellines had deserted Florence, very many more, reluctant to have their property confiscated, remained behind, paying a facile lip service to the triumphant commune. That these secret enemies were prepared to co-operate with the avowed traitors, who had gone to Siena and who under the leadership of Farinata degli Uberti were fighting the battles of the upland city, goes without saying. It is on this indubitable private understanding between the Ghibelline groups outside and inside the Florentine walls that Villani's story of the battle is founded; and if he makes somewhat more of it than it deserves, he is guilty of no worse misdemeanor than an exaggerated patriotism. For, aside from enabling him to pass lightly over the warrior reputation which accrued to the despised Sienese because of their victory, the treason theory held the distinct satisfaction for a man of Villani's colossal bias of proving that it was, after all, his own countrymen who defeated his countrymen and that nobody else could have turned the trick.

After declaring that the Sienese launched their attack unexpectedly and that their sudden appearance spread immediate confusion in the Florentine ranks, Villani continues:

> And what caused particular alarm was that the Ghibellines in the Florentine camp, both mounted and on foot, when they saw the enemy approach took to flight, as had been agreed beforehand; and among them were members of the Pressa, Abbati, and other families. Moreover, they did not permit the Florentines and their allies to

[6] No one interested in the factual basis of Montaperti can afford to overlook what Davidsohn has assembled in *Forschungen*, Vol. IV, pp. 143-72. It is an amazing piece of scholarly detective work. However, when Davidsohn in his turn undertakes to describe the battle (Vol. II[1], p. 500), we are made aware that a pen strictly governed by a body of imperfect facts will never do justice to the vivacity of life.

form rank and join battle. And just as the squadron of Germans violently struck the troop of Florentine knights, whose banner-bearer was Messer Jacopo del Nacca of the family of the Pazzi and a man of great valor, that vile traitor, Messer Bocca degli Abbati, who rode close to his side, struck the said Jacopo with his sword, cutting off the hand which supported the banner. And immediately Bocca was set on and killed. Seeing the banner on the ground and themselves betrayed at the very moment when they were powerfully assaulted by the Germans, the knights and foot soldiers were in brief order put to rout. But because the horsemen of Florence were the first to learn of the treason, they had only thirty-six casualties distributed between dead and captive. A great butchery ensued, however, of the Florentine infantry as well as of the Lucchese and Orvietans, who had shut themselves up in the castle of Montaperti. And such as were not killed were taken. More than twenty-five hundred remained dead on the field and more than fifteen hundred of the best commoners of Florence, Lucca, and the other allies were led away into captivity.[7]

An apology if you will; certainly not the full story of that famous rout. Yet he would be rash indeed who, in the face of the corroborative touches supplied, not by the emotional chroniclers, but by impeccable contemporary documents, should set down Bocca degli Abbati's treason as a myth.[8] Nor may the evidence of Dante, one of the most candid souls that ever lived, be overlooked. On reaching the lower depths of hell, where men who have been guilty of treason suffer punishment by being imbedded in eternal ice, the poet, accidentally perhaps, but with deep inner satisfaction nonetheless, drove his foot into the traitor's face. Bocca and his misdeed were as real and indubitable to the Florentine wayfarer through the underworld as the beloved San Giovanni in which he had been baptized.

However, to concede Villani a respectful hearing is not to free him from the charge of attempting to belittle the Sienese triumph. His figures of the losses suffered by the Guelphs are preposterously low in view of the circumstance that a Tuscan, not just a Florentine, army of approximately seventy thousand men had been literally pulverized. True, the cavalry suffered comparatively few casualties for, as Villani explains, they spurred their horses from the field at the very beginning of the battle. But the infantry, more particularly the commoners of Lucca and Florence, who bravely stood their ground when the high-born gentlemen ran for their lives, were savagely broken. Instead of the modest losses reported by Villani, we must conclude that close to ten thousand dead covered the field and that no less than twenty thousand captives were jammed into the improvised hell-holes of Siena made to serve as prisons. In this connection authentic documents inform us that the prisoners languished for years in these noisome quarters, unfit habitations for dogs and even swine. Happy they who, overcome by black despair, swooned off into eternal sleep.

When all is said, the battle of Montaperti signified an overthrow which for completeness invites comparison with that of Frederick Barbarossa at Legnano. Whether its consequences would prove as durable was another matter and re-

[7] Villani, VI, 79.
[8] Davidsohn, *Forschungen*, Vol. IV, pp. 152-53.

mained for the future to disclose. Certainly for the time being King Manfred's vicar-general in Tuscany, Count Giordano, ruled the land, and with him triumphed Siena and the Ghibellines. Crushed and exhausted Florence did not have the strength to offer the slightest further resistance. Its fugitive Guelph knighthood rode into Florence only to ride out again. Confronted with the bottomless despair of the shattered remnant of the citizens, they saw they could not count on further support. On September 12 the victorious Ghibellines returned to their native city headed by Farinata degli Uberti and followed by Count Giordano with his German mercenaries. Not a protest was voiced when, in the name of King Manfred, they took over the government. The democratic interlude of 1250 had come to an abrupt end. Let us take leave of it with Villani's just and moving words: "And thus was broken and annulled the old democracy (*Il Popolo Vecchio*) of Florence which had won so many victories and boasted such power and grandeur for ten years."

X. The Fall of the Hohenstaufens and the Ghibelline Collapse in Tuscany (1260–70)

WHAT happened at Florence after Montaperti was promptly reenacted throughout Tuscany: the Guelphs abandoned town after town, leaving the government in the hands of their Ghibelline rivals. Exactly as in the Arno city, the people as distinguished from the magnates belonged as yet neither to the one party nor to the other and could therefore readily enough accommodate themselves to the new situation. Besides, in this instance the success of the Ghibellines signified the end of Florentine control and the resumption of an independence which all alike eagerly craved. So great was the resentment against the former proud mistress now humbled to the dust that the demand even made itself heard in some quarters for her total destruction. At a Ghibelline congress held in the flush of victory at Empoli, Count Giordano, at the urgence of King Manfred himself and with the passionate support, we may be sure, of the Sienese, brought this extreme retributive measure to discussion. Then arose Farinata degli Uberti, who, having just regained his fatherland, was not minded to lose it again at the bidding of its enemies. In his immortal poem Dante has celebrated the deed of the gallant nobleman, who, laying his hand to his sword in that hostile parliament, covered his native city with his body and so saved it from destruction.[1]

As soon as it was decided that Florence should be spared, it became necessary to provide for its government. The simplest course was to ignore the recent democratic episode and to return to the earlier communal constitution. Accordingly, Manfred's vicar-general appointed Count Guido Novello as podestà, and Guido in conducting the affairs of his office consulted with the usual councils of the citizens. This gave the government a certain air of being independent, although it is clear that, with an appointee of Manfred in control, nothing could be undertaken that ran counter to the king's interest.

This Guido Novello belonged to the famous family which had for generations been one of the great landholders of Tuscany. Its fortunes, as we are aware, had begun to decline with the rise of Florence, but it still boasted numerous castles and estates, especially in the Casentino, the hill country of the upper Arno. In the course of time its possessions had become divided among several branches and, no longer held together by a single authoritative

[1] *Inferno,* X, 91-3. Dante has just told Farinata why he and his clan are held in such abhorrence at Florence. This draws the proud rejoinder: *ma fui io sol colà* (single-handed I saved her from destruction!).

chief, each branch followed the course best adapted to promote its particular fortunes. Thus there were now Guelph Guidi and Ghibelline Guidi; and these divided relatives had arrived at the inflamed state of mind which prompted them to regard their common blood less as a bond than an added grievance. While the new podestà of Florence, Count Guido Novello, was a passionate Ghibelline, his cousin, Count Guido Guerra, was the acknowledged leader of the Florentine Guelphs. On the occasion of the recent clash at Montaperti the cousins had fought on opposite sides, and Guido Guerra had led the defeated Guelphs back to Florence and thence into a resentful exile. The situation serves to illuminate the descending road which all the great Tuscan feudatories traveled in the thirteenth century. With domestic division added to the expansion of the towns their extinction would not be long delayed.

The most pressing concern of the returned Ghibellines was to revenge themselves on their Guelph enemies. The form of that revenge had by this time become so well established as to be automatic. Not only were the fugitives sentenced to death as rebels and their property confiscated, but their houses and towers, in town and country alike, were ruthlessly leveled with the ground. Within the walls of Florence alone about two hundred structures fell victim to this hateful folly. Since a large complex of Ghibelline dwellings had gone the same road a few years before on the occasion of the Ghibelline exodus of 1258, considerable sections of the town must by the end of 1260 have been in ruins. A chance visitor would have received the impression that he had come to a city erratically devastated by an earthquake.

The fugitive Guelphs congregated in Lucca, the only city of Tuscany which refused to bend its neck under the Ghibelline yoke. It followed therefore that Manfred's intrepid and victorious vicar-general could not rest content till he had driven the enemy from this last foothold and transferred Guelph Lucca to the Ghibelline column. This was the immediate political objective of the victors; and since it involved a struggle not with passive walls of stone but with determined human beings, it cost several campaigns before it was crowned with success. Count Giordano was after a while recalled by Manfred for service in the southern kingdom, and in his place Count Guido Novello was advanced to the Tuscan vicarate-general. It is a not uninteresting personal detail that, wed to an illegitimate daughter of Emperor Frederick II, he enjoyed the distinction of being the brother-in-law of the Sicilian monarch. To this connection rather than to his merits he must have owed his high appointment, for he was plagued with indecision and, first and last, made a very mediocre showing as captain of the Tuscan Ghibellines. In his military capacity his first care and duty was to hold the German mercenaries together, for they were the strong pillar on which the whole Ghibelline superstructure rested. Since their cost was apportioned among all the Tuscan towns enrolled in the Ghibelline league, their upkeep occasioned no insuperable difficulties. Exclusively a cavalry, they were not particularly effective against a walled town like Lucca. However, after a few campaigns, in which infantry contingents from the Ghibelline towns participated at the side of the German knights, Lucca was at last, in 1264, brought to terms. To save itself from threatened destruction the town agreed to banish the Guelph refugees from Florence and the other Tuscan localities and to take the oath of allegiance to Manfred and his vicar-general. As the sad train of his dejected enemies wound slowly up the Apennines to seek shelter among the Guelphs of the Romagna, Guido Novello may be imagined viewing that tragic exodus with partisan satisfaction. Tuscany had become a united province under his rule and from every city of the land waved the eagle banner of the empire.

While Manfred triumphed in this signal manner in Tuscany, difficulties which gathered volume like a swiftly descending avalanche arose in another quarter. The king's most implacable enemy was, as need hardly be said, the papacy. Stubbornly refusing to recognize him as sovereign in Sicily, Pope Alexander IV had made the vain effort to replace him with an English prince. Not long after the battle of Montaperti, which greatly strengthened the hated Manfred by putting Tuscany also in his control, the baffled Alexander died, to be succeeded first by Urban IV (1261–64), a Frenchman, and then by another Frenchman, Clement IV (1265–68). Intelligent and resourceful men, both these popes were inflexibly determined on ridding the papacy, once and for all, of the intolerable incubus of the house of Hohenstaufen. The English solution of their predecessor having failed, they evolved a French plan on which they did not scruple to stake every moral and material resource of their office.

The contemporary French king was the famous Louis IX, afterward raised to the honors of sainthood. He took an interest in the papal project to the extent of permitting his younger brother, the count of Anjou, to accept the proffer of the Sicilian crown and of putting no difficulties in the way of raising the funds necessary for the enterprise by papal levies on the ecclesiastical properties in his kingdom. The count of Anjou, Charles by name, was a man of unbounded political ambition, a good soldier, and, though without as much as a trace of his brother's saintliness, a correct and orthodox believer. A nose, bold as a hawk's beak, betrayed a fierce and impatient masculinity.[2] If the pope would provide him with the sinews of war, the count agreed to attend to the rest. The head of Christendom had therefore to put his financial mills to grinding; and as the measures which produced the desired golden grist were responsible for a vast expansion of Florentine banking, we are obliged to give them a strict attention.

With the intensification of the struggle between church and empire in the days of Frederick II, the financial operations of the papacy had become exceedingly important. Cruelly pressed for money, the popes sought to increase their revenues by levying on the various national churches on the ground that the war against the excommunicated emperor was equivalent to a crusade. In case of a crusade, let us recall, the pope was privileged to tithe the church. The important work of collecting the crusading tithes and forwarding them to Italy had been intrusted to the great trading companies of Siena and Florence, which through their permanent agents in France, England, and the

[2] Dante, who, as a youth, must have seen Charles during one of his visits to Florence, pictures him as "colui dal maschio naso." (*Purg.*, VII, 113.) See also Villani's interesting characterization, VII, 1.

Netherlands were satisfactorily equipped for the service. It is hardly possible to overestimate the extent to which the ecclesiastical riches of Europe deflected into the papal treasury had contributed to the defeat of the great Hohenstaufen. However, the recent victory of Montaperti had made Tuscany Ghibelline; and although the bankers, after the accommodating manner of their kind, would have been pleased to serve both sides, the reigning pope, Urban IV, was unwilling to lean upon avowed enemies. Clever politician that he was and familiar with the nature of money-lenders, he saw in the situation an opportunity for driving a wedge into the Ghibelline solidarity of Tuscany. Hardly therefore had he assumed the keys of St. Peter, when he put Florence and Siena, now officially Ghibelline, under interdict. Not content with this measure, he excommunicated their merchants and ordered their debtors throughout the world to refuse to make payment on loans and goods on pain of being excommunicated in their turn. Only in case the merchants made formal submission to the pope and could show a letter of pardon from the curia or one of its authorized agents certifying the fact, was the satisfaction of the debt declared to be permissible. It followed that the Sienese and Florentine trading houses were condemned to bankruptcy unless they sought and obtained the pope's favor. Under this ecclesiastical pressure the big business men, though naturally as inconspicuously as possible, went over to the Guelph side. If we now remember that it was the Sienese and Florentine merchants who were the outstanding figures in papal banking, we can see that by the unscrupulous application of his power of excommunication the pope had gained the inestimable advantage over Manfred of marshalling the Tuscan money interests behind his cause.

The next measure carries us to France. Urban first, and Clement after him, having stipulated with King Louis IX that the French church was to bear the bulk of the expense of Charles of Anjou's armament, commanded the bishops and abbots of the realm to tithe themselves during three successive years. As in the earlier case of Frederick II, the tithing was based on the theory that the projected campaign against Manfred ranked as a crusade. Not able to raise the tax fast enough to suit the impatient pope, the French prelates were obliged to borrow from the Italian bankers. Money advanced under these pressing circumstances brought anywhere from 20 to 60 per cent annual interest, thus extending to the canny Tuscan traders an opportunity for enormous profits. No wonder we find them scurrying to secure the pope's pardon and falling on their knees before him at Rome or his deputies in France to protest that they were to all eternity his humble servants. Tuscany might be officially Ghibelline, but its business leaders, the bankers and merchants, were secretly or openly Guelph and enlisted their money power on the papal side.[3]

When, in the spring of 1265, the careful preparations in France of Charles of Anjou were approaching completion, he proceeded with an advance guard of five hundred knights and one thousand bowmen to Marseilles. Embarking in twenty ships, he sailed to the mouth of the Tiber and passed thence to Rome. The main army of some thirty thousand men did not get under way

[3] On the reckless financial activities of the pope and his Italian agents in France, see Davidsohn Vol. II[1], pp. 566-69.

till the autumn, when it moved leisurely across Lombardy to proceed via the Romagna and the Marches of Ancona to its rendezvous with Charles at the papal capital. It remains a riddle why Manfred, who had exhibited a most energetic character in conquering his throne, showed a slackness in meeting the French attack which must have greatly discouraged his followers. The sea power of the Pisans, who were his allies, was more than sufficient to have scattered to the winds the small flotilla which had pushed out from the harbor of Marseilles with Charles himself on board. But the Pisans rested on their oars on account of a quarrel they had with Manfred's vicar-general in Tuscany, Count Guido Novello. When they had at last wrested from Guido the concessions they considered their due, it was too late to intercept the pretender. Again, with his numerous adherents in Lombardy, Manfred would seem to have been in an excellent position to harass the march of the main army; but here, too, no resistance worthy of the name was made against the invader.

Such hesitations and delays show conclusively that something had gone wrong in Manfred's camp. Perhaps the key to the secret is the strong oriental trait in Manfred which he shared with his famous father and which manifested itself in a capricious alternation of sensuous languor and feverish activity. In any case it is a fact that he did as good as nothing to hinder the junction of the main French army with the advance guard under Charles already at Rome. Heartened by the apparent paralysis of the enemy, the count of Anjou joyously celebrated his coronation as king of Sicily in the ancient capital on the Tiber and immediately afterward pushed south to seize the prize. On February 26, 1266, the eager pretender encountered King Manfred's forces not far from Beneventum. In the fierce fight that followed the Florentine Guelphs, who had been wanderers on the face of the earth since Montaperti, took a distinguished part; but, consistently sluggish under Guido Novello's inept leadership, the Florentine and Tuscan Ghibellines shone by their absence. The rest is too well known to require elaboration. Manfred's army was routed and himself killed. When after a close search of the battlefield the hacked and disfigured corpse was recovered and brought before Charles, he had the dead monarch's captive barons brought from their prison cells to identify the body. Full of fear, they hesitated to speak in that hostile company; but high-hearted Count Giordano, the gallant victor of Montaperti, at the first glimpse of his mutilated lord dropped his face into his hands and sobbed: "Omè, omè, signor mio." [4]

The effect of Beneventum on the political situation of Tuscany was not so sudden and overwhelming as might have been expected. Undeniably the pope's credit rose promptly to such a pitch that all the Tuscan towns expressed a desire to be reconciled with him. Willing to meet their pliant mood halfway, he offered to remove the interdict with which they had been smitten, in return for a vow of submission to himself. This conciliatory offer Florence accepted, without, however, exhibiting the least haste to meet the additional commands of the pope. What Clement wanted, above all, was the withdrawal from the city of the German mercenaries, who constituted the formidable standing army

[4] Villani, VII, 9.

of the still dominant league of Tuscan Ghibellines. The league had remained intact after Beneventum under its commander, Guido Novello, and was naturally looked on askance by victorious Charles and his eager papal mentor. If Guido maintained his German host at Florence, the strategic center of Tuscany, and resolutely stood his ground, Pope Clement could not get control of the province short of open war. Resolution, however, was the very quality Count Guido had always conspicuously lacked; and when on November 11, 1266, there occurred in Florence a rising of the people against the Germans engineered by papal partisans, rather than fight in the narrow streets unsuited to the style of mounted troops, the quaking Guido led his foreign cohorts out of the city.

It was a fatal act of pusillanimity. Even so, although the departure of the Germans gave the city back to its citizens, it did not hand it over to the pope and the Guelph faction. Promptly reasserting themselves on the disappearance of the foreign troops, the Florentine popolani returned to their normal policy of independence from all outside control coupled with internal peace. While the two noble factions, the Guelphs and the Ghibellines, had by this time acquired a certain following among the masses, the people in general were still of neither party and hoped in the common interest to bring the hostile magnates to an accommodation. Consequently the departure of the Germans was not followed by a move to drive out the Ghibellines. On the contrary, they were permitted to stay, while at the same time an invitation was issued to the exiled Guelphs to return to the city. To this policy of reconciliation the pope was strongly opposed, for he wanted Florence to be delivered exclusively into Guelph hands and no mercy to be shown to his Ghibelline enemies Clement took the view that the Hohenstaufen snake, which had been scotched at Beneventum, was not killed as yet by any means because in Germany there lived the boy Conradin, who would only have to appear in Italy to bring the Ghibellines back to life. It naturally confirmed him in his set hostility to a Guelph-Ghibelline pacification to learn, early in the year 1267, that the prince, a spirited youth of fifteen, was about to embark on the attempt to recover his Sicilian kingdom.

As soon as the situation was complicated by this new factor, Clement IV with characteristic swiftness of decision gave his negotiations with the Florentines a different character. He would no longer attempt to persuade them to submit to his will, he would employ force. Having, however, no military power of his own, he was obliged to turn once again to his French champion, to Angevin Charles. He commissioned him to be his representative in Tuscany to the end of "pacifying" the province in the papal interest. The ambitious Sicilian king had been impatiently waiting for this very call. Already master of the south, he could now with the consent and at the behest of the pope advance his foot into the heart of Italy. He dispatched a troop of French knights northward, to whom the exiled Florentine Guelphs, who had fought at Beneventum, added their strength as they crossed the boundary of Tuscany. On *Sabbato Santo,* the day before Easter of the year 1267, and five months after the convulsion which had rid the town of its German occupation, the combined forces appeared unexpectedly before Florence.

The Ghibellines in the city, afflicted with the feebleness which had been their curse ever since Guido Novello had become their head, at once resolved to give up the city. Would it have been different with them if the fiery Farinata degli Uberti, who had died three years before (1264), had still been among the living? All that we know of him justifies the surmise that his indignation would have exploded against the craven slackness of his fellows. If we linger for a moment over the ignominious retreat, it is because, as the event proved, the Ghibellines lightly surrendered the last chance they ever had to make an exit from the Florentine stage in honorable accord with the traditions of a military caste. By their cowardly evacuation of the city at the coming of the French, they did indeed for the moment save their lives; but instead of falling like heroes in a gallant charge, they died in dispersion, munching as impecunious beggars the scant crumbs tossed them by a resentful charity. Once again in the long seesaw of Guelph-Ghibelline strife, as the Ghibellines rode out by one gate the Guelphs rode in by another. And just as the Ghibelline rule, now ended, had been built on German troopers, the new Guelph rule, which succeeded it, rested on King Charles and the horsemen of France. The bloodless revolution which made Florence Guelph (and kept her Guelph for as long as her independence lasted) took place on Easter Sunday, the fifty-first anniversary of the famous murder of Buondelmonte at the head of the Ponte Vecchio.[5]

Once more in accordance with the ruthless *vae victis* of Italian politics the Guelphs began their rule with a wholesale proscription of the departed Ghibellines and with a general confiscation of their goods; again, in lieu of the escaped individuals, their houses, which could not escape, were dedicated to destruction. As the Guelphs owed their triumph to the intervention in their behalf of King Charles, whatever reward he might demand would have to be conceded. Pope Clement promoted him to the vicarate-general of Tuscany, while the Florentine Guelphs elevated him to the podestàship of their city. However, since at the time of the Guelph revolution he was still in the south, and since at best he would be only occasionally in Tuscany, he filled these two important offices with trusted followers charged to carry out his policies. On taking over the rule of Florence, he instituted a system identical with that of Manfred's time with the single difference that the roles of Guelphs and Ghibellines were now reversed. The acting podestà, who was always Charles's personal appointee, duly observed the form of consulting the two councils traditionally attached to his office; but as only approved Guelphs from the upper and middle classes were permitted to sit in these bodies, the government presented the picture of a strictly partisan regime. The renewed organization of the people under the captain, a conspicuous democratic feature of the Primo Popolo, was prohibited. The people as such counted for no more in the new Guelph than in the late Ghibelline system. This deserves to be expressly said since the view propounded by Villani and echoed by all his imitators to the

[5] The political plans and intrigues that agitated Florence from the summer of 1266 to the Guelph triumph of Easter (April 17), 1267, have given rise to grave controversies. They are discussed with a grateful resultant clarification by Davidsohn, Vol. II[1], pp. 598-612; *Forschungen*, Vol. IV, pp. 174-97.

effect that the victorious Guelphs, as distinguished from the defeated Ghibellines, exhibited popular leanings still enjoys general acceptance. Every act of the new rulers proves that they were fundamentally as anti-democratic as their rivals and that they had a heart that beat as one with that of their energetic patron, King Charles. This grand personage, who assumed the podestaship in 1267 and retained the office for an unbroken stretch of thirteen years, regarded all commoners, whether in his native France or in Italy, the land of his adoption, as laborious clods whom God in his goodness had provided in order that sovereigns and their barons, the true elect of the earth, might lead an honorable and dignified existence. In short, he was a faithful exponent of his class and age.

Untroubled by either urban-democratic or evangelical-Franciscan leanings, Charles had a firmness of character and a political understanding which raised him far above the average ruler of the day. It was largely to his own high qualities that he owed his Sicilian throne; and now that that throne was threatened by the descent into Italy of Conradin, in the eyes of strict legitimists the lawful heir, he was resolved not to leave a stone unturned to repeat his victory over Manfred. Therefore a month after his troops had occupied Florence, he came in person to Tuscany with the purpose of organizing the province as the first line of defense against the German claimant. Although the Guelph league was now clearly dominant and boasted the support of the majority of the Tuscan towns, the Ghibellines were still formidable since, besides the many castles of their noblemen, two considerable communes, Pisa and Siena, and a number of smaller settlements, like Poggibonsi, obstinately refused to recognize Charles as vicar-general. When in the summer of 1267 it became known that Conradin with a small but well-equipped body of knights was on the point of setting out from Germany, the resistance of the Tuscan Ghibellines was naturally stiffened by this news; and when, in October, the prince actually appeared in Verona, warmly acclaimed by his Lombard adherents, a hope was lighted in every Ghibelline breast in Tuscany that induced the enemies of Charles to resist his authority more vigorously than ever. Quick to see that under the prevailing circumstances the decision rested with the sword, he resolved to bring the recalcitrants to terms before Conradin should arrive upon the scene. But little Poggibonsi, his first object of attack, heroically resisted him for five months; and when on its surrender he turned against Pisa, his forces were too exhausted to take it by assault. Could he have captured the great seaport, he might very probably have halted Conradin's advance, for it was through the territory of Pisa, habitually friendly to his family, that the young prince planned to march southward into the kingdom which he hoped to wrest from the usurper. No fault can be found with Charles's strategy. It failed because of the resistance he encountered, chiefly from Poggibonsi and from Pisa. Accommodating himself to the altered situation, he determined to retire to his kingdom and settle the issue with his rival on the soil they both claimed.

It was in the early spring of 1268 that Charles abandoned his central Italian position as militarily untenable. Shortly after, young Conradin led his band of German knights, strengthened by numerous Lombard partisans who had eagerly flocked to his standards, across the Apennines above Pisa. On April 7 the inhabitants of the Ghibelline seaport gave him a welcome as clamorous as any they had ever offered to his imperial ancestors. He was a youth of sixteen, blond and of goodly figure, and his comeliness, added to his exalted birth, stirred the quick sympathies of the people wherever he appeared. His most intimate friend and adviser, Frederick, duke of Austria, was only three years older than himself. Launched without preparation upon the wild sea of Italian politics, the two inexperienced young men must at times have been utterly bewildered by the party passions which roared and grimaced about them in uncontrolled fury. Had they not known the goal toward which they were steering and had they not resolutely pointed their course southward, they would have lost their way as on an uncharted ocean. From Pisa the journey led onward to Siena, which tried to outdo Pisa with its acclamations; and from Siena the Ghibelline host, steadily increased by fresh volunteers, streamed southward and ever southward in search of the French rival. Charles's great patron and ally, Pope Clement IV, unable to hold Rome, had sought refuge in well-fortified Viterbo. From the battlements of his Viterban palace he saw on a hot summer's day the luminous cloud of dust some miles to the west which marked the passing of the hostile army. Not for a moment even did doubt assail the stout heart or flit across the features of the inflexible old man. "He will vanish like that golden dust," he prophesied of the young Hohenstaufen to the cardinals intently gazing westward; and after a pause, "They are leading him like a lamb to the slaughter." [6]

From Rome still pressing southward, the Ghibelline army entered the southern kingdom to be confronted at last, on August 23, by the Guelph champion in a valley not far from Tagliacozzo. Conradin's forces were more numerous, but Charles handled his army with greater skill, and victory, as sweeping as two and a half years before at Beneventum, again perched upon his banners. The Suabian lad attended by the duke of Austria and a handful of Italian lords, who remained faithful to the last, made his escape from the battlefield; but to no avail. Betrayed to the conqueror in the hope of gain, at the command of the resentful Charles, he, together with his devoted friend and a stalwart band of Italian Ghibellines, was beheaded on the market square of Naples. He was the last of the Hohenstaufens, a line of kings, who, as in a Greek tragedy, had been carried to the sun-lit summits only, because man may not vie with the gods, to be swallowed up in darkness and defeat.

Although the death of Conradin signified the fall of the strongest pillar of the Ghibelline cause, the Tuscan Ghibellines did not on that account at once give up the struggle. As King Charles was obliged to remain in the south in order to stamp out the rebellion which had here and there sporadically raised its head, he dispatched a representative at the head of a French force to Tuscany charged to resume the policy of reducing the province to a single Guelph mass. The preliminary step to this end would have to be to bring to terms Siena and Pisa, ever the enthusiastic champions of the Ghibelline cause. In spite of the bitter cup of Tagliacozzo the two towns were so little inclined to submission that they impertinently braved the Angevin sovereign.

[6] Davidsohn, Vol. II[2], p. 36.

Siena even had the audacity to lay siege to little nearby Colle, like Montalcino and Montepulciano always a thorn in the flesh of the larger town. At this provocation the French vicar attended by the Florentine host started for the scene of action and on June 17, 1269, under the walls of Colle, signally defeated the Sienese and their Ghibelline allies. It was the Red Lily's revenge for the rout at Montaperti some nine years earlier. Reluctant even now to accept its fate, Siena continued to offer resistance; but when, in the following year, Pisa, seeing no prospect of Ghibelline help from any quarter, entered the Guelph system, the upland town, in order to escape the grinding siege that threatened, also came to terms (August 4, 1270). Into the hands of Guido of Montfort, official representative of Charles, she swore fealty to the Guelph cause, agreed to take back her Guelph exiles, and, in conclusive token of submission, accepted a Guelph podestà. No sooner had the Sienese Guelphs re-entered the city in accordance with the treaty than they drove out the Ghibellines amidst retributive measures as familiar as they were revolting. In this manner did Siena become Guelph and bid farewell forever to its Ghibelline age, the period of its greatness. Continuing on its triumphant course, the Guelph league broke down the steadily weakening resistance of its remaining adversaries until only occasional castles in the inaccessible mountain areas floated the Ghibelline pennant. Approximately two years after Conradin met a felon's death at Naples, Tuscany had been welded into a Guelph dominion obedient to the pope and King Charles.

For Florence the Guelph triumph involved a number of such important social-political changes that we are obliged to give them close attention. Granting that the local Guelphs owed their success to Charles and his French knights, and granting further, that the Angevin exercised a more or less autocratic authority through his right to appoint the podestà, it was also true that he could not maintain himself in the town without the backing of the Guelphs, organized as the parte Guelfa, and that he was therefore constrained to accept their partnership. In sum, Charles and the parte Guelfa shared the government between them. Since Charles had numerous general interests up and down the Italian peninsula and was usually far away, while the parte Guelfa, as exclusively Florentine, was always on the ground, it followed also that the king and the party could co-operate without a perilous amount of friction. What rendered the partnership particularly harmonious was the fact that Charles was willing to hand over the entire domestic field to the Guelphs, provided he was permitted to retain control of Florentine foreign policy. The situation has been oversimplified by writers who are content to describe Florence as subjected to the king of Sicily. Undoubtedly it was; and yet the immensely important internal developments went forward under the impulsion, not of Charles, but of the parte Guelfa, resolved, first, to revenge itself on the defeated Ghibellines and, second, to maintain its new-won power at all costs. Revenge had been a feature of the Guelph-Ghibelline feud since its inception a half-century before, but organization for continued power, at least in the rigorous form now adopted, was a novelty.

We have learned that the Guelph and the Ghibelline parties came into being when the ancient society of the nobles, the societas militum, could no longer be maintained. All the evidence which has come down to us confirms the belief that the two parties were organized along identical lines. But as we know much more about the parte Guelfe than about the parte Ghibellina, and as the parte Guelfa played a much more conspicuous and continuous role in the history of Florence, we are justified in concentrating our attention on this truly extraordinary organization.[7] The executive or governing committee consisted of six captains, all of them members of magnate families. While this indicates an aristocratic association, rich popolani were by no means excluded from membership in the party, for the nobles may have remembered that their own ancestors had once to a large extent been popolani and that their present exalted station represented a relatively recent achievement. The parte Guelfa was frankly a union of birth and wealth. If the executive power represented by the captains was reserved to birth, wealth received recognition in the department in which it was certain to have the greatest interest, the treasury. This was intrusted to a committee of six, three of whom were required to be popolani. Final authority rested with the general assembly of the party, which elected the officials and voted on all important measures. In all matters pertaining to their office the six captains sought the advice of a small secret council of fourteen members, called *credentia.* Among the officials there stood out one with the ominous name of Accuser of the Ghibellines. He was in effect the head of the detective service with the whole party membership serving under him as volunteer informers. This officer alone should suffice to convince us that if the end sought by the party was power, the means adopted to achieve the end was a continued terror.

Although the repressive measures of the party were directed against the Ghibellines, the latter were not by any means all of one kind, for there were Ghibellines and Ghibellines. The most dangerous group of Ghibellines were the *ribelli* (rebels). This uncompromising designation was attached to all those who had voluntarily left the city. They were condemned to death, their houses were subject to destruction, and all their possessions, real and personal alike, were confiscated. By far the greater number of Ghibellines, however, did not go into exile but stayed on in Florence in the hope of somehow weathering the storm. In the eyes of their Guelph adversaries they constituted a body of the suspect and consequently were fair game for the Accuser of the Ghibellines and his following of patriotic spies. When such a resident Ghibelline was denounced to the captains of the party, he could at the discretion of these potentates be required to leave the city for a place assigned him as a residence, which would be near or far from Florence according to the degree of suspicion he had incurred. There was no trial and the sentence was indeterminate as to time. In distinction from voluntary exile, which rated as rebellion, imposed exile was called *confino* and its victims *confinati.* If the confinati abandoned their allotted residence, they automatically became rebels, subject to the rebel's lot of death and confiscation. Rebels and confinati, distinct legal

[7] Villani, VII, 17; Davidsohn, Vol. II[1], pp. 618-20. The earliest statute of the parte Guelfa which has reached us bears the date 1335. It was published by Bonaini in the *Giornale Storico degli Archivi Toscani,* Vol. I, pp. 4-41. A valuable contribution is by U. Dorini, *Notizie Storiche sull'Università di Parte Guelfa in Firenze.* Florence, 1902.

categories but hardly distinguishable in the misery of their lot, henceforth loom large in Florentine political history.

It remains to describe the feature by which the Guelphs completed the ruin of their adversaries. As the victors desired, above all, to make sure that their vanquished opponents should never again return to power, they were not satisfied with the death sentence *in absentia* and the sweeping sequestration of goods. These measures had in the past been imposed by the Ghibellines on the Guelphs and, notwithstanding, the Guelphs had come back and regained their position and their property. Plainly the fatal thing for the future of Ghibellinism would be to dispose of its wealth, first by turning it into money, and then by distributing the money beyond any chance of recovery. With the clairvoyance inspired by hate this radical measure was with some unavoidable exceptions put into execution and the resultant revenue divided into three parts: one part for the commune, one part for the party, and one part for individual Guelphs claiming indemnity for previous losses at the hand of Ghibellines. If the plutocratic element was well represented in the party from the first, we may assume that it was not weakened when the liquidation of the immense Ghibelline properties in town and country got under way and the money-changers were invited to seat themselves at a unique banquet of percentages and commissions. The one-third share diverted into the party treasury deserves particular attention; it had the effect of providing the party with ready money, while giving it besides the credit and authority of a great bank.

The political ruin of the Florentine Ghibellines resulted from many causes which the foregoing pages have illuminated. The main cause surely was that they aimed to perpetuate their rule in their native city with the help of the empire, which proved a broken reed. But their financial ruin, which made their political failure irretrievable, was brought about by a relentless economic persecution by which their victorious opponents undermined their existence and reduced them to the level of homeless beggars.

XI. The Second Democracy: The Priors and the Ordinances of Justice (1282–93)

THE developments in Florence following the sweeping Guelph victory cannot be grasped without a preliminary understanding of the effect of that victory on the papacy. The papal court was still celebrating the fall of the Hohenstaufens when it was visited by an uneasy foreboding that it had avoided Scylla only to be threatened by Charybdis. In order to escape the German and Hohenstaufen grip the popes had drawn France and the Angevins on the scene; and promptly, on the execution of Conradin, they learned that they were now hardly less dependent on King Charles than they had once been on his Suabian predecessors. Another development complicated the crisis. By leaning heavily through several decades on France and its royal house the papacy had been unable to escape the consequences of this association, and in both outlook and personnel had become markedly gallicized. To mention a single but significant item: in the college of cardinals the French representation had steadily increased; and this growth in numbers, abetted by the impalpable spread of French sentiments through the whole body of the Roman clergy, brought it about that candidates of French nationality tended with waxing frequency to emerge as popes from the papal conclaves. We have taken account of the decisive role played by the two French popes, Urban IV and Clement IV, in the last act of the Hohenstaufen tragedy. They were both of them men of sterling quality, unflinchingly devoted to the papal cause. But if they had not been Frenchmen we may doubt whether they would have committed themselves with the ardor that characterized their policy to the establishment of a French king in southern Italy. When the death of Conradin put the political destinies of Italy into the hands of King Charles, Pope Clement IV began to show signs of uneasiness and, had he lived longer, he might not improbably have become sufficiently fired by the formidable tradition behind his office to attempt to clip the wings of the protégé who had waxed too strong. But he died a month after the Suabian boy's execution while still exulting over the manifest intervention of the Lord of Hosts in his behalf.

When the cardinals met at Viterbo to elect Clement's successor, the hidden crisis within the papal institution burst irresistibly into the open, revealing itself to all the world. The college split disastrously into a French and an Italian faction; and so evenly matched were the opponents that the ensuing deadlock was not broken for almost three years. The prolonged contest signified that the French group of cardinals was under Angevin influence and wanted a pope friendly to the Angevin alliance, while the Italian group, alarmed at the growing French dominance, was determined to return to the Italian tradition and to raise to power a man of their own nationality who would bestir himself to ban the Angevin specter.

When an Italian, who took the title of Gregory X (1271–76), at length emerged as victor, Europe did not have long to wait in order to learn that the eminence achieved by King Charles was not to the papal taste. Gregory was not in Europe but at Acre in Syria at the time of his election. During his residence at that seaport he had been deeply distressed by the waning power of the Christians in the east. It was a particularly insufferable circumstance in his eyes that the infidels had been permitted again to possess themselves of the Holy Places of Jerusalem, which had been regained for the occident a generation before by Emperor Frederick II. No sooner therefore had Gregory been elected pope than he returned to Europe, single-mindedly resolved to initiate a new crusade. With a minimum of delay he issued a call for a General Council of Christendom at the city of Lyons to consider and prepare a united expedition. Having reached this decision, he saw that if his proposal was to enjoy the universal support at which he was aiming, a necessary preliminary would have to be the pacification of Italy, and that, as a first step to this end, a reconciliation must be effected between the Guelphs and Ghibellines of Tuscany. Although he was aware of the opposition to any such plan of the Guelphs and their ally, King Charles, who were unwilling to surrender any of the fruits of victory, he would not let himself be deterred and firmly informed these partisans, and the Ghibellines as well, that he was determined to act as peacemaker between them. While the beaten Ghibellines naturally welcomed the proposal, the Guelphs, although stiffly hostile, could not openly reject the initiative of the ecclesiastical ruler in whose name their league was concluded and for whose benefit it was supposed primarily to exist. When, on proceeding leisurely to the assembly to be held at Lyons, Gregory, in June, 1273, arrived on the Arno, he was permitted with sulking reluctance on the part of the ruling Guelphs to negotiate between them and their Ghibelline victims.

The presence of Gregory X in Florence is chiefly notable because it bore witness to his perception that, if he continued to identify himself with the Guelph faction, he was destined to remain a client of King Charles, while if he succeeded in strengthening the Ghibellines in Florence and throughout Italy, he might hope to raise himself to the level of an arbiter. Besides, the settlement of the Guelph-Ghibelline feud would greatly aid the crusade on which he had set his heart. Owing to the untiring zeal with which he pursued his project of reconciliation Gregory achieved the apparent miracle of bringing the rival factions to an agreement; and after its terms had been laid down in an elaborate document, the event was celebrated by one of those public spectacles in which the Florentines, like all medieval Italians, took a naïve delight. Its climax was reached when chosen representatives of the two venomously estranged groups exchanged, with what dark looks and private reservations may be left to the imagination, the conventional kiss of peace (July 12, 1273).

The plaudits of the spectators were still ringing in his ears, when Gregory began to suspect that he had been tricked. A man more versed in the ways of the world than he would never have committed himself to so futile an undertaking. Such a man would have known from the beginning that a party as vindictive as the Guelphs and exercising so unchallenged an ascendancy would never surrender its advantage save as a consequence of defeat on the field of battle. Even more than the Guelphs was the resolute, iron-nerved Charles opposed to letting the reins slip weakly from his hands. He had come in person to Florence in order that his Guelph friends might learn from his own mouth that, in spite of the lip service he paid his papal patron, he had not changed in his heart. Under these circumstances Gregory was so effectively baulked by his tricky antagonists that he was not able to give the treaty of reconciliation a really equitable character; and what few advantages it contained for the Ghibellines were quickly nullified when Gregory, on departing from the city, intrusted its execution to none other than his vicar-general in Tuscany, to Charles himself. We must conclude that this last partisan action was forced on the pope by his Guelph allies. When on leaving Florence he reviewed the recent events, he gradually convinced himself that he had been the victim of a cleverly spun plot. To this belated illumination the outraged Ghibellines contributed their share, for their complaints at the vindictive treatment accorded them followed him into the hills of the Mugello, whither he had retreated during the summer heat in order to restore his shattered health. In September, only two months after blessing a sham fraternization, he exhibited his irate state of mind at having been duped by the Guelph rulers of Florence by laying their city under an interdict.

In the light of the pope's Tuscan plans his interdict signified his strong disapproval of the local parte Guelfa; and although the anathema did not embrace Charles, it might well be taken to mean that all was not well between the pope and his secular advocate. Even before coming to Florence Gregory had taken another step not calculated to improve the relations between the two men. Deeply convinced that the most effective counterweight to the power of Charles would be the restoration of the fallen empire, he had opened negotiations with the German princes, pleading with them in fatherly tones to end the anarchy which had prevailed since the death of Frederick II by electing a successor. Pope Gregory had turned Ghibelline! At least that is what the disgusted Guelphs said, first in whispers and finally aloud to all the world. In their passionate partisanship they forgot that since the popes of the past had become Guelph for no other reason than to escape the control of the emperor, they might with impeccable consistency throw themselves on the Ghibelline side as soon as it became necessary to break the shackles of a Guelph master. Regardless of the confused happenings on the restless human stage, the unalterable lodestar of the papacy was and would remain complete independence from temporal control.

In response to unremitting papal pressure the German electors on September 29, 1273, acclaimed an inconspicuous south German count, Rudolph of Hapsburg, as German king; and although the authority of the German king had in the course of recent decades declined beyond recovery, Gregory wholeheartedly rejoiced that there was now again someone in the world whom h might hope to play off against the overbearing Angevin. He went so far as t plan for Rudolph's early descent into Italy in order to invest him with th imperial crown; but first one event and then another intervened, causin repeated adjournment of the project. In the end Rudolph confined himself t Germany and never crossed the Alps. He was the first of the new, th diminished German kings, who were conscious of being so feeble in thei homeland that the dangerous Italian adventure, although it never ceased t exercise a powerful fascination, persuaded only a few of them ever again t stake their lives and happiness upon it.

After presiding over the General Council held at Lyons and inauguratin numerous negotiations concerned with the prospective crusade, Gregory turne his face again toward Italy to undertake the final preparations for the even which, according to his devout intentions, was to make his pontificate foreve memorable. During his absence the Florentine Guelphs had finally and com pletely sabotaged the treaty they had at his behest negotiated with the Ghibel lines and held more exclusive sway than ever in their city. Toward the inter dict with which they had been punished they maintained an attitude of stub born insolence. Not even when, some two years after it had been imposed Gregory again entered Tuscany on his way to Rome, did they condescen to seek the forgiveness of the offended pontiff. With Florence under his curse Gregory planned, in sign of his displeasure, to give the city a wide berth an to cross the Arno on his southward journey by an upstream ford. But a sudde downpour—it was the month of the December rains—rendered his plan im practicable. Obliged for reasons of safety to use one of the Florentine bridges he found himself under the necessity of lifting his ban, since it was imprope for a pope to enter an excommunicated town. Accordingly he suspende the interdict for the limited period of his traverse. Thereupon, preceded an followed by a numerous suite, he entered the gate and moved as fast as hi porters could carry his litter through the narrow streets, along which dense kneeling crowds implored the blessing which the baffled pontiff, alread stricken with a mortal disease, languidly accorded. When he had crossed th river and left the city by the eastern gate, he ordered his litter to be set dow and the long procession halted. Then turning his face toward the town, wit raised hand he solemnly renewed the suspended curse: a scene so mediev as to be not easily forgotten. The broken old man got no farther on his Rome ward journey than Arezzo, where on January 10, 1276, his troubled earthl pilgrimage touched its final goal.

Three popes followed each other in rapid succession until on Novembe 25, 1277, an Italian of the great Orsini family of Rome, who assumed the nam of Nicholas III, mounted the chair of the chief of the apostles, and with fa greater energy than the well-intentioned but feeble Gregory, but also wit far greater lack of scruple, resumed his predecessor's policy. A handsome ma of princely bearing and tradition, Nicholas was much more interested in push ing the fortunes of his family than in reviving the failing crusading fervor o his Christian flock. But, first and foremost, he wished to withdraw the papac from under the mailed fist of the doughty Charles; and since in a reign tha lasted less than three years he succeeded in doing the thing that Gregory had tried but failed to do, he invites our hesitant regard. One of his earliest acts was to renew the invitation to King Rudolph to come to Italy to assume the imperial crown; however, as a born bargainer, he was not minded to extend a favor without asking a favor in return. He let Rudolph know that he expected by way of payment for his support the cession of the great north-central province of Italy, commonly called the Romagna. A bold demand indeed, which would have made the eyes of the predecessors of the puny count of Hapsburg blaze with indignation! However, as the reduced aspirant to the empire could not maintain himself even in his German kingdom without the help of the pope, he yielded, and on June 30, 1278, issued the diploma which carried the temporal power of the papacy beyond the Apennines far into the Lombard plain. The thought which prompted Nicholas to insist on this expansion is perfectly transparent. It was, in final analysis, the grave temporal weakness of the papacy which had caused it during the recent decades to be tossed, like a ball, from Hohenstaufen to Anjou. The ruling pontiff, a man dominated exclusively by political considerations, held the opinion that, while an even balance between Rudolph and Charles might contribute to his independence, this desirable condition would not be definitely and finally secured until the papacy itself had come into possession of sufficient territory to serve as the basis of an adequate secular dominion.

No sooner had Pope Nicholas acquired title to this new and extensive territory than he sent thither his nephew, Cardinal Latino, as legate with full powers. He was to reduce the province to obedience by ironing out the cantankerous Guelph-Ghibelline feuds which it shared with Tuscany and the rest of Italy. Although the cardinal-legate achieved a clamorous success, it cannot be denied that it was hollow since it fell to pieces a few months after his departure. Latino heads the long line of papal legates destined to learn that the Romagnoles, regardless of a feigned submission to their new liege lord, were born to rebellion as the sparks fly upward. However, these unhappy developments were as yet hidden behind the veil of the future, when, with the aureole of his Romagna triumph about his head, the cardinal-legate turned his face to Tuscany, there to repeat his recent miracle of civic pacification.

In order to understand the activity unfolded in Tuscany by the papal nephew we must grasp that this province held a central position in the plan of Pope Nicholas to strengthen the papacy and to diminish the power of King Charles. Nicholas had therefore, even before dispatching Latino on his Romagna mission, terminated the Tuscan vicarate, on the strength of which the Sicilian monarch had dominated central Italy during the past decade. In place of the deposed Charles, Latino was to exercise the powers of a vicar-general for the pope, who by this means planned to bring Tuscany under the immediate control of the papacy. As a preparatory measure the papal representative was ordered once more to attack the thorny problem of persuading the Florentine Guelphs to an accommodation with their Ghibelline foes. The reign of a single faction was to be brought to an end to be succeeded by the peaceful rule of both factions under the guaranty and blessing of the pope. On October 8, 1279, the cardinal made his formal entry into Florence.

Cardinal Latino was a Dominican friar, a man of upright character, famous for his learning and eloquence. If he is, as is widely believed, the author of the *Dies Irae,* a medieval hymn of unrivaled majesty, we are obliged to acclaim him also as a great religious poet. To enable him to play his role of arbiter, that ancient democratic mechanism, the parlamentum, was brought from the municipal lumber-room, and in a great public assembly the papal emissary was by popular acclamation endowed with full political powers. Thus elevated above the battle, he made such good headway that after a few months he was able to announce a settlement. Its first feature was the reconciliation of Guelphs and Ghibellines in a public ceremony culminating in the exchange of oath and kiss between chosen representatives of the two embittered factions. The spectacular event, a close imitation of the scene staged by Pope Gregory X seven years before, took place on January 18, 1280. It was followed a month later by the publication of a new constitution, by the terms of which the two hostile factions were henceforth amicably to share the government of their native city between them.

There is no denying that, at least so far as the first, the pacificatory feature of his settlement is concerned, the cardinal achieved a certain measure of success. According to the treaty the exiled Ghibellines were to be repatriated after reasonable delays and by groups, carefully spaced, in order to avoid a too sudden and therefore dangerous influx; they were even to receive back their confiscated property insofar as it had not yet been sold and the proceeds distributed. It is this significant qualification to the amnesty accorded them which particularly invites our attention. Had not their spirit been broken by their long exile and its attendant misery, it is inconceivable that they would have accepted the loss and injury implied in this condition. For under its terms they cannot, in the main, have entered into possession of anything other than the heaps of stone and brick, to which their demolished houses had been systematically reduced. Deterred by the appalling prospect, a considerable number of Ghibellines, the proud Uberti among them, curtly declined to take advantage of the invitation to return. This unreconciled group continued therefore to constitute a nucleus of fuorusciti (exiles). They sought refuge in the more inaccessible parts of the Apennines, where, joined by the purely lawless elements to be found in all medieval societies, they remained a source of provincial disturbances for many decades to come. Undeniably, however, the majority of the Ghibellines came back to their native city, where, reduced in numbers and prestige and economically ruined, they gradually dropped out of sight. There is no reason for withdrawing or even modifying the statement made in the previous chapter that the Ghibellines signed their death warrant as a political party when, in 1267, they abandoned the city to the Guelphs without lifting a hand in their own defense.

Notwithstanding their having been ousted from exclusive control by the arbitral decision of the cardinal, the Guelphs remained an organization of practically undiminished might. In view of their wealth and their powerful connections at home and abroad, there was no reason at any time why they should despair; and no sooner had the hostile Pope Nicholas expired some six months after Latino had instituted the new political order, than their spirits, as well as those of their steadfast ally, King Charles, registered an immediate improvement. Not only had the late pontiff deprived the Angevin king of the vicarate-general of Tuscany, but as soon as the cardinal's new constitution was put into effect, the king had also been forced out of the podestàship of Florence. Doubtless Charles confidently looked forward to his early restoration to the two posts so necessary to the continuance of his Tuscan supremacy. All such hopes were blasted, however, by an unexpected succession of events. For one thing, Rudolph, the newly elected German king, came forward to demand he Tuscan vicarate for himself. It was a claim which, constitutionally, was incontrovertible. If, following the demise of Emperor Frederick II, the popes had asserted and exercised the right to appoint the representative of the empire n Tuscany, they did so on the assumption—a most questionable assumption, oo, let it be said—that during an imperial vacancy they were empowered to ct in the emperor's stead. While the feeble and distant Rudolph might not ucceed in getting the Tuscans to recognize the vicar whom he dispatched to heir province, no successor of Pope Nicholas could fail to acknowledge that, vith a German king once more on the throne, the head of the church no onger possessed the slightest constitutional pretext for interfering politically in Tuscany.

A second event fell even more heavily into the scales against Charles and he resumption of his Tuscan hegemony. At the Easter festival of the year 282 occurred the famous general massacre of the French occupying forces on he island of Sicily known as the Sicilian Vespers. Unexpectedly and over ight, as it were, one half of his southern kingdom shook off the yoke of the Angevin tyrant. The rebels promptly offered the island to King Pedro of Aragon on the theory that, as husband of Constance, the daughter of former King Manfred, he was the legitimate heir to the Sicilian crown. Thus, after King Charles had so effectively laid the Hohenstaufen ghost that he had ost all fear of it, it made a vengeful reappearance in his declining years. Not ven his enemies will say that he blenched at the sight. He took up the war gainst the usurping king of Aragon with the same vigor he had displayed gainst Manfred and Conradin, but in his old age Lady Luck, who, womanke, favors the young, turned her back on him and he died in 1285 after aving experienced a succession of grave disasters. His son and successor, Charles II, continued the struggle, but to no avail. The island of Sicily became n independent kingdom; and although the Angevin rulers succeeded in preerving the peninsular half of their monarchy for themselves, the title, king of icily, to which they clung, became a transparent mockery of the facts.

The blow administered to the power and prestige of Charles by the Sicilian evolt put an abrupt end to whatever dreams he and the Guelph party may ave entertained to recover their lost Tuscan supremacy. But the fact stands ut that Guelphism survived the elimination from municipal control of the riginal Guelph champions, for Florence now became Guelph by its own ecision. No development in the town is more important than this, and none more easy to grasp the moment we direct our attention to the economic tuation. During the period of a little more than a decade of Guelph rule, lorence had experienced an economic boom involving an immense expansion of trade and population. By the year 1280, according to a conservative estimate the town had come to embrace some 45,000 people,[1] a multitude so great tha it could no longer be confined within the second circle of walls. Real estat values and shop rentals registered an uninterrupted advance. The prime caus of these encouraging, if socially disturbing, phenomena was the growing vol ume of trade, overwhelmingly due to the favors extended to Florence by th Guelph bloc of powers, consisting of the pope, King Charles of Sicily, an the king of France. It was Florentine houses which were intrusted with th immensely lucrative banking of the pope, and it was these same houses which in their double capacity of bankers and merchants, enjoyed special tradin privileges within the dominions of the two powerful Guelph sovereigns Every citizen noted the mounting curve of prosperity and every citizen capabl of reflection was aware that its continuing to mount depended on keeping th town politically aligned with the Guelph powers. To be sure, the profits of th economic expansion accrued chiefly to the enterprisers and capitalists, wh became immensely wealthy, while the common people continued to wrestl with poverty, hunger, and squalor; but this unequal distribution of the com mercial returns did not keep the unreflecting masses from sharing the Guelp sentiments of their superiors. With business flourishing on account of th Guelph connections of the town, Florence became instinctively and rabidl Guelph.

Matters standing thus, the time had come for the steadily expanding me chant element of the citizenry to take over the government. No violence wa necessary and none occurred. In view of the fact that the rich traders wer strongly represented in the parte Guelfa, this group, in spite of its nobiliar origin and tendencies, possibly even favored the movement. As for the Ghibe lines, they were, even after the partial repatriation of 1280, too feeble eithe to promote or to hinder political change. All that was necessary to bring abou merchant control was imperceptibly to supplant the shaky government whic had been imposed by Cardinal Latino and which, an artificial creation e cogitated by a learned divine, was laughably out of touch with the Florentin actualities. In the view of Latino the two dominant city groups were st as in the past the parte Guelfa and the parte Ghibellina, and the governme he dictated divided the power between them as equitably as conditions pe mitted. As, owing to continued Guelph predominance, the new governme never really operated along Latino's lines, we shall spare ourselves the effo of examining its extraordinarily complicated details. What the cardinal ha failed to grasp was that the two parties between which he divided, or rath tried to divide, the power belonged essentially to another era, and that th present was dominated by the great traders, who, though Guelph in sentime and therefore well disposed toward the Guelph party, had become sufficient self-conscious to take the protection of their interests into their own hand Now the traders were organized in gilds or arti. However, long before the associations began to make their power felt the merchants as individuals ha exercised considerable influence. During the democratic interlude of 1250, f

[1] Davidsohn, Vol. II², p. 171, discusses the conflicting estimates. See also Caggese, Vol. I, p. 48 note 15.

xample, it was they and not the gilds as such that had exercised political ontrol. At that, economically speaking, still relatively backward period a ubstantial equality seems to have reigned among the gilds, and trade and andicraft associations, co-operating together, constituted a single and harnonious democratic mass. By 1280 the Guelph boom had taken place and the arlier harmony and equality had disappeared. The immensely expanded noney power was now concentrated in the merchant gilds, against which the raft gilds, although they too had not stood still, were no longer able to hold heir own. It is this situation which explains why, beginning in 1282 and irectly under the nose of the feeble authorities created by Latino two years efore, the merchant gilds were able to nominate representatives, called priors, vho quietly began to appropriate the functions of government. Meeting no pposition, they became bolder, and in the course of the following year (1283) ney liquidated Latino's absurd constitution completely by establishing their wn government, which from its chief executive has received the name of the riors.

When we realize that with ups and downs and with certain subtractions nd additions the new government of the priors lasted for two hundred years, nat it lasted in fact as long as Florence remained a free commonwealth, we annot escape a conclusion of absolutely central importance. It is that Florence wed its material greatness to its merchant gilds and that it achieved somening as close to stable government as was possible under the complicated play f the municipal, provincial, and world-forces to which it was exposed, when 1 1282 its merchant gilds seized the political power. The merchant gilds were ocally not called merchant gilds but greater gilds (*arti maggiori*) and were even in number. They were (1) the gild of judges and notaries; (2) the Calimala gild, comprising the dealers in and refiners of foreign cloth; (3) the Cambio or gild of money-changers; (4) the Lana or wool gild, which dealt 1 cloth of local manufacture; (5) the Por Santa Maria gild, in which the eading retailers of the shopping street, called Por or Porta Santa Maria, were oined with the silk merchants; (6) the gild of physicians and apothecaries *speziali*), the latter including the dealers in oriental spices; (7) the gild of urriers, the importers of pelts and manufacturers of fur garments. While the ild of judges and notaries was manifestly not a gild of traders, it comprised ne important legal group, which at Florence and everywhere else became so ntimately associated with the rising bourgeoisie as to be inseparable from it. The other six gilds embraced the men of affairs and captains of industry, vhose clever capture of the rapidly multiplying economic opportunities of the nirteenth century had succeeded in making Florence a leading focus of alian and world-trade.

It was the seven arti maggiori which by instituting an executive of six riors to be chosen from its membership took over the government in 1282–83. However, they preferred to exhibit a certain moderation in respect to their ictory. The little bourgeoisie of shopkeepers and artisans was organized at ne time in certainly no fewer than twenty-five lesser gilds (*arti minori*) and robably in many more. The members had little or nothing in common with ne great traders, who held them in contempt but feared them nonetheless because of their numbers. On this account the merchant gilds on seizing power resolved to hold out an olive branch to the artisan element by inviting five of their gilds to share the power with them. The gilds so honored were doubtless the strongest of the minor gilds and for this reason are frequently referred to as middle gilds (*arti medie*). They were (1) the butchers; (2) the shoemakers; (3) the blacksmiths; (4) the builders, including both carpenter and masons; (5) the *rigattieri,* the second-hand dealers, a much more re spectable category in the Middle Ages than among ourselves, largely owing to the solid and durable character of medieval goods. As these five were ac cepted by the seven as co-rulers, we may with some justification speak, for the time being at least, of twelve greater gilds. But that the five middle gilds were never anything more than a decorative flourish on the system of merchan domination is proved by the fact that in the first decade (1282–92) of the existence of the priorate it was exercised exclusively, or all but exclusively, by members of the merchant oligarchy.[2]

Again as on previous occasions when the constitution had undergone a change in order to bring it abreast of the altered social situation, it was no reshaped from the bottom. The podestà, for instance, was not disturbed, no were his two traditional councils modified in any way. The podestà was stil to be a foreigner, appointed for a year to act as chief judge and to lead the army in war. However, he was now understood to be immediately responsible to the priors, who were the new executive charged with initiating legislatior and directing the policy of the commonwealth. Six in number, the prior served for two months, during which time they lived together as a single family in a private house hired for the purpose, until a generation later whe they moved into their own splendid palace, the Palazzo dei Signori, now the Palazzo Vecchio and still the most impressive reminder to native and vis itor alike of the former greatness of the city. Toward the close of thei term they elected their six successors in a session in which the heads o the twelve ruling gilds participated together with a number of wise mer (*sapientes*) chosen at pleasure among the six wards (*sesti*) of the city. To fortify the control achieved by the twelve arti maggiori they were organized into a militia under a captain and defender of the gilds. This militia, purely political in character, must not be confused with the citizen militia, which from the early days of the commune had been and still was the Florentine population mobilized for war. The gild militia rendered a purely domes tic service, which consisted in assembling at the call of its captain in order to protect the regime of the priors against the attack of its local enemies Like the podestà, the captain, who was rated as one of the heads of the state, was provided with two councils completely dominated by gildsmer in good standing. In comparison with the aristocratic Guelph and Ghibel line governments that had preceded the priors, the new government may with some justification be called democratic; but as it was a democracy strictly

[2] N. Ottokar, *Il Comune di Firenze alla Fine del Dugento*. Florence, 1926. On p. 25, note, th author gives the figures revealing the gild connection of the priors in the decade 1282-92 and show that the priors belonging to the middle gilds were so few as to be all but negligible. In thi period, and in almost all the subsequent periods as well, the priorate was the prerogative of th great merchants.

USES OF THE ALIGHIERI FAMILY AS RECONSTRUCTED EARLY IN THE TWENTIETH
NTURY AROUND AN AUTHENTIC CORE

ft: DANTE. FROM A MANUSCRIPT OF THE FOURTEENTH CENTURY IN THE RIC-
DIAN LIBRARY AT FLORENCE. *Right:* PETRARCH. FROM A MANUSCRIPT OF THE
URTEENTH CENTURY IN THE MEDICEAN LIBRARY AT FLORENCE

Left: ANDREA PISANO. THE LABORS OF OUR FIRST ANCESTORS. *Right:* ANI
PISANO. THE ART OF WEAVING

Left: PANEL (TREE OF LIFE) FROM THE PULPIT IN SAN LEONARDO IN ARC
Right: ANDREA PISANO. BURIAL OF ST. JOHN. A PANEL OF THE FIRST BR
DOOR OF THE BAPTISTRY

limited by membership in twelve ruling gilds, it would seem to be more properly described as a gild democracy. Such was the only kind of democracy of which Florence was at this time capable, and such, as a matter of fact, was the only kind which, in spite of occasional movements to broaden its base, Florence ever attained.

Although we have no knowledge of any disturbances attending the establishment of the new constitution, it had hardly been set up when it encountered opposition from the nobles. Owing to the shrinkage in the Ghibelline ranks the most conspicuous members of the nobility were now Guelphs, who, associated together in the powerful Guelph party, were far from looking on themselves as representatives of a lost cause. Enriched by the Ghibelline confiscations, the parte Guelfa occupied extensive club quarters, from which as a center it exercised a vast social and financial influence. The day of the old tower associations was over; and although many of the towers, deprived by civic enactment of their dizzy upper stories, still stood and vendetta continued to be the unwritten law of the land, men now conducted their feuds on a smaller scale and with less disturbance of the public peace. We cannot doubt that the civic order was already in far better case than in the rude consular age.

Owing to the almost stealthy establishment of the new government, the nobility did not at once realize that they were no longer the ruling power in the state. Then, with the gild democracy firmly consolidated by means of an armed militia, all that remained for the aristocrats to do in order to signify their displeasure was to vent their spite on the people by manifestations of contempt and individual acts of violence. Undoubtedly they had treated their social inferiors in this way in the past and with entire impunity. But the people, or at least a part of the people, were now in power, and a cry went up that this insufferable conduct must cease and that the nobles should at last, if necessary by special legislation, be brought into the common civic frame. As early as 1281, during the short-lived government instituted by Cardinal Latino, an effort had been made toward this end by a law which required individuals designated as magnates to give surety for their good behavior to the amount of two thousand *librae*. The law was resented by the individuals so designated and only irregularly enforced. On being re-enacted in a much stiffer form in 1286 it again remained very largely a dead letter. This persistent nullification can be accounted for only by the wavering attitude of the new government of the priors. It was made up of merchants with material interests, to defend which the new system had been devised; but many merchants, indeed the richest and most influential of the town, were members also of the parte Guelfa and connected by marriage and business partnerships with the Guelph nobiliary families. Consequently they became involved in a moral ambiguity. While their membership in the merchant gilds pushed them to defend popular interests and to support legislation directed against the lawless nobility, their kinship with the former ruling group filled them with a secret sympathy for this order and impelled them to soften whatever blows might be aimed at its arrogance. In short, confronted in its first phase with the problem of an unruly upper class inherited from the past, the government of the priors blew hot and cold for the simple reason that the leading individuals in the seats of power stood avowedly in the popular, but secretly also in the aristocratic, camp.

The whole first decade of the new government is troubled with this confusion.[3] But while, with secret allies in the priorate, the magnates were able to nullify some of the measures taken against them, there were other measures, behind which there was such a pressure of an aroused public opinion that resistance was impossible. In a class struggle, such as in essence we are here confronted with even though the class lines were not yet clearly drawn, the economic weapon is as certain to be brought into play as the political weapon and may, if effectively wielded, do quite as much damage. It has been contended by Salvemini but denied by Ottokar that it is in this sense that we must interpret the tendency more frequently to levy the tax on real property, the common form of nobiliary wealth. Be that as it may, a measure much more indisputably aimed at the nobles was the law of August 6, 1289, which liberated the serfs on the estates throughout the Florentine dominion. But here, too, considerable caution is in place. Without doubt the liberation of the serfs had begun in Tuscany with the earliest appearance of the commune. The towns with their copious opportunities for getting on in the world exercised a subtle lure, to which so many serfs had responded that Dante, the scornful and aloof scholar and poet, was moved contemptuously to refer to the numerous additions to the Florentine population in his day as a vile peasant breed. To keep the agricultural laborers from abandoning the countryside in a solid mass, the lords themselves had been compelled to improve the lot of their dependents by conceding them a better tenure through a contractual relation. This usually took the form of owner and peasant sharing the wheat, wine, olive oil, and other products grown by the peasant at some agreed ratio. The arrangement, called *mezzeria* or *mezzadria,* the more usual form, is to this day the common form of agricultural production in Tuscany. To all intents and purposes it was gradually worked out in the age of the communes when the serfdom of the earlier, the feudal, age could no longer be maintained.

Conceding that the liberation of the serfs had been making headway from as far back as the eleventh century, especially in the areas close to the towns, we must not forget that in the less accessible upland regions there were still vast noble properties where serfdom was rigorously enforced. It was these more remote noblemen whom the liberation law of 1289 was intended to smite; but in order that no lord, near or far, should escape, the law in question was declared to apply to the whole Florentine jurisdiction. It may be that, since medieval enactments were rarely carried into prompt effect, there was still sporadic serfdom even after the new law was passed; but that serf-

[3] That the social-political situation during the crucial decade (1282-93) was very complicated is proved by the unusually divergent opinions regarding it of scholars and historians. Few periods of Florentine history have been more intensely studied. The fundamental archival publication is the work of A. Gherardi, *Le Consulte della Repubblica Fiorentina dell'anno 1280 al 1298.* 2 vols. Florence, 1898. The consulte are in effect the minutes of the various Florentine councils. See also: G. Salvemini, *Magnati e Popolani in Firenze dal 1280 al 1295.* Florence, 1899; Davidsohn, Vol. II^2, chaps. 9-10; Caggese, Vol. I, chaps. 6-7; N. Ottokar, *Il Comune di Firenze,* etc. This last work is a detailed study of the cross- and under-currents that churned the Florentine social and political waters in the period in question.

dom, already long before 1289 a moribund institution, moved thenceforward precipitately to its demise can no more be doubted than that its passing in Tuscany antedates by generations and even centuries its end in the countries north of the Alps.[4]

In this same critical decade (1282–92) the current of opinion did not always and in all respects run against the magnates. They were a warrior group who fought on horseback and made their value felt the moment the city became involved in active conflict. Since the end of the Suabian line, the whole land of Tuscany had, largely under Florentine guidance, become Guelph, and the peace of the province undoubtedly depended on maintaining the Guelph predominance. Notwithstanding that the once vigorous and enterprising Florentine Ghibellines had dwindled to a pale and innocuous remnant, there were still enough virile Ghibellines left in other Tuscan towns, such as Pisa and Arezzo, as well as among the upland nobility, to constitute a perpetual threat to the established Guelph ascendancy. This was made manifest when, in 1287, the Ghibelline group of Arezzo ejected their Guelph rivals from the city and appropriated the government. The Florentine Guelphs, desiring to help their Aretine brothers, immediately clamored for war; and the citizenry and the priors were sufficiently averse to seeing a Ghibelline outpost set up at the head of the Arno stream to be themselves infected with bellicose sentiments. War followed, during which, with the nobles enthusiastically serving their country, it would not have been a handsome procedure to enforce the special code enacted against them as though they were enemies. The Aretine war culminated in the battle of Campaldino, fought not far from Arezzo on June 11, 1289; and when the Florentines won a crushing victory, owing in large measure to the reckless charge of their cavalry, they could not hinder the nobles on their return from conducting themselves in the streets and public squares with a more brazen swagger than ever.

The war at the source of the Arno was followed by a war at its mouth against Pisa. Clinging more than any other town of Tuscany or even of Italy to its Ghibelline memories, Pisa needed only the example of Arezzo to persuade it to restore (1288) its Ghibelline government. At the same time it had the good sense to intrust its defense against the Guelphs, sure to resent this backsliding, to a great soldier, the Ghibelline nobleman, Guido of Montefeltro. The result was that when the Florentines, thinking to repeat their Aretine triumph, began a war against Pisa, they made no headway against the clever defensive tactics of their opponent. They returned to the assault in three successive campaigns and on the failure of the third campaign suffered the not unusual revulsion characteristic of democratic communities. They complained they had been drawn into an unnecessary war by their Guelph nobles, all sense of gratitude for the Campaldino victory disappeared, and the resentment they had so long been nursing against the arrogant brawlers in their midst erupted volcanically.

This is the plausible version rather than the documented certainty touching the fresh and decisive outburst against the magnates which occurred in the

[4] The interesting act of liberation is printed in Villari, *I Primi Due Secoli*, etc., Vol. I, pp. 268-70.

winter of 1292–93. Even now nothing might have been done, if the outraged people had not found a leader capable of giving effect to their angry sentiments. This was Giano della Bella, descendant of one of the most ancient families of the city and a member of the Calimala, the oldest and richest of the great trading gilds. Much has been conjectured about Giano, very little is securely known. As certain we may set down that, animated by hatred of his fellow-nobles, to many of whom he was bound by ties of blood, he resolved to spare no effort to put an end to their excesses. Recognizing that if his attack was to be successful, he would have to broaden the base of the democratic regime, he inaugurated his campaign by drawing the remaining gilds, which by a process of fusion were reduced to nine, into the existing system. These least important gilds, called arti minori, were, to name them by their leading members: (1) the retailers of wine; (2) the innkeepers; (3) the sellers of salt, oil, and cheese; (4) the tanners; (5) the armorers; (6) the ironworkers (other than blacksmiths); (7) the girdlemakers; (8) the woodworkers (other than carpenters); (9) the bakers. The nine were given a military organization, which was added to and incorporated in the already existent militia of the twelve greater gilds. Thus strengthened, the government launched a new attack upon the magnates of a far more uncompromising character than any that had yet taken place. It assumed the form of the promulgation on January 18, 1293, of the most famous act of Florentine constitutional history, the Ordinances of Justice.[5]

The early articles of the Ordinances of Justice are strictly constitutional in nature, for they are concerned with defining the outstanding features of the government, particularly the priors, the captain, their respective councils, and the political brotherhood of the twelve major gilds enlarged by the recent addition of the minor gilds to the number of nine. There follow the interesting regulations regarding the election of the priors and their fraternal living during their two months' term of office. An important addition to the six priors authorized by the Ordinances deserves particular attention. This addition was a seventh prior with the special designation of a gonfalonier or banner-bearer of Justice (*vexillifer justitiae, gonfaloniere della giustizia*). The function of the banner-bearer was to execute the sentences pronounced in the court of the podestà against the magnates and to this end he was assigned a force of one thousand men. This special force was required to assemble, properly armed, at the order of the gonfalonier and to follow his special banner of white silk conspicuously marked with a red cross whithersoever he carried it in execution of the podestà's judgment against an offending magnate.

By far the largest section of the Ordinances of Justice is concerned with the magnates (*magnati, grandi*), who furnished the immediate occasion for this sweeping constitutional document. It is notable and somewhat surprising that the older term "nobles" was in this law completely replaced by the newer word. The change may be taken to signify that by 1293 it had become well understood in Florence that the highest citizen group was no longer noble

[5] Published first by Bonaini, in *Arch. Stor. It.*, Nuova Serie, Vol. I, pp. 3 ff. A better edition, with the emendations of 1295, will be found in Salvemini, *Magnati e Popolani*, etc., pp. 384-432.

or feudal in the true sense of the word but merely a limited body of families whose wealth dated farther back than that of the growing mass of successful traders. In strict accord with human nature from the beginning of time the families of older wealth gave themselves feudal airs, cultivated horsemanship, practiced themselves in arms, and sought the honor of knighthood. It is this last-named distinction, knighthood, on which the law fastened when it came to drawing up the list of families who, designated as magnate, were to be put under special restraints and subjected to special penalties. We know, not from the Ordinances themselves but from another source, that on the strength of the knighthood provision not quite one hundred and fifty families of Florence and its county had the magnate or grande stigma put upon them. As each family was really a sum of related families, that is, a clan, it is difficult to estimate the number of individual males that may have been affected by the measure.[6] To put their number at a thousand would hardly seem to be an exaggeration.

Each male member of each family designated by the law as magnate was obliged to swear a special oath of obedience to the government of the priors and to give bond in the sum of two thousand librae that he would keep the peace. In case he failed to pay, his next of kin was liable, since the law laid down the principle of familial responsibility. If from the act of violence committed by the grande against the popolano death did not follow, the aggressor might be fined up to the total amount of the surety, depending on the gravity of the wound. In the case of death, however, the law knew no paltering. On the outrage being reported to the podestà, this official was obliged with the least possible delay to pronounce the death sentence against the offending magnate together with the confiscation of his goods and the destruction of his houses. At this point the banner-bearer of Justice and his special militia of one thousand men entered into action as executors of the sentence. Even more irksome to the magnates than these financial and social disabilities were the political disabilities imposed on them. They could not be elected to the priorate (Article III); they could not sit in the councils of the captain (Article XV); and, although they might continue to belong to a gild, they could not exercise authority within the gild by serving as consul or rector (Article XXXIV).

Although Giano della Bella did not sit in the priorate that passed the Ordinances of Justice, as the spiritual father and prime mover of the fuller democratic system with its special edge against the magnates, he was bound in honor to show his countrymen that the teeth he had put into this legislation were effective. He therefore had himself elected into the subsequent priorate which began its bimestrial term on February 15, 1293. As, in accordance with the requirements of the constitution, the six priors were distributed among the six wards or sesti in such a way that each sesto always boasted a prior from its territory, we learn on this occasion that Giano represented the sesto Porta San Piero, in which the houses of his family were located. A high-spirited, impulsive man, persuaded that it was his mission to bring jus-

[6] Salvemini, *Magnati e Popolani,* p. 376, gives the list of *town* magnates—seventy-two families in all.

tice to his city, he saw that the success of the reform hinged on making a good start; and when it was reported that a member of the Galli, a family inscribed under the requirements of the law on the roll of magnates, had murdered two Florentine commoners, he resolved on immediate action, even though the crime had taken place in distant France and the murderer himself could not be apprehended. The case was brought before the podestà who pronounced sentence according to the Ordinances. Thereupon, the new official, the gonfalonier of Justice, doubtless under pressure from the watchful Giano, had his bell sounded as the law prescribed, his guard of one thousand men streamed together before the residence of the priors, and with his banner of white silk marked with a red cross leading the way, the functionary specially appointed to deal with magnates marched upon the houses of the Galli. They lay along Por Santa Maria, one of the streets most densely crowded with the towers and houses of the old families. Under the direction of skilful masons the work of destruction was promptly taken in hand, while the banner-bearer and his militia maintained a sharp lookout against a possible diversion on the part of the outraged magnates, and the trumpeters of the commune added to the solemnity of the occasion by sounding their instruments as though the Day of Judgment had arrived.

The Day of Judgment for magnates. For thus had Giano della Bella and his following of commoners highly resolved. It remained to be seen whether the magnates took the same view of their impending doom and were prepared to give up the ghost without further struggle.

XII. A Tragic Interlude: The Blacks, the Whites, and Pope Boniface VIII

THE crisis precipitated in Florence by the Ordinances of Justice may, without doing violence to the facts, be dramatized as a duel between a tribune of the people and the order of patricians; but to understand the resolution of the crisis we must go beyond these simple terms. Giano della Bella's following consisted of the lesser gilds and the unorganized proletariat, an excitable mass which from the beginning of time has proved a most unreliable support. Undoubtedly, too, he had the backing of some of the upper gildsmen; but many members of this group openly, and even more of them secretly, took the view that the Ordinances bore too heavily on the magnates, who in their majority not only were merchants like themselves but were also actually associated with them in business. The leaders among Giano's merchant opponents were men of the soft-treading, vulpine type and, as masters of intrigue, were able to render invaluable assistance to their more forthright allies, the magnates, who, prompted by their feudal habits, were not averse to appealing to the sword. Finally, the character and role of Giano must not be overlooked. In the ungoverned pursuit of what was to him a great cause, he had become a demagogue; but he was not a wholehearted demagogue, for he had too many moral scruples and too much personal delicacy to identify himself with the mob in all its aspects and activities.

We are remarkably well informed about these hidden elements in the situation by one of the most spirited works of the whole range of Florentine historiography, the chronicle of Dino Compagni.[1] A member of one of the greater gilds, Dino was the type of the mounting trader instinctively hostile to merchants of an older date than himself who had the bad taste to play at being gentlemen of ancient lineage by the adoption of military customs. He could fairly regard himself as one of the founders of the new democratic government, for he had served as prior as early as 1282; and naturally when Providence deigned to give the plain people in Giano Della Bella a leader resolved to bridle the overbearing magnates, Dino, like the simple and honest soul he was, hailed him as a deliverer. In afteryears when, as a sequel to the Ordinances, Florence had gone through a painful agony and Dino himself had been politically snuffed out, he sat down to write his recollections. By that act he became the producer of a type of literature of which there were

[1] The standard edition is that of I. Del Lungo, *Dino Compagni e la sua Cronica.* 3 vols. Florence, 1879-80. For an evaluation of this work see Introduction.

as yet few, if any, examples. The unfamiliarity of the age with Dino's kind of document is proved by its having been passed on to us under the name of a chronicle, a traditional form to which it no longer bore any resemblance. Like all memoirs, those of Dino, owing to his reliance on the ever treacherous human memory, are crowded with innumerable errors of detail; nonetheless they disclose so many piquant and picturesque incidents that they constitute quite the most precious single source we have on the rise and fall of Giano della Bella and on the subsequent ferocious feud between the Blacks and the Whites. Present-day writers have been greatly encouraged to lean on Dino by the fact that the abundant documents recently brought to light have almost invariably confirmed the old merchant's veracity.

Having served as prior from February 15 to April 15, 1293, Giano della Bella became, in accordance with a requirement of his own Ordinances, ineligible for re-election to the priorate for two years. However, since he was now the head of the dominant party, his retirement from office did not interfere with his exercise of an indirect control. It was this continuing power that persuaded his enemies that the first step toward getting rid of the new system would be to get rid of him. Many of the magnates, as might be expected, favored an armed uprising. Apart, however, from its certain failure so long as the people presented a solid front, the upper class was so little united, owing to its interminable private feuds, that anything resembling a generally accepted plan of action was out of the question. It was therefore agreed to adopt a suggestion originating with a group of clever, intriguing lawyers. Associated from the start with the new regime as members of the gild of judges and notaries, the lawyers in the main had no patience with the recent democratic turn of events, and, like most of their kind throughout the ages, were animated with a strong conservative preference for inherited privileges and established wealth. As their chosen weapon was not the sword but the word as sharp as and sharper than the sword, they urged a whispering campaign against Giano which would picture him as a tyrant and fill one group after another with suspicion of his designs. It greatly helped their purpose that the tribune was an ardent spirit given to the habit of easing his mind by passionate outbursts against his opponents. By picking up these temperamental utterances and giving them a subterranean currency a definitely hostile atmosphere could be gradually created. All that would then be needed to explode the bomb was the spark supplied by some chance event.

Most appropriately, the needed happy accident was furnished by the most daring, picturesque, and uncompromising member of the class which the new fundamental law designated as magnates and enemies. Corso de' Donati had led the cavalry attack which smashed the Ghibellines at Campaldino in 1289. His consciousness of having deserved well of his country did not tend to reduce his class pretensions, which, deeply bred in the bone, had, even before Campaldino, brought him into repeated conflicts with the new social order. The average gildsman consistently regarded Corso as his enemy; the common people, on the other hand, were alternately for and against him. We owe to Dino a sharply etched vignette giving evidence that the lower orders were often carried away by the glamor emanating from Corso's ancient name and feudal bearing. For, says Dino, when, armed and mounted on his charger, Corso rode grandly through the streets, he was greeted on all hands with a spontaneous *Viva il Barone!*

Superfluously, one is tempted to say, but inevitably in view of his violent character, the head of the Donati family had involved himself in half a score of feuds with other magnate houses. It was these innumerable divisions among the grandi which hindered their effective union and greatly accelerated their decline. By this time, when the Ghibellines had practically vanished from the local scene, to avoid the threatening tedium of existence Guelphs had begun to quarrel with Guelphs and, not content with this new viciousness, a single Guelph family often fell into two implacable factions. Thus it was with the Donati. The swaggering Corso was not the man to regard a relative who had rebelled against his headship with a culpable leniency; and when, on a December day of the year 1294, he encountered his hostile cousin, Simone, in the streets, a fracas followed in which Corso wounded Simone and killed one of Simone's grooms. The case came under the Ordinances of Justice for the sole reason that the unfortunate groom was a popolano. At the hearing before the podestà, a foreigner and a knight as both law and custom demanded, the brazen Corso succeeded in presenting the incident in such a light that, although he was smitten with a money fine, it was not himself but his cousin who was condemned to loss of life and property as the guilty party. The sentence was pronounced on January 23, 1295; and no sooner did the report of it spread among the people whom the sensational trial had drawn in a dense mass to the gates of the podestà's palace than an outcry arose over this monstrous miscarriage of justice, ending in an uprising. By setting fire to the wooden doors of the grim stone fortress the mob forced an entrance into the interior. Only by swift and ignominious flight over the neighboring house roofs was the podestà able to save his life. The cheated victors vented their rage by plundering his residence from cellar to garret.

This orgy of popular lawlessness greatly shocked the instincts of the propertied classes and produced a sharp mental reaction. No sooner therefore was order restored than the priors were invited by the councils to institute an investigation in order to discover and punish the leading culprits. The inquiry disclosed that a brother of Giano della Bella's, Taldo by name, had taken a prominent part in inciting the people against the podestà. Giano himself had adopted exactly the opposite course. Mounting a horse, he had forced his way into the crowd to dissuade it from committing violence, but the maddened people had turned their spears against their erstwhile idol and had obliged him to desist. His spell had been broken and his enemies took heart. When, a few days later, the election of a new group of priors took place, his opponents dominated the situation and put in power a magistracy uncompromisingly hostile to his person and cause. On the very day (February 15, 1295) on which they took the oath of office, they ordered Giano's arrest on the impudently false charge that he had caused the recent public disorder. Dino Compagni, who loved his leader deeply but not uncritically, afterward declared that in his opinion the champion of the people should have met the challenge by one last effort to rally his followers about him. Giano was of another mind, perhaps because of disgust with the fickle populace he had so wholeheartedly served. He decided to leave the country, and the government, happy to bring the issue to a close without a trial of strength, threw no difficulties in his way. But as soon as he was well out of reach, in accordance with that bitter irony which has rung down the curtain on the career of so many public men, he was condemned under his own Ordinances of Justice to loss of life and goods. He retired to France, where he continued to live for more than a decade, a true Florentine to the end, for he attempted to recoup his shattered fortunes by a fresh trading venture.

On Giano's disappearance from the scene, Corso Donati and his magnate following imagined it would be an easy thing to dispose of the Ordinances. But they were mistaken. When in the summer of this same year they tried a sudden rising, they encountered so vigorous a resistance on the part of a united people that they were obliged to resort to negotiations. Undeniably, however, they prospered in these more than they had reason to expect because of their secret friends in the government. While they agreed once again to submit to the Ordinances, which thus triumphed as the law of the land, they were accorded a few mitigations, of which one at least was not unimportant. The original requirement regarding eligibility to the chief magistracy had been that the priors must be chosen from such gildsmen as actively exercised their profession (*de artificibus continue artem exercentibus*). After the revision of July 6, 1295, all persons carried on the gild rolls were eligible, regardless of whether they were actively engaged in the business of the gild or not. This opened a way for such members of the old families as chose to give up their feudal habits to be absorbed into full citizen fellowship. However, the central and essential article of the Ordinances, excluding from the priorate and the various institutions that had arisen with the priorate all families, any individual member of which had acquired the honor of knighthood, remained untouched by the revision.[2]

On the heel of the foiled magnate uprising of the summer of 1295 a new difference appeared among the great houses which, by spreading gradually to the other classes, ended in a rupture culminating in a fresh set of devastating calamities. Ever since Corso Donati had raised his head as a spokesman of the magnates a close neighbor of his of the Porta San Piero quarter, Vieri de' Cerchi, had put forth pretensions of his own to magnate leadership and had gained a considerable following. Vieri, too, was a knight who on the field of Campaldino had ridden furiously into action. However, his knighthood was only a garment for festival wear, for he was the richest and shrewdest banker of his day and the head of the most flourishing trading company of the city. This immersion in business invited the scorn of Corso Donati who, as the representative of an older, prouder, but impoverished family, was bent on presenting himself to view exclusively in the role of a great baron. The opposed interests and attitudes of the two men had produced nothing worse than back-biting and ridicule until the renewed acceptance of the Ordinances forced on the magnates in 1295. With that date a political divergence made its appearance over the policy by which the magnate interest would hence-

[2] Article III. Salvemini, *Magnati e Popolani,* p. 390.

forth be best served. Vieri, the banker, intimately linked with all the far-flung business of the town and exercising an indefinable influence among all the merchant gilds, made up his mind that the time had come to give up the struggle against the Ordinances. The people regarded them as their Bill of Rights and, fickle though they might be in other matters, flew to arms the moment this palladium of their liberty was threatened. Moreover, the movement within the government since the fall of Giano della Bella showed that, with the lower orders deprived of a leader, political authority had slipped back into the hands of the lawyers and merchants of the arti maggiori. Of these, the head of the great banking house of the Cerchi was the intimate associate, and among them he could hope, even though as a knight he was excluded from the priorate, to exercise a commanding influence. A not inconsiderable number of magnates, who, though magnates, were also business men, fell in with these views and, joining themselves to Vieri, created a Cerchi party. To the intransigent Corso such conciliatory action was no better than treason. When his fellow-irreconcilables gathered under his banner, he found himself at the head of a rival party of the Donati. True, the two parties were loose political rings rather than parties in a modern sense, but they represented a definite split among the magnates with ramifications reaching far down into the people. Above all, the split signified a division among the dominant Guelphs and this undoubtedly held a threat for the continued Guelph character of the city.

The invaluable Dino affords us vivid glimpses of how the Guelph feud developed amidst an atmosphere of constantly increasing tension. The following scene befell on December 16, 1296, although Dino does not say so, since, as a rambling memoirist, he has a mind elevated above dates.[3]

One day many citizens came together in the Piazza de' Frescobaldi to assist at the funeral of a woman, it being the custom of the country on such occasions for the men of title to sit on wooden benches, while the simple citizens sat on the ground on straw mats. [This was the usual form of mourning among well-to-do Florentines. While the men honored the dead acquaintance by solemnly gathering in the manner here described, the women, gathered around the corpse in an inner room, demonstrated their sorrow by loud weeping.] With the Cerchi partisans on one side and the Donati partisans on the other, someone stood up either to smooth out his garment or for some other reason. At once, from suspicion, those of the opposite party stood up and laid hand to their swords. Their opponents did the same and blows fell. The neutrals who were present interposed and stopped the fight. Notwithstanding, many people rushed to the houses of the Cerchi, demanding to be led against the Donati; but the Cerchi refused.[4]

Still further to enlighten us touching the charged atmosphere, Dino follows this episode with another, which probably befell in the ensuing year, although the careless author again vouchsafes us no date. The story introduces us to Guido Cavalcanti, poet and friend of Dante Alighieri. The Italian title "messer" is the equivalent of the Latin "dominus" and was reserved for the highest social order, the knights and judges.

[3] Davidsohn, Vol. III, p. 27, supplies the date from another source.
[4] This and the following episode in the Del Lungo edition, pp. 88-92.

There was a noble young knight, Guido by name, son of messer Cavalcante Cavalcanti. He was courteous and brave but contemptuous of the common people and given to solitude and study. He was an enemy of messer Corso and had repeatedly attempted to do him an injury. Messer Corso feared him greatly because of his intrepid spirit; and once, while Guido was on pilgrimage to Santiago de Compostella, Corso plotted to have him assassinated. But the attempt failed. On which account, having on his return to Florence heard of the plot, he incited many youths against Corso, pledging them to come to his aid. And being one day in company with some youths of the house of Cerchi mounted and with javelin in hand, he spurred his horse against messer Corso, trusting he would be followed by the Cerchi. . . . And as he rode past Corso he threw his javelin and missed. With messer Corso at the time were Simone, his son, a brave and powerful youth, and Cecchino de' Bardi, and many others, all armed with swords. And they pursued Guido but, unable to reach him, threw stones at him. And from the windows stones were thrown so that Guido was wounded in the hand.

It must have been becoming harder and harder for the government of the priors to maintain the peace between the two inflamed factions. Secretly the rulers leaned toward the Cerchi because the Cerchi had accepted the situation; but this only made the Donati more implacable. Nor were these latter without weighty support of their own. As the temper of the official organization of the Guelphs, the parte Guelfa, was uncompromisingly aristocratic, it did not hesitate to throw its considerable influence into the scales on the Donati side. Besides, the resourceful, turbulent Corso was a host in himself. In the winter of 1298–99 he even managed by means that remain unrevealed to acquire a dominant influence in the government. At any rate the appearances favor this view, for he succeeded in having a podestà elected who, when he arrived in Florence, regarded himself as Corso's personal agent. He was messer Monfiorito da Coderta, a native of Treviso and of course a knight. Possibly it was his class feeling which explains his friendship with Corso and which led him to commit an act of outrageous malfeasance. In a civil suit brought by Corso against his mother-in-law the obliging podestà went the partisan length of condemning the defendant to the loss of all her property. So monstrous was the sentence and so general the indignation over it that messer Monfiorito was arrested, deprived of office, and assessed a fantastic fine. And, once aroused, the public wrath was not appeased till the insolent Corso, who had so manifestly tampered with the leading official of the state, was himself brought to justice. He was smitten with a heavy money penalty and sent into exile (May, 1299). The unscrupulous magnate had overplayed his hand and had lost.

The elimination of their leader so weakened the Donati that the Cerchi gained an unchallenged ascendancy in the town. The government continued as before to rest with the priors and the gilds, but the appointment to office fell more and more in accordance with the wishes of an inner ring made up of the Cerchi and their friends. While the mass of the Florentines accepted this turn of affairs, at least for the time being, the Donati, their banished leader, and the allied parte Guelfa had thoughts only of restitution and revenge and searched the sky in every direction for a helper. They found him in the pope, who in point of fact had already for so long a time been pondering interference that he did not have to be importuned to be induced to act.

The pope who now thrust himself as a leading character into the Florentine drama was Boniface VIII, one of the most eminent and problematical, though certainly not one of the worthiest, successors of the Apostle Peter. Boniface was elected to the papacy in December, 1294, after having gained a wide experience in the varied business of the church. Like so many of his greatest predecessors, he was by both temperament and education a canon lawyer and, thus equipped, became the exponent of the most extravagant claims of the ecclesiastical jurists. If, as was freely whispered among his countrymen, he did not believe in the immortality of the soul, it might be argued that, in rejecting this central tenet of Christianity, he had removed himself, in an ideal sense, from the Christian fold. On the other hand, we should not forget that the Christian fold had long ago been institutionalized as a church, and that for Pope Boniface to play his magnificent part it was much less important for him to be a true believer than a strict and energetic churchman. It was certainly as a churchman that he has established his place in history, for his name is forever associated with the culmination of the papal claims to world-control. The early medieval view that the rule of Christendom was to be shared equally between pope and emperor had gradually, under the strain of conflict, been replaced by the doctrine of papal supremacy. Certainly it is difficult to see how the position taken by such vigorous authoritarians as Gregory VII and Innocent III can be interpreted other than as outright abandonment of the original balanced dualism. When Boniface VIII in his turn faced the problem, he cannot be said to have done more than give the Gregorian theory of the relation of church and state a more precise and ringing formulation than it had yet received. His declarations were absolutely uncompromising and left not the least doubt that he regarded emperors, kings, and princes throughout the Christian world as holding their positions subject to his good pleasure. The pope derived his power from God, but the heads of states derived their power from the pope.

While it is not permissible even to mention Boniface VIII without indicating his eminence in the field of politico-ecclesiastical theory, his importance for Florence derives much less from his papal than from his personal ambitions. To be sure, he took toward the Florentine government the attitude imposed by his view of papal supremacy. That meant, as regards the ruling clique identified with the Cerchi, that they must do the papal bidding or suffer the consequences. However, he was principally moved in regard to the Cerchi by a consideration of a more personal sort, which was to subject Florence and, together with Florence, Tuscany to himself in order to hand them over to one of his relatives. For—and now we are touching on a side of his character hardly less important than his unswerving canonical dogmatism—Boniface VIII was a ferocious nepotist. In this respect, too, he cannot be said to have been an innovator. Almost from the earliest days of their great office, occasional incumbents of St. Peter's chair had yielded to the temptation of using their power to advance the fortunes of their families.

The great feudal clans of Rome, the Colonna, the Orsini, the Savelli, owed their vast wealth and historical status exclusively to this evil practice. If we now remind ourselves that Boniface VIII belonged to a lesser clan of the Roman Campagna, the Caetani, and that throughout his early life he had been exposed to the slights of the greater lords, we have no difficulty in understanding that from the moment he commanded the unbounded resources of the papacy he resolved to use them to raise the Caetani to a level with the oldest and most powerful barons of the capital.

The procedure most commonly followed by the popes to enrich their relatives was to endow them with manorial properties within the papal state. While Boniface adopted this measure, and that, too, with such characteristic legal thoroughness that the Caetani are to this day the lords of the largest aggregate of lands in central Italy, he followed also another course, which may have been suggested to him by Nicholas III. In this pope we meet another Roman magnate, a member of the Orsini clan. Animated with all the characteristic Roman ambitions, Nicholas, as has been noted in the previous chapter, had taken advantage of the enfeebled empire to induce Rudolph of Hapsburg to make over to him the province called the Romagna. The ultimate purpose of Nicholas had been to endow one of his nephews with the Romagna, and only his premature death had kept him from carrying out the plan. To Boniface VIII it seemed that Albert, son and successor of the accommodating Rudolph, might with equal ease be persuaded to repeat Rudolph's act of self-denial by surrendering to the head of Christendom another portion of his Italian kingdom, the province of Tuscany. He, Boniface, might then enfeoff with it some member of his family to help magnify the Caetani name.[5]

This analysis of Boniface's motives will serve to explain the disastrous role he came to play in Florentine affairs beginning with the assumption of power by the Cerchi faction. If this ruling junta had been willing to submit to his orders, it is quite unlikely that Boniface would ever have quarreled with it. But his orders, based on the view that the Donati were sound Guelphs and deeply devoted to his person, consistently ran to the effect that the Cerchi were to make peace with the Donati and share with them the offices and honors. And this the Cerchi refused to do, for selfish reasons in the first place, but also because they had become perfectly clear in their minds that the pope planned to use the Donati as his means of acquiring personal control of the city. In resisting the pope they were therefore following the policy which was as old as the Florentine commune, and which regarded independence as more precious than life. They twisted and turned, like the crafty democratic politicians they were; they protested their eternal devotion to his Holiness; but his bidding they would not do, conscious that in defending Florence against a planned papal encroachment they were doing their patriotic duty in accordance with the hopes and prayers of the vast majority of their fellow-citizens.

To a man of so autocratic a temper as Boniface the instinctive response to a rebuff is an appeal to force. And Boniface might have resorted to force at

[5] G. Levi, *Bonifazio VIII e le sue Relazioni col Comune di Firenze*. Rome, 1882. This author was the first to disclose Boniface's Tuscan ambitions. In their light the pope's resolve to subdue Florence, the capital of Tuscany, to his will becomes much more intelligible.

once, had it not been that when the Florentine deadlock occurred the Christian world had arrived at the turn of the century. For the year 1300 the pope had proclaimed a great Catholic Jubilee to be celebrated in the city of Rome; and if the capital of Christendom was to be visited by the expected masses of pilgrims on horse and on foot from all over the world, it was absolutely necessary that the highways of Italy should not ring with the shrill alarms of war. In order to further the Jubilee, Boniface was therefore willing to adjourn his reckoning with Florence. And when, amidst conditions of unusual peacefulness, the great festival occurred, it carried his self-esteem to its acme. It was estimated that 200,000 people visited Rome to pray at the shrines of the martyrs and to receive the papal blessing; and Boniface, a man in many respects more pagan than Christian, again and again presented himself to the pilgrim multitudes enthroned majestically above them and inhaling their adulation like a rich incense.

There was therefore peace between Florence and the pope in the year 1300. But at Florence itself it was a peace electrically charged. Aware that the pope was on their side, the Donati faction never ceased to annoy their antagonists in the seats of power. On May Day, when the city was in the habit of celebrating the return of spring with feasting in the homes and dancing and merry-making in the streets and public squares, a group of Donati youths wantonly attacked a company of the Cerchi assembled to watch a group of girls delicately treading a measure on the Piazza Santa Trinità. In a moment there was an uproar, but before the combatants could be separated the young Ricoverino de' Cerchi had suffered the shocking indignity of having his nose cut off by a Donati sword. Other similar clashes kept the city at a feverish temperature, informing all who were not deaf and blind that the Roman Jove had suspended but not cancelled his wrath. Indeed it was public knowledge that he was busily preparing a military expedition to break the stubborn Florentine resistance to his will.

In order to understand the new turn of the papal policy, we shall have to take note of still another of the varied activities of the restless pontiff. He had hardly been elevated to power when he spurred his Angevin protégé, King Charles II, to renew his efforts to conquer the island of Sicily; and to prove his sincerity he lavishly provided Charles with subsidies in support of naval and military forces assembled to drive out the Aragonese usurper. When these mighty efforts had proved vain, the undiscouraged Boniface evolved a fresh plan which looked to the king of France for help. This was Philip IV, called the Fair, the only man in the contemporary world who in bold self-esteem and frenzied ambition might be called a fit match for the pope. Their sharp tempers had already clashed over the king's attempt to tax the French clergy in the interest of the royal purse. Pope Boniface had promptly interposed his veto but, with so many other quarrels on his hands, he had adjourned the issue by agreeing to a provisional settlement. When, in the year 1299, he approached Philip with the project to lend a hand in the conquest of Sicily, he hoped the flattery of the invitation would not be lost on the king. Specifically, he requested that Philip send his brother, Charles of Valois, to Rome with a band of French knights to serve as the nucleus of an army to be recruited at the expense of the pope and to be sent to Sicily to end at last the struggle which had now been going on for twenty years. The bargain was struck and the coming of Charles of Valois fixed for the summer of the year after the peaceful Jubilee. It was the subjugation of the Sicilians for which the French prince was engaged; but by way of curtain-raiser Boniface planned, as soon as he would have his agent under his hand at Rome, to send him to Florence to settle the score with the recalcitrant Cerchi.

All this was so well known on the Arno that there was no doubt in the minds of the ruling group that in the year 1301 they would have to fight for their existence. It is this consciousness which accounts for the action the Cerchi now took in regard to Pistoia. This nearby town had for many years been riven with a local strife of so terrible a character that one is at a loss to account for it except on the ancient Greek theory that whom the gods wish to destroy they first make mad. The struggle had its origin in a division of the leading local family, the Cancellieri, into two camps, the White Cancellieri and the Black Cancellieri. By degrees the quarrel had spread like an insidious contagion to the whole population which, with every man's hand against his brother, was threatened with extermination. In the year 1296 the government of Florence interfered, assumed supreme control over Pistoia for five years and, by dividing the offices equally between the Whites and the Blacks, and at the same time by enforcing order, established a precarious truce. In the spring of 1301 the Cerchi faction, peering anxiously into the future, became alarmed by the thought that the expiration of the Florentine control over Pistoia exactly synchronized with the prospective struggle for independence with the pope. Should the Florentines surrender control over Pistoia, and should this town then put itself under the protection of the curia, Florence would, in a military sense, be greatly imperiled. On this account the Cerchi staked their safety on a very dangerous plan. They conspired with the stronger, or at least the better disposed faction of the Pistoiese, the Whites, and with the aid of these allies and amidst a renewal of the horrible local atrocities, in May, 1301, drove the leading Blacks from the city. It was this identification of the Cerchi with the Pistoiese Whites which led to their having the label of "Whites" now applied to themselves; and naturally with the betrayed Pistoiese Blacks calling desperately to the Donati for help, this Florentine party came soon to be known as "Blacks." Although it was never forgotten in Florence that the new civil struggle with which the city was tormented originated in a conflict of opinion between the families of the Donati and the Cerchi, beginning with the summer of the year 1301 the old party names were completely superseded by the newer and more colorful designations borrowed from Pistoia.

The only possible way in which the Cerchi could have justified their monstrous breach of faith toward Pistoia would have been to make it appear as the inaugural act of an energetic struggle for independence against a power-maddened pope. But that is precisely what they failed to do. After the wholly isolated act of daring connected with Pistoia, the Cerchi or, as we shall call them henceforward, the Whites, were smitten with complete paralysis. In the late summer, in accordance with the bargain struck with Pope Boniface,

Charles of Valois reported at Rome with a small force of French knights, and again, exactly as had been planned and generally foreseen, the pope, before sending him off to conquer Sicily, dispatched him to Tuscany to bring the Whites to heel. Agreeing that the Whites, if they stood for anything, stood for the freedom of their city, we are bound to declare that they made as despicable a defense as any recorded in history of a cause which men have universally acclaimed as noble. The miserable truth is that the leading Whites were in the main prosperous merchants who had no stomach for the grinding realities of war. At their head was Vieri de' Cerchi, the great banker, and Vieri's financial interests made him pitifully tremulous for the safety of his investments. When, in moments of danger, feebleness sits at the helm, discouragement quickly masters passengers and crew, and Vieri's timidity was not long in communicating itself to the priors and the other governing bodies. They seized on the idea that the French wolf advancing against them was possibly no wolf at all. They even encouraged one another to view him as a lamb, and to fortify their willing credulity lent an eager ear to the prince's ambassadors who announced that their lord was coming with the single object of making peace among the citizens. Peace! In their terror they fastened on this fiction, although at the bottom of their hearts they knew with absolute certainty that the mission of the scion of the house of Valois was to depose the Whites and put the Blacks in power. Tremulously the priors receded from position after position, until on November 1, 1301, the papal forces of less than a thousand men rode through the southern gate without having flung at them so much as a hostile cry. The central figure of the military pageant of that fatal day was the contemptible French prince and executioner, whom the most famous of his Florentine victims did not fail duly to gibbet in his great poem. He pictured Charles of Valois riding into Florence not with the loyal weapons of a *preux chevalier,* but "armed with the lance that Judas swung." [6]

Solely because of this victim, the austere thinker and unrivaled poet, Dante Alighieri, the revolution precipitated by the coming of the French prince has induced so thoroughgoing an investigation of every scrap of the surviving evidence that we are exceptionally well informed about the tragic incidents following the occupation of the city by the Franco-papal army.[7] The poet was a member of an ancient Florentine family which, though noble, had never been particularly conspicuous and which in its recent representatives had consistently aligned itself with the Guelphs. Seventeen when the priorate was established in 1282, Dante enjoyed the advantage of having been obliged to adjust to the democratic victory while he was still undeveloped and flexible. There can be no doubt that the young man made his peace with the new system, for, in sign of his acceptance of it, he joined the gild of the *Medici e Speziali.* Membership in a gild, it will be remembered, was the prerequisite for the enjoyment of political rights. However, to be carried on a gild roll did not

[6] *Purgatorio,* XX, 74.

[7] The first modern presentation by Del Lungo (in Vol. I of his edition of Dino Compagni) was followed by numerous studies dealing with special aspects of the event and crowned by a searching recapitulation by Davidsohn, Vol. III, chap. I; *Forschungen,* Vol. III, p. 2 ("Die Schwarzen und die Weissen"); *Forschungen,* Vol. IV, pp. 259-68.

necessarily signify (after 1295) that the member actively exercised the occupation the gild in question denoted, and Dante of course has never been suspected by anyone of being either a physician or an apothecary.[8] He was a scholar, poet, and gentleman of leisure who, like his forebears, derived his living from a modest property. In spite of his eligibility to public office, he did no more than occasionally participate in politics till the independence of his beloved city was threatened by Pope Boniface. Then, with a quick decision, he took his stand with the Whites. By serving as a prior in the June 15 to August 15 period of the year 1300, when the Cerchi were in full control, he made himself forever hateful to the Blacks. His attitude in the following year to the pressing problem of how to meet the papal force advancing under Charles of Valois is not revealed by any document. If we strongly incline to free him from responsibility for the course pursued, it is first, because he did not sit in the inner ring of the ruling merchant group, and second, because his upright and energetic nature presents the strongest possible contrast to the cowardly evasion consistently practiced in that year by his party affiliates.

The story of the White disaster and the Black triumph is told by Dino, himself a leading White, with such strong feeling and such touches of vivid detail that in his pages the past again becomes alive for the moved reader. As it would be foolhardy to attempt to compete with the chronicler's simple and instinctive art, the present writer will content himself with an unadorned record of the catastrophe which overwhelmed the city. When, after prolonged parleys, Charles of Valois was permitted to enter the gates, he took a solemn engagement to assume the part of peacemaker (*paciarius*) and not forcibly to change the government. Of course he broke his word, thereby demonstrating not only to Dante but to the whole world that he boasted the name but not the honor of a knight. Four days after the French force had occupied the town and at nightfall of the very day on which the prince renewed in a particularly solemn form his oath to uphold the civil order, Corso Donati with a handful of followers appeared under the walls of Florence and in the early dawn forced an entrance at one of the gates. Sentenced to exile over two years before, he had by leaving his place of banishment, automatically become a rebel, condemned, as the phrase ran, in goods and person (*in avere e persona*). If the outlawed magnate now ventured violently to repossess himself of his native city, it was for the single reason that he enjoyed the special protection of the pope and had been privately assured of the support of the pope's Florentine representative. Nothing short of this assumption will explain the effrontery with which, once within the walls, he regarded the town as his prize. Rallying his Black intimates, he went the rounds seeking out his personal enemies and sacking their houses. To increase the confusion and terror he opened the prisons and incited the delivered criminals to make the most of their freedom. Next, he descended on and drove from their respective residences the priors and the podestà. And finally, to crown his iniquitous labors,

[8] He appears on the roster of the gild in 1297 in the following form: Dante d'Aldighieri degli Aldighieri, poeta Fiorentino. C. Fiorelli, "Dipintori a Firenze nell'Arte dei Medici, Speziali, e Merciai." *Arch. Stor. It.*, Vol. II, 1920, p. 7.

he set up a podestà obedient to his will and inducted into office a group of hand-picked priors of proved Black faith.

For five terrible days following Corso Donati's vengeful return the town was given over to plunder, arson, and violence. Unless the defeated Whites inhabited impregnable towers, they were made the helpless victims of every imaginable outrage. Their warehouses were looted, their women abused, their children captured and held to ransom. At last the papal peacemaker bestirred himself to put an end to the disorders. The pope, too, tried to make himself heard above the din in the interests of that accommodation between the two warring Guelph factions which he had always advocated. Far-seeing statesman that he was, he wanted a united Guelph Florence and not a Black Guelph ascendancy of so relentless a character that the White Guelphs would either leave the city of their own free will or else be driven out in a solid mass. In either event they would have no choice but to join the Ghibellines, thereby greatly raising the fortunes of this anti-papal party throughout Tuscany.

Under strict papal orders the Valois prince tried to temper the victory of the Blacks and to issue to the Whites the necessary guaranties of safety. It was too late. His plan, so often tried before, to appease the passions by a formal reconciliation of the leading families miscarried; and when the Blacks insisted that nothing short of their appropriating to themselves the undivided fruits of victory would assure the Guelph triumph, the Frenchman abandoned an opposition which had never been other than perfunctory. The new plan of Corso and his partisans was to resume the destruction of their enemies under the cloak of the law. In seizing the power after driving the Whites from office they had not changed the constitution; they had not even abrogated the Ordinances of Justice. With good Black Guelphs in all the leading positions it was not necessary to abolish this hated legislation, for the accommodating Black priors would see to it that it was not enforced. By summoning the Whites before a Florentine court manned by a Black podestà, the victors could demonstrate to the pope, and to all the world besides, that they were lovers and practicers of "justice," while at the same time they would resume the pleasant, momentarily interrupted game of annihilating their enemies.

The new plan was inaugurated on January 18, 1302, by a summons issued to a group of Whites to appear for trial. Fresh lists followed at short intervals and showed that it was the intention of the victors to let no leading enemy escape. As the defendants entertained no illusion as to what was in store for them, most of them saved their lives by flight. This served as an excuse to declare them in contumacy and to condemn them in a sweeping sentence to loss of life and property. An examination of the lists of the proscribed makes plain that the leaders of the Blacks vengefully resolved that no citizen who had served as a White prior or who in some other official capacity had identified himself with the White government should go unpunished. It was because of his priorate in the summer of 1300 that his fate now overtook Dante. Summoned to trial by an order of January 27, 1302, he left the city, whereupon a new decree of March 10 condemned him with a roster of thirteen other victims to death by fire. The sentence, which, if executed, would have extinguished as though he had been a common felon one of the most luminous spirits of all the ages, has prompted the hearts of later generations to deep indignation. The sentiment will be shared with particular vivacity by the readers and lovers of his great epic; and yet to this same group another thought is unescapable. Dante became a wanderer on the face of the earth and suffered every grief and hardship to which man is heir. Without this racking experience and the accompanying single-minded dedication of himself to the poetic mission in which he sought oblivion for his loss of ease, family, friends, and country, he would never have risen to the intense vision which endowed our western culture with the unique splendor of the Divine Comedy.[9]

Throughout the year 1302 an organized reign of terror, which reached its greatest intensity after the month of April, held Florence in its grip. It was in April that Charles of Valois finally took his departure, and his going marks an intensification of Black persecution because his presence had, after all, imposed a measure of restraint upon the victors. In the course of this year two successive podestàs pronounced five hundred and fifty-nine death sentences by either hanging, decapitation, or the fagot. If in their vast majority the verdicts were not executed, it was only because, like Dante, the intended victims had saved themselves by flight. The names of the condemned, preserved by the documents, summon before us no more than a long file of pallid ghosts. As we let our eye glance over the list of what must have been the leading citizens of Florence, our attention, if we except one immortal name, is likely to be caught by just one other, that of ser Petracco. The title "ser" indicates a notary, and the notary in question had made himself obnoxious by serving the White regime as a governmental secretary. Two years after his condemnation he was living as an exile at Arezzo, where he begot a son, Francesco, who afterward changed his family name to Petrarca as having a more pleasing sound. The linking through the medium of a common death sentence of the two men hailed as the supreme poets of the Italian people is an arresting caprice of blindly groping Chance.

In addition to the almost six hundred citizens sentenced to death, other hundreds were sent into confino throughout the length and breadth of the peninsula. As such exiles were usually ruined in health and fortune, their lot can hardly have been happier than that of those who, as rebels, had been smitten with the sterner verdict. In the eyes of the triumphant Blacks all White Guelphs alike had become Ghibellines, and it was by this argument that Corso and his followers justified their ferocious proceeding.

Designated and condemned as Ghibellines, the defeated Whites played into the hands of their enemies. For though it would be difficult to indicate any other course they might have followed, on being driven from Florence they made their way to such Ghibelline centers as Arezzo, Pisa, and Pistoia, which joyfully bade them welcome. There, uniting with their former enemies, they became before long completely fused with them. Like them they

[9] In connection with Dante's condemnation it is proper to point out that the house, hard by the little church of San Martino and commonly accepted as his birthplace, cannot have been his, since in virtue of the sentence pronounced against him his house was destroyed. Undeniably, however, the existing structure, erected in the fourteenth century, occupies the *site* of a house of the Alighieri family. See the impressive demonstration of Davidsohn, Vol. III, pp. 198-99.

spent their days dreaming of the revenge which would be theirs, should they ever return to power. The consequence for Tuscany of the White exodus was therefore a new war of Guelphs and Ghibellines, which owed much of its vigor to the initiative of the latest converts to Ghibellinism, the Whites. Fortune on the whole favored the Blacks; or, to resort to a more human judgment, the lack of manly resolution characteristic of the Whites continued to tell against them. They found their mainstay in the great Ghibelline families of the upper Arno, such as the Ubertini and the Pazzi—the latter not to be confused with the urban family of the same name—but these fine lords were naturally more interested in their own welfare than in that of their needy and often troublesome guests. More than once the new allies launched an attack which carried them to the very walls of Florence, but they were pursued by ill luck and at the last moment something regularly went wrong.

Throughout his first year of exile Dante, who, like his humble friend, ser Petracco, had taken refuge in Arezzo, abode with the militant Whites. Then, disgusted with the wrangling and incompetence served up to him as a daily spectacle, he withdrew from their company and, as he put it proudly in his poem, formed a party by himself (*averti fatta parte per te stesso. Paradiso,* XVII, 69). Thenceforward we may think of Dante as a convinced, theoretical Ghibelline, but divorced both in flesh and spirit from the many successive plots of the Whites and their Ghibelline allies to reconquer Florence by force of arms. To follow the activities of the group he deserted is to share in his contempt for their meager endowment with decisive gifts of heart and brain. We suffer no loss by dispensing ourselves from tracing their repeated futile assaults on this and that military position of the Blacks. Suffice it that the latter maintained the advantage they had won and continued to hold the City of the Red Lily in the hollow of their hand.

The unqualified supremacy of the Florentine Blacks—such was the net result of the interference of Pope Boniface. It was a conclusion far removed from his original purpose, for Boniface, as has been said repeatedly, schemed to bring the city under his own control, and when, on that November day of the year 1301, Charles of Valois, acting as his agent, entered the city gate, the pope must have thought that the game was won. In reality it was already lost, though no contemporary, however sharp-witted, would have ventured to assert as much on that day of the apparent papal triumph. Yet, before two more years had passed, the whole world reverberated not only with the relatively unimportant matter of Boniface's failure to acquire Florence and Tuscany, but with a papal overthrow so enormous that to his innumerable impassioned enemies at least it was comparable only to the fall of Lucifer.

Because the catastrophe of Boniface, though belonging to the general history of the occident, bears also directly on the fortunes of Florence, we are not permitted to neglect it. Its fated instrument was that self-willed Philip IV of France, with whom Pope Boniface, almost from the beginning of his reign, had developed differences of opinion regarding the royal claim to tax the clergy and whom, with a blind worship of his own superior acumen and authority, he imagined he need not fear. It must have been this sense of an inviolable security that moved him to solicit the aid of Philip's brother,

Charles, for the realization of his Italian plans, even while refusing to abate a jot or tittle of his assertions regarding the immunity of the church from secular control and the ultimate subjection of all civil sovereigns to himself. Thus it came about that the military activity in Italy, with which the Valois prince was charged, went on side by side with the development of the acrimonious ecclesiastical controversy between Boniface and the Valois prince's brother, and that at the precise moment when one member of the house of Capet triumphed at Florence, the conflict with another and greater Capet entered a final bitter phase. No more than a short month after the Arno city had been captured the pope issued the bull, *Ausculta Fili Carissime,* in which he affronted his royal opponent past every chance of reconciliation by categorically asserting his subjection to St. Peter's chair.

Here in its essence, if not in its details, was the issue back again which had rocked the occident to its foundations in the days of the Hohenstaufen emperors! But the world had moved on to new thoughts and sentiments since that time. A succession of venal and worldly popes had put Rome under a cloud; and the development of the royal authority in France had concentrated in a single hand the strength of a great people firmly resolved to be a nation. Philip did not hesitate therefore to defend his crown. He boldly burned the obnoxious bull and, on summoning the three estates of his realm, had the satisfaction of seeing them range themselves unanimously behind him. Popular support of such energy had never cheered the emperors in their earlier struggle with the papacy. Indeed it was because both their German and Italian subjects had preponderantly sided with the spiritual power that the sovereigns from Henry IV to Frederick II had practically without exception gone down in defeat. A nation united behind its monarch against the claim of priestly control of its secular concerns was a novelty on the European stage and provided the French ruler with an invulnerable armor.

Unconcerned with the details of the clamorous conflict between Philip and Boniface, we shall pay attention only to a few central and decisive circumstances. An almost immediate effect of the intensification of the struggle was that the pontiff dropped his ambitions with regard to Florence and Tuscany. For, overconfident though he was by temperament, he did not fail to recognize, as soon as Philip had committed the *Ausculta* bull to the flames, that he now had so crucial a controversy on his hands that for its sake he would have to sacrifice every minor interest he had been pursuing. He did not at once break with Philip's brother. With the Florentine mission brought to a conclusion, the papal impresario ordered the French prince to proceed with the Sicilian campaign, the original purpose of his descent into Italy. Accordingly, in the spring of 1302 Charles of Valois abandoned Florence and conducted an invasion of the contested island from which he reaped no honor. After a brief struggle with the Aragonese incumbent, against the express wishes of the pope he brought the war to a close with an ignominious treaty. Thereupon beating a hasty retreat to the mainland, he continued his northward march without interruption until, before the year was over, he had recrossed the Alps and stood again on French soil. Doubtless even Boniface was glad to see the last of this shifty and unimpressive champion of the papal interests in

Italy. Besides, he was a French prince and the whole French royal house by this time had, like the Hohenstaufens to Boniface's predecessors, become a race of vipers to be trodden under foot.

With the deliberate, measured tread of fate the struggle between Boniface and the French king now moved to its issue. In another famous bull, *Unam Sanctam,* the pontiff affirmed that he wielded both the spiritual and the temporal sword and, after a further interval, he put his antagonist formally to the ban of the church. Still closely supported by his people, Philip countered this thrust by declaring the pope a heretic and demanding an ecumenical council for his trial and deposition. As pontiff and king glared at each other across Europe, each equally firm and equally unwilling to yield an inch of his position, it became clear that one or the other would have to break. Against every medieval precedent it turned out to be the pope. But if the lordly Boniface was overtaken by a nemesis, which myriads of his contemporaries, with Dante at their head, hailed as proof that justice, though laggard, still endured, even these enemies were shocked by the unexampled combination of perfidy and treason which brought about his overthrow. A political agent of King Philip, Guillaume de Nogaret by name, conspired with the savage brother of a Colonna cardinal to seize the pope's person; and on September 7, 1303, their forces were, with the connivance of traitors in the papal inner circle, admitted to the fortress of Anagni, where Boniface as usual had set up his summer residence. After a brief resistance the armed horde burst into the chamber of the pope, and Nogaret, in the name of his master, summoned the head of Christendom to acknowledge the charges which had been preferred against him and resign. The Caetani was an old man of over seventy years. There is no denying that he had lived his life as a worldling with little thought given to his Nazarene exemplar. But it is also true that he had manifested a quality of Roman grandeur which on meeting his supreme crisis he did not betray. For three days Nogaret and the fierce Colonna brigand kept him closely imprisoned in his room without bending him to their will. Then a revulsion of feeling among the people of Anagni in favor of the defiant old man drove the conspirators from the town. Boniface was free. He promptly removed to Rome, where, on October 11, he died, doubtless of natural causes but in part no doubt too, consumed by a helpless rage over the unparalleled indignity of which he had been the victim.[10]

When the defeated Boniface VIII was buried, his extravagant papal claims were buried with him. In the eyes of all the world the French crown had emerged as victor from the conflict. Ever since the day a pope had called on a French ruler to help him against Emperor Frederick II the influence of France in the government of the church had been on the increase. Seen in historical perspective, the triumph of Philip IV therefore appears as the logical culmination of a movement long under way. The French king was not the man to miss the significance of his victory and on his adversary's death took steps to bring the papacy completely under his control. He was not at once

[10] Inside the cathedral of Florence between the two main doors there is a seated statue of Boniface VIII in the act of blessing. It once adorned the original façade of the edifice and is a worthy memorial of the great pope in the grave Gothic spirit.

successful, for a reaction against the perpetrators of the Anagni outrage prompted the conclave to elect a moderate adherent of the dead Boniface who took the title Benedict XI. After less than a year Benedict departed this life in his turn (July 7, 1304); and with King Philip using his influence with a devoted faction among the cardinals to hold out for a French candidate, the new conclave, in which the French and the Italian parties were well matched, did not elect a new pope till the following summer. Then it was a French prelate, the archbishop of Bordeaux, who carried off the victory. Taking the title Clement V, he never even gave himself the trouble to cross the Alps and quietly resigned himself to accept King Philip as his master. Before long he set up his residence at Avignon on the Rhone, thus inaugurating the chapter of papal history familiar as the Babylonian Captivity. It is a period of French domination during which the pope, estranged from Italy, played a diminished part, politically speaking, in Tuscan and Florentine affairs. But let us make no mistake. So ingrained in the western mind was the concept of a single church under a single head that the purely spiritual power of the pope over Christian believers either in Italy or elsewhere showed little impairment during the period of abasement when not Rome, but Avignon, served as the papal capital.

XIII. The Last Emperor

ON THE transfer of the papacy to Avignon, Florence was, at least for the time being, affected neither favorably nor unfavorably by an event which was fraught with so many grave consequences for the Catholic church. The Blacks were in power, and under their tutelage the city enjoyed, if no more, surely no less, security and freedom from outside control than under the many preceding governments. Since the Whites, on being violently hunted from the town, had joined forces with the Ghibellines, the law classified them as Ghibellines and did them all the injury to which a ferocious, time-honored custom lent an evil sanction. It sounds like a perverse dream, but is no more than the bare truth to say that almost over night these two colored factions had exchanged political principles. The Whites, who were driven into exile because they had dared to oppose the plot of Pope Boniface to bring the city under his yoke, became committed by the mere act of turning Ghibelline to the policy of subjecting Florence to imperialist, that is to say, to German, influence, while the Blacks, who had not scrupled to betray their country to Boniface, now ruled the city as the proud champions of its independence against their imperialist adversaries.

That the central purpose of the Ghibellines of Tuscany, like that of the Ghibellines of all the other provinces of Italy, was to revive the might of that power which had sunk into its grave with Frederick II, does not admit of the slightest doubt. To this end each Ghibelline provincial group maintained a fighting organization which carried the eagle of the empire on its banner. The Guelph provincial leagues were equally warlike and proclaimed as their point of union their common devotion to the church. Exactly like the Guelph leagues of Lombardy, Tuscany, Liguria, and the other provinces, the corresponding Ghibelline leagues kept in close touch with one another by exchanging information and rendering military aid. Party loyalty, however, did not go deep. The individual members of each league habitually put their selfish advantage above every other consideration and held themselves to be at liberty to desert the common cause without alleging a reason and even without first serving notice. In spite of such unprincipled practices there were always enough members left in a given organization or enough fresh recruits were won to its ranks for the various leagues to maintain a continuous political existence. Hence, from a general peninsular point of view, the substance of Italy's history during most of the fourteenth century continued to be, exactly as in the previous century, the struggle between the Guelph and the Ghibelline factions. While, generally speaking, the latter party supported the empire and the former the church, the single member of either faction sought in the main nothing but his own advancement and looked on the league of his adherence as the convenient ladder by which to raise himself above his fellows. In spite of the uncertain loyalty commanded by the Guelph and Ghibelline leagues and in spite of their consequent instability, it remains a fact that they provided the only existing principles of national coherence. The unceasing civil war between the rival groups was indeed devastating, but without the party bond extending from province to province, every commune would have been a separate center of anarchy and the peninsular chaos would have been unmitigated and complete.

Ever since the restoration of the German kingship in the person of Rudolph of Hapsburg the partisans of the empire in Italy had been in the habit of sending embassies across the Alps to urge the monarch to undertake the journey which would refurbish the tarnished imperial crown and bring aid and comfort to his Italian followers. But the successive German rulers had remained deaf to these siren calls, chiefly because they lacked the resources necessary for an expensive transalpine expedition. Before venturing to look abroad, they would have to fortify their enfeebled position in Germany. When Rudolph I died in 1291, he was followed by Adolph of Nassau, who, on meeting death in battle in 1298, was succeeded by Rudolph's son, Albert. It was this Albert of Hapsburg who occupied the German throne when the crisis occurred in Florence which substituted a Black for a White government. As soon as the banished Whites had joined the Tuscan Ghibellines, the two fused groups made Albert the target of renewed impetuous petitions. Together with the Ghibellines of Lombardy and the Romagna they implored him to rouse himself and come to the assistance of his Italian adherents. And when their humility failed to make the desired impression, they did not hesitate to sound stronger accents. We have already touched upon the conduct of him who, among the earliest of the White exiles, became the leading Ghibelline of his generation, nay, of the whole Middle Ages. In speaking of him in these superlative terms we assign him to the place to which he has been raised by the judgment of posterity but which the inconspicuous, powerless wanderer was far from enjoying in his own day. We have learned that after a brief experience in the fighting ranks of his party, he abandoned the heat and dust of battle in order to promote the cause he had at heart by his unaided effort and in his own way. Under the spur of a profound inspiration he became, as it were, the disembodied voice of Ghibelline idealism. Undoubtedly his utterances were at the time hardly heard amidst the clash of arms around him; but for a later age, when the profane clamor of his own day has long since been silenced, they ring out with a celestial clearness. In his immortal poem the Florentine exile apostrophizes the delinquent Albert of Hapsburg in a passage which he prefaces with an unforgettable picture of the political anarchy reigning in Italy during the first decade of the fourteenth century.

Ah, servile Italy, abode of woe!
Bark without pilot in a stormy sky!
Queen once of fair domains—now fallen low! . . .
For now thy living ones are constant foes,
And each one gnaws the other, even they
Whom the same moat, the self-same walls enclose.
Search, wretched one, thy sea-girt shores around,
Then inward turn to thine own breast and see
If any part in joyous peace be found. . . .
And ye,[1] who should to things divine be given,
And let Augustus in his saddle sit
(If ye had listened to the voice of Heaven),
Look how the beast, refusing all command,
For want of spurs obeyeth not the bit,
Since to the bridle ye have put the hand.[2]

There follows, without interruption, his apostrophe to the laggard German sovereign:

O German Albert, who desertest her,
Ungovernable now and savage grown,
When most she needed pressing with the spur,
May on thy race Heaven's righteous judgment fall!
And be it signally and plainly shown,
With terror thy successor to appal,
Since by thy lust yon distant lands to gain,
Thou and thy sire have suffered wild to run
What is the garden of thy fair domain.

To gain lands in distant Germany Albert and his sire before him neglected Italy, the paradise of their realm. Cannot Albert be persuaded to open his eyes to the ferocious civil wars that are turning over every Italian province as with a giant plough?

Come, see the Capulets and Montagues,[3]
Monaldi and Filippeschi, reckless one! . . .
Come, cruel man, behold what ills endure
Thy nobles and avenge their injuries. . . .
Come and behold thy Rome, how she doth mourn!
A lonely widow, day and night she cries,
"When will my Caesar to my arms return?"
Come and behold thy people, how they love!
And if no pity our distress inspire,
Let blushes for thyself thy pity move.

[1] Ye—the pope and his clergy who have usurped the temporal power.

[2] *Purgatorio,* VI, 76 ff. Translated by I. C. Wright.

[3] These are the two factions whose implacable hostility disturbed their native city of Verona and furnished the plot for Shakespeare's tragedy of Romeo and Juliet. They and a second pair of opponents, the Monaldi and Filippeschi, serve as a reminder that every city of Italy was riven by the same disastrous Guelph-Ghibelline feud.

If distant Albert was a potential factor in the Italian situation, he fell from this role on May 1, 1308, when he was assassinated by his nephew. In the following autumn the German electoral princes raised to the throne the count of Luxemburg, who figures in history as Emperor Henry VII. Viewed from the angle of personal resources and inherited lands, Henry was a sovereign as little impressive as his immediate predecessors; and exactly as in their case, his only chance to be something more than a feeble symbol of unity in a Germany which had fallen apart into many scores of all but independent principalities was to increase the territory under his immediate control. Owing to the fact that the ruling dynasty of Bohemia was at the moment of Henry's accession opportunely reduced to a single female heir, the newly elected king, by betrothing his son to this princess, acquired at a stroke a very considerable sovereignty for his house. Without this fortunate accession to his strength it is most unlikely that he would have been in a position to play an active part even in Germany; and for him to lead an expedition into Italy would have been entirely out of the question. Affirming this much does not mean that from the moment of his election Henry's heart was not set on the Italian venture. Nonetheless it is true that he could not have got his expedition under way without the lucky addition to his purse of the Bohemian revenues. It was also a help, and by no means a negligible feature of the general situation, that Germany happened just then to be enjoying an unwonted interval of peace and could be temporarily abandoned by its sovereign without the pressing fear of losing it.

The county, later the duchy, of Luxemburg, Henry's original possession, lay on the western border of Germany and embraced a population partly of French, partly of German language and culture. In the person of Henry both influences met to produce a happy mixture. While he was German in appearance, being blond, high-colored, and of vigorous frame, he had been brought up at the court of France and bore himself in speech and manners as a Frenchman. A fine product of the age of chivalry, he was a courteous, brave, and pious knight, who impressed whomsoever he met with his candor and sincerity. Nonetheless he belonged to a culture that was passing and by reason of his very merits was ill equipped to cope with the new culture only just dawning in his own north and already well established in the Mediterranean basin.

The mental estrangement between the new sovereign and his Italian subjects did not augur well for the success of his transalpine journey, for even if he should bring himself to a certain measure of accommodation to the novel social and intellectual conditions of the peninsula, he would not be willing to renounce his imperial rights. It is a central feature of Henry's outlook that he held as grand a conception of the place assigned to an emperor in God's inscrutable plan as any of his Saxon or Suabian predecessors. He was the heir of ancient Rome called to universal rule to the end of bringing peace and justice to all the peoples of the earth. Was there in the Europe of the fourteenth century still room for this conception? Could Italy with its free communes dedicated to trade and engaged in developing a specifically urban culture cancel its immediate past and reconfine itself within the legal frame of an agrarian feudal kingdom? Merely to put these questions is to answer them: Henry's courageous attempt to revive a glory for which the living generation had no longer any understanding was foredoomed. Happily for his own peace of mind he did not experience the full force of the failure which was in store for him, for he died of a fever contracted in the field before his defeat was clearly manifest. Even before attacking the details of his Italian intervention let us therefore admit that it represents a labor of Sisyphus and by sober, matter-of-fact standards deserves to be classified as romantic folly. But that is not the whole story, since it is always a question on this earth of ours not only of what it is that men do but also of how they do it. And of Henry it may fairly be said that he went his difficult way with such nobility of purpose and such unwavering courage that his defeat is transformed into a spiritual victory.

In support of this judgment we may appeal to the much more striking case of Henry's greatest contemporary. For even more convincingly than Henry the poet Dante brings home to us that outworn conceptions and crushing defeat are fully compatible with personal distinction and high moral integrity. At the mere rumor of the coming of the German king, the Florentine exile, in tones more like those of a prophet than of a political partisan, uttered his delirious joy at the approach of the divinely appointed universal judge and ruler. "Behold now the acceptable time which brings consolation and peace. For a new day is dawning which shall scatter our darkness," he declared in a letter issued like a royal proclamation to the princes and peoples of Italy. And in the same ecstatic vein, he added: "Rejoice, oh, Italy, . . . for thy bridegroom cometh, the hope of the world, the glory of thy people, the ever clement Henry, who is Caesar and Augustus."[4] The man who expressed himself in these extravagant terms was looking backward to a past that could not be recalled. However, by defending the civil power against the excessive claims of the church he was also looking forward to an Italy cured of its terrible divisions by the creation of a national sovereign standing firmly on his feet and freed in all respects of papal tutelage. It is this prophetic note disengaging itself from Dante's medieval message, it is the strong patriotic sentiment within the antiquated form that explains why the poet is enshrined in the hearts of the living generation of Italians not only as their greatest singer but also in hardly less degree because he was the champion and herald of their political unification.

Let it never be forgotten that if Henry erred, he erred with Dante and has linked his name forever with that greater name. But let it not be forgotten

[4] *Dantis Alagherii Epistolae.* With Introduction, Translation, Notes, and Indices by Paget Toynbee. Oxford, 1920. Epistola V, pp. 46-62. Three of these Dante letters bear on Henry's expedition and reveal the Ghibelline idealist.

Either at this time (1309-10) or somewhat later—the authorities are in disagreement—Dante composed his famous political treatise, *De Monarchia,* in which he championed the conception of an empire wholly independent of the church and, like the church, deriving its power directly from God. In the *De Monarchia* Dante returned to the dualistic position of an empire and a church, equal and independent each of the other, which was the commonly entertained medieval doctrine until supplanted by the theory of papal supremacy championed by the great popes from Gregory VII to Boniface VIII. While by his tract the Florentine poet strengthened Ghibellinism theoretically, it was of course too late to save the cause in fact and practice.

either that, in spite of the glamor with which these two, each in his own way, invested the king's coming, the venture was a hopeless anachronism. Nobody felt this more instinctively or deeply than those Florentine burghers, who, though infinitely beneath their exiled fellow-citizen in gifts of heart and mind, had the advantage over him of being, through their daily duties in the home and shop, in touch with the most immediate verities of existence. They looked from the start with cold distrust upon this first imperial expedition since the death of their great enemy, Frederick II. Before long their instinctive opposition hardened into so settled a hostility that Florence became the very nub and focus of the forces which were resolved not to be dominated by the ghosts of the past, even though those ghosts walked in clanking armor and spread a very actual terror. The farther Henry got on with his Italian expedition the more he became aware that it was Florence which he would have to overcome, Florence, which, refusing to be seduced by a mirage, clung obstinately to the benefits immediately in hand, such as an ever-widening trade, industrial enterprise, self-government, and the proud first-fruits of a new and vital urban culture. For us engaged on the task of tracing the development of the free commune of Florence, the main interest of the attempt of Henry to revive the feudal age lies in the circumstance that it culminated in a duel between himself and that same commune, which by Henry's time had become the foremost representative of the new Italian civilization.

For the first two years of his reign Henry was occupied with fortifying his position in Germany and in making preparations for his Italian expedition. He then crossed the Alps at the head of an army and in October, 1310, stood upon Lombard soil, the first monarch to take seriously the task of exercising rule in the peninsula since the fall of the Hohenstaufens. And at first his success was highly gratifying. He let it be known that he had come not as a partisan but as a kindly disposed judge; and for a time even the Guelphs were sufficiently impressed with his attitude to sheathe the sword and cheer him on his way. Moreover—a circumstance bound to count heavily with the Guelphs—he had arrived in Italy with the express indorsement and blessing of the pope. Clement V, the first of the Avignon popes, had chiefly his own feeble disposition to thank if he had sunk to the level of a mere chaplain of the French king. But since, after all, he was the Roman pontiff and head of Christendom, his subservience to a temporal sovereign was not wholly to his liking. He came to see that only through the restoration of the empire could he hope to regain control of the papal dominions in Italy and to recover even in part his lost independence. With a view to creating a counterweight to France, become too potent for his self-esteem, he had therefore, secretly at first and then more openly, encouraged Henry's plans. Finally, he went so far as solemnly to promise Henry to do everything within his power to promote his coronation as emperor at Rome. It was this novel solidarity of pope and German sovereign that took the wind out of the Guelph sails. We may adduce it as the leading explanation of the all but universal acclaim with which Henry was received by Guelph and Ghibelline towns alike, when he marched through Lombardy on his way to Milan, where on January 6, 1311, he assumed the iron crown of Italy.

Then, with the first item of his comprehensive program happily realized, difficulties sprang up like armed men in Henry's path and abruptly ended his Italian honeymoon. Cremona raised the banner of rebellion and had to be brought to obedience by a show of force. Undismayed by the harsh punishment meted out to the rebel commune, neighboring Brescia followed suit and made renewed submission only after a siege which detained the imperial army in Lombardy through the hot and disease-breeding months of an Italian summer. With much of the enthusiasm evaporated which his coming had aroused, Henry turned toward Genoa to pass the winter and refit his reduced forces for the crucial southward thrust toward Rome set for the coming spring. There, on the Tiber, his coronation would place a divine seal upon his labors. As the proposed march would take him through Tuscany and was likely to meet with the greatest obstacles if the leading Tuscan city proved unfriendly, the obligation arises at this juncture to examine at some length the contemporary Florentine situation. And being less interested in the details of municipal politics than in the outstanding social and political trends, we shall select such events of the period between Henry's election and his expected passage through Tuscany as are calculated to give us a better understanding of the temper of the citizens and their daily life within the walls.

At the very time the German princes were preparing to confer the German crown on Henry of Luxemburg, Corso Donati, the indomitable roysterer, met a characteristic end. It was Corso who had been chiefly responsible for driving out the Whites in order to put his own Black faction in control. By reason of the forceful leadership he had supplied, a large place in public affairs was his not unreasonable expectation. But he failed to take into account the jealous temper of his fellow-magnates. Afraid of his reckless courage and suspecting that he was planning to make himself the tyrant of the town after the usurping fashion already general in Lombardy, these heads of rival houses checked and hindered him at every point, and by the use of a cunning with which the forthright warrior could not cope succeeded in keeping his authority well within bounds. To be sure, only good Black Guelphs were permitted to fill the public offices, but they were the appointees, not of Corso, but of his envious partners. With developments so little in keeping with his expectations the indignant nobleman refused to be content. Perpetually revolving plots for his aggrandizement, he was regularly balked in their execution by the subterranean activities of his cleverer opponents. Sooner or later the protracted undercover conflict was bound to burst into the open and be brought to a decision.

In the autumn of 1308 Corso's personal finances, which had a way of getting out of hand not unusual in noblemen of his irregular habits and spendthrift disposition, gave his enemies the opportunity of threatening him with trial and imprisonment. Incensed beyond endurance by this indignity, he openly assembled men and arms. When the news of these preparations got abroad, the people became excited and armed themselves to fight, some for, others against, the stormy petrel who for almost two decades had been the chief disturber of the local peace. The issue was decided by the hired troops of the government. Controlled by the Black faction in power and vigorously supported by the armed forces of the gilds, they enveloped the cluster of Donati houses which fronted on the Piazza San Piero Maggiore in the eastern section of the town. The plan of the attackers was to secure Corso's person and execute him as a rebel. Although tortured by gout, he managed during the confusion of the struggle to mount a horse and make his escape by the Santa Croce gate. When a troop of fast-riding Catalan mercenaries overtook him, rather than be led back to Florence a captive for his enemies to mock at, he threw himself from his horse and, after being dragged a short distance, was dispatched by a thrust through the throat of a Catalan lance (October 6, 1308). By way of stating his opinion of the iniquities of the destroyer of the Whites, Dante in his poem assigned his adversary to the everlasting pains of hell; but the historian is moved to express a milder judgment. He recognizes in Corso Donati a not unimpressive representative of the warrior virtues and vices of the dying Middle Ages. In a city which, in the course of recent generations, had undergone so thorough a commercialization as had Florence, he had become impossible. In point of fact he was the last of his kind. Never after his exit from the scene did Florentines of other than the banker-merchant type play a conspicuous part in the politics of the town.

In the summer of 1310, the Guelphs in control of the city were for the first time obliged clearly to define their stand toward Henry of Luxemburg. About to cross the Alps, Henry had sent ambassadors ahead to announce his coming to the towns and princes of Italy and to ask for the appointment of commissioners to be dispatched to him to take the customary oath of fealty. In July these emissaries arrived at Florence. Since the pope was lending Henry his support, a friendly policy might have seemed an advisable preliminary flourish; but so much more Guelph than the Holy Father were the Florentines that the royal agents were given a prompt rebuff. A leading Black magnate, Betto de' Brunelleschi, charged by the priors to speak for the government, uttered the rude boast to the ambassadors that "his countrymen had never yet bowed their sharp horns to any master."[5] Joining deeds to words, the commune resumed the construction of the new, the third circle of walls, inaugurated some twenty years before; and so rapidly did the work progress that before many months had passed the main section, which gave protection to that part of the city lying upon the right bank of the Arno, was completed. While paeans of welcome were arising from every town and province to greet the arrival of Henry in his kingdom, the uncompromising Guelphs of Florence, and of Florence alone among Italian cities, refused to be deluded and, expecting war, looked to their defenses.

It is a tribute to the courage of the Florentine rulers that they tossed the gauntlet to the monarch in spite of immediate local difficulties that might well have whispered compromise. Already in 1308 the two great banks of the Mozzi and Franzesi had failed and badly shaken the whole business structure of the city. Two years later, before more than a partial recovery had been effected, the bank of the Cerchi, which notwithstanding its connection with the banished Whites had continued to operate from Florence as its center,

[5] Dino, *Libro Terzo*, 35.

GNA. DEATH AND ASSUMPTION OF THE VIRGIN. OR SAN MICHELE

Left: CIMABUE. ENTHRONED MADONNA. UFFIZI GALLERY. *Right:* GIOTTO. THRONED MADONNA. UFFIZI GALLERY

GIOTTO. CORONATION OF THE VIRGIN. ALTARPIECE. SANTA CROCE

went the same road. As these and similar firms, which put the Arno city at the head of international banking, rested not only on the capital of the well-to-do but also on the savings of the small tradesmen, every bank crash brought loss and misery to many scores of families. In 1311, with the closer approach to Florence of the emperor, the local difficulties became even greater. A partial failure of the harvest doubled the price of wheat and obliged the government to alleviate the situation by making purchases in distant markets. Under these adverse circumstances it would have been prudent to reduce expenses by dismissing the mercenaries who formed the nucleus of the city's military establishment. The pusillanimous thought was not seriously entertained. Instead of being reduced, the army was on the contrary steadily increased, and to meet the heavy costs incurred by these open preparations for the coming struggle the property tax called *estimo* was repeatedly levied within a single year.[6]

In its swelling self-esteem and growing hatred of its adversary, the commune resolved to remove the last emblem in its midst of its former subjection to the empire. The symbol of the empire was the eagle. In earlier times it had been carved on the town gates or been painted or cut in stone on the house fronts by all citizens who desired to make a public avowal of their loyalty. A general order now went forth that all these imperial birds must be removed; and Dino, to whom we owe this interesting detail, adds that "a fine was assessed on whosoever refused to erase them."[7] But let it not be imagined for a moment that the prevailing burgher mood was just a senseless rage. Fully aware of the gravity of the impending struggle, the government recognized the advantage of reducing its very numerous local enemies in order to present as united a front as possible to the enemy. Only a prudent consideration of this sort will account for the relatively liberal amnesty for political offenses issued at this time (1311). It made possible the repatriation, on the payment of no more than a small money penalty, of those many hundreds of exiles who, though of White affiliation, had not figured conspicuously in the late civil war. The pardon, it need hardly be said, was not broad enough to include exiles who, like Dante, were considered to be White leaders and who had been condemned to death.

In spite of scarcity and bankruptcies, in spite of war preparations and multiplied taxes, the local feuds never rested. It would not have been Florence had it been otherwise. If it was chiefly the magnates to whom vendetta was a sacred obligation, the complete propriety of the ancient practice of retaliation was accepted without question by the whole citizen body. On Corso Donati's death it became incumbent on his family to avenge the spilling of his blood; and although he was actually killed by a Catalan soldier, it was known that some of his magnate rivals, and more particularly messer Betto de' Brunelleschi, were the instigators of the plot that culminated in his death. The surviving relatives of Corso maintained a close watch of the supposed guilty parties, but some years passed before they found an opportunity to strike. The eminent Betto, whom they particularly singled out as their victim,

[6] For these local problems and entanglements see Davidsohn, Vol. III, pp. 422-24.
[7] Dino, *Libro Terzo,* 35.

had reached still greater eminence by reason of Corso's disappearance. Owing to his local prominence and his merited reputation as an orator, it was he who was intrusted with the reply to Henry's ambassadors; and, as we have seen, he did not hesitate to give his words the brusque character of a declaration of war. Although a passionate patriot, he had the magnate's typical contempt for the common people, and when the food scarcity of the winter 1310-11 occasioned a wide suffering, he used his wealth to hoard grain and added insult to injury by openly mocking at the misery of the poor. In short, messer Betto was not an attractive type of magnate and no great public lamentation followed when two Donati youths made an end of him. On a day in February, 1311, when both the scarcity of grain and Betto's profits were at their height, the avengers burst upon him in his house while he was quietly playing at chess and dispatched him with their poniards. In this manner Corso, who in obedience to the local mores had in his day avenged many a murdered relative, was avenged in his turn. At the time the murder of his adversary occurred the popular hatred Corso had aroused in his lifetime was so far forgotten that he could at last be accorded the funeral honors which custom prescribed as his due. When, following his death at the hands of city troopers, his mutilated corpse was left lying in the dust of the road a mile beyond the eastern gate, it had been picked up by the monks of the nearby monastery of San Salvi and hurriedly put away within their precincts. Now since, with Betto's murder three years after Corso's death, the Donati honor was restored, the family removed Corso's remains from their temporary burial place and amidst pompous ceremonies, as if he had just died, laid the old warrior to rest in the family vaults in Florence.[8]

From this varied assortment of local items we may gather that, in spite of the vast reverberation caused by the emperor's presence in Italy, the daily life of the Florentines went on much as before. However, not for a moment did the ruling Guelph clique relax its watch on the movements of their imperial opponent or waver in their hostility to his person and undertaking. On Christmas Eve of the year 1311, Henry, while residing at Genoa, put an end to the negotiations he had been patiently conducting for over a year with the City of the Red Lily regarding the oath of allegiance to which he was legally entitled. By formal sentence rendered in his court he declared Florence outlawed, ordered the seizure of the goods of its citizens throughout the imperial dominions, and, for good measure, loaded the town with a fine amounting to no less than five thousand pounds of gold. When, some months later, the emperor proceeded from Genoa to Pisa, it was feared by the Florentines and expected by the rest of Italy that he would at once lead his army up the Arno Valley and make good his threats against the city. The Tuscan Ghibellines, who crowded to Pisa to honor their champion, outdid one another in urging this punitive measure upon him. We still possess the flaming epistle which Dante addressed to Henry recommending an immediate advance on guilty Florence. But the Luxemburger was of another mind. He had an eye only for the imperial crown which glowed mysteriously in the distance and

[8] Dino, *Libro Terzo,* 39, supplemented by Villani, IX, 12.

was impatient to be invested with the magic round. Simple child of the medieval fancies which still ruled the north, he held to the belief that the effulgence with which he would be clothed at Rome would of itself suffice to bring rebellious Florence to obedience. Thus inspired, he pressed southward from Pisa by the Maremma route only to be shaken rudely from his dreams as he neared the goal of his ambition.

Such success as had thus far attended the Luxemburg sovereign was, as has been noted, primarily owing to the circumstance that his expedition enjoyed the backing of the pope. But in measure as Henry prospered, Clement V, who was far from being a free agent, turned cold, and under pressure from the royal court of France prepared to put obstacles in the German sovereign's path. When King Robert I of Naples, who had succeeded his father, Charles II, in 1309, sent his younger brother with an armed troop to occupy the Tiber city, the pope did not dare affront either the French king or that king's Neapolitan relative so far as to signify his displeasure with this act of war.[9] Here was the turning-point of Clement's policy, here the first unequivocal evidence of that papal opposition to Henry which Dante has branded as abominable treason against his *alto Arrigo,* the messenger from heaven. Under these altered auspices "high Harry" had to force his way into Rome under constant fighting and met with such formidable opposition from the Neapolitan troops that the crucial Vatican quarter containing St. Peter's church and the grave of the chief apostle remained unconquered. In the end Henry was obliged to content himself with holding the less distinguished eastern section of Rome, where lay the church of St. John Lateran; and there, contrary to tradition, he was crowned on June 29, 1312, by a committee of three cardinals, who had been delegated to this service by the pope before his French master had obliged him to change his mind.

Thoroughly aroused to the insecurity of his situation by this partial failure, Henry resolved to stake fame and fortune on the capture and punishment of that town which ever since his coming to Italy had been the head and front of the opposition. The most recent outrage of Florence had been to send all its available troops to Rome in order to co-operate with Robert of Naples in the plan to defeat the Luxemburger's coronation. On departing from Rome, Henry moved northward through Umbria and in September entered Tuscany by the valley of the upper Arno. Owing to losses in battle and, still more, to the ravages of disease, his forces had shrunk till his heavy cavalry, always regarded as the decisive branch of the service in those days, amounted to no more than two thousand knights, divided equally among Germans and Italians. As it was impossible with so limited a troop to lay siege to a town of the formidable circumference of Florence, Henry must have hoped that the Florentines would offer battle and bring their dispute with their lawful lord to that form of decision favored by the feudal world and celebrated as the Judgment of God. Or perhaps in his unconquerable romanticism he imagined his adversaries would think better of their recalcitrancy and abruptly change their evil course now that the Roman chrism sanctified his

[9] On the vehemence of the pressure brought to bear on Clement V by the French royal house, see the dispatch of the Aragonese ambassador quoted by Davidsohn, Vol. III, p. 469.

brow. He simply could not grasp that these solid, earth-rooted merchants shopkeepers were forever done with the political flummery of the Midc Ages and thought only of their priceless communal freedom, determined to defend it by hook and by crook without the least regard for the frayed values of an outmoded ideology.

Buoyed by such sentiments, the Florentine rulers had, as soon as Henry's design against their town became clear, left no stone unturned to give him a reception that he would remember. They breathed new life into the league of Tuscan Guelphs, drawing into the fold every town within the province save those two impenitent hearths of Ghibellinism, Pisa and Arezzo. They established fruitful contact with the neighboring leagues of Lombardy and the Romagna and called on Robert of Naples to repay the aid so freely given in keeping Henry out of the sacred precinct of the Vatican. Finally, by ambassadors dispatched to France they assured themselves of the sympathy and, if the need arose, of the active help of King Philip and of Philip's obedient tool, the pope. As a result of this wide agitation and indefatigable energy it came about that when, on September 19, Henry appeared before the eastern gate of Santa Croce and established his headquarters at the Vallombrosan monastery of San Salvi, a composite Guelph army at least twice the size of his own was gathered at Florence to turn him from his prize.

Even with this preponderance in numbers the army of the Guelphs was discreetly kept behind the sheltering walls of the town in the assurance that lack of supplies, disease, and the inclement season would effect the ruin of the besieging host more quickly and decisively than the sword. And as they hoped and planned, so it befell. The imperial horsemen, though foraging far and wide, were soon without food; the autumn rains set in, turning the fields to swamps and raising the Arno to flood height; dysentery and similar camp diseases, against which the primitive medical science of the age afforded no protection, mowed down the harassed warriors by the score. When the emperor himself fell ill, his physicians gathered at his bedside to argue in their learned Latin the breathless question whether it was a quartan or a tertian fever which had laid him low. Henry had but lately turned forty and boasted an exceptionally vigorous constitution. While the savants were still disputing over the right name for his affliction, he mastered his weakness, rose from his sickbed, and, seeing the disastrous situation of his army, raised the siege, if siege it may be called.

Florence had stayed the imperial advance and turned the tide. Deliberately, with many pauses to show that they had not been routed, Henry's forces rolled down the Arno Valley toward faithful Pisa. Since the imperialists lived on the country, harrying it in their disappointment to the best of their ability, we may believe that the Florentine countryside for many miles around the capital was reduced to sorry desolation. The evidence which has come down to us proves overwhelmingly that the long campaign of attrition wrought burghers and peasants incalculable damage. But they remained stanch. And they had every right to rejoice for, without having risked the hazards of battle, they had been victorious.

When, once more safe within the walls of Pisa, Henry reviewed his present uation, he no longer underrated the difficulties connected with his purpose of raising the empire from its grave. Although in his unteachable simplicity he flatly refused to believe that his professed friend, the pope, had betrayed him, he at least ceased to count further on Clement's active support in carrying through his program. Henceforth he relied only on what was reasonably sure and that was the armed might of his willing vassals in Germany and Italy. With their reduced resources he was obliged to face a powerful bloc of enemies, whose concerted action had already proved too much for him at Rome and Florence and whom their recent successes had filled with soaring confidence. We cannot but think that throughout the winter spent at Pisa he must have been assailed with heavy doubts; but, if so, he kept them to himself. A pious and brave cavalier, he knew no other course than to go on with what he had begun till death should intervene; and therefore, instead of going back to Germany, which would have signified a public admission of defeat, he made extraordinary efforts to assemble a new army in order to deal his enemies a fresh blow. Pisa, the ever true, aided him with a liberal grant of funds, fresh troops came from across the Alps, and by the early summer of 1313 he was again the commander of an army, larger and better equipped than that with which he had assaulted Florence in the previous autumn.

Contemporaries have recorded the opinion that if Henry had again directed his spear against the Red Lily, he would not have been turned back a second time. When we reflect that the countryside had been laid waste and that the town itself had been drained of its resources, we must agree that the emperor's chances against the rebel city had considerably improved. But who will say that the dying Guelph fires would not once more have been fanned to flame at the enemy's approach? In any case the emperor, with that unsteadiness of objective so generally characteristic of feudal warfare, did not return upon his steps. He resolved instead to fling his new army on the king of Naples. In his guileless way of viewing politics, he saw, not the French pope, but Angevin Robert, with whom he had come to blows at Rome, as the villain of the piece, and desired to be revenged on him for his unchivalrous attempt to exclude a divinely called sovereign from his capital. Stirred to his depths by the Neapolitan's seizure of Rome in the previous year, Henry did not even desist from his plan when the double-tongued Clement now ventured into the open and forbade the expedition against Robert on pain of excommunication. With stern resolution he set his face to the south.

In August, 1313, the imperial host left Pisa, moving slowly up the Elsa Valley. Henry had never made a full recovery from the malarial attack which had prostrated him near Florence some ten months before. While cutting a circle around Siena, a stanch Ghibelline town in Hohenstaufen days turned Guelph these many years, he was again stricken. He had to be carried in a litter thenceforward, but did not get far. We are assured by the chroniclers that his mystified physicians, deeply alarmed by his condition, conscientiously purged and bled him, but on August 24, at the little hamlet of Buonconvento, he dispensed with their further services. He died as he had lived, an honorable Christian gentleman, consoled upon his deathbed by the last sacrament administered to him by his Dominican confessor. Although the monstrous charge that he was poisoned with the holy wafer laid upon his lips by the same friendly priest was widely credited at the time and is still repeated by uncritical historians, it may be dismissed as an invention wherewith the grief-stricken Ghibellines expressed their sense of the irrational manner in which fate interferes in the affairs of men.

The army, bearing the dead monarch in its midst, flowed sadly back to Pisa, and there the body was bestowed in the cathedral and a monument erected over it, the remnants of which may still be seen in the right transept of that famous edifice. The funeral over, the imperial forces dissolved like mist before the sun. They had been assembled to support the project of their liege lord, and as much time would have to pass before his successor could be elected in distant Germany, there was no authority in sight capable of holding the army together. Before many seasons rolled by the brief Italian adventure of Henry had become a memory which served to strengthen the already general impression that the Holy Roman empire had paled to a shadow and was extinct in all but name. An occasional German sovereign in the years ahead still showed that he was under the spell of the old imperial idea, and one or another of them even fared across the Alps in search of the imperial crown which only Rome could bestow. Henry VII was the last emperor who unquestioningly believed in the remarkable political institution which went back to Charlemagne and Otto and which in the general view had Julius Caesar as its founder. Because of this faith of his, Henry staked his all on forcing an antiquated order on a changed Italy and lost.

We cannot take leave of the defeated Henry laid to rest in his sepulcher in Pisa without returning to the much more arresting case of Dante, the last and greatest exponent of a universal order, of which Henry was but the political representative. Living at the close of the Middle Ages, when the thought of the period had been given a full and rounded formulation by the great schoolmen culminating in Aquinas, the poet and thinker made himself the mouthpiece of their view that the central concern of life was the problem of salvation. In Dante's solemn conception of our earth as the proving-ground of souls there was little, if any, place for the travel, commerce, experimentation, and other activities of a mundane kind which had transformed his native Florence from a nameless, sleepy hamlet to a lively metropolis with material and intellectual interests covering the known world. It was in substance these very innovations which Dante rejected when he declared for the coherent system by which the medieval philosophers had, or thought they had, provided for every legitimate aspiration of the sons of Adam by harmonizing faith and reason. Persuaded that the medieval way of life was prescribed by revelations vouchsafed the saints and prophets and supplemented by the ratiocinations of great thinkers, he had nothing but contempt for the novel political, social, and economic attitudes which were triumphantly asserting themselves among his fellow-citizens. The sum of these novelties came at a later time and with a somewhat misplaced emphasis to be called the Renaissance. We assign to Dante his distinctive place in the unfolding of European culture when we declare that, owing to his spiritual inheritance and temperamental preferences, he identified himself with the theology and outlook of the Middle Ages and indignantly rejected the rising secular philosophy inherent in the exploratory activities of his Florentine and Italian contemporaries. By this same judgment it becomes clear that they and not he were in line with the fated forward movement of occidental civilization.

XIV. Florence Encounters the Problem of the Despot (1313–43)

EVER since the rise of the towns their leading concern had been the growth of their power at home and abroad. Each had started existence with the plan of conquering its county and, as soon as that objective had been won, each with the characteristic unrestraint of youth had extended its operations into the county of its neighbors. We have seen that Lombardy, the Romagna, Umbria, and Tuscany were from the twelfth century on torn with this relentless strife. If the Hohenstaufen emperors had occasionally brought it to a halt, it had broken out again with elemental vehemence the moment the imperial overlord relaxed his vigilance. On the death of the high-spirited Frederick II the empire fell into such feebleness that it no longer counted in the Italian situation. When the attempt of Henry VII to revive the fallen empire failed, more emphatically than ever the towns were left to work out their territorial and other similar problems by their own strength.

The uninterrupted warfare among the towns throughout the flourishing town area lying between the Alps and the fringe of ancient Latium had a marked effect on their domestic constitution. Normally each town aspired to self-government, and in its first or consular stage of emancipation from feudal bondage had resorted to representative institutions as evidenced by an elected executive, consultative councils, and a parliament of the people. While this democratic machinery was overelaborate and the responsibilities under it too widely distributed, it might conceivably have worked had it not been for the martial and aggressive policy the towns saw fit to adopt. War calls for swift decisions and concentrated authority; and in measure as the struggle of each town against its neighbors assumed larger proportions and became a permanent feature of its foreign policy, the original constitution with its democratic elements was found to be inadequate and progressively broke down. As frequently before and after the Italian communal era, democracy was found to be hopelessly incompatible with war conceived as a legitimate and indispensable tool of policy.

A second consequence of the unceasing intercommunal struggle forces itself on our attention when we survey the general Italian scene. The democratically oriented communes had at first employed democratic armies, the organized forces utilized in their early enterprises being nothing other than the male population mobilized at the call to arms. Such a popular army sufficed for the work immediately in hand, which was to assault and break down the feudal castles in the contado and to encounter the onslaught of the similarly constituted army of a neighboring town. Moved by a passionate patriotism, it might even on occasion charge with irresistible abandon and overcome the proud chivalry of a Barbarossa. But undeniably there were defects in an army of this kind which in the long run would prove disastrous. There was always the likelihood, instanced by scores of actual cases, that the infantry or pedites, who were poorly equipped and inadequately trained, would at an unexpected turn of events disintegrate into a panicky mob, while a campaign unduly drawn out would be resented as an intolerable hardship, because it separated the citizen from his livelihood and exposed his family to suffering and starvation.

Much more dependable than the infantry was the cavalry made up of the milites and recruited from the well-to-do citizens, more particularly from the urban nobility. However, on social grounds the expanding democracy very generally turned against the quarrelsome and arrogant gentry and, after canceling its political rights, very often, for good measure, hounded it from its territory. The consequent reduction in numbers of the nobility did not necessarily signify a decline in the number of the urban horsemen. In the case of most towns, and certainly in the case of Florence, the duty of every man of means to maintain a horse for the commune and perform cavalry service in wartime remained an inalterable obligation. But when, with the accelerated expansion of Florence before and after the year 1300, many citizens, formerly poor, became well-to-do, they were found to have neither the desire nor the ability for effective equestrian service. The traditional obligation of the man of means to supply a horse in time of war was designated by the term *cavallata.* While the numerous new-rich admitted their liability to the cavallata, they often proposed and, in view of the sorry figure they cut on horseback, the authorities gladly accepted, a substitute rider. In this manner the cavallata already by the early fourteenth century commonly comprised two separate services, the one the maintenance of a horse in peace time, the other the riding or having it ridden into the field at the call to war. This bifurcation undermined the tradition of serving in person and brought about an indefinable loss of pride and patriotism. Where and whenever the old nobility, or even some part of it, survived, its fighting spirit was slow to be extinguished. However, the very opposite was true of the *popolani grassi,* the fat burghers, who came more and more to preponderate among the citizens subject to the cavallata. Taken up with money-making and personally averse to arms, they succeeded to a steadily increasing degree in being dispensed from the cavallata obligation by having it commuted into a pure money payment. The commutation came to be designated with a touch of wry humor as a *cavallata morta;* and it is with this supply of "a dead horse," already in full development by the early decades of the fourteenth century, that the once famous cavalry arm of the original municipal army came to an ignominious end.[1]

[1] As long ago as 1865, C. Paoli made a study of the *Cavallate Fiorentine* based largely on that inexhaustible source for all military matters pertaining to the republican army, the *Libro di Montaperti.* See *Arch. Stor. It.,* Serie 3, Vol. I, pp. 53-75.

In view of the steadily diminishing value of both branches of the popular army, it was inevitable that the town governments should begin to experiment with professional soldiers, with mercenaries. In this development the emperors had led the way. Disgusted with the self-will of the feudal levies which, as soon as the number of weeks' or months' service required by their feudal contract had expired, would turn their faces homeward without regard to military exigencies, they had formed a nucleus of hired troops calculated to stick with their commander at least as long as their wages were paid promptly. Such troops, well horsed, adequately armed and trained, and bound besides into an effective unit by an impalpable *esprit de corps,* came gradually to dominate the military situation.[2] Their leader or captain was at first regularly a nobleman born to the profession of arms. As such he would be disposed to comport himself with some regard for the conventional obligations of decency imposed by the theory and practice of knighthood. Inevitably, however, with war become an occupation in which soldiers were engaged for hire, the moral standards of the mercenary leaders declined until they and their following presented themselves to view as nothing more than profit-seeking, brutal adventurers serving whosoever offered the most pay and inaccessible to the appeal of honor and humanity. At first prevailingly of German nationality, the mercenaries we encounter in the Italian wars were before long recruited from the fighting stock of every country of Europe. A commune would hire a troop of men-at-arms for a particular campaign and turn them loose the moment the campaign was over. Or if, because the situation remained permanently critical, the troopers were retained on the municipal pay-roll, they assumed the character of a standing army and became an important factor in the local situation. In these circumstances it might easily happen that an unscrupulous political group within the town, or the ambitious head of such a political group, would try to manipulate them for selfish ends. In case the cunning plotter happened to be a nobleman practiced in feudal warfare, he might succeed in attaching the hired horsemen to his person; and by loosing them at a given moment on the city he could terrorize the community and hold it at his mercy. From such military bullying to the seizure of political power was but a step and the successful captain, native or foreign, would crown his career by becoming a despot or tyrant. The usual fourteenth-century Italian designation for such a usurper was *signore,* which is to say, lord or master.

We thus see that under the impact of many forces, political, military, and social, the free governments of the twelfth and thirteenth centuries tended to be replaced by a military chief with autocratic power. And just as the towns of the rich Lombard plain had been the ones to inaugurate the movement of communal liberty, so they were the first to exhibit the phenomenon of the signore. Throughout the second half of the thirteenth century the despotic movement continued to gather force in the Po Valley with the great Lombard metropolis, Milan, acting as pacemaker. And before the opening of the fourteenth century the development had begun to spread with the un-

[2] On the growing use of mercenaries by Florence, as well as on other military developments of the fourteenth century, see Davidsohn, Vol. IV[1], chap. 3. A lively account of Italian military history is bv E. Ricotti. *Storia delle Compagnie di Ventura in Italia.* 3 vols. Milan, 1929.

reasoning authority of a new fashion to all the provinces bordering on Lombardy. We have already looked at the picture which, shortly after the year 1300, Dante painted of the distracted peninsula. While he is particularly distressed by the ruinous civil and provincial wars and their attendant misery and chaos, he does not fail to cry out also against the murder of the communal liberties by the rising despots.

> Che le città d'Italia tutte piene
> Son di tiranni ed un Marcel diventa
> Ogni villan che parteggiando viene.
>
> (For all the towns of Italy are full
> Of tyrants, and becometh a Marcellus
> Each peasant churl who plays the partisan.)[3]

If he called passionately on the absent emperor to come to Italy and exercise his sovereign rights, he certainly expected, among other benefits, to have an end made of the mad self-exaltation of Italy's countless military adventurers.

But when an emperor came in the person of Henry VII, he proved himself incapable of riding the storm and making himself master of the situation; and no sooner had he been buried with appropriate pomp at Pisa than Tuscany, which thus far had not been greatly influenced by the Lombard example, experienced the rise of so vigorous a succession of tyrants that the communal liberties of every town, including Florence, were gravely jeopardized. The story of tyranny in Tuscany starts with Pisa which, as the chief support of Henry's Ghibelline expedition, found itself exposed to a combined Guelph attack the moment Henry's army, following the death of its leader, began to disperse. The Guelph league embraced practically all the other towns of Tuscany with Florence at their head and was not likely to let the opportunity slip by to punish the impenitent Ghibelline nucleus of Pisa. Thoroughly alarmed for its safety, the maritime town invited one of Henry's trusted Italian lieutenants, the nobleman Uguccione della Faggiuola, to assume its defense. As his family estates lay in the highlands of the upper Arno, Uguccione was by tradition both a Ghibelline and an enemy of Florence. In a long and agitated military career he had proved himself a mighty warrior and carouser and, alert to the many possibilities of advancement offered by the political anarchy of the peninsula, had fixed his mind on carving out an urban signory for himself. At the same time that the Pisan commonwealth turned to him for help it persuaded a body of eight hundred German knights, who had lost their paymaster when they buried Emperor Henry, to enter its service. By this fortunate coincidence the energetic nobleman, who personally commanded no following, found himself at the head of an experienced troop of fighters.

Uguccione lost no time in launching his program. He declared war on Lucca, ever a popular measure with the Pisan populace owing to the immemorial feud between these close neighbors. When some Pisan merchants, anxious about their profits, protested against the unnecessary disturbance of

[3] *Purgatorio,* VI, 124-27. Marcellus is the Roman general, M. Claudius Marcellus, and serves here as the perennial military type.

the peace, he arrested and executed a number of their leaders. Thereupon, summoning a public parliament, he persuaded it to offer him the lordship of the city for ten years. The action signified the abolition of constitutional government and its replacement by Uguccione's despotism. Immediately after, on June 14, 1314, he justified his dictatorship to his Pisan partisans by capturing Lucca. The unhappy town was put to the sack for three interminable days. For many generations past the famous industrial specialty of Lucca had been the manufacture of fine silks, in which it stood foremost among all the towns of Italy. As a result of the havoc wrought by an unloosed horde of plundering mercenaries, hundreds of silk artisans emigrated, chiefly to Florence and Bologna, which welcomed them with open arms. When quiet was again restored the manufacture of silk was resumed by the Lucchese who had survived the recent crisis, and, before long, the town had again acquired a certain standing as a commercial and industrial center. But there can be no doubt that the disaster of 1314 administered a blow to the industrial prestige of the old Tuscan capital on the Serchio from which it never recovered.

With the combined resources of Pisa and Lucca at his disposal, Uguccione could assume the offensive against the Guelph league of Tuscany. And at once he directed his attention to Pistoia as the point from which the security of Florence itself, the fiery head of the league, could be most successfully threatened. The ever-watchful metropolis was not caught unawares. Already in the spring of 1313, at which time the Arno city was expecting a fresh attack from Emperor Henry, it had tightened the bonds which joined it to King Robert of Naples by granting him the *signoria* over it for a term of five years. The submission must be interpreted as an emergency measure, for it was carefully safeguarded by the citizens, resolved, as soon as the immediate danger had passed, to resume the reins. In exchange for his all-important military help, King Robert was to be allowed to appoint the Florentine podestà, without otherwise altering or setting aside the constitution. While the king was thus to be represented in the town by a leading official as well as by a body of Neapolitan troops, he was obliged to acknowledge that there were constitutional bounds which he must under no circumstances overstep. How far this was from the typical tyranny of the period is made clear by referring for comparison to the case of Uguccione, who, from the day of his seizure of power at Pisa, was its unquestioned sovereign. Nonetheless by its acceptance of King Robert as overlord the Arno city experienced its first taste of subjection to the rule of a master since the inauguration of the government of the priors. And this first taste was destined not to be the last. Although her historians have delighted in extolling Florence as the most stubborn center of self-government in Italy, and although the town fully deserves to be singled out in this respect, it is an exaggeration to repeat with some too fullsome admirers that Florence never felt the yoke of tyranny till it was fastened on her neck by the treachery of a family nursed in her own bosom.

The war begun by Uguccione against the league of Tuscan Guelphs reached a climax on August 29, 1315, in a great battle fought just west of Pistoia, near Montecatini. It was a signal victory for the Ghibellines who administered such a rout to the Guelphs as they had not suffered since Montaperti, half a century before. However, the lord of Pisa failed to squeeze all the expected advantages out of his victory, probably because of difficulties that had arisen in his own camp. His chief lieutenant was a young warrior, Castruccio Castracane by name. Castruccio belonged to a noble family of Lucca, the Antelminelli, the members of which had been banished, when Castruccio was a lad, because of their Ghibelline sympathies. The young exile had tried to retrieve his fortunes by the usual avenue of war, had joined the forces of Henry VII on the descent of that monarch into Italy, and, with an ambition that allowed no chance to slip by unused, had co-operated with Uguccione on the day when the Pisan signore took Castruccio's native town by storm.

Since that capital event Castruccio had secretly aspired to nothing less than to the independent rule of the city to which he belonged by birth and to which he had returned by force of arms. He was as capable a soldier as the much more experienced Uguccione and every whit as eager to achieve an independent sovereignty. At the same time he had the advantage over his much older chief of a cooler head and a wider political vision. By sheer military serviceableness he made himself so indispensable that, although Uguccione watched him with the usual suspicion of the tyrant, he delayed action until it was too late. Then, on the day before Easter of the year 1316, the lord of Pisa suddenly ordered Castruccio, who was residing in dependent Lucca, under arrest. By accident or, much more probably, by Castruccio's secret machinations, a rebellion occurred on the same day in Pisa, which the young Antelminelli utilized so cleverly that he was able to bring down the whole edifice of Uguccione's power. It was one of those sudden upsets so characteristic of the period. Pisa promptly resumed its independence, while Lucca, to mark its gratitude for having been liberated from the yoke of its hated neighbor, gratefully conceded the scepter to the vigorous warrior who was its own beloved son. It does credit to Castruccio's moderation that he permitted the defeated and crestfallen Uguccione to pass safely out of the country.

Castruccio was thirty-five years old when he found himself the adored ruler of his Lucchese countrymen. Moving cautiously at first, he accepted the offer of the Guelphs to discuss the points of difference between them and him. As a result an agreement was reached which, in May, 1317, led to the pacification of Tuscany. Needless to say there were too many incurable animosities between the two ancient factions for the peace to prove lasting. Besides, the dominant Tuscan figure was now the young Lucchese despot, and he was animated by too unbridled an ambition to be content with the territory already won. In 1320 he became involved in a war against Genoa, which city the Guelphs had recently acquired and which the rasped and angry Ghibellines desired to bring back into their ranks. To help their friends, the Genoese Guelphs, the Florentines invaded the contado of Lucca and obliged Castruccio in self-protection to hurry home. Thereupon for a number of years Lucca and Florence with their respective allies cruelly harried each other's territory. At the same time they were quick to spring to the aid of friends beyond the limits of Tuscany. Avoiding the always tiresome details of these local conflicts, we should not fail to note that more and more the struggle between the Tuscan Guelphs and Ghibellines tended to enlarge its field of action. Each group entered on increasingly close relations with the related groups of Liguria, Lombardy, and Umbria with the result that when war broke out in one of these provinces, it quickly spread to all the others. With this widening of the political horizon no Tuscan government could any longer afford to shape its policy with sole reference to the local situation.

So little faith, and justifiably as the events just recounted prove, did the Florentines put in the Tuscan pacification of 1317 that when the five-year term of King Robert's signory expired, they renewed it for four years more. It was agreed that it should run till 1322. However, when that year rose upon the world, even though, as we shall presently see, the Ghibelline danger had again become acute, the men of Arno were so thoroughly tired of the Neapolitan guests in their midst that they refused further to extend King Robert's term and resumed control of their affairs. Florence was herself again! And to signalize her return to popular sovereignty, she reinstituted the capitano del popolo, the particular official whom the people regarded as their leading defender, and who for this very reason had been obliged to disappear from the political scene when the king of Naples with his anti-popular tendencies took hold. Being now newly appointed, he was, according to custom, supplied with a constitution drawn up to define his office and its obligations. The instrument of 1322 enjoys great honor among scholars because it is the earliest constitution of the capitano to come down to us. Three years later (1325), a periodic revision provided a new *statuto* also for the podestà; and this document, as being the oldest surviving record of an even more ancient and dignified office than that of the capitano, has very properly been accorded a position of honor at the side of the captain's document. The two documents together supply the solid basis for every serious inquiry into the constitutional history of Florence.[4] In this connection it may be well distinctly to point out what should be already apparent from the facts just recounted, that there is no single document which may be called *the* Florentine constitution. It was customary to provide a statuto for every official or set of officials, on which he or they took the oath of office and by which their respective duties were defined. We have just seen that such was the case with the podestà and the capitano del popolo. Since the leading governing body from the year 1282 consisted of the priors, the priors of course had a constitution of their own. It is in this light that we should regard the Ordinances of Justice (1293) with their prescriptive statements touching the manner of election of the priors, their term of office, their power of legislative initiative, and other similar matters. Under the ruling system of statutory regulation the officials charged with the indirect taxes (*gabelle*) and with the supervision of the grain market at Or San Michele (*I Sei del Biado*) also had their special constitutions. All

[4] The two constitutions have been published by Romolo Caggese in two volumes under the title *Statuti della Repubblica Fiorentina*. Vol. I, "Statuto del Capitano del Popolo degli anni 1322-25." Florence, 1910. Vol. II, "Statuto del Podestà dell'anno 1325." Florence, 1921. Failure to meet the requirements of an advanced scholarship has been charged by several authoritative critics. See a review of Caggese by G. Rondoni in *Arch. Stor. It.*, Series 5, Vol. XLVII, pp. 181-95; also a body article by R. Palmarocchi, "Contributi allo Studio delle Fonti Statuarie," in *Arch. Stor. It.*, dispensa 3 of 1930, pp. 56-107. Consult also Davidsohn, Vol. IV, *Anmerkungen zum Zweiten Theil*, pp. 1-4, "Die Aeltesten Statuten von Florenz."

ese documents with the records of the council sessions, the *Provvisioni* and *Consulte,* thrown in for good measure, make up the fundamental constitutional material of the republic of Florence. They will have to be collected, analyzed, and interpreted, a work that has as yet been no more than begun, before we can reach a full understanding of the public law and private practices of the sons of the Red Lily in the period of their most vigorous self-expression.

It cannot be truthfully said that as soon as Florence in 1322 again took over its own affairs, it prospered more vigorously than had been the case under Neapolitan direction. If throughout the peninsula republican forms were giving way to despotism, the reason, as cannot be too often repeated, was that democracies are in their very nature ill adapted to the successful conduct of war. Again and again in the years ahead Florence was to have this truth brought home to it, but never more crushingly than in the pending struggle with the unusually capable lord of Lucca. Like Uguccione before him, Castruccio aimed to reduce Pistoia to obedience in the persuasion that the capture of this strategic post was the necessary preliminary to the overthrow of Florence and the subjection of Tuscany to his person. For nothing less than the conquest of the whole province had become the goal of his ambition; and Florence, he argued, though too strong to be directly attacked, would fall like ripe fruit into his lap as soon as he had made himself master of Pistoia and the many small supporting fortresses among the rolling hills of the Pistoiese contado. On May 5, 1325, Castruccio won the Pistoian prize by a sudden stroke, which would hardly have been successful had he not been helped by traitors within the walls. Traitors or no traitors, he had captured the city and news fell upon the ears of his Arno enemies like a peal of thunder. They realized that they were as game stalked by a cunning hunter and angrily resolved to bring the issue to a quick decision.

By this time it had already become the settled practice of Florence to hire foreign horsemen as soon as war hove in sight. Under the same impulsion it had become usual to name a special war captain (*capitano di guerra*), to whom rather than to the podestà, as had formerly been the case, the conduct of the campaign to be undertaken was intrusted. Accordingly, within a day after the capture of Pistoia, the government appointed the Spaniard, or rather Catalan, Raymond of Cardona, to the post of war captain and invited him to increase the mounted mercenaries already in hand as rapidly as possible by new enlistments. These preparations illustrate perfectly the military revolution which was sweeping Italy at this time and on which we enlarged at the beginning of this chapter. The core of the Florentine army, as that of every other town, was by now the body of heavily armored horsemen recruited on the open market at a wage determined by the law of supply and demand. When, after a month of hurried preparations, Raymond inaugurated the campaign, he commanded about twenty-five hundred knights representing a veritable Babel of tongues, for the recruits who had flocked to his banner hailed from France, Spain, Germany, Italy, and England. But note well: four hundred of this cavalry body were native Florentines, of whom some were rich popolani patriotically resolved to satisfy the ancient cavallata requirement, and the others survivors from the depressed and declining nobility who still fough in the wars of Florence as a matter of pride and pleasure. But how had the importance of the native cavalry diminished! By 1325, as the figures show, the local horsemen were completely overshadowed by the mercenaries. And with such giant footsteps did the decline of the old republican army proceed that in the course of the next few decades the native horsemen dropped altogether out of sight. Therewith the military revolution, a social revolution in its origin, had reached its logical goal. Machiavelli writing some two hundred years later, when Italy exhibited a painful helplessness before the assaults of France and Spain, ascribed the absence of a fighting spirit in his countrymen to the systematic uprooting of the nobility by such measures as the Ordinances of Justice. Had it not been for this legislation, he argued, the town cavalries would never have run to such sorry seed as they did. The great political thinker erred in this opinion because he did not consider all the factors of the situation. Without any doubt whatever, the main reason for the decline and extinction of the urban cavalry was not the Ordinances of Justice but the circumstance that, with the fourteenth century, war became the affair of professional soldiers. Compared with them the local milites, even when they had not abandoned the exercise of arms, looked and acted like an awkward squad. The Florentine army system of republican days fell by the wayside—and the statement holds for both infantry and cavalry—owing, in the main, to a feature invariably accompanying social change and increasingly in evidence through all the subsequent phases of occidental civilization. We may call it refinement of function or specialization.

In point of fact the infantry was even less capable of meeting the severer fighting standards of the new age than the horsemen. Nonetheless the democratic army did not die easily and at once; and just as we find Florentine milites still mobilized for the campaign of 1325, so also do we encounter Florentine pedites in the army led into the field by the Catalan captain. On a brilliant day of the month of June, when Raymond had completed his preparations, some fifteen thousand citizen foot-soldiers marched out of the western gate with the bells of all the churches ringing madly to speed them on their way.[5] Quite the most curious, because the most anachronistic feature of this host marching forth to battle for the honor and safety of Florence was that ancient emblem of the free commune, the caroccio. Drawn by white oxen swathed in crimson cloth and carrying a mast and bell—the famous *martinella*—upon its ample platform, it drew the reverent gaze of the populace strung out along the line of march. What Cardona's steel-clad mercenaries on their heavy barbs may have remarked on this gay carnival float would constitute an interesting comment on changing manners if someone had been sufficiently interested to preserve their words.

Throughout the summer the Florentines were occupied with the siege and capture of the numerous small castles held by the enemy in the region between Lucca and Pistoia. Offering no active opposition, Castruccio kept his

[5] Villani, IX, 300. The chronicler's burgher pride moves him to enter into picturesque details and statistical data regarding this great host which the interested reader will do well to look up.

army intact in a central position among the foothills above Altopascio, from where he could forestall an attack aimed at either Lucca to the west or at Pistoia to the east. Thus passed the hot summer days with Raymond's effectives steadily declining through disease and desertion. Nonetheless a number of small successes were chalked up for the City of the Baptist. These caused the Florentines to swell with such confidence that they insisted, before ending the campaign, on measuring swords with the Ghibelline lord, apparently grown timid in the face of the bold Guelph initiative. Under these circumstances the campaign was brought to a head with a battle fought on September 23, 1325, near Altopascio, in which Castruccio enjoyed the advantage of occupying higher ground and commanding a less exhausted army. In a very short time the Florentine resistance was broken and in the rout that followed many thousands of knights and foot-soldiers, together with the rich equipment of the camp, were captured by the enemy. Of course that lumbering relic of other days, the caroccio, also fell into the enemy's hands and without doubt filled the hearts of the people of Lucca with more pride than the sight of all the other trophies when, following his victory, Castruccio held a triumphal entry into his capital. In the seared hearts of the Florentines, on the other hand, Altopascio took its place beside those two other names of evil omen, Montecatini and Montaperti.

The vigorous Castruccio pursued the fleeing enemy to the very walls of Florence and during the subsequent weeks occupied himself with laying waste the fertile fields around the city. He did not undertake the siege of so vast a town for the excellent reason that he lacked the necessary forces to surround it. Moreover, in connection with the recent intensification of the war, the Florentine government had been spurred to complete the new circumvallation of the town, thereby rendering it impregnable to direct assault. We are aware that the third circle of walls had been begun more than a generation ago and that it had gone forward with often prolonged interruptions ever since. The year 1310, when Henry VII descended into Italy, had brought about a revival of activity; and so far had the work been pushed on that occasion that, when the mortal crisis connected with the name of Castruccio arose, the whole costly structure could between 1322 and 1325 be brought to completion. We are well informed on this crowning phase of the undertaking because our leading chronicler, Villani, acted as one of the municipal overseers and is happy to communicate the results of his labors to his readers.[6] Castruccio paid the new defenses a fine compliment in his way by declining to try them out.

That the dejected Florentines harbored the gravest anxieties, however, in regard to the Lucchese lord is proved by the renewed surrender of their liberties into the hands of a Guelph signore. Long accustomed to look for succor in periods of stress to the house of Anjou, they now (December, 1325) offered themselves to King Robert's son and heir, Charles, duke of Calabria. In the

[6] Villani, IX, 137. "Ed io scrittore, trovandomi per lo commune di Firenze uficiale con altri onorevoli cittadini sopra fare edificare le dette mura." . . . See also IX, 256, 257. For the fully documented record of the construction of the third circle beginning as far back as 1284, see Davidsohn, *Forschungen*, Vol. IV, pp. 447 ff.

agreement as ultimately ratified Charles was made regent and protector for te. years; he was to maintain a body of one thousand French knights and be paid an annual stipend of 200,000 gold florins; he was to nominate the podestà, the priors, and all other officials; and finally, he was to exercise that most sovereign of all rights, the right of peace and war. Comparing these sweeping terms with those of the very qualified submission of 1313 to Charles' father, we are forced to admit that they come close to abject surrender. In seeking safety from the attack of one tyrant the frightened republic had thrown itself into the arms of another. In July, 1326, Duke Charles arrived in person from the south at the head of a splendid cavalcade. It was not the least ominous feature of the new venture in despotism that on the duke's taking up his residence in the palace of the podestà, it was promptly rechristened Palazzo Ducale. In spite of this act of shoddy servility, the republican spirit was not so dead that it did not command many votaries who looked with barely concealed ill-will on the royal ruler in their midst and who prayed earnestly for the day when the city might again free itself from the noose into which it had thrust its head.[7]

Meanwhile an event was ripening in another quarter of the world which must have tended to confirm the Florentine merchants in the wisdom of their surrender to a master who was a tried and impassioned Guelph. Another German sovereign, Ludwig of Bavaria, was making ready to cross the Alps and hearten his Ghibelline following. Having traced in some detail the fortunes in Italy of Henry VII, we need not hesitate for a moment to declare that every imperial intervention after his time was foredoomed to failure. The coming of Ludwig was therefore no more than an empty gesture. However, that the Italians alive at that time should be disturbed by his arrival may be readily admitted. The Ghibellines would rejoice at the strength about to be added to their ranks, while the Guelphs would register a corresponding flutter of alarm. Especially in Tuscany, dominated by Ghibelline Castruccio, the depressed Guelphs would show concern and Guelph Florence would not unnaturally feel the need of nestling more closely than ever under the wing of its Angevin protector. While still beyond the barrier of the Alps, Ludwig had taken note of Castruccio's success and had rewarded him with the title of imperial vicar. His usurpations thus legitimized, the Antelminelli might entertain as not too extravagant the hope of making his lordship hereditary in his house. The potential strength added to their dangerous provincial enemy was the main reason for alarm on the part of the Florentines over the coming of the Bavarian. In every other respect the event left them entirely unmoved.

In the spring of 1327 Ludwig crossed the Brenner pass and came to Milan, where on the last day of May he was crowned in the church of Sant' Ambrogio with the iron crown of Italy. He owed this initial success to the Ghibellines of Lombardy, for he had brought with him only a small force of his own Germans. When, in the autumn, he proceeded into Tuscany, he passed from under the protection of the Lombard Ghibellines to that of the Ghibellines

[7] For a close study of the episode connected with the name of Charles of Naples see *Arch. Stor. It.*, Serie 5, Vol. XLII (1908), pp. 45 ff., 259 ff. The author, G. degli Azzi, has illustrated his study with many documents.

. Tuscany and was accordingly met and welcomed at the Tuscan border by Castruccio. Though playing ostensibly the part of his sovereign's obedient servant, the successful adventurer was in reality the guardian of his master; and when he now requested of that master to be made hereditary duke of Lucca, he could not be denied. This was a first step. Others would follow in due course until the lord of little Lucca had expanded into the duke of the great province of Tuscany. Tuscany was without doubt Castruccio's goal, although he was content for the present to keep the thought locked closely in his bosom.

The new duke's immediate purpose was to make himself indispensable to Ludwig by speeding him on his way to Rome, where the Bavarian desired to be crowned emperor. In this connection it will be necessary to set forth a literary controversy which arose at this time and which is just about the only feature of this Roman expedition with a real claim on our attention. The controversy in question had its origin in the renewal of the papal declaration that the church is superior to the empire and consequently can make and unmake emperors at its pleasure. The pope reigning in Ludwig's time was the Frenchman, John XXII (1316–34). He was disliked by many Italians, not necessarily Ghibellines, because he refused to give up his residence at Avignon and return to Rome; and he was looked at askance by pious Christians generally because of his gross financial exactions and his ferocious persecution of that faction of the followers of the Assisan saint called Spiritual Franciscans. These Spirituals had become the object of the papal wrath for no other reason than their fanatical devotion to the evangelical doctrine of poverty. John had opposed the election of Ludwig as German king and, when it took place in spite of him, promptly declared it null and void. In his counterblast to this thunder Ludwig enumerated the sins of his Avignonese enemy and, because of John's fanatical opposition to the doctrine of poverty preached by the Spirituals, roundly declared that his opponent was a heretic. As one defamation calls for another, pope and king continued to fire reverberating broadsides at each other until they had exhausted the objurgatory resources of the Latin language and destroyed every prospect of an amicable settlement of their differences. It will convey a sense of these rancorous amenities if we remark that the pope habitually referred to Ludwig not as king or emperor but as "the accursed Bavarian." He even corrected Ludwig's pedigree by confidently affirming that his real father was none other than Beelzebub.

Similar pleasantries having been exchanged between the two putative heads of Christendom for some centuries past, this latest version of an old controversy might be overlooked were it not for the fact that, when it was about two years old, it gave birth (1324) to something new, a book to wit, indicative of the dawn of a new era of political thought. It was written by Marsilius of Padua (with the probable assistance of the Frenchman, John of Jandun) and bore the intriguing title, *Defensor Pacis* (Defender of the Peace). It projected a philosophy which, though held as yet by few men, signified a lively response on the part of the author to such tremendous recent happenings as the growth of towns, the emergence of national monarchies, and the overthrow of Pope Boniface VIII by Philip IV of France. In view of the va expansion of secular interests indicated by these events, Marsilius, who, be sides being an Italian townsman, was a physician of a scientific bent, found it impossible further to subscribe to the opinion that the civil development of Europe must continue to be subjected to the direction of the church. He went back to the Aristotelian position that the state is a purely mundane institution created for the protection and happiness of its members; and from this premise he deduced that, instead of the state being the civil department of a church which might claim to be omnipotent because instituted by God, the very opposite was true and that the church was rather the religious department of an all-powerful state. He pushed his claim far beyond the Reformation leaders of the sixteenth century, and in effect anticipated a position which enjoyed no general support till the French Revolution. He was thus some centuries ahead of his time, and as the champion of a doctrine that would have dragged the clergy from its eminence aroused a furious resentment in ecclesiastical circles. Nor did he content himself with moving with academic caution in the tenuous realm of theory, for he climaxed his exposition with a vitriolic denunciation of the ignorance, avarice, and worldliness of priests and prelates and particularly of their head, the pope. Although the papal anathema fell promptly on the revolutionary agitator, his book continued to circulate widely for the excellent reason that it expressed a viewpoint which was in accord with some of the leading movements of the age. In short, the *Defensor Pacis* is a literary monument of the first order.

To save himself from clerical persecution Marsilius, who was living at Paris when he composed his great work, had been obliged to put himself under the immediate protection of Ludwig in Germany. He was a big factor in pushing the Bavarian into the Italian venture and, in complete accord with his secular doctrine, he took the position that it was not at all necessary for an emperor to be crowned by the pope. Such radicalism was not easy for any medieval person to accept, and we may take it as certain that Ludwig himself would not have accepted it, if he could have discovered any other way out of his difficulties. As long as Pope John XXII took the hostile stand he did, Ludwig could not hope to have the imperial crown set upon his head; and all that remained, if Ludwig clung to his Roman project, was to subscribe to the Marsilian teaching that the true and legitimate bestower of the imperial diadem was the purely civil group of the Roman people.

It was with the resolution to act on this idea that Ludwig, after receiving the Italian crown at Milan, pushed southward into Tuscany, where we have found him making the most of Castruccio's ascendancy. With the Tuscan's strong support he pressed onward to Rome, where on January 17, 1328, he received the coveted imperial diadem from Sciarra Colonna, acting as syndic of the historic populus Romanus. This Sciarra Colonna, we may note in passing, is the very dubious character who, a generation before, had managed the ambuscade of Anagni, to which the arrogant Boniface VIII had fallen victim. It is interesting to learn that a purely secular coronation did not, after all, satisfy Ludwig, as would have been the case had he been wholeheartedly converted by Marsilius, now in constant attendance on him as his personal cian. The medieval man was still strong in Ludwig and even stronger his followers. Not content therefore with the civil act, he had himself onsecrated at the same time by two bishops. True, they did not claim to represent the pope and the pope for his part did his best to discredit them by declaring them to be heretics; but they wore the robes appropriate to the occasion and applied what passed for holy chrism to the Bavarian's brow. Thereafter every good Ghibelline who cared to argue the point might affirm that Ludwig was emperor *both* by the grace of God and of the Roman people. The chronicler affords us a glimpse of Castruccio at the Roman ceremonies which is so precious that we may not pass it over. Castruccio knew, and everybody knew, that it was he, Castruccio, who had enabled Ludwig o win the imperial diadem. As there was no false modesty about the Lucchese ord, he presented himself to view during the coronation ceremonies in a flame-colored robe, which bore across the front in golden letters the inscripion: He is what God ordains; and across the shoulders, also in letters of gold, an the legend: And he shall be what God shall ordain.[8] He wished to tell he world that, while it had already seen wonders, it might expect still greater wonders in the future.

While Castruccio was at Rome, the Florentines resolved to take advantage of his absence from their neighborhood. They made a sudden night attack on Pistoia and captured the city. The loss drew the discomfited signore speedily back to Tuscany determined to retake the stronghold. The siege that ollowed did not yield its prize till early August, and in the hour of his riumph the conqueror was himself laid low. A fever contracted during the operations before Pistoia slowly undermined his strength and on September 3 brought his brilliant career to a close. On his deathbed he made provision to have his young sons succeed him, but they were not of his mettle and after only a few weeks were obliged to abandon Tuscany. Even Emperor Ludwig, forgetting what he owed their father, turned against them; had they, however, enjoyed his support instead of his enmity, they would not have gained greatly by the exchange. For the emperor had hardly left Rome when his opponents took over the city on the Tiber; and as, in the course of the summer and autumn, he slowly retreated northward to Pisa, the whole rail edifice of his might began to crack in all its joints. During the winter 1328–29 he did his best to hold Tuscany in submission but, with Castruccio gone, he found the Guelph tide flowing too strongly for him successfully to stem it. In the spring he withdrew to Lombardy, whence, with his partisans falling away from him in increasing numbers every day, he escaped, a orely tried and beaten man, across the Alps. In February, 1330, he was back n his capital of Munich.

The jubilation of the Florentines at the passing of Castruccio shook the welkin. Death, as Machiavelli maliciously remarked at the sudden demise of another enemy, was ever his countrymen's best ally. Two months later he impersonal Reaper rendered them another egregious service, for on November 9, he mowed down the Florentine signore, Charles of Calabria. When,

[8] Villani, X, 59. The two inscriptions read: *E quello che Iddio vuole;* and *E si sarà quello che Iddio vorrà.*

in the previous winter, Ludwig had left Pisa for Rome, the duke had a
doned his Florentine residence in order to help defend his father's kingd
against a possible invasion. In the capital city of Naples he died, still a youn
man; and instead of being obliged to overthrow by force of arms the maste
whom they no longer needed now that Castruccio was no more, the Florentines had the good fortune of having their freedom returned to them as a
pure gift. They at once resolved to revert to the old constitution, of which
the emblem was the priorate, although not without adopting, in the restles
manner pilloried in Dante's immortal verse,[9] a few supposed improvements
The revision of 1328 may not be overlooked because it added to the popula
government inaugurated in 1282 a last characteristic feature. Not that othe
features were not excogitated and tried later on. Of some of them we shal
be obliged to take at least passing notice. However, of all constitutional re
forms after those of 1328 it may be safely said that either they proved ephem
eral and promptly disappeared or else that they did not in any notable wa
modify the established machinery.

Since the priorate was based on the gild system, eligibility to office wa
reserved to the membership of the twenty-one gilds recognized by the con
stitution. Of the twenty-one, seven had been originally classified as arti mag
giori, five as arti medie, and nine as arti minori. But the association of th
middle with the greater gilds in the first stage of the revolution had brough
it about that in the Ordinances of Justice these two classes had been groupe
together as the twelve greater gilds. To a certain extent this was misleadin
since only the seven upper gilds were engaged in the export business, an
since only among their members were to be found individuals possessed o
considerable resources. In any case, regardless of whether we consider th
greater gilds to have been seven or twelve in number, there were rich gilds
men and poor gildsmen, and, as might be expected in a period of commercia
domination, it was the rich and not the poor who preponderantly served a
priors and banner-bearers. While the greater gildsmen may have owed thei
preponderance to their greater ability and wider experience, it was also du
to their secret and unscrupulous manipulation of the elections. The resul
was that from the very start the priorate showed a tendency to circulat
among a relatively small number of families of the new-rich, designated b
their less fortunate fellow-citizens with a mixture of admiration and contemp
as *il popolo grasso,* the fat bourgeoisie.

Davidsohn has closely studied the prior lists for the years 1310 to 1313 an
noticed the occurrence and recurrence of names belonging to families destine
to dominate the next two centuries of Arno history.[10] He enumerates, amon

[9]. . . . . che fai tanti sottili
Provvedimenti, ch'a mezzo Novembre
Non giugne quel che tu d'Ottobre fili.
Purgatorio, VI, 142-44.

(. . . . . who makest such fine-spun
Provisions, that to middle of November
Reacheth not what thou in October spinnest.)

[10] Davidsohn, Vol. III, p. 401.

..ers, such characteristic surnames as Soderini, Valori, Albizzi, Foresi, Strozzi, Machiavelli, Corsini, Acciaiuoli, Peruzzi, and Medici. The great families of the previous century were slowly sinking below the horizon, certainly not wholly because of the Ordinances of Justice. They had passed their meridian and were encountering that law of decline which rules all living organisms. The families which replaced them owed their wealth to exactly the same sources as their predecessors, that is, to money-lending and barter. However, they followed a different course from their predecessors since, owing to the taboo put upon knighthood in the Ordinances, they were in growing measure willing to forgo the use of arms and to concentrate on the two engrossing concerns of business and politics. In the generations to come the proudest boast of a good Florentine sprang not from the number of his ancestors who had ridden to battle or gone on crusade but from the number who had served as priors and banner-bearers. With this exaltation of the new republican magistracies it is intelligible that from their first appearance a small clique should have attempted to monopolize them. When criticism became disagreeably clamorous, a reform might be effected which for a time would carry a larger percentage of lesser gildsmen into the priorate. But before long the good resolutions would weaken, and the "fat" burghers, resuming control, would with their intelligence and persistence aided by their money bags successfully render null and void their theoretical equality with small shopkeepers and dependent craftsmen.

Even before the resumption of self-government on the death of the duke of Calabria the suggestion had been repeatedly made to reduce the predominance of the new-rich in office by replacing the existing method of election by a system of drawings by lot. Proposed again in 1328, the measure was so confidently recommended as a sure cure for past evils that it was enthusiastically adopted. Under the new enactment the names of those eligible for the various magistracies were selected by an extraordinarily complicated procedure, called the *scrutinio* or scrutiny, from the membership of the twenty-one gilds possessed of political rating, and put into *borse,* leather purses or bags. From these borse, at the expiration of the terms of the various officials in service, the names of the new officials were extracted by lot. The borse were to be periodically renewed by means of a new scrutinio and they were secured against fraudulent manipulation in their place of deposit with the same elaborate precautions as were used in their preparation.[11] In view of the fact that that will-o'-the-wisp, the democratic equality of all gildsmen, great and small, rich and poor, continued to elude its pursuers, it is impossible to avoid the conclusion that all these involved arrangements represent an enormous futility. Since there was no change in the Florentine social order, we may reasonably ask how the borse could be expected to produce an equalitarianism which did not exist. Not many months after the citizens had adopted the great ballot reform of scrutinio and borse, mutterings were heard to the effect that the same old clique was still on top. Instead of "guiding" the elections, as had been the case in the past, it now, by means best known to itself,

[11] The intricate safeguarding devices, absolutely unique in the history of democratic government, may be consulted in Villani, X, 108, and in Davidsohn, Vol. III, pp. 862 ff.

juggled the lists of the eligibles before and after they got into the borse. sum, we may agree that from the inauguration of the priorate in 1282 there was in Florence so persistent a drift toward an oligarchy of a plutocratic type that we are obliged to conclude it constituted a reasonably correct expression of the city's social structure. However, neither the slighted members of the lesser gilds nor the steadily growing body of the unorganized and, let us never forget, wholly disfranchised workers were willing to accept the situation. By continuing to demand rights for themselves they projected an element of unrest into the play of politics which successfully kept Florence from hardening into such a comfortable, set oligarchy as already before the end of the thirteenth century had succeeded in monopolizing the government of that other great Italian republic, Venice. In spite of powerful oligarchial tendencies, democratic aspirations never ceased to stir among the common people. They were even vigorous enough to unseat the oligarchs from time to time and to oblige them at all times to be on their guard.

It should not be overlooked, although it was not exactly an epochal event, that in connection with the reform of 1328 the system of councils was genuinely simplified. Instead of the traditional two councils of the podestà there was to be henceforth but a single council of the podestà composed of two hundred and fifty members; and instead of the traditional two councils of the captain, there was to be a single council of the captain composed of three hundred members. Furthermore, in place of the council of One Hundred hitherto attached to the priors, this governing committee was held to be sufficiently advised by Twelve Good Men (*boni uomini*), to whom, a little later, were added the Sixteen Captains of the Military Companies. The Twelve Good Men and the Sixteen Captains (*gonfalonieri*) constituted what was called the college (*collegium*) of the priors. Following this reorganization, a bill, after having been approved by the priors and their collegium, was transmitted to the councils respectively of the captain and the podestà and, on being passed by them, became a law. Though it is not a novelty introduced by the revision here discussed, it deserves to be recorded that the priors and gonfalonier of Justice were by this time no longer housed in a private residence hired for the purpose, as had originally been the case. The palace of the priors, in our day still the proudest landmark of the city under its later designation of Palazzo Vecchio, was begun in 1299 and already in 1302 was far enough along for the new executive to take possession.[12] When we think intimately and humanly of the seven heads of the government, we may visualize them as living together during their two months' term of office in the quarters provided in the new municipal center. The constitution closely and elaborately regulated their lives. They ate together with some ceremony at the expense of the republic, which for purposes of pomp surrounded them with numerous servants. They were prohibited from leaving the palace on private business and no one of them was permitted to conduct official negotiations to the exclusion of his colleagues. The priorate was a commission form of

[12] It was in 1302 still far from its present appearance. The stages of its construction may be traced from the documents given by Davidsohn, *Forschungen,* Vol. IV, pp. 499 ff.

, vernment and every conceivable difficulty was put in the way of any one prior exercising a greater authority than his fellows.

The decade following the resumption of Florentine self-government was a period of prosperity, indeed in Villani's eyes his beloved city reached a peak from which it greatly declined in the subsequent decade, the last of the chronicler's life. Between 1328 and 1338 trade and industry visibly advanced, the population grew by leaps and bounds, important public works were undertaken, and a life pulsed through the streets and squares which filled the solid burgher that Villani was with patriotic exultation. And since, as a trader who passed many hours each day bent over a ledger, nothing was more eloquent to his mind than figures, he resolved to take a census of his native town at the close of its most prosperous interval. It is not likely that any medieval man before him ever planned an undertaking so difficult and withall so modern. He had to assemble his material as best he could without authoritative help from any quarter. Admittedly his private researches cannot be accepted without important reservations; let it be said, however, that whenever modern investigators have discovered data enabling them to test Villani's statements, they have been moved to voice their admiration of the old chronicler's veracity and accuracy.

On the basis of the consumption of grain Villani arrived at a figure of ninety thousand men, women, and children within the walls.[13] There were usually about fifteen hundred strangers in Florence, a figure indicative as much of the commercial eminence of the city as of the medieval love of travel. This well-attested passion of our forefathers we moderns, who are inclined to associate travel with the conveniences resulting from steam and electricity, are wont to overlook. From eight to ten thousand children, boys and girls, attended the elementary schools which taught the rudiments of reading and writing, while some six hundred boys were enrolled in four schools of a higher grade which introduced them to the mysteries of grammar and logic. That means of course that they were made acquainted with Latin and dialectics, the recognized foundation of all medieval intellectual culture. There were one hundred and ten churches in the city and its suburbs, of which fifty-seven served as parish churches; the remainder belonged to the various religious orders. Thirty hospitals with a capacity of more than one thousand beds served the poor and the sick. Two hundred shops of the wool gild, giving work to about thirty thousand hands, turned out annually between seventy and eighty thousand bolts of cloth worth more than one million two hundred thousand gold florins. This bit of information alone suffices to show that it was the textile industry which gave Florence its economic eminence. But while once upon a time it had been the merchants of the Calimala gild, the importers of coarse

[13] Villani, XI, 94. He speaks picturesquely of *bocche* (mouths). Modern students, statistically trained, have indorsed Villani's figures. In view of the new suburbs, which had already grown up around the third circle of walls only recently completed, they favor a total population for 1339, including city and suburbs, of one hundred and fifteen to one hundred and twenty thousand. N. Rodolico, *La Democrazia Fiorentina nel suo Tramonto,* chap. I. Bologna, 1905. G. Pardi, "Disegno della Storia Demografica di Firenze," *Arch. Stor. It.,* Serie 5, Vol. I, pp. 3 ff., 185 ff. Rodolico discusses the population figures for the town through the Middle Ages and Renaissance; Pardi discusses them from the beginnings to the present time.

Flemish or French cloth for the purpose of refining it, who had been the le[illegible]ing manufacturers, shortly after the turn of the thirteenth century the merchants of the wool gild, who made an excellent native cloth, though generally from imported, more particularly from English, wool, acquired a supremacy over the Calimala merchants which they never again lost. In other words, the *arte di Lana* dominated the trecento much as the other woolen gild, the *arte di Calimala,* had dominated the dugento. In abstracting as our final items from this part of Villani's census that Florence was served by eighty banks, six hundred men of law, sixty physicians and surgeons, and one hundred apothecaries, we get a picture that obliges us to conclude that here on the middle Arno we encounter a society already so richly differentiated as to be no longer medieval.

It is when our annalist takes up the revenues and expenditures of his beloved town, that his bosom swells with a very special pride.[14] The form of tax favored and almost exclusively used by the city fathers was the indirect tax, the *gabella.* Most of the gabelle were collected at the town gates on merchandise, both as it entered and passed out of the city, and on the food of the people, grain, wine, salt, and meat. The total revenues, constituted overwhelmingly of gabelle, came to three hundred thousand gold florins, a sum, according to the enraptured statistician, which would be a magnificent income for a kingdom (*sarebbe gran cosa a un reame*). Indeed King Robert of Naples, whom the Florentines were pleased to think of as their protector, had no such sum as that to jingle in his pocket. As no more than fifty thousand florins were required to meet the ordinary costs of administration, the remainder, constituting about five-sixths of the annual budget, was swallowed up by war. It happened that in the years of which Villani has written most fully war had practically become chronic, for first, there were the defensive wars against Castruccio Castracane, and after Castruccio's death came the offensive wars (of which we shall presently hear) to acquire Castruccio's Lucca and to confirm the Florentine mastery of Tuscany. We receive ample evidence from Villani's data touching the military revolution, to which we have repeatedly referred in this chapter. While the chronicler speaks of the continued liability to service in the field of every son of Florence between the ages of fifteen and seventy, he makes it perfectly clear that the citizen militia was only rarely summoned and that at least in his declining years the wars of the Arno city were mainly fought by hireling troops. When the campaign was over, the mercenaries were, as a rule, discharged, but the responsibilities which Florence had assumed as an expanding power made it necessary to retain a portion of them on the pay-roll at all times to assure peace and order throughout the ever-widening dominion of the state. If we realize that the city kept even in time of peace a small standing army of from seven hundred to one thousand horsemen, we are prepared to admit that the republican system inherited from the consular days has been superseded. These changes, above all, the continuous wars with their inordinate cost, stirred humanitarian regrets in the historian's heart. He was a bourgeois of the moralizing type who approved the democratic system of the gilds but grieved that it tended to produce magistrates too fond of power and overprompt

[14] Villani, XI, 92, 93.

nake war. In fact so thoroughgoing was his humanitarianism that he reveals himself at times as a theoretic pacifist. This will explain why, in concluding his account of the disproportionate expenditures for military purposes, our usually matter-of-fact trader and statistician was shaken by an emotional paroxysm. In a furious apostrophe addressed to the rulers of Florence, with whom, et us not forget, he was closely tied up, he cries out: "O Signori Fiorentini, what a perverse and wicked policy is this of yours to increase the revenues of he commune from the substance of poor citizens by means of increased taxes and to invest them in insane undertakings! . . . Moderate, most beloved, your nordinate ambitions, for thus you will please God and will cease to burden an innocent people."

Villani's presentation of the Florentine budget opens up the whole imporant matter of taxation. As a recent work[15] has at last presented the issue in its historical perspective, we can now find our way through the intricate financial abyrinth of the young commune, although many of the developments antelating the triumph of the Blacks still remain obscure. As in the case of one and ll of the services and institutions created by the commune, the taxes have a haphazard, accidental, and empirical beginning. Their origin must be sought n certain feudal dues wrested from the empire, more particularly a hearth-tax of twenty-six pennies (*denarii*), and in way-tolls collected at the town gates and commonly called *pedaggi*. Since the hearth-tax was a direct tax and the pedaggio an indirect tax, we observe that the two great categories of taxation igure in the communal finances from the start. It was with an increase of the eturns from the indirect taxes that the young republic attempted to meet the vaxing burdens of government. Even in full feudal times the town had reorted to imposts on ovens, wine, grain, and similar consumption taxes, and hese dues, added to the tolls on goods in transit, increased automatically in measure as commerce and population expanded. The generic name for indirect axes being gabelle, we may think of the growing commune as operating argely with them. However, toward the middle of the thirteenth century a new direct tax put in an appearance, the *estimo*. It represented an attempt to raduate the tax burden according to the wealth of the individual and thereby o moderate the injustice of the consumption taxes, which fell with crushing everity on the common people. Commendable in intention, the estimo caused nending complaints, in part because from the beginning of time men have een averse to paying direct taxes, but also because the assessment, based on oth capital and income, varied so greatly from man to man and was so subect to fraud and favor that it developed monstrously inequitable features. There was as yet no great body of statistical material on hand from which it vould have been possible to arrive at acceptable norms for a scientific income ax, even if such an ideal had lain within the mental range of the taxing bodies f that age. When the imperfect estimates, called estimo, were ready, the govrnment, acting on resolutions passed by the councils, levied a tax called *libra* ased on the estimo and naming a rate of payment calculated to bring in the um of which the treasury stood in immediate need. Owing to the ever-widen-

[15] B. Barbadoro, *Le Finanze della Repubblica Fiorentina: Imposta Diretta e Debito Pubblico fino l'Istituzione del Monte*. Florence, 1929.

ing range of action of the commune and to the consequent growth oi penditures, chiefly for war, it might often happen that the owners of propert, were *allibrati* several times within a year. In 1315, when Florence was obliged to meet the danger which threatened her ascendancy owing to the sudden rise of Uguccione della Faggiuola, a financial crisis was precipitated which enables our authority, Barbadoro, to give us the first clear view of the principles and practices underlying the taxation structure of the state.

By the year 1315 the Blacks had been in power for over a decade and the rule of the Blacks had worked out as the triumph of the popolo grasso, the "fat" bourgeoisie. It was these well-to-do rulers who had to submit to a disgusting inquisition into their possessions for the purposes of the estimo and who had to arrange to pay the libra as often as it was voted in order to meet an extraordinary expense. In 1315, in the very face of the peril threatening from Pisa, they revolted, and with an apparent unanimity in all the councils sweepingly rejected the combination of estimo and libra as a means for balancing the budget. Never did a possessive bourgeoisie more neatly than on this occasion reveal its intimate mind and heart. Far removed from giving up the policy of an expanding control in Tuscany and Italy, the dominant merchants were firmly resolved to continue the wars which their policy made unavoidable, but they would no longer finance them by a method obliging their class to bear a large portion of the tax burden. Their war finances—and Florentine taxation throughout the Black period falls substantially under this head—were based on a conception so typically bourgeois that it has reappeared ever since when and wherever a bourgeoisie has exercised control. The men who dominated the priorate and the councils determined to meet the war costs by spreading them among the people through increased indirect taxes (*gabelle*) and among themselves through loans (*prestanze*) carrying an interest rate of 8 or more per cent. Since the course adopted in 1315 was still followed twenty years later when Villani took his census, we are not surprised to learn that the immense regular revenues, amounting to three hundred thousand gold florins, were almost exclusively raised by gabelle. The most considerable exception which he lists is the estimo of the countryside. On abolishing the estimo for the city, where they had their residence, the self-seeking burghers did not extend the favor to the agricultural population. Apparently an impost based on possessions was a welcome source of revenue, provided it fell on magnates and country yokels and not on the urban lords of trade.

If we keep in mind the hardly ever interrupted wars of the decades immediately following the adoption of the new financial plan, we are prepared to understand the crisis that slowly gathered around the policy of loans, the second string to the bow of taxation. The prestanze were numerous, they bore an engaging rate of interest, and in order to effect their redemption they were assigned on issue to one or another of the many gabelle. But when the wars not only gave no sign of coming to an end but grew steadily more expensive, the repayment of the loans had to be adjourned, while the interest they drew was subjected to reduction or indefinite postponement. With the campaigns of the late thirties and early forties connected with the attempt to capture Lucca these unhappy effects made themselves violently felt. By considering them at

..is point we are forging ahead of our story, but the procedure is justified by the need of bringing our financial argument to a logical conclusion. The point to keep in mind is that at the beginning of the forties there was an immense public debt, which was no longer being redeemed according to contract and on which even the interest payments were but irregularly made. The only way to save the whole device of the prestanze from collapse was by a consolidation of the old loans, together with a slash in the interest rate and by at least a partial abandonment of the feature of redemption. By a series of measures belonging to the period 1343–47 this reform was carried through[16] and an orderly administration of the public debt created, picturesquely called *Monte,* from the single heap or "mountain" to which the varied items of indebtedness had been reduced. Considered purely as a technical operation in public finance, the Florentine Monte represented a notable achievement. By means of it the system of loans was re-established in the public confidence, thereby enabling loans together with indirect taxes to remain the characteristic features of Florentine taxation for many years to come. The dark side of the successful consolidation of the national debt signified by the Monte was that it indefinitely adjourned the return to the estimo, the direct tax, by which individuals contributed to the support of their government in some reasonable proportion to their means.

Appropriating Villani's habitual way of marking a transition, we shall now leave the issue of taxes and resume our interrupted political narrative. As soon as, with the death of the duke of Calabria in 1328, the Florentine oligarchs had reacquired control, they took up again their plan of territorial expansion, which the successive, meteor-like appearances of Uguccione della Faggiuola and Castruccio Castracane had obliged them to abandon. Their instrument for extending their power over Tuscany had now for some two generations been the league of Tuscan Guelphs. While this was a useful device, it represented a very loose federation, and from the angle of a power aspiring to an unchallenged mastery, was much less satisfactory than direct control. From the first, therefore, Florence had not hesitated to impose its immediate rule whenever the opportunity offered, with the result that, in addition to the scores of castles seized and garrisoned by it at various strategic points, it had gradually acquired possession of most of the small markets and communes of its county and district. It tried to make its yoke as light as the circumstances permitted by contenting itself with sending an executive or podestà and a small troop of men-at-arms under a captain to the subjected town and by conceding, in return for this hegemony, a considerable measure of self-government.[17]

Another and a higher stage in the growth and consolidation of the Florentine state would be reached when the great towns, once the equals and still the jealous rivals of the Red Lily, should in their turn be brought beneath its sway. More than once in the past it had seemed that this stage had been reached, but always some unexpected event had intervened and saved the intended victim from Florentine dominion. However, when at the death of

[16] Barbadoro, chaps. VIII, IX.

[17] A typical case of submission is that of the small town of Colle. Its people agreed to receive "podestà e capitano di Firenze e la guardia della rocca alle loro spese." Villani, XI, 81.

Castruccio his loosely joined state fell apart, the desired day dawned at la. The chief object of contention between Castruccio and the Arno city had been Pistoia; and one of the first consequences of the collapse of the lord of Lucca's miniature empire had been the resumption of its independence by the cantankerous little neighbor of Florence which enjoyed the dubious honor of having given birth to the Black-White feud. But Pistoia was too utterly drained of its vitality by the frequent sieges it had recently undergone to be able to stand securely on its feet. On its own initiative it now accepted the supremacy of Florence, first by permitting its neighbor to appoint its chief official, and later by receiving a small Florentine garrison. The main effect of this welcome increment of power was to stimulate the Florentine appetite. So complete was the disintegration of Castruccio's state that Lucca itself, exhausted by its superlative effort, seemed ripe for subjection. For over a decade after this prospect dawned, the Florentines directed their gaze at the rival city on the Serchio with a kind of hypnotized intensity. Their waking and their sleeping thoughts were concerned with the capture of Lucca; and when in the end all their greedy plans miscarried, the political confusion and economic exhaustion caused by the long Lucchese effort led, as a similar crisis had already twice done in the past, to another signore or tyrant.

So amazingly tied up with the political upheaval throughout Italy was the long-drawn-out Florentine enterprise having Lucca as its object that it almost defies unraveling. The Visconti of Milan, the Scala of Verona, the astute oligarchs of Venice, and even King John of Bohemia, son of Emperor Henry VII (the same John, who, falling afterward at Crécy, left his three-plumed helmet on the ground for the Black Prince to pick up), play a role *pro* or *contra* Florence, while a score of minor city tyrants and feudal potentates, whom it would only add to the confusion to enumerate, make a sporadic appearance in the complicated plot. And yet the story in its essence is simple enough, for it turns on the helplessness of Lucca after Castruccio's fall and the greedy expectation of its neighbors, near and far, to appropriate the enfeebled state. It told against the Florentines that they were not the earliest bystanders to take advantage of the confusion produced in Lucca by the death of its signore. The first group of profiteers was a body of German mercenaries. Having deserted Ludwig of Bavaria when he was no longer able to pay them their wages, they occupied Lucca by force and set themselves up as its owners. Overwhelmed before long by the practical difficulties of government, they sold their possession for a lump sum to a rich Genoese banker. This gentleman, a member of the famous house of Spinola, transferred it for a consideration to the aforementioned son of Emperor Henry VII, who, a typical knight-errant, had come to Italy in the early thirties ready to try his hand at any adventure that might happen to come his way. After having met with a number of rebuffs that signally dampened his romantic ardor, John in his turn sold (1334) the Serchio city to the Rossi of Parma. The Rossi, too, did not hold it long, for under pressure from the powerful lord of Verona, Mastino della Scala, they handed it over to this leading Lombard signore; and when Mastino, owing to his frequent wars, stood in need of money, he entered into negotiations with the Florentines who all along had watched this succession of dizzy transfers of title with the liveliest anxiety. But the Veronese lord proved as slippery as an eel. While he craved the bills of exchange of the Arno merchants, he wanted just as eagerly to keep his new-won political foothold in Tuscany. He therefore blew alternately hot and cold in the Lucchese matter. Vastly indignant at this double-dealing, the Florentines in 1336 made an alliance with the republic of Venice in the hope of extracting Lucca from Mastino by military pressure from two sides, and once again they met with disappointment. For no sooner had the allied Venetians gained their own particular end than they made a separate peace with the Scala tyrant and obliged Florence to come to terms or meet the concentrated attack of the enemy (1338). Apparently regardless of whether they followed the course of bribery or war the Florentines were destined to be balked of the Lucchese prize.

Unwilling to concede themselves beaten, they now returned to their original plan of buying Lucca from Mastino with a chest of good gold florins and straightway ran into a new difficulty. The closest neighbor of the Serchio city was Pisa; and Pisa, indisposed to have Florence established at its gates, opened negotiations of its own with Mastino and followed them up with an attack on Lucca in the hope of capturing it. Thus matters stood in 1341. After the Florentines had wasted large sums in attempted bribery of the slippery Mastino and after they had lost even larger sums in levying war on him, the Pisans had the impertinence to come forward in order to reap where the Florentines had sown. In their desperation the Arno burghers suspended the constitution and intrusted a committee of twenty citizens (*I Venti*) with full powers for one year. To no avail; for when on October 2, 1341, the Twenty authorized an attack on the Pisan host besieging Lucca, the Florentine army suffered a capital rebuff. This accumulation of disasters prompted the lugubrious Villani to raise the theological issue as to why God was so hard on his native city; and, as a good, believing Christian, he found the answer in the heaped sins of his fellow-citizens.[18] But though the merchants might lament and beat their bosoms, they were not even yet prepared to abandon the prize on which their heart was set. In the spring of 1342 they made a new attempt to raise the siege of Lucca by the Pisans which ended in a new failure; and on July 6 Lucca surrendered to the Pisan commander. The coveted town was lost and all Florence groaned aloud. Half crazed with rage and disappointment, it resolved as a last desperate measure to try its luck with a military adventurer.

On August 1, 1342, immediately after the expiration of the power conceded to the Twenty, the Frenchman, Count Walter of Brienne, called duke of Athens, was put in charge of the war as *capitano di guerra*. This office had become a feature of the constitution some years before and was in no way irregular. Indeed it was the priors, the guardians of the democratic system, who appointed Count Walter to the command of the army. They chose him, it is true, less for his own sake than because of his relationship by marriage to that house of Anjou to which Florence had long ago contracted the habit of appealing in periods of stress. In this French nobleman we encounter another characteristic figure of that age of swift political flux. His father had actually

[18] Villani, XI, 135.

been lord of the duchy of Athens, one of those curious states of the Byzantine east created by the combined prowess and treachery of the knights of the Fourth Crusade. But he had fallen in battle against a band of Catalan mercenaries, who, having seized the duchy, obliged his young son and heir to seek shelter under the wings of King Robert of Naples. Brought up at court and married to a royal princess, Count Walter employed the now empty title of duke of Athens as a stimulus to his ambition. With antecedents such as his it was inevitable that he should cast himself for the role of knight-errant in an Italy teeming with opportunities for *ogni villan che parteggiando viene*. In the passing of the years he had seen much military service, but, apart from his knowledge of war and a certain tenacity of purpose, he possessed no qualities whatever calculated to recommend him to his contemporaries. Villani, who, while detesting him, does not indulge in vilification, describes him as a dark-skinned, undersized man with a long, scraggy beard and a furtive eye completely incapable of arousing a generous enthusiasm.[19] Encouraged by a Florentine merchant group abroad to offer his sword to the Red Lily, he arrived at the precise moment when the city, disorganized and panicky, was looking about for a savior. Appointed as capitano di guerra, he was no sooner in office than some of the magnates with a following of rich popolani began to urge him not to rest content with his limited position but to make himself absolute lord of the city. While the leading contemporary chronicler insists on regarding the magnates as the main instigators of the intrigue, a recent investigator has adduced sufficient documentary material to oblige us to see the event in a somewhat different light.[20] However, to give due weight to this new evidence we must halt our narrative for a moment, while we examine the grave economic crisis which struck Florence at the very moment when it was receiving blow on blow in connection with its Lucchese enterprise.

The economic crisis of these years was in its origin a purely financial crisis and sprang from the reckless grant of loans on the part of the great Florentine trading and banking companies to various European governments for the unproductive purpose of waging war. The trading companies, great international concerns with branches in all the leading cities of the west, had made Florence the world's leading money center. If, toward the end of the dugento, such great houses as the Mozzi, the Scali, the Spini, and the Cerchi held the lead in supplying needy governments with funds, in the course of the first third of the trecento their places had been taken by the even larger and more flourishing establishments of the Frescobaldi, the Bardi, the Acciaiuoli, and the Peruzzi. Business was severely competitive, and while some firms had succeeded in making themselves particularly strong at the papal court or in the kingdom of Naples, others had gained a commanding position in Flanders, in England, and in France. In England, beginning with the reign of Edward I and reaching a climax under Edward III, the Bardi and Peruzzi had acquired a status that gave them a practical monopoly of the export of wool, the leading raw product of English origin figuring in the world-market. The two houses owed their eminence to the favor of the sovereign, to whom they made a return

19 Villani, XII, 8.

20 A. Sapori, *La Crisi delle Compagnie Mercantili dei Bardi e dei Peruzzi*. Florence, 1926.

TTO. THE RAISING OF DRUSIANA. SCENE FROM THE LIFE OF ST. JOHN THE
NGELIST. FRESCO. PERUZZI CHAPEL IN SANTA CROCE

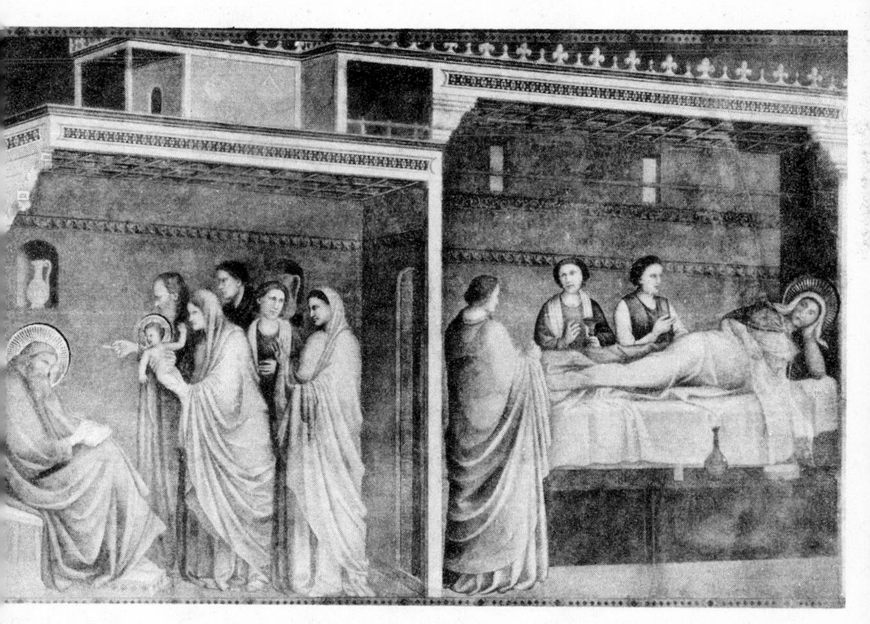

TTO. TWO SCENES FROM THE LIFE OF ST. JOHN THE BAPTIST. FRESCO. PERUZZI
APEL IN SANTA CROCE

ORCAGNA. ALTARPIECE
THE STROZZI CHAPEL
SANTA MARIA NOVELL

ORCAGNA. PARADISE. FRESCO IN THE STROZZI CHAPEL IN SANTA MARIA NOVELLA

by supplying his treasury with the cash whereof it was in perpetual need. When Edward III was seized with the ambition to conquer France, he proposed to meet the cost of the enterprise with loans from his Florentine servants; and although they knew that the investment was dangerous, they had by gradual stages become so involved in the royal finances that a retreat was impossible. After extending themselves to the limit in Edward's early campaigns, by 1339 they were completely exhausted; and when the king, drawing only inconsiderable revenues from his as yet poor and backward realm, was unable to pay his creditors either interest or principal, there was nothing for the English branches of the two houses to do but to go into bankruptcy.

When the news of this disaster reached Florence, it produced a run not only on the Bardi and the Peruzzi banks but on all the banks of the city, large and small. The general confidence was shaken, and it required a series of moratoria on the part of both government and depositors before the public became somewhat calmed and orderly business could be again resumed. But without any doubt whatever, owing to Edward III's default on his enormous war debt, the Florentine financial structure was in perilous case as early as 1339. Had the budget of the Florentine state been on a sound basis, there might presently have been a pick-up. But Florence, too, had just squandered vast sums on war, and what is more, it continued to squander them long after the crisis of 1339 had sounded a first warning. The government was in the hands of the popolo grasso, and there was nothing for the bankers to do, so long as they were an integral part of the system, but to support the Lucchese enterprise to which the whole city had become rapturously committed. When the hard-pressed authorities were forced by the state of the treasury increasingly to suspend payment on the city's obligations, a second and a final financial convulsion could not be long delayed. It was under these circumstances that the great trading companies, wishing to avoid the catastrophe that threatened them, turned to the plan of giving the city a tyrant of their own choosing. Having raised him to power, they hoped as their reward to be intrusted with the shaping of his foreign policy and with the exclusive control of his finances.

This, in substance, is Sapori's theory regarding the origin of the tyranny of the duke of Athens, and it differs from that of contemporary Villani in bringing the role of the bankers into greater relief. But it cannot be said to contradict Villani, for the alert eyewitness was fully aware that the magnates and bankers co-operated in foisting the French nobleman on the city. In offering his version of the event he was confronted with the ambiguity which we have repeatedly pointed out and which remains a source of confusion to this day: the magnate and rich popolani classes in Florence were largely indistinguishable. The Bardi and Frescobaldi, for instance, were magnates, while the Peruzzi and Acciaiuoli were popolani. Doubtless they and many other traders of both legal categories acted together in the great emergency of the summer of 1342 for the unexceptional reason that they had an identical interest to defend. In reporting the event Villani makes too much of the purely magnate element, on which account Sapori's correction may be welcomed since it shows that the conspirators were, economically, a single class induced to act together by the commonest of class motives, self-interest.

Thus oriented in regard to the hidden powers behind the duke of Athens, we arrive at a much clearer understanding regarding the events following his appointment as capitano di guerra. The plotters, magnates and rich traders as Villani truthfully states, in private audiences with the new commander-in-chief urged him to make himself signore. At the same time they prompted the common people, more ill-disposed than ever to the popolo grasso after the accumulated political failures of the foregoing decade and the accompanying economic crisis, to greet him with wild acclamations whenever he appeared in public. Fearing a revolutionary outbreak, the intimidated priors sought to save the situation by offering the war captain the signory of Florence for the duration of one year. But when on the day after this offer, on September 8, a parlamentum was called in the great public square before the palace of the priors (the present Piazza Signoria) in order to have the people confirm the bargain, the popolo minuto, instigated by the magnates, raised a deafening shout *a vita, a vita* (for life, for life); and suiting their action to their words, they lifted the duke to their shoulders and triumphantly carried him into the palace. It was an act emblematic of the acquisition of sovereignty. By the work of a packed and disorderly parliament Walter of Brienne had become the despot of the City of the Baptist for the length of his natural days.

Raised to power in this manner, the duke might be supposed to have adopted the policy of leaning heavily on the highest and the lowest classes of the population. And such indeed seemed at first to be the case. Owing to a desperate attempt on the part of two of the leading magnate-banker families, the Bardi and Frescobaldi, to seize the power two years before, in 1340, they had been banished from Florence. Of course they had not ceased to exercise influence, owing to their essential solidarity with the great mass of monied men left behind. Nonetheless they desired to have the ban against them canceled and this favor the new ruler promptly accorded. At the same time he made peace with Pisa in order to stop the heavy financial drain which had gone on for years and had in the main been met by forced loans from the Florentine banks. And finally, he protected the slipping trading companies from the molestations of their creditors by conceding them a moratorium for a period of three years. As for the popolo minuto, who looked upon him as their man and cheered him to the echo, he showed his sympathy for them by filling the priorate largely from their ranks. It was a feature of his tyranny that, while leaving the constitution intact, he operated it in his interest by appointing the officials. The priors having in this way become a purely ornamental feature of the government, there was no reason why he should not flatter the vanity of butchers, wineshopkeepers, and wool-carders by inviting them to serve as a mock executive. But while prepared to favor the groups to which he owed his signory, he had no mind to be ruled by them or to conduct his government on any counsel or in any interest save his own. Before long the noble plotters found the doors of the palace shut against them and themselves excluded from every exercise of power. And when, on November 20, the duke sanctioned the suspension of payment on all the city's war loans on the ground that the gabelle, from which the loans were to be paid, were needed for current expenditures, he straightway transformed his banker-supporters into his enemies. The proclaimed suspension of payments was really a veiled bankruptcy of the Florentine state. It would have been followed at once by the bankruptcy of the trading-houses, if the duke had not already conceded the three-year moratorium, which kept their creditors from flying at them like angry hornets. It is an interesting detail that the tyrant returned to the direct tax, the estimo, as a convenient means of raising revenue. In this he may have acted merely from avarice, as the good Villani claims; but the student of a later day will not fail to recall that despotism was the political form toward which all Italy was feeling its way, and that despotism, in spite of the evils inseparable from personal rule, usually bestirs itself to end the domination of a privileged class by reducing the whole population to a common level before the law.[21]

Without believing that the new despot was as malevolent and avaricious as his enemies afterward made out, we should find no difficulty in persuading ourselves that the Florentines, after the manner of fickle man, soon tired of their master, and that the group, particularly eager to get rid of him, were the heads of the trading-houses disappointed in their hope that he would be content to act as their tool. The group below the great traders, the broad middle class, had never looked on him with favor; and as for the lower orders who unquestionably had helped him seize the power, they too began to grow cool when they discovered that he could not master the economic crisis, which was deepening every day and spreading a disastrous unemployment. By the spring of 1343 three separate conspiracies against the tyrant were under way, hatched by rival groups of magnates and rich popolani. On the duke's somewhat belatedly getting wind of one of them and taking action by arresting its promoters, in self-defense the three movements coalesced, armed their followers, and on July 26, 1343, set them in motion against the palace. With such celerity was the rising effected that the duke was not able to assemble more than a fraction of his troops scattered over the Florentine dominion. Even the common people, whether from disillusionment, as already hinted, or from thoughtless abandonment to the excitement of the moment, rallied to the rebels. With the apparent hearty co-operation of all its social elements Florence laid siege to its ruler in the palazzo, which he occupied with four hundred soldiers hurriedly gathered together and scantily supplied with food and water.

As his precarious situation put victory out of the despot's reach, he was not long in opening negotiations with his besiegers. But the population, aroused to frenzy and thirsting like wolves for warm blood, would not hear of a surrender which permitted their ruler to withdraw with the honors of war and which cheated them of their vengeance. They called for victims, and on the sixth day of the siege the duke, broken in spirit and resolved at all costs to save his precious person, was obliged to sacrifice the man who had acted as his chief of police, and to push him, together with his eighteen-year-old son, through the palace gate into the arms of the waiting mob. Let Villani re-

[21] On these measures of the duke see Sapori, pp. 146-50. On the whole incident of the duke of Athens, the work of C. Paoli is still invaluable. See *Giornale Storico degli Archivi Toscani,* Vol. VI, pp. 79 ff., 169 ff.; also *Arch. Stor. It.,* Serie 3, Vol. XVI, pp. 22 ff.

count what followed: "In the presence of the father and for his greater sorrow they first dismembered the son, cutting him into small bits (*minuti pezzi*); and this done, they did the same to the father. And one planted a piece of flesh on a lance and another on a sword, and in this manner they made the rounds of the city. And some there were so cruel and possessed of such bestial fury that they ate of the raw flesh."[22] With its savagery placated by this revolting demonstration, the multitude began to disperse, permitting a Committee of Fourteen, to which full powers had been given by a parlamentum hurriedly assembled in the church of Santa Reparata, to make the final arrangements with the fallen signore. Accordingly, on August 6, under safe conduct from a body of Sienese, who had rushed from their hills to help their Florentine friends, the duke with his dependents made his departure from the palace and the city. It was the closing act of the third and most substantial experiment in despotism on the part of the republic since the beginning of the century.

The Fourteen, intrusted with the reorganization of the government, were made up half of magnates and half of leading burghers. This composition of the committee tells us without further argument that it was the trading-houses that overthrew the tyrant, as it had also been they who had installed him in the palace. In the sessions they held to discuss the composition of the new government their central concern must have been the continuation of their power. But as, for the moment, they had the whole city behind them, it was the part of wisdom to exhibit a certain moderation. They therefore re-enacted the old constitution of the priors with a few alterations. Some of these belong to the mere mechanics of administration, as, for instance, the article which replaced the old division of the city into sixths with a new division into quarters; and another article which raised the number of priors from six to twelve, three for each of the new units. What alone mattered to the victors was their own adequate representation in the priorate, and to bring this about they took the bold step of abolishing the Ordinances of Justice. With the magnates, after half a century of political ostracism, again made eligible to the chief executive, the Fourteen ordained that henceforth the priorate should be composed of four magnates (one for each quarter) and eight popolani (two for each quarter), selected from the membership of the twenty-one gilds.

Great as must have been the exultation of the magnate-bankers over the revamped constitution, they made the error common to the upper classes of every age of paying too little attention to the feelings of the people. Consequently, the priors of the new dispensation had been in office only a few days when, on September 22, a mob of immense dimensions gathered around the palace, declaring that it would storm the building unless the four sitting magnates were immediately ousted from the priorate. There was nothing to do but to yield, and thus the planned rehabilitation of the magnates came to naught. The lords of trade saw the last chance of saving their ailing firms slip from their hands and, as an extreme measure, resolved to resort to arms. Warned

[22] Villani, XII, 17.

by the open preparations of the magnates at several centers of the town but particularly on the left bank, the quarter of Oltrarno, the people were not taken by surprise and resolutely attacked their enemies wherever they found them (September 24). When the Bardi, easily the leading magnate clan and occupying with their clustered houses a dominant position along the steep hill of San Giorgio, found themselves entirely enveloped by a raging multitude, they gave up the struggle. The associated banking heads had been beaten all along the line and the people were free to carry through another reorganization.

The reform effected in the course of deliberations conducted by the victors during the month of October was much more moderate than might have been expected in view of the revolutionary character of the uprising against the magnates. The old priorate constitution was retained, together with some of the surface changes recently introduced, as, for instance, the division of the town into quarters instead of sixths. With the priorate again limited to popolani and with two priors assigned to each quarter, there resulted a college of eight priors, to whom the gonfalonier of Justice was added as a ninth member. Of course the Ordinances of Justice were re-enacted, not, however, without a mitigation of some of the features which the passing years had made imperative. A considerable number of families designated as magnates back in the days of Giano della Bella had become so greatly impoverished that it was ridiculous to regard them as still constituting a peril to the state. Accordingly, they were stricken from the magnate rolls and reintegrated with the Florentine citizenry. It throws an interesting light on the mad whirligig of Time to learn that in the countryside a number of individuals rightfully carrying the title of counts had so declined in the social scale that they made their living as agricultural laborers (*lavoratori di terra*). Far and away the most significant change brought about in connection with the reaffirmation of the traditional gild rule was that the seven greater gilds were deprived of their too exclusive control. In view of the fact that the political and economic system associated with the "fat" bourgeoisie had suffered shipwreck, no other result was to be expected. The five middle and nine lesser gilds insisted on being given an opportunity to pull the city out of the mire; and finding themselves on account of the revolution at the helm, they were able to carry their point. When the new borse were prepared for the various offices, the heads of the fourteen lesser gilds managed to get enough names of small artificers into the purses to assure this class a respectable representation in the future. To clinch the matter it was ordained that of the eight priors, two were to be henceforth members of the seven upper gilds, three of the arti medie, and three of the arte minori. While the popolo grasso was thus not completely shelved, small shopkeepers and craftsmen in the main took over the government. It was a dislocation of power within the established framework of the gilds. That it was but a mildly revolutionary change will appear the moment we reflect that the great body of workingmen, chiefly wool workers, remained as completely disfranchised after 1343 as before.[23]

[23] I have followed the usual interpretation of Villani's description of the new government given in XII, 22. Some recent students have favored an interpretation in accordance with which the control remained, after all, with the greater gilds.

Under a government responsive to the pressure of a petty bourgeoisie the fate of the trading-houses was soon sealed. They had been tottering ever since the crash of the London branches of the Bardi and Peruzzi in 1339 and had managed to keep afloat only by means of extensions granted by their creditors and of moratoria conceded by the government. Their desperate situation, growing worse with every year, was reflected in their numerous criminal designs to get possession of the Florentine government and treasury. But with the crushing of the September rising and the taking over of the government by their enemies they had arrived at the end of their tether and the bankruptcies, so long expected, could no longer be delayed. The series of failures was opened by the Peruzzi and Acciaiuoli and continued without interruption till practically all the houses, great and small alike, had gone the same road. It was an unexampled financial collapse.[24] As the house of the Buonaccorsi, of which our friend Villani was a member, crashed with the rest, we have an explanation of the note of bitterness which crept into his account of the new government. The new rulers were obliged to struggle with the evil heritage left on their hands by the popolo grasso and, as is not unusual in a conflict among envenomed political groups, were charged with the sins of their predecessors. That they were not unmindful of their responsibilities toward the sorely tried commonwealth intrusted to their care is proved by their liquidating the Lucchese fiasco by renewing the peace which the duke of Athens had concluded with Pisa and which left Lucca in Pisa's hands. At the same time, instead of repudiating the public debt, as the duke had done, they officially recognized it by carrying through those conversion and consolidation measures already described, which culminated (1347) in the establishment of the Monte. The last bank to fail was the greatest of all, the house of the Bardi. It managed to struggle along till 1346, when it at last surrendered its assets into the hands of its creditors. If Florence should ever rise again to play a part in international commerce and finance, it would have to be under the leadership of new men capable of making the very ruins by which they were surrounded serve as the foundations of daring new ventures.

The period following the tyranny of the duke of Athens was not a happy one either for Florence itself or for the new government. The terrible financial convulsion with its extinction of credit forced many small industrialists, chiefly manufacturers of woolen cloth, to go into bankruptcy, and the shutting down of so many shops was attended by widespread unemployment and starvation. To fill the cup of local woe to overflowing the Tuscan crops were frequently inadequate and the attendant undernourishment prepared the ground for a succession of death-dealing contagions. They reached their climax when, in 1348, there descended on the city, on Italy, and on all Europe the greatest pestilence known to history, the famous Black Death. Even if the number of victims in Florence did not reach one hundred thousand, as the novelist Boccaccio reports, and even if the dead, according to the more moderate figures of living scholars, did not come to more than two-thirds of the population, the toll exacted overwhelms the mind, especially if we take into

[24] The most convincing account of the long banking crisis of 1339-46 is still that of Villani, XII, 54, 56.

account that the havoc at Florence was repeated in every city of Italy and Europe. Among the leading victims of the pestilence in the Arno city was the historian, Giovanni Villani. Before taking final leave of one to whom every lover of Florence owes an inestimable debt of gratitude, let us turn again the pages of his book, this time not to hear him give his, on the whole, amazingly illuminating version of political events, but with the very human purpose of recovering the daily aspects of the town he loved and of catching the pulse beat of the citizens whose hopes and fears he shared and faithfully recorded.

XV. Seeing Florence with Giovanni Villani

BEFORE consulting Giovanni Villani's book in order to note some of the many familiar aspects which he records of his town and its inhabitants, it may be well to supply a biographical sketch of the man whom we have already learned to honor as an invaluable guide through the mazes of the commune's political fortunes. He was born at Florence around the year 1280. The date is exceedingly important because two years later, in 1282, there began that democratic revolution which led to the creation of the priorate and culminated in the Ordinances of Justice (1293). As his father, Villano di Stoldo, was a well-to-do merchant, the family belonged to the class which the revolution had made supreme in the state. In the household of the successful trader there abounded a vigorous burgher self-esteem, which became the very breath of young Giovanni's nostrils. By achieving a minor partnership in the great company of the Cerchi, Stoldo found himself incorporated in the political party of the Whites, and in 1300, the year of the Jubilee so critical for the Arno city, shared in the triumph of his group by sitting among the priors. In good Florentine fashion Giovanni followed in his father's footsteps. He was destined to be a merchant and normally would have become a White Guelph, if the great disaster of 1301 had not overtaken the party. With the responsible leaders of the Whites dispersed and persecuted, the young man found it convenient to disappear from view for a time by representing Florentine trading-houses in distant Flanders and afterward, nearer home, at Naples. On his return to the banks of the Arno, he quietly affiliated himself with the victorious Blacks and was established in the same world of trade as his father before him by a partnership in the firm of the Peruzzi, which he later gave up to join his fortunes with the Buonaccorsi. That he did not shirk the responsibilities of citizenship is proved by his serving, at one time, as an official of the mint and, on another occasion, as a member of the commission intrusted with completing the third circle of walls; but his high standing in the ruling merchant world and in his own gild of the Calimala is best attested by his appointment to the highest office of the state, the priorate. Indeed he was prior no less than three times. In his old age he was overtaken by misfortune, for he went down with his firm, the Buonaccorsi, in the great financial crash of the early forties. A relentless creditor even had him incarcerated for a while in the infamous prison, Le Stinche. Not long after his release, the terrible Black Death invaded the occident and on reaching Florence carried off the honorable burgher and industrious chronicler when he was not far from seventy years of age.[1]

While Giovanni, as the son of a well-to-do merchant, was doubtless sent to one of the several grammar schools that flourished at Florence and there made acquaintance with Latin and dialectics, his real education came to him from the wide practical experience growing out of his commercial contacts and his quickening travels through Italy and Europe. He had a natural gift of observation coupled with an insatiable curiosity about the world in which he lived. It is to this factual turn of his mind that we owe the abundance and variety of his information. But inevitably he colored whatever he saw and reported with a very personal point of view. He was a passionate patriot devoted to the honor and glory of Florence, and he believed that his country possessed in the gild constitution elaborated in his youth the precise government it needed. That under the practical working-out of this system the merchants of the arti maggiori largely monopolized the offices seemed to him to be wholly right and proper in view of their higher social station and broader knowledge of the world. Perhaps because of the sad fate of his father's friends, the Whites, who had had the audacity to oppose the pope and were punished by the loss of home and fortune, he became an unswerving papal partisan, who never ceased proclaiming that opposition to the church was a sin sure to be punished in both the Here and the Hereafter. With the same intellectual submissiveness he accepted the role which the Middle Ages ascribed to the movements of the stars and to the wiles and plots of an ever-watchful Satan. In short, on the reflective and speculative side of his mind he remained contentedly a medieval man. On the other hand, when it came to business and politics, in which he felt securely at home, he did not hesitate to use his personal judgment and to buttress it with rational analysis. In these related fields he has all the essential earmarks of one who has left the medieval outlook behind him. Whoever is inclined to contend that the social and economic revolution connected with the rise of the communes represents the first stage in the supersession of the Middle Ages, and that the second stage, which carried the revolution into the realm of abstract thought, is nothing other than a belated but inevitable development from the first stage, should find strong evidence supporting this view in so manifest a transition figure as that of Giovanni Villani.

Villani himself has told us how he came to be the historian of his city. When Pope Boniface VIII proclaimed the Great Jubilee of the year 1300 and the thought of all the world turned to the Roman pilgrimage, Giovanni, a young man of twenty, found his heart swelling with promptings mixed of devotion and adventure and, yielding to his inner voices, set out for the Eternal City. Let him tell us in his own words what happened to him in the papal capital.

And being on that blessed pilgrimage in the sacred city of Rome and seeing its great and ancient monuments and reading the great deeds of the Romans as de-

[1] Elogio di Giovanni Villani attached to Villani, IV, 189-207; Davidsohn, Vol. IV^3, pp. 159-60.

scribed by Virgil, Sallust, Lucan, Livy, Valerius, Orosius, and other masters of history . . . I took my prompting from them although I am a disciple unworthy of such an undertaking. But in view of the fact that our city of Florence, daughter and offspring of Rome, was mounting and pursuing great purposes, while Rome was in its decline, I thought it proper to trace in this chronicle the origins of the city of Florence, so far as I have been able to recover them, and to relate the city's further development at greater length, and at the same time to give a brief account of events throughout the world as long as it please God, in the hope of whose favor I undertook the said enterprise rather than in reliance on my own poor wits. And thus in the year 1300, on my return from Rome, I began to compile this book in the name of God and the blessed John the Baptist and in honor of our city of Florence.[2]

This very personal statement with its strong patriotic note calls for no comment unless it be to say that Villani occupied himself during many years with the task of assembling his materials before he began the actual composition of his *Cronica*. In proceeding now to make selections from the work with a view to illustrating the life of Florence in the first half of the fourteenth century, occasional explanatory comment will be unavoidable, although our plan will be to yield the floor so far as possible to our guide. In preparation for the next excerpt it will be necessary to recall that in the very year following the Jubilee Charles of Valois rode into Florence as the military arm of the ambitious Boniface VIII and that in the wake of that invasion the Whites succumbed to their foes, the Blacks. As the Whites refused to accept their defeat, the city remained gravely convulsed for many years to come. Nonetheless life went on much as before: people went to church and market, and the customary festivals were punctually observed. Among them was May Day; and when the first of May of the year 1304 dawned, it was celebrated in the usual manner with dancing and merrymaking in the streets and public squares. However, on this particular occasion the residents of Borgo San Frediano resolved to provide a special entertainment of their own and sent a herald through the town to invite their fellow-citizens to a representation of hell on the waters and banks of Arno. Whoever was eager to have authentic news of the other world (*novelle dell'altro mondo*) was to betake himself to the Carraia bridge and its approaches for a good view of the spectacle.

And on barges and boats moored in the Arno they erected platforms and thereon pictured hell with its fires and punishments and sufferings; with men in the likeness of demons horrible to see; and with other men acting the part of naked souls. And the demons subjected their victims to various tortures amidst a hurly-burly of cries and shrieks hateful and terrible to see and hear. And many citizens crowded together to view the novel spectacle, and the Carraia bridge, which was constructed of wooden planks laid from pier to pier, became so burdened with people that it broke in several places and crashed into the river with its load. For which reason many people were drowned and many others suffered injuries so that play turned to earnest and, exactly as the public crier had announced, many went to get news of the other world. . . .[3]

[2] Villani, VIII, 36.
[3] VIII, 70.

Thus was the merry month of May ushered in *con grande pianto e dolore* and we may believe that the furious strife between the Blacks and Whites was temporarily forgotten. But only very temporarily, for five weeks later, on June 10, 1304, it flared up anew and led to a conflagration so disastrous that it threatened the whole city with destruction. The background for the event is supplied by the fact that on his death in October, 1303, Pope Boniface VIII had been succeeded by Benedict XI and that the new pope was resolved to heal the division caused by his predecessor by effecting a reconciliation between the two envenomed factions. To this end he dispatched a cardinal to Florence with full powers. Only a few families credited with Black sympathies, the powerful Cavalcanti among them, were willing to give ear to the proposal. In order to frustrate the cardinal's plan an intransigent group of Blacks began an attack on their enemies, who unexpectedly made so vigorous a defense that it seemed likely they would capture the city. In their acute alarm the Blacks commissioned a dissolute member of the Abati family, a priest by profession, to divert the attention of the victors by setting fire to the city at several places and particularly to the mass of the Cavalcanti houses on or about the Mercato Nuovo.

And so impetuous was the accursed fire fanned by a north wind, which blew hard on that day, that there burned the houses of the Abati and of the Macci and the whole loggia of Or San Michele and the houses of the Amieri, the Toschi, the Cipriani, the Lamberti, the Bachini, the Buiamonti and the whole street of Calimala. And then attacking the houses of the Cavalcanti, it traveled round the Mercato Nuovo and consumed the church of Saint Cecilia, whence it made its way down the street of Por Santa Maria as far as the Ponte Vecchio. . . . In sum, it destroyed the medulla and core (*midollo e tuorlo*) of the city of Florence, consuming a total of one thousand seven hundred palaces, towers, and houses. The loss in furniture, treasures, and goods of every kind was incalculable inasmuch as in this area were all the merchandise and valuables of the town. And what was not burnt up by the fire was carried off by robbers, who were aided by the circumstance that civil war continued to rage throughout the city. By reason of which fire and sack many trading companies and clans and families were reduced to misery.[4]

Dismayed by the fire which, partly by design and partly by the accident of the powerful wind, destroyed the extensive real estate holdings of the Cavalcanti, these magnates became excited and took refuge in the country. They fortified themselves, among other places, in their castle in the Greve Valley called Le Stinche. Thereupon in the month of September the government, again securely controlled by the uncompromising Guelphs, ordered an expedition against this stronghold and captured it—a success which produced a strange transference of the castle's name to one of the more sinister of the city's institutions.

And when the castle had been destroyed, the prisoners were brought to Florence and incarcerated in the new prison erected by the commune on ground formerly owned by the Uberti next to the church of San Simone. And because the prisoners

[4] VIII, 71.

from Le Stinche castle were the first to be lodged in the new jail, the said jail received the name of Le Stinche.[5]

Le Stinche remained one of the notorious institutions of Florence for many centuries, although we have no reason to believe that the conditions in this particular prison were worse than elsewhere in Italy and Europe. In the fourteenth century and for generations afterward it never occurred to anyone to treat prisoners as other than social outcasts; and if we add that even the educated and well-to-do were ignorant of the simplest rules of private and public hygiene, we may leave the prison conditions obtaining in Florence and throughout the west to the imagination. The reader will not overlook another feature in the epithet popularly conferred on the new jail. The Cavalcanti castle in the valley of the Greve was a hated nobiliary stronghold, and it tickled the rising third estate to deride their enemies, the magnates, by attaching a high-sounding feudal title to a hideous domestic lockup. However, this defeat does not mark the exit of the Cavalcanti from Florentine history—far from it. A few years after their expulsion they became the beneficiaries of an amnesty, and such members of the great clan as were still alive again took up their residence in Florence. But they did not for that reason pardon their enemies. The blood feud was an aristocratic institution in good moral standing and, with murder begetting murder, largely accounts for the bewildering excesses which were commonplace incidents of every Florentine family history. Without any question their own bloody divisions were a big factor in the ultimate overthrow of the noble class. Let Villani tell us how in a manner possessed not even of a tincture of the boasted chivalry of the Middle Ages a returned Cavalcanti practiced vendetta upon a fellow-nobleman.

In the said year [1312], on January 11, it happened in Florence that messer Pazzino de' Pazzi, one of the small clique in control of the city [that is, he belonged to the ruling group of Black Guelphs], on going on a falcon hunt to the island of the Arno, without any guard other than his falconers and servants, was killed by Paffiero de' Cavalcanti with the aid of the Brunelleschi and certain mounted troopers in their pay. . . . It was an act of revenge in behalf of Masino de' Cavalcanti and messer Betto Brunelleschi, whose deaths were laid at the door of messer Pazzino. In order to bring the greater infamy on the Cavalcanti family, the body of the dead man was brought in state to the palace of the priors. Thereupon the whole city rose in arms and under the banner of the people rushed upon the houses of the Cavalcanti and, setting fire to them, once again drove their owners from the city.[6]

While our chronicler is chiefly interested in his own Florence, he does not fail to record striking events from all over Italy and Europe. Naturally the restless religious movements of the day do not escape his attention. Here is his account of one of those mass explosions of self-accusing penance which throughout the Middle Ages made a periodic appearance among all the European groups of the Christian family.

In the said year [1310] a great marvel made its appearance. It began in Piedmont, advanced through Lombardy and the Genoese littoral, and spread thence to Tus-

[5] VIII, 75.
[6] IX, 33.

any and almost covered all Italy. Many people of the commoner sort, men and women and children without number, left their occupations and their cares behind them and, with the cross to point the way, went from place to place beating their bodies and crying *misericordia* and turning people to penance by persuading them to make peace with one another. The Florentines and the inhabitants of a few other cities refused to let them enter their territory and drove them away saying that they were an augury of evil to the land.[7]

On this and some other occasions as well the hard-headed merchant governors of the Arno town showed that they were proof against the current religious excitement; but as the Florentines in the mass were undoubtedly true sons of the Middle Ages, they too were frequently swept off their feet by fervid, popular movements of an evangelical origin. Even at the height of the Renaissance, it will be recalled, in the brilliant and pagan age of Lorenzo de' Medici, a fanatic fervor seized the citizens at the call of Savonarola and, renouncing their worldliness in sackcloth and ashes, they offered a spectacle at which the rest of Italy gazed in mute astonishment. In dealing with Florence it will be well regularly to distinguish between a small, much-traveled, and relatively sophisticated merchant class and the stay-at-home conservative masses. While the former gradually developed an intrepid skepticism which became an important factor in shaping the new and modern European mentality, the latter, even far into the Renaissance, clung to the familiar attitudes and conventions of the Middle Ages.

Our journalistic guide records the outbreak of fire in his overcrowded town with monotonous frequency, although not many fires were so destructive as that of the year 1304, at which we have glanced. Nor were they, like that calamitous affair, started by incendiaries in the interest of a political group. They may be ascribed in the main to the simple circumstance that a large part of the city was, in Villani's day, still built of wood and highly inflammable. We are likely to overlook this detail by picturing Florence to ourselves as made up of picturesque feudal towers and palaces formidably constructed of masonry to withstand the assault of enemies. True, the nobiliary edifices were both numerous and durably built, but around them clung the wooden shops and miserable shelters of the common people, who contributed to the swollen revenues of the fortress-owners by the payment of rent for quarters which by our standards were unbelievably insubstantial, dark, and squalid. Villani, as a reporter who permits no event, great or small, to escape his attention, enumerates such a steady succession of fires that he furnishes ground for the belief that the city must have been in large part renewed with every generation. Opening the book almost at random, we get an alarming picture of the fire risks to which the rapidly expanding Florence of the fourteenth century was exposed.

In the said year [1331], on June 23, during the night of the vigil of Saint John, a fire broke out on the Ponte Vecchio, toward the left bank, and all the shops on the bridge to the number of twenty were burned with heavy loss to many craftsmen. And two apprentices perished in the fire. . . . Further, on September 12, at dusk,

[7] VIII, 121.

a fire broke out at the house of the Soldanieri by the church of Santa Trinità i: certain lowly structures housing some carpenters and a blacksmith. And six persons perished, who because of the furious blaze occasioned by the lumber and the horse-stalls were unable to escape. And again, on February 28 [1332], at oncoming night fire attacked the palace of the podestà and burned the roof of the old structure and two-thirds of the new palace from the first story up. On which account the government ordered both structures to be rebuilt in stone all the way to the roof. And a half year later, on July 16, the palace of the wool gild by Or San Michele took fire and everything was consumed from the first story up. . . . The wool gild thereupon ordered their palace to be reconstructed on a larger scale with stone vaults to the roof.[8]

All of which speaks so eloquently for itself that it requires no remark unless it be that even a great public structure, like the palace of the podestà, was long in assuming the all-stone, fire-proof guise in which it presents itself to view today. Villani's statement apprizes us that seventy-five years after the palazzo was begun—the foundation stone was laid in 1255—it still had a roof of wooden beams, and that the recent addition to the rear had only its first story built of stone and that the second and third stories had been hurriedly and provisionally raised of wood. Only after the alarm occasioned by the fire of 1332 did the residence of the podestà acquire that look of eternity which is perhaps its main distinction in the eyes of a present-day visitor of the Arno city.[9]

In a diary-like record of the external events of a lifetime there is bound to be frequent reference to tempests, hailstorms, drouths, floods, and other accidents of the weather. Villani brings home to us that in his day, as with all generations before and since, the natural phenomena engaged a large proportion of the thought and conversation of men. What is, however, peculiar to him and the medieval period to which he belonged is the explanation offered of the freakish and often disastrous behavior of the elements. Our simple friend shared all the views current in his age regarding the influence of the stars and planets on man and his multiple affairs. Just as we children of a later time have systematized our elaborate observations of the celestial bodies in the science of astronomy, so our medieval predecessors reduced their ignorance and superstition to a system in the pseudo-science of astrology. Of this highly elaborated body of misinformation Villani was more than a casual student, and he delights in consequence to weave its mysteries through the whole fabric of his chronicle. Over and over again he records eclipses of the sun and moon and the ever recurrent conjunction and opposition of planets and then very confidently ascribes a subsequent pestilence or flood or unexpected demise of a great personage to the celestial phenomenon. His theory of these supernatural influences is propounded in Book XI, 68, on the occasion of two comets which appeared in rapid succession in the year 1337. First he gives the view entertained of the wandering bodies by the *filosofi,* the students of nature, according to whom comets, being plainly un-

[8] X, 182.

[9] Even if, as Davidsohn contends (*Forschungen,* Vol. IV, p. 505), the fire of 1332 injured what is now the Palazzo Vecchio and not the earlier palace of the podestà, our comment loses none of its force.

assifiable as fixed stars, are of planetary origin, being "dry vapors . . . collected in the fiery atmosphere under the sky of the moon by reason of the dissolution [*corruzione*] of the celestial bodies called planets." Then he continues:

But whatever they may be, every comet is the sign of some event [*novità*] in the world and generally a malignant one; and sometimes it is the sign of the death of great lords or of revolution in kingdoms and among people more particularly in that planet which has given birth to the comet [by the above-mentioned process of *corruzione*]. And wheresoever the comet extends its mastery, it produces many evils, such as famine, pestilence, revolution, and other grave occurrences, as any man of good understanding may find out for himself by reading onward in this book.

By reading onward we encounter a general texture of happenings in the world wholly indistinguishable from what has gone before and, as "men of good understanding," are obliged to conclude that the deflection of human destiny from its appointed course owing to the two *stelle comete* of 1337 was precisely zero. But such modern skepticism should not hinder us from noting that Villani's faith in astrology considerably colors his narrative, as does in no less degree his and his age's opinion regarding the activity of God's ever busy and versatile adversary, Satan. The cloven-footed potentate and his myriad army of evil spirits are as tirelessly bent on the capture of human souls as are the shining battalions of their opponents, the saints and angels operating from heaven as their base. Our annalist, who, as a traveled, commonsense trader, is inclined to concede the dominion of the law of cause and effect in the fields of business and government, is nevertheless puzzled, as we unfortunately continue to be to this day, by the presence of a certain erratic and incalculable element in human events. This element, which we have decided non-committally to call chance or fate, Villani is prompted to refer to spirits, good and bad, who pull the strings behind the scenes. Of course he piously leaves the last word in the human drama to the commander of the good spirits, to Almighty God; but as innumerable undertakings manifestly go wrong in the world, he ascribes their deflection from their intended course to the devil, to whom he refers with genuine but superstitious respect as the enemy of the human race (*nemico della umana generazione*). In sum, Villani mixes with his often lucidly rational analysis of events, by virtue of which we recognize his closeness to ourselves, hidden causes, such as the stars, God, and Satan, with which the present-day historian with consequent severe loss of picturesqueness has been obliged to dispense.

On attacking the greatest flood disaster which ever visited Florence, Villani starts off in a very modern manner by ascribing the calamity to an extraordinary fall of rain over the whole watershed of the Arno. We learn that the rain began on November 1, 1333, and that it came down in cataracts without a break for four nights and days to the accompaniment of frightful lightning and thunder.

Wherefore everyone was filled with great fear and all the church bells throughout the city were rung continuously as an invocation to heaven that the water rise no farther. And in the houses they beat the kettles and brass basins raising loud cri to God of *misericordia, misericordia,* the while those in peril fled from roof to roof and house to house on improvised bridges. And so great was the human din and tumult that it almost drowned out the crash of the thunder.[10]

Although the whole chapter dealing with the flood is in one way or another remarkable, we shall have to be content with excerpts.

By Thursday noon, November 4, the Arno had swollen so vastly at Florence that it covered the whole plain of San Salvi to a depth of from ten to sixteen feet. [San Salvi lay to the east of the town and the water was dammed up on the plain by the stout city wall.] And at the first sleep of night the water washed away the city wall above the Corso de' Tintori . . . for a space of over two hundred feet. Thereupon the whole volume of the flood rushed into the city with such fury that it filled all Florence. It covered and drowned the streets, some more, some less, but it was worst in the sesti of San Piero Scheraggio and Porta San Piero and Porta del Duomo. . . . In the baptistery of St. John the water rose above the altar and reached to over half the height of the columns of porphyry before the entrance. [These were the columns presented by the Pisans over two hundred years before. They are to this day in the indicated place with a line scratched on them showing the level reached by the water in 1333.] And in the palace of the commune, where dwells the podestà, it rose in the courtyard, where he pronounces justice, to the height of ten feet. . . . And in Or San Michele and in the nearby Mercato Nuovo it rose to almost four feet. . . . And the Carraia bridge fell with the exception of two arches toward the right bank. And immediately after fell the Trinità bridge, save for one pier and one arch toward the church of Santa Trinità. It was now the turn of the Ponte Vecchio. When it was choked by the logs brought down by the Arno, the waters leaped over the arches and, rushing on the shops upon the bridge, swept everything away except the two central piers. And at the Rubaconte bridge the water washed over the top at one side and destroyed the parapet at several places. . . . And the statue of Mars, which stood on a pedestal on this side of the Ponte Vecchio, fell into the Arno. . . . And when Mars had fallen and all the houses between the Ponte Vecchio and the Carraia bridge had come down and all the streets on both banks were covered with ruins—to look at this scene was to stare at chaos.

By the afternoon of the next day the worst was over and the waters began rapidly to recede. Our conscientious chronicler follows the flood downstream and shows that, although it brought serious injury to every village and town as far as Pisa, it wreaked its chief spite on Florence. His bill of particulars for his native city includes three hundred dead, the loss of innumerable domestic animals, the ruin of uncounted houses, bridges, mills. He does not forget the many kinds of supplies which were carried off, such as the cloth of the weavers, the casks of wine, the stores of grain. He confesses his inability to state the total loss in money value, but he illustrates the damage by going to the municipal account books for the information that Florence paid out for the single item of repair of walls and bridges the sum of one hundred and fifty thousand gold florins. And he concludes his tale of woe with the statement "that not since its destruction by the Gothic king, Totila, the scourge of God, did Florence suffer *si grande avversità e dammaggio come fu questo.*"

[10] Villani, XI, 1.

The great flood had a curious intellectual aftermath. A people so alert and inquisitive as the Florentines were stung to raise the issue of the why and wherefore of this disaster; and it characterizes the fourteenth century as an age of slowly advancing reason that the theologians, who categorically explained the flood as a judgment of God upon the wicked, no longer had it all their own way. We hear that a group of "philosophers" put up a stiff fight in favor of the view that the flood was just a natural event (*venuto per corso di natura*). The position signified a notable measure of rational enlightenment, although the arguments with which it was supported were borrowed from astrology and have an undiluted medieval character. Villani himself, as we have seen, a passionate amateur astrologer, patiently rehearses the "natural causes." "On May 14 there was an eclipse of the moon in the sign of Taurus . . . and then at the beginning of July there followed a conjunction of Saturn with Mars at the end of the sign of the Virgin. . . . And, added to all this, the planet Jupiter, which is sweet and kind and brings good luck, found itself in the sign of Aquarius so that its favorable action was eliminated," and so forth through a long, solemn section unrelieved by so much as a fugitive twinkle of the eye.[11] But with a single sweep of their mighty arms the theologians brushed aside both the naturalist hypothesis and the astrological cobwebs in which it was entangled. Corso di natura? Tut, tut! The corso di natura is a matter of God's will and pleasure. And very certainly the laws of nature and the actions of the elements and the demons as well are nothing other than divine scourges and hammers to punish men for their sins. We gather that the correct theological position is that the great concern of God is to punish the accursed seed of Adam for its innumerable derelictions, and that in pursuit of this high purpose he may act according to nature or above nature or even contrary to nature, exactly as he sees fit, since he is Lord Omnipotent. Of course the amateur theologian, who is even stronger in Villani than the amateur astrologer, gives the victory in the great debate between faith and reason to orthodoxy and the Catholic church. And in concluding his report of the controversy he adds his personal view: "I, the author, hold to this opinion on the flood, that by means of the laws of nature God pronounced judgment on us for our outrageous sins." A confession of faith, let us admit, of impeccable orthodoxy; but let us also take note that with his avowal of the existence of the laws of nature he has opened a crack in the conservative armor certain to prove dangerous in the future.

A grave concern of every medieval commune was its food supply. With its fast-growing population and limited territory Florence in particular was perpetually threatened with scarcity. A very intelligent grain-dealer, a contemporary of Villani's by name of Lenzi, calculated that the Florentine contado normally furnished about five-twelfths of the wheat annually required by the population.[12] The remainder had to be imported from the outlying districts of Tuscany; and when Tuscany, as frequently happened, failed to

[11] XI, 2.

[12] Davidsohn, *Forschungen,* Vol. IV, pp. 307-14, bases an interesting study of *Die Getreidepolitik der Kommune* on Lenzi's copious and reliable data. On the control of the food supply by the government see also Davidsohn, Vol. IV[1], pp. 130-33.

satisfy its considerable provincial needs, the Florentine market became dependent on shipments by land from the Romagna and by sea from southern Italy. Under these circumstances scarcity and its offspring, famine, always hovered on the horizon and the government was moved to intrust the very critical problem of the food supply to a standing committee of six men with extraordinary powers, *I Sei della Biada.* The grain market was located in Villani's time on the piazza of Or San Michele, and the specially constructed loggia, under which the dealers met and over which the Six had jurisdiction, was always a lively place, and in periods of scarcity, when the price shot up like a rocket, a veritable inferno. The standard measure for grain was the *staio,* which has been calculated as the equivalent of seventeen and two-thirds kilograms. Reduced to our standard, the staio would thus represent a weight of thirty-nine pounds. During the first half of the fourteenth century the normal price of the staio of wheat was about twelve soldi. At any rate both Lenzi, the professional grain-dealer, and Villani, the sharp merchant observer, agree that wheat is abundant if the price sinks below twelve soldi per staio and that a scarcity is in the wind if it tends to rise above that figure.

Now one of the most interesting aspects of Florentine life reflected by Villani's chronicle has to do with the recurrent scarcities. It has been argued by some modern economists, familiar with a free market of world-scope, that the medieval scarcities were primarily due to the prohibitions to export, by means of which the governments of the time, and Florence with the rest, attempted to safeguard their limited local supply. That these prohibitions wrought a certain mischief may be admitted, but to make them account for the permanent food shortage of Florence is absurd. That phenomenon must be referred, as already indicated, to the town's fast-growing population and the inability to feed it from the limited grainlands of Florence or of Tuscany as a whole. In seasons when the crop suffered either from too much or too little rain or sun, a crisis in a crowded center like the Arno city was inevitable. Owing to the prevailing primitive means of transportation, grain could not be brought from distant countries nor could the amounts drawn from relatively accessible points, such as the Romagna and Naples, be indefinitely increased. For one thing these provinces, to which Florence frequently resorted as granaries, might be afflicted with a scarcity of their own and, for another, the mules and ships which served as carriers moved very slowly and possessed a painfully small carrying capacity. If, in addition to all this, we allow for the hazards of the sea route due to piracy, and of the land route because of the innumerable wars, we must conclude that a sum of conditions prevailed in the fourteenth century which, rooted in the civilization of the time, made the Florentine nervousness over the bread question as perennial as it was incurable.

The situation is copiously illustrated by our faithful guide. Throughout the book we find him giving a hawklike attention to the fluctuations of the food prices chalked up at the local produce exchange of Or San Michele; and we gather from his statements that a scarcity of a more or less severe character put in an appearance on an average of about three times each decade. About once each decade the scarcity became so intense as to assume the proportions a famine. When this pitiless, unbidden guest visited the city, he caused unspeakable misery and confusion. Not only was Florence a proletarian city, most of whose wage-earners dwelt habitually on the margin of starvation, but it was also crowded with beggars living upon the charity which medieval Christianity inculcated as a duty and which was habitually dispensed by well-to-do individuals and even more bounteously by numerous religious institutions founded in part for this very purpose. Famine prices at once tended to put the cost of bread beyond the reach of the workers and perforce checked, and in the end completely dried up, the stream of charity. Speaking of the year 1328, Villani reports a growing scarcity which became steadily more acute until by Easter, 1329, the staio of wheat cost forty-two soldi; and just before the new local crop was in, which would be toward the end of June, the price had reached sixty soldi and therewith the equivalent of a gold florin. This figure, the highest that was reached on the occasion of this particular famine, represented a 500 per cent advance on the normal price.

The famine was felt not only in Florence but throughout Tuscany and a large part of Italy. And so terrible was it that the Perugians, the Sienese, the Lucchese, the Pistolese, and many other townsmen drove forth from their territory all their beggars because they could not support them. Guided by wise counsel and divine pity, the commune of Florence did not do this; in fact it received and provided for a large fraction of the poor mendicants of all Tuscany. . . . It sent for grain to Sicily, ordering it to be brought to the port of Talamone in the Maremma and transporting it thence to Florence at great risk and expense. The government sent also to the Romagna and to the contado of Arezzo; and as long as the scarcity lasted, disregarding the heavy charge upon the public purse, it kept the price of the staio at half a gold florin [which would be two and a half times the normal figure] although to effect this reduction it permitted the wheat to be mixed to one-fourth its volume with coarser grain. In spite of all the government did, the agitation of the people at the market of Or San Michele was so great that it was necessary to protect the officials by means of guards fitted out with ax and block to punish rioters on the spot with the loss of hands or feet.

And in mitigation of this famine the commune of Florence spent in those two years more than sixty thousand gold florins. Finally, it was decided not to go on selling grain in the piazza but to requisition all the bakers' ovens for the baking of bread in order to sell it on the following morning in three or four shops in every sesto at four pennies for the loaf of six ounces. This arrangement successfully tamed the rage of the people since wage-earners with eight to twelve pennies a day could now buy bread on which to live, whereas formerly they had been unable to find the sum necessary to buy a whole staio of wheat.[13]

In the wake of a medieval famine there generally followed a pestilence, which attacked the enfeebled population and carried them off by the hundreds. It must not, however, be supposed that contagious diseases took root only when undernourishment had cleared the way for them. The sanitary conditions in a town like Florence can hardly be painted in sufficiently dark colors. Water was supplied first, from public fountains, of which there was one for each of the fifty-seven city parishes, and second, from numerous private wells

[13] Villani, X, 118.

with a capricious action and of a very doubtful purity. Not only was there underground sewage system but the government recognized no obligation to collect and dispose of the city refuse. Everybody tossed the household waste into the street, where it lay till it was eaten by wandering hogs or washed by the rain into the river. If on this score alone Florence would receive a very low rating from a modern health commission, it would be declared completely outside the pale by the way the people satisfied their private necessities. Only the houses of the well-to-do had cesspools, while the mass of the population, without causing the least scandal, utilized for their needs the less frequented streets, the plentiful ruins of the houses of magnates destroyed under the Ordinances of Justice, and the vast circle of the city walls. If we add that the very numerous poor were housed either in skimpy, wooden shacks or in damp cellars without light and air except from the open door, we shall understand that diseases like typhoid, tuberculosis, and influenza were endemic in the population. In fact it was in the Florence of the trecento that the name influenza was invented for the catarrhal affection which, then as now, periodically became epidemic and levied a heavy toll on all the communities it smote.

Wholly unconscious of the to us incredible deficiencies of the personal hygiene and public sanitation of his time, Villani innocently ignores them in his record. But he neither does nor can ignore the pestilences which periodically descended on his city and which the complete neglect of even the most rudimentary health provisions alone made possible. With his uncommon intelligence he suspects that the abundant filth has something to do with the recurrent plagues, but in the end he falls back for their explanation, exactly as he did in the case of the flood of 1333, on the will of an offended God supplemented by the astrological mysteries. His account of the *grande mortalità* of 1340 is typical.[14] He introduces it by reference to the comet, which in March of that year appeared in the eastern sky. Brief, we are told, was the stay of the celestial wanderer, but the ills which followed his visit lasted a long time.

> For at once began a great pestilence, from which, if one fell ill, he but rarely escaped. And more than a sixth of the citizenry perished, among them the best and most beloved of our men and women. There was no family which did not lose one and even two and three of its members. And the pestilence lasted till the approach of winter. And in the city alone more than 15,000 corpses of men and women were buried. Wherefore the city was full of grief and lamentation and people hardly attended to anything other than burying the dead. . . . In the county the mortality was not so great but there too there died a plenty; and with this pestilence there came a new scarcity on top of that of the preceding year and, in spite of the decrease of the population, the staio of grain was sold at thirty soldi. And the price would have risen higher if the commune had not made provision by importing grain by sea. . . . And on account of this pestilence the bishop and the clergy advised the holding of a great procession. It took place on June 18 and almost the whole body of citizens, men and women, followed the relics of the body of Christ, which are

[14] XI, 114.

preserved at Sant' Ambrogio, and marched through the city till nones [3 P.M.] carrying more than one hundred and fifty lighted candles as large as torches.[15]

In spite of this fine demonstration of piety the pestilence persisted till the November chill. Villani, now a man of sixty, was greatly depressed by the calamity, in which he lost innumerable dear friends. Indeed at this juncture disaster followed disaster both for him and his beloved city, enveloping his closing days in deepening shadows. He grieved over the interminable war for the possession of Lucca and the long string of disappointments the war brought in its train. When the capture of Lucca by Pisa led to the Red Lily's subjection to the debasing tyranny of the duke of Athens, he felt that the bottom had been touched in public turpitude. His private fortunes, however, did not reach their lowest depth till, with the casting off of the yoke of the despot, the series of bank failures began which included his own firm of the Buonaccorsi and lodged him for a period in the debtors' prison. He could not have been long released when a new plague began to throw its shadow, this time not only over Florence but over the whole world. The fresh affliction was the famous Black Death, the most widespread and sweepingly destructive pestilence in the annals of Europe. Villani, now greatly broken by the continued buffets of adversity, watched its oncoming with undiminished curiosity, especially as it was an epidemic different in its nature from any with which he was familiar. He gives the new disease no name but from the symptoms he enumerates, supplemented by the report of other witnesses, of whom the novelist, Boccaccio, is the most famous, we know it was the dread bubonic plague, which on this occasion made its way for the first time from its home in the orient into the west.

Villani reports that the disease put in an appearance at Florence in the year 1347 but that its violence diminished with the winter season. As in this preliminary visit it carried off only four thousand persons it did not impress him at the time as deeply as the epidemic of 1340 had done which, according to his figures, had mowed down some fifteen thousand people and which, although he does not tell us clearly what it was, in no case was the bubonic plague. But with the returning spring of the year 1348 the havoc began again.

The said plague was greater than among us in Pistoia and Prato . . . in Bologna and in the Romagna. It was greater also at Avignon, where the pope keeps court, and throughout the kingdom of France. But where it reaped the greatest harvest was in Turkey and among the countries beyond the sea and among the Tartars. . . . Having grown to vigor in Turkey and Greece and having spread thence over the whole Levant and Mesopotamia and Syria and Chaldea and Cyprus and Crete and Rhodes and all the islands of the Greek archipelago, the said pestilence leaped to Sicily and Sardinia and Corsica and Elba, and from there soon reached all the shores of the mainland. And of eight Genoese galleys which had gone to the Black Sea only four returned, full of infected sailors, who were smitten one after the other on the return journey. And all who arrived at Genoa died, and they corrupted the air to such an extent that whoever came near the bodies died shortly after. And it was a disease in which there appeared certain swellings in the groin and under the armpit,

[15] XI, 114.

and the victims spat blood, and in three days they were dead. And the priest who confessed the sick and those who nursed them so generally caught the infection that the victims were abandoned and deprived of confession, sacrament, medicine, and nursing. . . . And many lands and cities were made desolate. And this plague lasted till . . . . .[16]

So far did the diarist get in his tale of the ravages of the Black Death. He left a blank space after the word "till," planning to fill it in when the curse had been lifted from Florence and the world. But before that happy day dawned the old merchant himself had been carried off by the relentless pestilence. No particulars touching his demise have reached us. We know just this: the pen fell from his hand because together with thousands of his fellow-Florentines and hundreds of thousands of men and women throughout all the countries of the occident he perished in the *annus terribilis* of 1348.

However, we are not yet prepared to bid farewell to our crotchety and kindly cicerone. We have not tasted his most precious honey, the pages wherein he conveys to us the proud story of how Florence was rebuilt in his day. For it was within the span of Villani's life that the manifold activities, on which the Arno city had embarked since the revival of commerce in the eleventh century, began to flower in the spiritual culture, which is the occasion for the intense preoccupation of the world down to our time with this, quantitatively considered, fairly negligible state. To some of the more delicate aspects of this burgeoning, the plodding Villani, deeply entangled in business and politics, presented a tightly sealed mind. Accordingly he took no notice of them in his book. He failed, for instance, to give an account of the new school of poetry, though there stood at the head of it so tragic and dynamic a figure as Dante Alighieri. The chronicler's silence in this matter is particularly revealing as to his limitations, since we may assume that, although he was a somewhat younger man than the austere visionary, he knew him personally. The assumption seems reasonably safe not only because within the narrow bounds of Florence everybody knew everybody else, but more particularly because Giovanni's father, when Giovanni was a youth of twenty, was closely associated with the poet in the same political party of the White Guelphs. When Giovanni grew up and in due time himself joined the writing fraternity, he displayed, it is true, a certain patriotic pride in the fame acquired by his exiled fellow-countryman. On the occasion of the poet's death in 1321 he even devoted a chapter of his chronicle to a review of Dante's literary labors. It is the statement of a conscientious pedant, its even tone of respectful gravity being unruffled by as much as a flicker of imaginative understanding.[17] In short, Villani lacked the ear to catch the more delicate voices abroad in the trecento, but it would not on this account occur to us, who have looked somewhat into his mind, to charge him with rusticity. His undeniable refinement was of a social rather than an individual order and drew its strength from the root of the new burgher mentality. The aspirations to which he gave voice derived without exception from community living and culminated in the hope that Florence would express the wealth and power to which it was visibly

[16] XII, 84.
[17] IX, 136.

adding every day by an impressive outer garment of brick and stone. He wanted the Arno town not only to *be* the first in the world but also to *appear* as such. It is this patriotic passion which flutters his pulse with a subdued fever and envelops his pages with a much richer than merely a counting-house atmosphere. Had he been only the merchant absorbed in his balance sheet, he would have smothered his text under a leaden blanket of common sense.[18]

We remarked at the beginning that the great event of our annalist's youth was the seizure of political power by the twenty-one gilds. Spiritually this meant, if it meant anything, the coming of age of that civic spirit in which, as just stated, Villani's culture had its roots. However, just as the commercial expansion which culminated in the burgher victory of 1282 had gone on for many previous generations, so the civic spirit had begun to unfold long before the chronicler's birth. There therefore existed in Villani's boyhood concrete evidences of its long incubation and when, as a youth, he roamed through the city, he was brought face to face with them. Certain to arrest his attention would be the two walls encircling his native town. The inner wall, though largely removed in the interest of traffic, could still be traced without difficulty. Traditionally as well as by palpable evidence, it went back to Roman days and served to remind the thoughtful boy that his city was the authentic daughter of the great mother on the Tiber. But the first wall had been superseded by a second wall. Begun in 1172, in the days of Emperor Barbarossa, the new inclosure had trebled the original walled area of the city.[19] In his *Cronica* Villani for some undisclosed reason lets the second circle of walls be erected a hundred years earlier than was the case.[20] Perhaps he was led astray by older chroniclers from whom he drew his information. His error is unimportant for the purpose in hand, for at this point we are solely concerned with the civic impressions of Villani's boyhood and with the pride that swelled his bosom at the recognition that the city of his birth was a steadily expanding organism. And the evidence on this head continued to pile up, for the Florence under his youthful eye had already outgrown its second circle. Before each major city gate he saw stretching a populous *borgo* or suburb not without the alarming thought that all these people, their houses, and their possessions were exposed to destruction in case of an assault on the town. Over this situation grave burghers, such as Giovanni's father, would wag their heads when they met in the market-place and would declare, not without secret exultation, that the erection of a third and still more ample circle of walls could not be long adjourned. As we shall presently see it was in the son's lifetime and finally, under his supervision that the third circumvallation of Florence was carried to completion.

In addition to the walls there were only two public buildings in the Florence of Villani's boyhood likely to stir his civic imagination. They were the baptistry of St. John and the palace of the podestà, respectively the leading ecclesi-

[18] The private life of the Florentines, of which Villani affords us glimpses in this chapter, has been treated by two experts: G. Biagi, *Men and Manners of Old Florence*. London, 1909; A. Schiaparelli, *La Casa Fiorentina . . . nei Secoli XIV e XV*. Florence, 1908.

[19] Davidsohn, *Forschungen,* Vol. I, pp. 113 ff.

[20] Villani, IV, 8.

astical and the leading secular structure of the town. Around the history o the Florentine baptistery, which is to this day one of the most distinguishe Christian monuments in Europe, a good deal of mystery gathers. Was i built in the period of declining Rome, or in the seventh century during th Lombard domination, or did it rise to view in the eleventh or twelfth centur as the first fruits of the communal movement? The issue has released a heate debate among the experts into which it will not be necessary to enter. Suffic it that such slight *documentary* evidence as exists would seem to refer th structure to the Lombard period. On the other hand, the *artistic* evidenc supplied by the building itself would make the fifth century the more prob able period of origin.[21] Dante, Villani, and the local members of the writin tribe down to recent times have voiced the opinion that the baptistery wen clear back to the pagan era and that it had originally been a temple of Mars, th god of war. Owing to the great age of the Mars legend, it continued to fin stout champions until excavations conducted during the last generation estab lished beyond a doubt that the baptistery was erected *ab origine* as a Christia house of worship and that it never had had a pagan predecessor. The excava tions established also that the structure goes far back of the eleventh century We would thus seem to be reduced to a choice between the fifth and the sev enth centuries, between an early Christian and a Lombard origin. As i either case we have to predicate an architect who, steeped in the Roman tradi tion, produced an outstanding Roman-Christian monument, the question a to the preferable date is not particularly important. Moreover, in view o the fact that the unknown architect must have assembled his unusually fin columns, capitals, and architraves from abandoned pagan temples, we are, afte all, obliged to ascribe much of the merit attaching to this manifestly classica structure to pagan Rome.

Over innumerable other issues, chiefly of construction and ornamentation the controversy among the experts continues to rage unabated. It will serv our purpose if we take note that, like every other structure of venerable an tiquity, the baptistery has experienced many changes. From an early time i had an administration called *opera,* and from at least the twelfth century o the opera, in evidence of the growing interest of the citizens in all the con cerns of the town, was under lay management. As each new *operaio,* or hea of the works, would be prompted to outdo the achievements of his predeces sor, there were carried out with the advent of lay management numerou alterations and improvements which are rendered indubitable by survivin documents. Thus, for instance, the apse was given its present square forn in place of the semi-circular form which it had had originally, and the incrusta tion of the interior in white and green marble was either renewed or brough to completion. As the incrustation, inside and outside, is the chief decorativ feature of the baptistery, the question presents itself but cannot be answere whether on the occasion of the twelfth-century incrustation of the interio

[21] Davidsohn reviews the controversy and at the same time adduces the evidence for his opinio of a Lombard origin in the following passages: Vol. I, pp. 72, 736; Vol. IV, p. 3; *Forschungen* Vol. I, p. 144; *Forschungen,* Vol. IV, p. 461. The case for the supporters of the fifth-century origi is persuasively put by E. W. Anthony, *Early Florentine Architecture and Decoration.* Cambridg (Mass.), 1927.

he original pattern was adhered to or whether a different pattern, more leasing to the living generation, was adopted. Then, in the thirteenth cen- ury, it was resolved further to enrich the interior by giving it the in- omparable glow of mosaics. In 1225—we have now reached the period of recise dates—the new apse with its triumphal arch received the fine mosaic nvelope which it still boasts; and a half century later, in 1271, the resolution vas taken to cover the lofty cupola with pictures in mosaic illustrative of triking scenes from the Old and the New Testament. Often interrupted, wing to lack of funds, the work on the cupola took some thirty years to ring to completion. The scaffolds on which the artists stood to do their work nust have obstructed the interior during a large part of Villani's boyhood, and s often as he entered the door, he must have lifted his eyes to such scenes as, aving just been completed, were disclosed to the public gaze and constituted he latest wonder of the town. We know for certain that a greater man than Villani gave the new work a most eager scrutiny. For when, an exile from is native city, Dante came to recount his epochal journey from hell to para- ise, he wove numerous remembered details of the striking illustrations of the upola into the imagery of his great poem.[22]

The mosaics of the cupola were not yet finished when the baptistery bene- ited from a new attention. The opera of San Giovanni had by this time been aken over by the wealthy merchant gild of the Calimala, which assumed all xpenses both of maintenance and improvements. In 1293 the Calimala gen- rously provided the means for removing the large tombs of stone and marble vhich, besides disfiguring the outer wall of the baptistery, constituted a indrance to the growing traffic of the town. These tombs belonged to certain eading families, which, in accordance with an old Florentine custom, re- erved them for the burial of their members. At the same time the Calimala upplied the funds for a new marble envelope of the exterior. Again we are n doubt as to how closely the new outer incrustation followed the original lesign. It is even possible that some parts of the exterior were now incrusted or the first time. Villani was perhaps thirteen years old when San Giovanni eceived its fine exterior garment of white and green marble slabs and bands, nd when he came to write his chronicle he did not fail to mention the re- nembered splendor.[23]

A few hundred steps eastward of the baptistery of St. John rose the only ther building in Florence in Villani's youth calculated to stimulate his local ride. This was the palace occupied at that time by the podestà, although it ad originally been erected as the *palatium populi Florentini* to house the city's irst democratic government. When, as far back as the middle of the thir- eenth century, the people had for the first time ousted the nobility from con- rol, they had resolved to celebrate the event by building a residence for their ew rulers. Hardly was it ready for occupation when, in 1260, the disastrous attle of Montaperti put an end to the democratic interlude by redelivering he city, first into the hands of the Ghibelline, and later, into those of the Guelph nobility. At this recession of the democratic tide the fine new palace

[22] E. H. Wilkins, "Dante and the Mosaics of his Bel San Giovanni," *Speculum*, Vol. II, pp. 1 ff.
[23] Villani, VIII, 3.

of the people was assigned to the podestà as his residence, and as such it wa still serving when Villani was growing to manhood. It was and remains t this day one of the most impressive piles reared anywhere in Italy in the ag of the emerging third estate. The spirit of the time was still feudal and th main concern of the great landowners as well as of the rising communes wa self-defense. The structure originally evolved for this purpose was the castle and in one form or another it dotted all the hills of Tuscany and, for tha matter, of all Europe with its rude piles of masonry. Although the burghers struggling into existence against the will of the feudal class, were obliged t spend much of their fresh energy on the destruction of castles, when the faced the problem of their own safety they could find nothing better suited t their end than the stronghold of their enemies. In consequence they gave thei towns something of the aspect of enlarged castles by equipping them wit gates, moats, drawbridges, battlements, and every other engineering devic developed by the feudality; and when they built their first town halls, agai thinking primarily of defense, they repeated the castle pattern. The result fo Florence of this outlook on the world was the massive structure, which erected by the people, became identified with the podestà, and which sinc the sixteenth century has been called the Bargello from the police official whos residence it had meanwhile become. With its imposing walls of rough-hew stone and its vigorous battlemented tower it seems prepared to defy a worl of enemies. But its architects did not forget that primarily it was intended t serve certain novel communal purposes. Hence the handsome inner court wit its columns supporting a spacious vaulted portico and with its ceremonia stairway leading to an impressive open loggia at the level of the first story. I this palace, planned as a house of the people, was still a feudal castle, it ha felt a breath of that urbanity which it was one of the many functions of th communal revolution to bring into the world.

The two strong girdles of stone, the baptistery, the palace of the podestà— with these items we exhaust the monumental features of the Florence o Villani's boyhood. Parish and monastery churches, some of them of great ag were of course sown thickly through the town, but they were the handiwor of a poverty-stricken generation and, as a rule, were completely devoid of distinction. Even Santa Reparata, the cathedral church fronting the baptister on the east side, was a modest, commonplace edifice, which so little met th new opinion the Florentines were beginning to entertain of their importanc that they were eagerly discussing ways and means for replacing it with a mor magnificent pile. As for the two great begging orders of St. Dominic an St. Francis, they too possessed as yet quite unimpressive churches assigned t them on their first establishing themselves on the Arno. With these humbl structures also neither the friars nor the citizens were any longer contented, an the plans under way for their enlargement elicited enthusiastic popular support. Our living generation, looking into these matters, will be struck by th fact that the inhabitants of Florence, as well as of the other rising towns o Italy, made no distinction between the ecclesiastical and the civil buildings i their midst. They embraced them with an equal love, in part because al structures encompassed by the same wall were manifestly municipal an above all, because medieval people experienced no difficulty whatever over the double allegiance owed by them to church and state. The two institutions might clash and clash vigorously by taking opposed positions in issues of politics and taxation. Florence, for instance, so frequently resisted the demands of the Roman curia of a political import that it lay sometimes for months and years together under the papal interdict. But such a conflict did not shake the confidence of the people in the soul-saving mission of the church nor diminish their devotion to the shining company of the saints and martyrs. They were convinced, rich and poor alike, that the blessed spirits dwelling in the shadow of God's throne would favor their worshipers both individually and as a nation, provided they were approached with a humble heart and honored with loaded altars and far-seen temples.

And now we are prepared to deal with the building era which was inaugurated in Florence with the democratic triumph of the decade 1282–93, and which in the course of the next half century gave the city a new aspect. Because this architectural transformation coincided almost exactly with Villani's lifetime, we are in the fortunate position to extract from his own minute record the story of how the City of the Baptist adorned itself with most of the monuments constituting its fame among the cities of the world. While making Villani our guide, so often as it is necessary to correct an error into which he has fallen or to round off a story which he has not completed, we shall draw on the many other authoritative sources which have become available.[24]

In the year 1296,[25] when the city of Florence was in very tranquil state after the revolution associated with the name of Giano della Bella, the citizens agreed to renew their leading church, which was a rude affair and small for such a municipality. They resolved to lengthen it by extending it eastward [*di trarla addietro*] and to make it of marble and sculptured figures. And the foundation was laid with great solemnity on the day of St. Mary of September [26] by the cardinal legate of the pope and many bishops. And there were present also the podestà and the captain and the priors and all the officials of Florence. And the church was consecrated to the honor of God and St. Mary and given the name of Santa Maria del Fiore, although the people continued to call it by its former name of Santa Reparata. And in aid of the construction of the said church the commune ordered a subsidy of four denari on each libra paid out of the city treasury and a head-tax of two soldi on every male. And the legate and bishops endowed the church with liberal indulgences and pardons to whosoever should aid with alms.

Let us admit that this is a disappointingly dry and colorless report of a great event, but we are by now aware that Villani was more of a chronicler and a statistician than an artist. Nonetheless the bare statement contains some interesting particulars, as, for instance, that church and state co-operated in the dedication and that the new cathedral, as the expression of the new burgher

[24] A remarkable compendium of all the established facts concerning the history of Florentine buildings is W. Limburger, *Die Gebäude von Florenz*. Leipzig, 1910. It is an indispensable vademecum for the student in this field.

[25] VIII, 9. Villani gives the date 1294 for this event but Davidsohn shows (*Forschungen*, Vol. IV, p. 457) that 1296 is correct.

[26] St. Mary of September would be September 8.

pride, was to be erected by the taxes and free-will offerings of the citizens. In this financing of the project we have the explanation why the work was so often interrupted and took so many generations to bring to completion. Owing to local disturbances and expensive wars civic resources were sometimes for protracted periods simply not available. The architect to whom the new cathedral was intrusted and whom Villani does not name was Arnolfo di Cambio, a native of the val d'Elsa and a Florentine by adoption. He was without question the most famous builder of his day. Taking advantage of the fresh enthusiasm of his fellow-citizens, he made rapid headway and in a comparatively short time had raised and vaulted a number of bays at the western end and provided them with a façade. In the early fourteenth century, owing to the disturbances occasioned by the civil war between the Blacks and the Whites, work ceased completely. Unfortunately Arnolfo's façade, which must have been one of his notable creations, no longer exists. A little more than half a century after its erection, in 1358, it fell victim to one of those changes in architectural taste which are always taking place. It was ordered to be destroyed in order to permit Francesco Talenti to erect a façade more in the ruling Gothic style. Over two hundred years later Talenti's façade was in its turn sacrificed to a new revolution in taste and was replaced (1587) by a wretched late-Renaissance makeshift. This was endured for three hundred years, till 1887, when the present front, the extravagant dream of an expert sugar-baker, was substituted, without any perceptible improvement, for its feeble predecessor.

From this recital of the vicissitudes of a single feature of the new cathedral we may divine how complicated is its total building history. Probably the earliest façade was the best of the four, and the whole church, had it been erected according to Arnolfo's original plan, would have had a unity which was lost by reason of the many hands and periods destined to leave their mark upon the pile. However, medieval cathedrals were never built in a single, uninterrupted effort, according to an inalterable plan, and, everything considered, they usually compensate for their lack of stylistic harmony by a flexibility and variety which are extremely ingratiating. Arnolfo died, certainly before 1310. Exactly how far eastward toward the choir he had succeeded in carrying the new Santa Reparata, no surviving document reveals. We know merely that, owing to the above-mentioned disturbances supplemented by lack of funds, all work on the structure had been discontinued some years before Arnolfo's death.

Construction was not resumed for a quarter of a century. Villani reports the advent of a new building period under the year 1330 and informs us that the commune, besides reviving the former tax levies in the cathedral's favor, put the opera in charge of the arte di Lana, the richest gild of the city, in the hope of expediting the work.[27] On this occasion a more ambitious plan was substituted for that of Arnolfo and a few bays of a more ample span than those already completed were constructed which carried the nave eastward to its point of junction with the choir. This, in the form of a vast octagon, was projected as the outstanding feature of the new edifice. As its construction and

[27] Villani, X, 192.

that of the famous cupola over it is a story carrying us well into the Renaissance, we shall leave it to a later chapter.

Less than three years after the commune had committed itself to the formidable cathedral enterprise, it undertook another work of hardly inferior magnitude. Here is Villani's report of the transaction.

In the said year 1299[28] the commune and people of Florence laid the foundation of the palace of the priors. They were moved to take this step because of the party divisions and the brawls resulting therefrom between the people and the magnates on the occasion of the renewal of the priors, which occurred every two months. And it did not seem that the priors, who ruled the people and the republic, were secure in the house they inhabited which belonged to the White Cerchi[29] and lay behind the church of San Brocolo. And there, where they laid the foundation of the said palace, had formerly stood the houses of the Uberti, rebels of Florence and Ghibellines. And the ground whereon the houses had stood was converted into a piazza to make sure that the houses would never be rebuilt. And the commune bought the houses of other citizens, as, for instance, those of the Foraboschi, and raised the said palace on the purchased ground. And for the tower of the palace of the priors they utilized the tower of the Foraboschi, which was almost one hundred feet high and was called La Vacca [the Cow]. And in order that the said palace be not built on the former land of the Uberti the committee in charge placed it askew [*il puosono musso*], which was a great imperfection inasmuch as the palace should have been given a square or rectangular shape and should not have been carried so close to the church of San Piero Scheraggio.[30]

The palace of the priors is the present Palazzo Vecchio, while the piazza created by clearing away the débris of the Uberti houses is, at least in considerable part, the present Piazza Signoria. It throws a curious light on the ferocity of the party spirit that these Uberti ruins had been permitted to encumber the city for a whole generation. As in this instance, too, Villani fails to name the architect intrusted with the new enterprise, we have to go to other authorities to learn that it was Arnolfo di Cambio. Plainly, after his success with the new cathedral, he was recognized as the master-builder of the city. Our chronicler offers the interesting information that the architect was obliged to submit to several serious limitations. Not only did he have to avoid utilizing as much as an inch of the accursed Uberti ground but he was required to incorporate the existent tower of the Foraboschi in his design. Villani, who like most simple souls was hypnotized by the regularities of geometry, was not particularly pleased with the result. But later ages, disagreeing with him, have given an enthusiastic approval to Arnolfo's solution of a difficult problem. Taking his inspiration from the earlier palazzo of the podestà, he erected a

[28] Villani, VIII, 26. The exact date of the foundation ceremony was February 24, 1299 (Davidsohn, Vol. IV[3], pp. 3, 270). Villani gives the year 1298, but as by the Florentine calendar the year began on March 25, the day of the Annunciation, Villani's 1298 is 1299 by the common Christian calendar.

[29] The clan of the Cerchi was at the head of the political party called the Whites. They were composed of two branches, distinguished because of the color and complexion of their respective founders as White Cerchi and Black Cerchi. White Cerchi and Black Cerchi belonged alike to the political party of the Whites.

[30] San Piero Scheraggio hugged the south wall of the new palace. It was removed in the sixteenth century to make room for the Uffizi.

second civic edifice which, while it clung, like its prototype, to the fortress form and uttered brazen defiance to the enemies of the commonwealth, was an entirely independent creation. Above all, it was a more imposing, a more soaring mass; and instead of letting the tower of the Foraboschi become a handicap, Arnolfo so successfully mortised this ancient landmark into his design that, lengthened and battlement-crowned, it became the most distinctive feature of the edifice. In contrast to the cathedral, work on the communal residence proceeded so rapidly that after three years the building was far enough along for the priors to take possession (1302). But both it and the new piazza were still far from their present appearance. The records assembled by Davidsohn show that every year brought some innovation, though often slight and unimportant.[31] In 1306, for instance, the piazza was carefully paved, and in 1307 a bell was ordered to be cast to call the councils together and for similar official purposes. Because Arnolfo's tower was not yet ready at that date, we learn that the iron summoner was installed on a temporary platform in front of the structure. Indeed Arnolfo had departed this life long before the tower was completed; and completed, it was not complete because in its case, as in that of the whole edifice of which it was a part, the subsequent generations considered themselves privileged to make alterations according either to their taste or their changing necessities.

Immediately on their founding in the dugento, the two great begging orders of the Dominicans and the Franciscans had become the most alive and pushing elements in the Catholic church. They simply radiated energy; and since their vigor did not diminish in the trecento they were bound to be represented by great monastic establishments in all the growing communes of Italy. We have already noted that from an early time, and therefore long before Villani's birth, the Dominicans were settled at Santa Maria Novella and the Franciscans at the opposite, the eastern, end of the town in buildings which had been repeatedly enlarged. But with the great forward stride of the whole city coincident with the seizure of political power by the gilds, ideas of grandeur manifested themselves among both friars and citizens which refused to be content with anything less than the total reconstruction of the two monasteries on a magnificent scale.

The Dominicans led the way. In 1279, at about the time of Villani's birth and when the poet Dante was a lad of fourteen, they laid the foundation of a new monastery intended to replace the old one; and, a few years later, on February 2, 1283, they laid the foundations of the present imposing church of Santa Maria Novella. As Villani could not report these happenings from his own experience, he mentions them in a brief and confused statement not worth quoting.[32] However, as they mark the initiation of an enterprise which continued for many generations and gave Florence not only one of its most distinguished churches but also cloisters, a refectory, a library, a chapter house, and a bell tower constituting as imposing a monastic group as may be seen

[31] Davidsohn, *Forschungen,* Vol. IV, pp. 499 ff.

[32] Villani, VII, 56. Among the most important documents assembled by Davidsohn in regard to the architectural history of Florence are those bearing on Santa Maria Novella. See *Forschungen,* Vol. IV, pp. 466-82. He shows that the traditional attribution of the great temple to the two Dominican brothers, Fra Ristoro and Fra Sisto, is a pure invention.

anywhere in the world, we cannot afford to overlook the story. The individual structures were built, apparently without exception, by architects selected from among the brothers themselves. This need cause no surprise, for the order exercised a powerful attraction on men of the highest station and the most varied gifts, who, after their adoption of the cowl, were encouraged to put their talents at the service of the brotherhood. Much more remarkable is the consistently Gothic inspiration of the many friars busy at one time or another on this monastic monument. Within the circumference of Florence there is no ecclesiastical edifice which conveys more of the feeling of true, that is, of northern Gothic, than the church of Santa Maria Novella; and the features subsidiary to the church, such as the cloisters and the chapter-house, are in general keeping with the lines and feeling of the temple. In short, Santa Maria Novella constitutes one of the rare areas in Tuscany dedicated to the Gothic spirit.

We may remind ourselves in this connection that the Florentines were, architecturally, a very conservative people and persisted in cultivating the traditions native to their soil. So far as we are able to go back in history we encounter this trait. As soon as they began to outgrow the extreme poverty of the Middle Ages and were able to abandon wood in favor of stone, they developed a "style" representing a fusion of Roman traditions and current elements of taste. As the process was duplicated everywhere in Italy and western Europe there sprang into existence many distinct but interrelated styles, which, from the element common to them all, are distinguished as Romanesque. In northern Europe, more especially in France, the crude Romanesque was gradually sublimated into Gothic and brought to perfection in such magnificent cathedrals as Rheims and Chartres. In these marvelously harmonized monuments Gothic represents the conquest of a strikingly new world of architectural forms. As the story of how the Gothic style arose in northern France is not our concern, we may content ourselves with noting that with its highly developed elements of expression, such as the pointed arch, the massive buttress, the audacious flying buttress, and the soaring vault, it achieved a lightness and grace in the sharpest possible contrast with the ponderous gravity of the best examples of Romanesque.

Measured by the Gothic standards furnished by the great French cathedrals, the Florentine church of Santa Maria Novella is a very imperfect creation. Its nave—to concentrate on a single but significant feature—lacks the characteristic lift and flight of true Gothic by reason of the total suppression of the triforium and the employment of a merely rudimentary clerestory. But only pedants who are lost when their familiar categories fail them will refuse to enjoy this church of the Dominicans. Is it not enough that it has a noble spaciousness admirably suited for the worship of a united population? And if it must perforce be classified, let us call it a Tuscan variant of Gothic. Obviously the brother or brothers who devised it were under the influence of the graceful, yet vigorous northern style which in their time was making a triumphal march throughout the extent of western Christendom. But as they were also Tuscans, born and bred, they could not escape the native traditions which ruled their environment; and they did not hesitate to fuse them with the northern borrowings.

The Franciscan foundation of Santa Croce grew somewhat more deliberately than its Dominican rival. To be sure, Franciscans and Dominicans equally enjoyed both the favor of the citizens and the financial support of the government; but the injunction of poverty was so special a feature of the Little Brother of Assisi that a considerable section of his followers continued for a long time to protest against property of any kind and, particularly, against sumptuous houses of worship. They constituted an evangelical and puritan group called the Spiritual Franciscans, which with constantly diminishing success opposed the powerful worldly faction in their order until in the first half of the fourteenth century they completely lost the battle. The climax came when Pope John XXII of infamous memory denounced them as heretics and brought all the rigors of the Inquisition into play to effect their suppression. When some decades before this tragic event the Franciscans of Florence resolved to construct a new Santa Croce on a much larger scale than its inconspicuous predecessor, by thus committing themselves to a program of material expansion they gave proof of having effectively silenced the Spirituals in their midst. Although Villani does not expressly say so, we may be sure that so stout a burgher and defender of property as he sympathized with the victors.

In the year of Christ 1295, on the day of the Holy Cross of May, the foundation was laid of the new church of the Brothers Minor of Florence, called Santa Croce.[33] And at the consecration of the first stone there were present, amidst great pomp and solemnity, many bishops and prelates and priests and members of religious orders as well as the podestà and captain and all the good people of Florence, men and women alike. And work was begun at the chapels at the east end in order not to disturb the old church which the friars needed for religious services until the new chapels should be ready.

Santa Croce, too, though we do not get the information from Villani, was committed to the city's foremost architect, Arnolfo di Cambio. In fact it was the first of the three public enterprises associated with his name to be intrusted to his care, Santa Maria del Fiore following in the next year (1296), and the palace of the priors three years after the cathedral. But owing to the rather languid flow of funds, this earliest work progressed more slowly than the other two ventures and Arnolfo never lived to see more than the bare beginnings of Santa Croce. It is impossible to say whether, when at successive intervals work was renewed, his plans were adhered to, although it is usually assumed that such was the case. We know that the small, original church was not demolished till 1336, when it was at last removed to make room for the nave and aisles of the new structure. On these being added to the chapels of the choir, where, according to Villani, the work had begun, Santa Croce had been brought to substantial completion. In 1336, however, Arnolfo had been dead for over a quarter of a century, and we have no way of telling whether the nave and aisles followed his plans or not. That even after these sections had been completed there remained much to be done and that the church

[33] Villani, VIII, 7. Holy Cross of May would be May 3. The chronicler gives the date 1294, for which Davidsohn substitutes 1295. For documents bearing on the construction of Santa Croce see his *Forschungen,* Vol. IV, pp. 482 ff.

marched forward at the usual deliberate pace is proved by the fact that the nineteenth century arrived and still found Santa Croce without a façade. The tawdry front which was then erected in a burst of mistaken municipal patriotism will never cease to evoke a profound regret.

To enter Santa Croce is to find one's self in a very different world of form and feeling from that of Santa Maria Novella. On being intrusted with his task Arnolfo must have resolved to depart very substantially from the gloomy, if impressive, churches of the Florentine tradition and to raise a well-proportioned structure carried on slender piers and permitting the light from choir and clerestory agreeably to flood a spacious interior. It may well be that the artist, thoroughly Tuscan though he was, strove in this instance for a certain elegance characteristic of Gothic. In no case, however, was he fully committed to this imported style or particularly proficient in it. Had the northern architecture been a deep concern with him, he would not have surrendered the most characteristic Gothic feature, the vault, which in all sound Gothic examples soars high above the nave and majestically crowns it. In its stead he raised a roof of open beamwork, such as may be found in most of the older Tuscan churches. Owing perhaps to its inexpensiveness, he must have had this feature in mind from the first, for his piers were so slender that they could never have been intended to support a ponderous roof of stone. Because of these and other departures from the accepted norms, Gothic fanatics have not hesitated to scoff at Santa Croce, while sworn followers of the Romanesque have been hardly less disdainful. Both groups of critics make the mistake of approaching this building with a fixed preconception, instead of enjoying it directly for such merits as it has. These, as already indicated, lie in the direction of a warm, even light playing through the wide spaces of a nave and transept lightly floating on the slenderest possible supports.

Unless we somewhat hasten our steps we shall never have done with gazing at the fine new garment which Florence gave itself in Villani's time. The church of the Badia, the oldest and most honored monastery of the town, was totally rebuilt in the early years of the new government of the priors (around 1284); but four hundred years later an age of false refinement utterly destroyed what must have been a veritable treasure-house of early art in order to replace it with the existing structure, which so perfectly expresses the mental vacuity of its projectors. Fortunately the graceful hexagonal campanile, which belongs to the year 1330, was spared by the elegant vandals and still delights the visitor.[34] In this same year the Calimala gild, which, as we may recall, administered the opera of the baptistery, ordered of Andrea Pisano the first of the three magnificent bronze doors which still adorn that celebrated edifice. We shall return to this door when we take up the story of Florentine sculpture. Its quiet beauty prompted our pedestrian friend and guide to indulge in what for him is a burst of unrestrained enthusiasm. Nor does he forget to record the proud circumstance that it was none other than himself who represented the Calimala gild in connection with this enterprise.[35]

[34] The erection of the campanile is recorded by Villani, X, 174. Consult also on the campanile, Davidsohn, Vol IV^3, pp. 271-72.

[35] X, 174. For the official records covering the gate consult Davidsohn, *Forschungen,* Vol. IV, p. 464.

A little later, in 1337, an important measure was taken regarding Or San Michele.[36] But before discussing it, let us review the changes effected in the course of the centuries at this spot in order to remind ourselves how colorful is the history of every square foot of the city's area. Originally there stood on the site of what in Villani's day was the grain market, a small church dedicated to Saint Michael. It went all the way back to Lombard days, and because it stood in a garden, was called San Michele in Orto or Or San Michele for short. In 1239 it was destroyed, probably in connection with a civil outbreak occurring in that year. Thereupon the commune removed the débris and appropriated the open space thus acquired to various uses of its own. In 1284 the piazza was reserved as the market for the trade in grain and, in order to protect the dealers from the weather, a roofed loggia was erected to serve as shelter. Shortly after, a Madonna, which had been painted in fresco on one of the piers supporting the loggia, was declared to have operated a number of miraculous cures and at once leaped into such popularity that the candles and wax images dedicated to her by the faithful before long almost hid her Ladyship from view. The huge incendiary conflagration of 1304 started by the Blacks to save their regime completely destroyed the loggia and greatly damaged the fresco. Nonetheless it was incorporated in the new loggia which was promptly erected to replace its predecessor. This was so skimpily built that frequent repairs were necessary, and finally, in 1337, the priors resolved, as mentioned *ad annum* by Villani, to reconstruct the loggia in a more substantial manner and to crown it with two vaulted stories serviceable for storing grain. The original Madonna in fresco must by this time have faded out entirely, for in 1346 Bernardo Daddi was commissioned to paint on wood and in the most substantial manner a new picture of the Virgin. When this was ready it elicited such admiration that the leading Florentine sculptor, Orcagna, was ordered (1349) to provide for it the most beautiful shrine of which he was capable. It was not till the fifties, when Villani was already dead, that the combined loggia and storehouse for grain, decided on almost twenty years before, began to approach completion. When the structure, which is the present Or San Michele, was finished, an agitation was started to have the grain market with its vulgar hubbub removed to another piazza in order to provide an atmosphere more in keeping with the magnificent tabernacle on which Orcagna was engaged. In 1357 the transfer of the grain market was carried out and, two years later, when Orcagna had completed his shrine, the loggia was dedicated as a church. As soon as the loggia had been converted into a house of worship, it became urgent to give it a protective inclosure and accordingly, beginning in 1366, the open spaces between the loggia piers were walled up as we see them today.[37]

The most interesting communal undertaking of Villani's last decade was the rose-colored, marble-incrusted campanile, very generally regarded as the loveliest architectural monument of the town.

[36] Villani, XI, 67. Davidsohn, *Forschungen*, Vol. IV, p. 510.

[37] C. Schubert-Feder, "La Loggia di Or San Michele," *Arch. Stor. It.*, Serie 5, Vol. VII, pp. 67-88. Davidsohn, Vol. II[1], p. 244; Vol. II[2], pp. 191-92; Vol. IV[3], pp. 265-70; *Forschungen*, Vol. IV, p. 510.

In the said year [1334], on July 18, was begun the new bell tower of Santa Reparata [we observe that Villani too, much like the common people, was slow in applying to the cathedral its newer, more pretentious name of Santa Maria del Fiore] close to the front of the church on the piazza of San Giovanni. And there were present for the blessing of the first stone the bishop of Florence with all his clergy as well as the priors and the other magistrates with many people and a great procession. And the foundation was made as solid as possible. And as superintendent and overseer of the opera of Santa Reparata the commune appointed our fellow-citizen, Giotto, the most sovereign master of painting in his time, who drew all his figures and their postures according to nature. And he was given a salary by the commune in virtue of his talent and excellence.[38]

Villani, who omitted to name the architect of Santa Croce, Santa Maria del Fiore, and the Palazzo Communale, an artist who stood at the head of his profession in his time, does not hesitate to distinguish Giotto as the builder of the campanile for the reason that his fame was so widespread that it could not be ignored. Giotto is correctly signalized as a great painter (*maestro in dipintura*), whom it may surprise us moderns to find appointed operaio of Santa Reparata and architect of Santa Reparata's new bell tower. That Villani finds nothing out of the way in the appointment is clear evidence that the arts had not yet become as specialized as they are with us and that in those days a man who called himself an artist was expected to be an all-around craftsman. Giotto's bell tower replaced an unimportant predecessor which stood at the northwest corner of Santa Reparata. Instead of remodeling this humble structure, an entirely new structure was planned and a site selected for it at the opposite or southwest corner of the cathedral front. The celebrated operaio died at the age of seventy, two and a half years after his appointment. He lived to carry his project no farther than just above the first row of sculptures; but so completely did he stamp his creation with his genius that although the work, interrupted by the usual delays, was not finished till half a century later, it was carried through with only unimportant deviations from his plans.

Undoubtedly the campanile employs Gothic elements of expression, as, for instance, in its engagingly varied fenestration, and yet it is as little a "correct" Gothic structure as Santa Croce, Santa Maria Novella, or any other Florentine monument of the trecento. Once again it brings home to us that the Florentines of this age clung stubbornly to their local tradition, modifying it with imported or freely invented features according to their pleasure. Granting that its racy, native style enables the campanile to fit harmoniously into the Florentine ensemble, nonetheless, like every other work of genius, it has the very individual touch of its creator. For this reason the bell tower, which rises with the ease and grace of a lily in the center of a city which has the lily for its emblem, has never been called other than Giotto's campanile.

As one more structure completes the list of the notable Florentine edifices of the medieval period, it must be added to the record at this point, although it was not erected in the life-span of our guide. When a new set of priors was inaugurated into office or when a foreign ambassador was to be formally received, the republic made a practice of conducting the exercises in public on

[38] Villani, XI, 12.

the platform or *ringhiera* in front of the palace. If it rained during the ceremony, the enthusiasm of the orators and, even more of the drenched listeners, suffered a considerable diminution. This inconvenience had started an agitation for a covered loggia, and although from a relatively early time the matter was frequently discussed in the councils, nothing definite was done till 1376, when a number of private houses close to the palace were bought and leveled with the ground. Shortly after the task of building a public loggia was intrusted to the opera del duomo and by 1382 the structure, called originally Loggia dei Priori (or Signori) was completed. As in the sixteenth century, when the republic had perished, Duke Cosimo used the loggia as a station for his German bodyguard called Lanzi (from the German *Landsknecht*), it came gradually to be called Loggia dei Lanzi; and Loggia dei Lanzi it has remained to this day. The Loggia dei Lanzi is an impressive open hall of three round arches of bold leap and wide span. With its clustered piers, its stone vaults, and its decorative motifs it fits perfectly into the picture of Gothic Florence with which we have become acquainted. However, in applying the term Gothic to our city let us always bear in mind an architectural system consisting of a native Romanesque kernel, to which have been added a number of imported Gothic features. The Loggia dei Lanzi is a perfect illustration of the fusion of these two elements. While there is no lack of Gothic decorative features, the three great arches with their all but spoken welcome to the visitor of the great square have not been pointed as would have been the case if the architect had possessed the true Gothic feeling; instead they are smoothly rounded, presenting themselves to view as the authentic descendants of the arch of triumph, so congenial to the monumental feeling of the ancient Romans. In his great history of the arts Vasari ventured the guess that the plans for the loggia were drawn by the painter-sculptor Orcagna. He was wrong, but his speculation has become a part of the impregnable Florentine legend. Modern investigators have shown beyond dispute that the loggia was built by the contemporary heads of the cathedral works, sound professional workers of good standing in their day but enjoying no such reputation among the later generations as the master of the tabernacle of Or San Michele.[39] Under these circumstances it is easy to understand why the ever active legendary spirit, wishing to connect a famous object with a famous name, should have hit upon Orcagna, although in point of fact Orcagna had died eight years before even so much as the first step toward the construction of the loggia had been taken.

We are aware that the four bridges of Florence were all severely injured, if not totally ruined, by the historic flood of 1333. The oldest of these, which belonged to the miniature Florence of the early Middle Ages and which went back to Roman times, was the Ponte Vecchio. The other three had been added in the first half of the dugento. The Carraia bridge bears the date 1220 and was followed in 1237 by the bridge called Rubaconte, in honor of the podestà of that year, under whose auspices the foundations had been laid. For the designation Rubaconte there was afterward substituted that of delle Grazie from the shrine of a much-visited Madonna, Santa Maria delle Grazie, who by her perpetual presence bestowed her blessing on the structure. The fourth

[39] C. Frey, *Die Loggia dei Lanzi zu Florenz.* Berlin, 1885.

and last bridge was erected in 1252 and named Santa Trinità after the church on the right bank, near which it terminated. The addition of three bridges to the original Ponte Vecchio within a stretch of some thirty years of the thirteenth century is excellent proof of the rapid and often insufficiently realized growth of Florence in that relatively early period. The impression of the degree of this expansion is deepened when we reflect that these four bridges satisfied the needs of the city through the subsequent flourishing periods of the fourteenth and fifteenth centuries. Following the catastrophe of the year 1333, the commune put in service provisional bridges of wood until sufficient resources had been accumulated to rebuild these invaluable links of traffic on a larger scale and with stronger foundations than their predecessors.

We may learn of the generous manner in which the destroyed bridges were reconstructed by looking into the single instance of the oldest and most celebrated of them, the Ponte Vecchio.

In the year 1345, on July 18, was completed the new bridge over the Arno which replaced the Ponte Vecchio. It consisted of two piers and three arches and cost . . . gold florins [space left vacant and never filled in]. And it was raised on solid foundations and had a width of thirty-two braccia with a roadway in the middle of sixteen braccia. It was too wide in my judgment since the width was the cause of the lowering of the arches by two braccia. [Villani evidently held that it would have been better to have the bridge high and narrow than low and wide.] And the shops at either end of the bridge were each eight braccia wide and eight braccia long and were raised of stone on the solid arches. There were forty-three of these shops, from which the commune drew an annual rental of eighty and more gold florins. Originally they had been constructed of wood and been extended out over the Arno on beams since the old bridge had been only twelve braccia wide.[40]

The shops were rebuilt in stone, instead of wood, in order to put an end to the fires which had repeatedly destroyed them in the past. To this day, as everybody knows, the Ponte Vecchio has retained the picturesque feature of a double line of *botteghe* at either bridge end. Particularly interesting in Villani's report is the evidence of the greater traffic capacity of the new bridge. If we reckon the braccio roughly at two feet—it was in reality somewhat less—the open roadway of the new bridge was eight feet wider than the whole earlier structure! With its forty-odd shops of stone, which rested firmly on the stone vaulting of the arches without any overhang, the new bridge must have struck Villani's contemporaries as a notable advance in size and dignity on the vanished structure.

By way of curiosity we may note that the equestrian figure of Mars, which had long stood at the head of the bridge on the right bank, was not fished out of the waters which swallowed it on the occasion of the great inundation of 1333. Already in an earlier flood of the year 1178 the statue, located at that time on the opposite or left bank of the Arno, had been washed away only to be salvaged and set up again on the right bank. That is where it stood when, on a certain Easter morning, the truculent Uberti and Amidei used it as an ambuscade, from behind which they leaped upon and brutally dispatched the

[40] Villani, XII, 46.

handsome Buondelmonte, that too casual lover. Neither Villani nor Dante nor any other Florentine of the Middle Ages doubted that the ruined and featureless rider, "quella pietra scema,"[41] represented the Roman god. Did not Florence boast in the baptistery a former temple of Mars and, dedicated as the city was supposed to be to the pagan god of battles, was it not highly fitting to possess his statue? These old Mars legends, which constituted so living an element of the thought of the divine poet and his contemporaries, have been shown by modern criticism to have little or no basis in reality.[42] That is of course not very important since what chiefly counts in building up a national mentality is not the truth but the quality, high or low, of what is deeply held to be the truth. However, in view of the proved attachment of the Florentines to their disfigured, putative Mars, it remains perplexing that neither Villani nor any other writer has recorded any attempt to rescue the ancient horseman, become a patriotic emblem, from his watery grave. We are forced to conclude that his last plunge from his pedestal reduced him to such a dilapidated state that every hope of further restoration was rendered vain.

It would be ungracious if, after taking advantage of the services of our ancient guide, we should dismiss him before he had been permitted to show us the structural addition of his day which constituted perhaps the chief object of his civic pride. From the very beginning of its rise as a commune Florence had never for a moment been permitted to forget that it was confronted with a hostile world and that to relax its efforts against its environment was to fall behind in the race. Of this perilous situation the constant reminder was the city wall, which bound the inhabitants into a single sheepfold and made them secure against their enemies. In considering Villani's youth we have dealt with the two circles with which, as a boy, he became familiar, the first going back to Roman days, the second erected in the reign of Barbarossa and embracing about three times the area of the first. We are also aware that, long before Villani's birth, the continuously expanding town had burst beyond the bounds of the second girdle and that populous suburbs or borghi lay along every highway leading from the city. Owing to this situation, as soon as the victory of the gilds had energized the government, a plan was considered to create a third girdle; and in 1284 the project was initiated by four new gates on the right bank raised as barbicans or outposts at a considerable distance beyond the second circle. The four gates were joined provisionally by palisades of wood, which traced the line the walls would ultimately follow. However, owing to the expense of so immense an undertaking coupled with the momentary abscence of danger, the work soon came to a standstill and was not resumed till fifteen years later, in 1299. An era of intense municipal construction had at that time been inaugurated, as Santa Croce, Santa Maria del Fiore, and the palace of the priors amply witness, and it was natural for the awakened civic enthusiasm of the citizens to turn again to the interrupted enterprise of the third circle. But again little was done, this time owing to the outbreak of the civil war between the Blacks and the Whites; and it was not till the descent into Italy of Emperor Henry VII coupled with the certain expectation of his enmity

[41] Dante, *Paradiso,* XVI, 145.
[42] Davidsohn, Vol. I, pp. 748-52.

that a new and feverish period of construction set in (1310). Florence counted on war with its sovereign and war came, the grimmest sort of war, culminating in the year 1312 in the city's siege by the imperial host. To Villani, reporting the event, it was only the improved eastern defenses toward San Salvi, where Henry spread his camp, that saved Florence from destruction.[43]

When Henry died in the following year (1313), the city heaved a sigh of relief and again discarded hammer and trowel not to resume them till another cloud rose on the horizon from which emerged the dread face and form of Castruccio Castracane. This threat stimulated the commune to renewed effort; and between 1322 and 1324 the walls of the right bank, which inclosed five of the six sesti of the town, were actually and finally brought to completion. It is a stroke of good fortune that our chronicler, on account of his having been one of the overseers of construction during this particular period, was prompted to furnish his readers with a detailed description of the finished work.[44]

> In order that the memory of the greatness of the said city be always kept alive . . . we shall give an ordered account of the building of the said walls together with the measurements made by myself, the author, who, in behalf of the commune, served as official of the walls.

There follow details and figures so unusual in a work of this period, when men were notoriously indifferent to accuracy, that we would be tempted to challenge them if we had not by now accustomed ourselves to Villani's very modern factual sense. In closing his minute description he sums up as follows:

> And thus we find that the new circle of walls measures, on the right bank of the Arno, seven thousand seven hundred braccia. And this section possesses nine gates, that is, four master gates and five posterns [*postierle*], each with a tower of sixty braccia and with a barbican in front of it. And along the wall rise forty-five towers, counting also those of the gates.

Turning thence to the wall of the left bank (which we may note was not completed till 1328) he follows the same precise procedure employed in treating the wall of the right bank. And in a final survey he informs us that the wall throughout its extent was three braccia, that is, almost six feet, thick and twenty braccia, that is, almost forty feet, high to the top of the battlements, and that the total circumference of this tremendous mass of brick, stone, and mortar was five miles. The picture in our minds becomes still more impressive on learning that there were fifteen gates in all (nine on the right, six on the left bank), seventy-three towers along the wall at four-hundred-foot intervals, and a broad circumambient moat. That provision was made for the future increase of the population appears from the statement that much garden and vegetable land (*orti e giardini*) was included within the new circuit.

Bristling with the imposing masonry of its third circle, Florence was for many generations regarded as the best fortified city of Italy. When, with the seventeenth century, artillery and high explosives gained an increasing ascendancy, the defenses declined in value, and by the nineteenth century they had

[43] Villani, IX, 10. "La qual cosa fu poi lo scampo della città."
[44] IX, 256, 257.

become completely useless. In the period of Italian unification it was therefore resolved that the wall on the right bank should be leveled with the ground except for the three gates of Al Prato, San Gallo, and Alla Croce. The site of the ancient girdle is at present marked by a wide, tree-lined boulevard. On the left bank, however, in Oltrarno, the wall was happily spared and to this day spills its red mass over the irregularly formed ground. Whoever wishes to recover the sentiment which made Florence a self-contained community set off against a hostile world and inspiring the citizens with an unconquerable resolution cannot do better than on some fresh spring or mellow autumn morning to climb the hill of San Giorgio and, issuing from the gate still expressively carved with the dragon-killer whose fame it celebrates, drop thence slowly along the path which follows the ancient wall to the bank of the Arno. His walk will take him by the side of quiet vineyards and silvery olive orchards, among which, losing the sense of time, he will be joined unawares by Giovanni Villani with the eager proffer of his services as guide, while not far behind will hover the gracious, more reticent ghosts of Arnolfo, Giotto, and Dante Alighieri.

INDEX TO VOLUME I

INDEX

HARPER TORCHBOOKS / The Bollingen Library

[*Selected Titles*]

Rachel Bespaloff — ON THE ILIAD. *Introduction by Hermann Broch* TB/2006
Joseph Campbell, *Ed.* — PAGAN AND CHRISTIAN MYSTERIES TB/2013
E. R. Curtius — EUROPEAN LITERATURE AND THE LATIN MIDDLE AGES TB/2015
C. G. Jung — PSYCHOLOGICAL REFLECTIONS. Edited by Jolande Jacobi TB/2001
C. G. Jung — SYMBOLS OF TRANSFORMATION. Illustrated. *Vol. I,* TB/2009; *Vol. II,* TB/2010
St.-John Perse — SEAMARKS. Translated by Wallace Fowlie TB/2002
Jean Seznec — SURVIVAL OF THE PAGAN GODS. Illus. TB/2004
Heinrich Zimmer — MYTHS AND SYMBOLS IN INDIAN ART AND CIVILIZATION. Illus. TB/2005

HARPER TORCHBOOKS / The Cloister Library

[*Selected Titles*]

W. F. Albright — THE BIBLICAL PERIOD FROM ABRAHAM TO EZRA TB/102
C. K. Barrett, *Ed.* — THE NEW TESTAMENT BACKGROUND: *Selected Documents* TB/86
Karl Barth — CHURCH DOGMATICS: *A Selection.* Edited by G. W. Bromiley TB/95
Martin Buber — ECLIPSE OF GOD: *The Relation Between Religion and Philosophy* TB/12
Martin Buber — POINTING THE WAY. Ed. with Intro. by M. S. Friedman. TB/103
R. Bultmann — HISTORY AND ESCHATOLOGY: *The Presence of Eternity* TB/91
Jacob Burckhardt — THE CIVILIZATION OF THE RENAISSANCE IN ITALY. Illustrated Edition. Introduction by B. Nelson and C. Trinkaus. *Vol. I,* TB/40; *Vol. II,* TB/41
Frederick Copleston — MEDIEVAL PHILOSOPHY TB/76
Mircea Eliade — COSMOS AND HISTORY: *The Myth of the Eternal Return* TB/50
Sigmund Freud — ON CREATIVITY AND THE UNCONSCIOUS: *Papers on the Psychology of Art, Literature, Love, Religion.* Edited by Benjamin Nelson TB/45
F. H. Heinemann — EXISTENTIALISM AND THE MODERN PREDICAMENT TB/28
Winthrop Hudson — THE GREAT TRADITION OF THE AMERICAN CHURCHES TB/98
Johan Huizinga — ERASMUS AND THE AGE OF REFORMATION. Illustrated TB/19
Immanuel Kant — LECTURES ON ETHICS. Intro. by L. W. Beck. TB/105
Søren Kierkegaard — PURITY OF HEART TB/4
G. Rachel Levy — RELIGIOUS CONCEPTIONS OF THE STONE AGE *and their influence upon European thought.* Introduction by Henri Frankfort. TB/106
H. Richard Niebuhr — CHRIST AND CULTURE TB/3
A. D. Nock — ST. PAUL TB/104
Teilhard de Chardin — THE PHENOMENON OF MAN TB/83
D. W. Thomas, *Ed.* — DOCUMENTS FROM OLD TESTAMENT TIMES TB/85
Paul Tillich — DYNAMICS OF FAITH TB/42
Ernst Troeltsch — SOCIAL TEACHING OF CHRISTIAN CHURCHES. *Vol. I,* TB/71; *Vol. II,* TB/72
Wilhelm Windelband — A HISTORY OF PHILOSOPHY I: *Greek, Roman, Medieval* TB/38
Wilhelm Windelband — A HISTORY OF PHILOSOPHY II: *Renaissance, Enlightenment, Modern* TB/39

HARPER TORCHBOOKS / The Science Library

[*Selected Titles*]

R. B. Braithwaite — SCIENTIFIC EXPLANATION TB/515
Louis de Broglie — PHYSICS AND MICROPHYSICS. Foreword by Albert Einstein TB/514
J. Bronowski — SCIENCE AND HUMAN VALUES TB/505
Walter B. Cannon — BODILY CHANGES IN PAIN, HUNGER, FEAR AND RAGE. Illus. TB/562
W. E. Le Gros Clark — ANTECEDENTS OF MAN: *Intro. to Evolution of Primates.* Illus. TB/559
R. E. Coker — THIS GREAT AND WIDE SEA: *Oceanography & Marine Biology.* Illus. TB/551
A. C. Crombie, *Ed.* — TURNING POINTS IN PHYSICS TB/535
W. C. Dampier, *Ed.* — READINGS IN THE LITERATURE OF SCIENCE. Illustrated TB/512
C. V. Durell — READABLE RELATIVITY. Foreword by Freeman J. Dyson. Illus. TB/530
Werner Heisenberg — PHYSICS AND PHILOSOPHY: *The Revolution in Modern Science.* Intro. by F. S. C. Northrop TB/549
Max Jammer — CONCEPTS OF FORCE: *A Study in the Foundations of Dynamics* TB/550
S. Körner — THE PHILOSOPHY OF MATHEMATICS: *An Introduction* TB/547
J. R. Partington — A SHORT HISTORY OF CHEMISTRY. Illustrated TB/522
H. T. Pledge — SCIENCE SINCE 1500: *Mathematics, Physics, Chemistry, & Biology.* Illus. TB/506
John Read — THROUGH ALCHEMY TO CHEMISTRY. Illus. TB/561
Paul A. Schilpp, *Ed.* — ALBERT EINSTEIN: *Philosopher-Scientist. Vol. I,* TB/502; *Vol. II,* TB/503
G. J. Whitrow — THE NATURAL PHILOSOPHY OF TIME TB/563